Gender, Media, and Organization

A volume in
Women and Leadership
Susan R. Madsen, Karen A. Longman, Faith Wambura Ngunjiri, *Series Editors*

Gender, Media, and Organization

Challenging Mis(s)Representations of Women Leaders and Managers

edited by

Carole Elliott
Roehampton University

Valerie Stead
Lancaster University

Sharon Mavin
Roehampton University

Jannine Williams
University of Bradford

INFORMATION AGE PUBLISHING, INC.
Charlotte, NC • www.infoagepub.com

Library of Congress Cataloging-in-Publication Data

A CIP record for this book is available from the Library of Congress
http://www.loc.gov

ISBN: 978-1-68123-532-5 (Paperback)
       978-1-68123-533-2 (Hardcover)
       978-1-68123-534-9 (ebook)

CONTENTS

Introduction... 1
Carole Elliott, Valerie Stead, Sharon Mavin, and Jannine Williams

PART I

WOMEN EXECUTIVES

1 Is She Really Into It? The Media as Misleading in Its Portrayals
   of Female Executives' Work–Family (Im)Balance............................. 19
   Maura J. Mills, Leanne M. Tortez, and Maria E. Gallego-Pace

2 Who's That Girl? The (Mis)Representation of Female
   Corporate Leaders in *Time*.. 37
   Sandra L. French and Lisa Baker Webster

3 A Fairytale Career: Media Representations of Australia's First
   Female Banking CEO.. 49
   Helena Liu

4 Pulling a Chair up to the Table: A Critical Analysis of the
   "Lean In" Self-Help Movement and Its Implications for
   Individual Women and Women's Equality at Work 63
   Judith A. Clair and Caela McCann

5   "There's Never Been a Better Time to Be a Woman": The
    Discursive Effects of Women on Boards' Research Reports 77
    Scarlett E. Brown and Elisabeth K. Kelan

PART II

WOMEN PROFESSIONALS AND LEADERS

6   Dress and the Female Professional: A Case Study
    of *Working Woman* 95
    Ann Rippin, Harriet Shortt, and Samantha Warren

7   In the Name of the Other: Nicknaming and Gendered
    Misrepresentation/s of Women Leaders 111
    Alison Pullen and Lucy Taksa

8   Caveman Meritocracy: Misrepresenting Women
    Managers Online 133
    Janne Tienari and Pasi Ahonen

9   Wynne Some, Lose Some: An Intersectional Approach
    to Media Prejudice Against Canadian Women Politicians 153
    Rita A. Gardiner

PART III

WOMEN IN FILM AND TELEVISION

10 The "Gogglebox" and Gender: An Interdiscursive Analysis
    of Television Representations and Professional Femininities 169
    Helen Rodgers, Liz Yeomans, and Sallyann Halliday

11 Mediating the Future: Women Political Leaders
    in Science Fiction Television 197
    Kimberly Yost

12 The Runway-Ready Ringleader and Other Media Myths:
    An Analysis of Common Television and Film Stereotypes
    of Women Leaders 209
    Shana Matamala and Stephanie Abrahim

13 Working in ShondaLand: Representations
of African American Women in Leadership 225
Carrie Wilson-Brown and Samantha Szczur

14 The Margin as a Space of Resistance: Transforming Gendered
Leadership Through Popular Film 243
Alexia Panayiotou

About the Editors 259
About the Contributors 263

INTRODUCTION

Carole Elliott
University of Roehampton

Valerie Stead
Lancaster University

Sharon Mavin
University of Roehampton

Jannine Williams
University of Bradford

The stimulus for this volume has emerged from a series of seminars in the UK, funded by the Economic and Social Sciences Research Council (ESRC). The research focus of the seminar series is to develop methodologies and networks to challenge gendered media misrepresentations of women professionals and leaders. The media plays a critical role in society and is a recognized global power: It has the power to shape individuals' realities, provide frameworks for interpretation, reproduce and influence culture, educate, influence politics and policy, and effect social change (Mazza & Alvarez, 2000). Representing and shaping the behavior of people, not least in workplaces (Czarniawska & Rhodes, 2006), the media therefore has significant influence on how individuals, and in turn organizations, business

Gender, Media, and Organization, pages 1–16
Copyright © 2016 by Information Age Publishing
All rights of reproduction in any form reserved.

networks, and communities, make sense of and give sense to (Hellgren, Löwstedt, Puttonen, Tienari, Vaara, & Werr, 2002) women as professionals and leaders. Media representations of women professionals and leaders are often absent or gendered, are sexualized, and communicate contradictory messages. For example, we notice that on the one hand women leaders are championed, but on the other hand the media passes judgment on how women professionals "do gender well" against their feminine sex-category (Mavin & Grandy, 2013), evidenced by an excessive focus placed on women's hair, makeup, clothes, children, and weight, thereby calling into question their presence and competence to serve in senior roles. Yet there remains a lack of critical attention in leadership research to how women leaders and professionals are represented in the media, and this gap formed the basis for the seminar series and this edited volume. The lack of research interrogation of gendered media representations of women leaders and professionals is a surprising omission given the wealth of evidence from stakeholders outside academia that reveals that women, and women leaders, continue to be underrepresented across all forms of media outlets. For example, the Global Media Monitoring Project (GMMP) reports on an international study of women's presence on television, radio, the internet, and in newspapers (Macharia, 2015). The findings highlight that only 24% of news subjects involve women, and that in news stories women are two to three times more likely to be portrayed as victims in comparison to men.

The Washington DC-based Women's Media Center report (2015) titled "The Status of Women in the U.S. Media" quotes statistics that similarly demonstrate the relative scarcity of women's media presence. This research shows that, while men accounted for roughly 74% of guests on major U.S. television networks' Sunday morning news shows, women comprised just 26% of the guest line-up. Concerning analysts and journalists, none of the live major TV networks' Sunday morning news shows had an equal representation of men and women. The live program that had the most women experts was NBC's "Meet the Press," where, in 2014, women accounted for 29% of its 422 guests. Meanwhile, 71% of the guests on that program were men.

Two key objectives of the seminar series are:

1. to contribute to social change, equality, and economic performance by raising consciousness about women's lack of representation in the media
2. to challenge gendered misrepresentations of women professionals and leaders by the media.

In so doing, we are advocating for greater representation of women at work and in positions of leadership that do not fall back on lazy and gendered stereotypes such as "Queen Bee" (Mavin, 2008), "Iron Maiden," or

"Selfless Heroine" (Stead & Elliott, 2009) to describe women who hold positions of power and influence. An important means to tackle these objectives is to expand the limited literature in management and organization studies that explores how women leaders and issues related to women's access to leadership positions are represented in the news media (Mavin, Bryans, & Cunningham, 2010; Tienari, Holgersson, Meriläinen, & Höök, 2009). This volume represents a significant first step in fulfilling these objectives and is a reflection of the commitment by the International Leadership Association (ILA), and Women and Leadership Affinity Group members in particular, to enhance knowledge about women's leadership for the purpose of improving women's leadership development.

VOLUME DETAILS

The chapters in this book are divided into three parts: women executives, women professionals and leaders, and women in film and television. Together they represent the first collection of studies dedicated specifically to the examination of the media's representation of women professionals and leaders. Collectively, the studies are located in empirical contexts that range from Dr. Rita Gardiner's investigation of the media's treatment of two Canadian women's political campaigns to Dr. Kimberly Yost's examination of women political leaders in science fiction television. The authors who have contributed to the volume share an assumption that the media's outputs play a significant role in socialization and construction processes. We view the chapters as cultural texts, allowing us to view the work through a lens that draws attention to how texts construct and produce meaning that affects how we think and talk about women and leadership. As Rippin, Shortt, and Warren note in their chapter about the role of a magazine produced to instruct 1980s women how *to be* a professional woman, the images and texts we are exposed to create a "performative heritage" of gender, which influences both men's and women's perceptions of what professional woman *are* and how they *do* it.

Part I: Women Executives

This section of the book is dedicated to research that explores the media representation of women in executive roles. A particular focus in the media in the UK, Europe, and the U.S. has been related to the number of women on boards. In the UK, for example, the year 2015 was identified in a review by Lord Davies as a target to achieve 25% women serving on the boards of the recognized top-performing Financial Times Stock Exchange (FTSE)

100 companies. Reports by Cranfield University known as the Female FTSE reports assess the representation of women on boards in the UK, and they show huge strides in gender diversity in UK top companies since the first Davies Review in 2011 (Vinnicombe, Dolder, Sealy, Pryce, & Turner, 2015); women's representation is almost doubled, and there are currently no all-male boards in the FTSE 100.

However, outside of the top performing 100 companies, in the top 250 companies, there are still 23 companies with all-male boards, providing a strong indicator of gender inequality in an advanced Western society. Gender inequality on company boards is being recognized in the UK through various interventions such as the 30% Club, Women on Boards UK, and the Board Apprentice Scheme launched at the House of Lords in 2015, which places board-ready women as "apprentices" onto company boards to gain the exposure and experience to which they would otherwise not have access. Thus, in the UK at least, there is momentum to increase gender equality at executive leader levels. However, government and activist interventions are taking place within a context where media constructions of women professionals and leaders remain highly gendered and largely unchallenged. Media constructions of women executive leaders are gendered and powerful in messaging women's (un)acceptability as leaders against embedded stereotypes. Making women invisible via tokenism and yet spotlighted on the basis of their gender, media constructions trivialize women executive leaders' contribution, thus detracting from their credibility as leaders (Mavin et al., 2010). Continued gendered media constructions of women executive leaders, which focus relentlessly on critiques of women leaders' physicality, femininity, and personal relationships create and perpetuate powerful discourses. These discourses remind society that women are positioned against a male norm; they are deemed inappropriate as executive leaders and continue to remain as the *other* leader. Therefore, despite the progress made in appointing more women onto company boards, ongoing challenge and activism are required in order to stop these gendered media constructions. We can observe such challenge and activism through the following chapters.

In the opening chapter of this section, Dr. Maura Mills, Dr. Leanne Tortez, and Maria Gallego-Pace in their chapter, "Is She Really Into it? The Media as Misleading in its Portrayals of Female Executives' Work–Family (Im)Balance," examine the ways in which the media treats the work–family axis when discussing women leaders. Their analysis reflects the assumption that the media plays a significant role in the ways in which women are perceived and stereotyped. Coupled with normative views about leadership as a masculine activity, it is little wonder, these authors argue, that women leaders are often misrepresented in the media. Mills and colleagues are specifically interested in a stereotype that has not received adequate critical interrogation—assumptions made about women leaders and their familial commitments. If women do have family commitments, it is assumed that this limits their competence and dedication to their jobs. This is especially damaging for women leaders' representations as they are more visible, receive greater media attention, and have more fluid work–family boundaries than employees in non-leader positions. The chapter analyzes the media's treatment of Carly Fiorina, Condoleezza Rice, Katharine Zaleski, Marissa Mayer, Jill Abramson, Hillary Clinton, and Elena Kagan, noting the discriminatory ways in which these women leaders have been represented, including how they are portrayed in relation to familial commitments.

As Mills et al. observe, the harm of these representations extends beyond women leaders. They send messages to girls, young women, and non-leader women that leadership positions are largely impossible for women who choose to have families.

Similar to the chapter by Mills et al., Drs. Sandra French and Lisa Baker Webster's chapter, "Who's That Girl? The (Mis)Representation of Female Corporate Leaders in *Time*," articulates the media's power to shape cultural opinions. These authors undertake a rhetorical analysis of the media's construction of female corporate leaders on the covers of *Time* magazine, also taking into account how women corporate leaders are visually presented. *Time* is particularly worthy of such analysis, French and Webster suggest, given that the magazine has a large proportion of women readers, has existed since 1923, and has a tendency to profile a single person on the front cover—thus offering a rich source of longitudinal material. The authors specifically focus on covers between 1923 and 2014 that feature women who were previously, or are currently, corporate leaders, including Elizabeth Arden (1946), the Wallaces (1951), Alicia Patterson (1954), Sheryl Sandberg (2013), Janet Yellen (2014), and Mary Barra (2014).

Strikingly, French and Baker Webster's interpretation of the layout and design of these *Time* covers adopts theoretical ideas (Jamieson, 1995) that examine symbols of femininity and masculinity and the extent to which the covers are similar or different. Outlining how the women leaders' portrayals illustrate sameness and difference, for example, five out of the six covers contain symbols of masculinity, thereby hinting that these women are not representative of women in general. The authors conclude that all the women corporate leaders featured on a *Time* cover must simultaneously "craft" a capable leadership persona while at the same time assuring the reader that they retain a culturally acceptable feminine stereotype.

Dr. Helena Liu, in her chapter "A Fairytale Career: Media Representations of Australia's First Female Banking CEO," investigates the media's presentation of Gail Kelly, the first woman to lead Westpac, an Australian bank. Liu is concerned to interrogate the role of the media in producing and disseminating social meanings related to the representation of high-profile women leaders. *Factiva*, a media database, was used to identify a wider selection of articles on Kelly, and an event history database was developed to explore the convergences between Kelly, the bank, and the broader context. Discourse analysis and visual analysis of the resultant data highlighted the gendered nature of media representations of Kelly and her leadership of Westpac. The chapter argues the importance of context in the media's framing of her leadership of Westpac, including the use of stereotypical representations of banking leaders. Liu suggests that the media positioning of Kelly was unsurprisingly gendered, following Kelly's sharing of familial responsibilities to counteract the distrust of banking leaders in the media; early representations focused upon her familial connections, her appearance, and Kelly as symbolic of all women—as a female champion and ideal. During a potential merger, the logo of a previous employer (St. George Bank) was used to construct a fairytale representation, with Kelly cast in various archetypal roles. This was followed by a growing concern triggered by the global financial crisis that led to archetypically negative representations of bankers as greedy and rapacious. Representations then returned to more favorable, yet feminized, images when Kelly launched initiatives to support employees on parental leave. Liu suggests that while women leaders may attempt to shape media representations, contextual factors such as the global financial crisis and stereotypical, essentialist notions of gender emerge to distort such efforts.

Dr. Judith Clair and Caela McCann's chapter, "Pulling a Chair up to the Table: A Critical Analysis of the 'Lean In' Self-Help Movement and Its Implication for Individual Women and Women's Equality at Work," reviews the impact of Sheryl Sandberg's Lean In movement as part of a self-help genre for women who want to advance professionally. The appeal of Lean In as a self-help mechanism is argued to be its meeting of desires for self-transformation and its female centricity. The authors argue that Lean In is reflective of an individualized focus and the belief that multiple individualized efforts will contribute to more women leaders who can promote institutional change. They observe that the modern format of the Lean In movement and the message of personal responsibility resonate with young women's desire for senior-level opportunities and preparedness to focus on individual effort. The potential longevity of Lean In is explored, suggesting that while there is some criticism of the movement as being deeply flawed, there remains potential for women to be motivated to assert agency, for individual actions to effect social change, and for keeping the concern for women's progress in the public domain.

Scarlett Brown and Dr. Elisabeth Kelan's chapter, "'There's Never Been a Better Time to be a Woman': The Discursive Effects of Women on Boards' Research Reports," focuses upon the effects of media portrayals in research reports into the absence of women directors on corporate boards. Brown and Kelan offer a significant contribution to the academic analysis of reports into the lack of women on boards (WoB). Their aim is to examine the discursive effects of these reports beyond simply increasing the numbers of women on boards. The chapter is underpinned by the premise that media representations of leaders have a powerful influence over cultural discourses surrounding business and leadership. An analysis of research reports concerning women on boards is presented, including findings from academic research into the experiences of men and women seeking non-executive director (NED) roles on corporate boards in the UK. The authors' findings show that while reports about women on boards are abundant and often convincing, there is little evidence to demonstrate a direct causal relationship between the appointment of women and board *success*. Examining the different ways in which reports represent women on boards, the chapter importantly draws attention to what is representative of *fact* or truth, the legitimacy of the research reports, and the durability of the discourses they produce.

Part II: Women Professionals and Leaders

Part II explores the media representation of women professionals and leaders. Professions have a growing occupational and economic significance, partially fueled by an influx of women (and ethnic/minorities) that have historically been excluded from professional work (Muzio & Tomlinson, 2012). One reason for a lack of women's representation in professional roles is attributed to a shift from private to public patriarchy (Walby, 1986). Key to the idea of public patriarchy is the notion of the ideal worker who is promoted as gender neutral and yet shares characteristics typically associated with men. For example, Acker (1990) illustrated how the ideal worker has no family responsibilities and is able to devote their time exclusively to their job. This supposed gender neutrality, Acker argued, is also present in organizational structures—for example, through networks that take place outside of work hours. Women professionals' marginalization is long documented; for example, Kanter (1983) noted that women have often been stereotyped into limited roles associated with caring responsibilities. Such stereotyping limits professional women from becoming fully associated with professional work. The media are recognized as contributing to how people think about women and professional work (Macharia, O'Connor, & Ndangham, 2010). Women are associated, or framed, *with* and *through* gender, in contrast to men, who are represented as genderless (Pantti, 2005). Women's marginalization in relation to professional work is well illustrated in the media. According to the 2015 Global Media Monitoring Report (Macharia, 2015), the number of professional women working in the media has changed little, with only 37% of stories across newspapers, radio, and television being reported by women professionals. The perpetuation of such limited representations of women contributes to a media that reinforces gender stereotypes while claiming to be gender neutral. It is within this context that this volume contributes insights into *how* the media presents gendered stereotypes and limited representations, as well as identifying the consequences for women professionals.

Dr. Ann Rippin, Dr. Harriet Shortt, and Dr. Samantha Warren begin Part II with their chapter titled, "Dress and the Female Professional: A Case Study of *Working Woman*." They use a visual social semiotic approach to their analysis of *Working Woman* magazine, a mid-1980s UK publication aimed at professional women. Positioning the magazine as an example of a cultural text, they argue that many of today's women leaders and managers were socialized into their understandings of what it means to be a "professional woman" during this era. Their analysis thus provides insights into what they call the "performative heritage of gender," particularly in relation to the way women dress, including the use of make-up and accessories.

The chapter describes two levels of visual analysis: the first, a visual social semiotic analysis; and the second, hand-drawn, stylized sketches based on specific images from the magazines to exemplify a particular element. These sketches are presented in the chapter and serve, the authors argue, to articulate the visual power of *Working Woman*'s original images devoid of their more frivolous semiotic associations.

The next chapter in Part II, "In the Name of the Other: Nicknaming and Gendered Misrepresentation/s of Women Leaders" by Drs. Alison Pullen and Lucy Taksa, takes a unique perspective to the cultural production of women's leadership constructions in the media by focusing upon how nicknaming mis/represents women leaders and women's leadership. Pullen and Taksa examine an elite group of women who are the first in their country's history to have senior leadership positions in a long legacy of male occupants—first political leaders. The authors approach nicknaming as a discursive strategy and document how mass media is a cultural producer that shapes and marks women's leadership roles, images, and, eventually, perceived success. In the chapter, Pullen and Taksa successfully outline how the gendered construction of nicknaming is a fruitful way of exploring power manifested in and through mass media and leadership bodies. The chapter focuses upon analysis of the "Iron Lady" nickname to show the ways in which women leaders are evaluated in relation to their male counterparts and the ways in which nicknaming marks and stereotypes women in particular ways. Pullen and Taksa conduct an analysis across cultures of the Iron Lady nickname, which was given to first political leaders in the UK, New Zealand, Australia, France, Germany, Lithuania, Israel, Pakistan, India, Brazil, Latvia, the United States, and Liberia. Through their analysis, the authors highlight how nicknaming becomes a specific, gendered barrier to leadership and perpetuates negative-gendered media constructions of women leaders. Pullen and Taksa set out a range of future research to advance knowledge about the ways in which gendered economies employ and produce particular nicknames. This includes exploring how nicknaming produces inequality; how women leaders identify with and resist the mass production of their gendered lives through representation in the mass media; the relationship between nicknaming and sexuality, race, and age; and the embodied nature of nicknaming.

Drs. Janne Tienari and Pasi Ahonen's chapter, "Caveman Meritocracy: Misrepresenting Women Managers Online," provides an in-depth reading of online comments made in response to a feature article published in a web-based Finnish business newspaper, *Taloussanomat* (Ranta, 2012). Their findings reveal a dissonance between the egalitarian image of Finland and misogynist misrepresentations of women that reproduce gender stereotypes and myths. Tienari and Ahonen's analysis reveals an online anti-women discourse that is often vitriolic, serving to essentialize gender differences. They propose the term *caveman meritocracy* to characterize the dominant logic of the commentary that claims an order based on "natural" reasons (i.e., management is a masculine activity, and women are, by nature, unsuited for responsibility and leadership roles). According to Tienari and Ahonen, this logic is supported by the anti-women discourse of *caveman talk*, in which women are represented as simultaneously untrustworthy in management roles and in contravention of the natural order. Thus, a lack of women in managerial roles is a natural outcome resulting from meritocracy, competition ("the battle of the sexes"), and the evolutionary traits of each sex. Social media, they conclude, provides a conducive environment for the reproduction of misogynist misrepresentation such as caveman talk, enabling real-time gushes of emotional outrage to become public and permanent social discourse.

In Chapter 9, "Wynne Some, Lose Some: An Intersectional Approach to Media Prejudice Against Canadian Women Politicians," Dr. Rita Gardiner undertakes an intersectional analysis, informed by an Arendtian phenomenological investigation, to theorize about the prejudice faced by women politicians. The political campaigns of Kathleen Wynne, Canada's first openly gay premier, and Olivia Chow, the initial frontrunner to replace the former Mayor of Toronto, Rob Ford, were the focus of Gardiner's analysis. Interrogating their campaigns through the dual lens of intersectionality and Arendtian phenomenology reveals, Gardiner argues, how prejudice is multifaceted and privileges some individuals and physical bodies over others. The complexity and variability of individual identity revealed through an intersectional lens leads to some striking findings. For example, Gardiner argues that Wynne's lesbian identity did not significantly influence her campaign as much as Chow's ethnic identity influenced her campaign. The chapter provides great detail in its analysis of the different ways in which Wynne's and Chow's appearances are treated by the media. While Chow presents in a more feminine way than Wynne, the media have labeled Wynne as "Premier SchoolMarm"—a term credited in large part to her wearing spectacles. This leads Gardiner to reach two conclusions:

1. women leaders' appearance matters, but in different ways
2. media prejudice reasserts the political status quo.

Part III: Women in Film and Television

The comprehensive annual report published by the U.S. Media Center on the status of women in the media of the United States depicted a gendered landscape where women in film and television remain underrepresented both on and off screen. The report documented that only 27% of creators, writers, producers, executive producers, photography directors, and editors of prime-time television entertainment shows are women. The numbers are even starker in the film industry, where the Media Center report noted that 83% of all directors, executive producers, writers, cinematographers, and editors for the 250 most profitable films made in the U.S. during 2014 were men (and typically White men). Julie Burton, President of the Women's Media Center, has drawn attention to how this disparity is reflected in the 2015 Oscar nominations, with women numbering fewer than one in five of all non-acting nominees, and with seven Oscar categories in which no women were nominated (directing, writing—original screenplay, writing—adapted screenplay, cinematography, original score, visual effects, sound mixing). Burton pointed to a study in the *Los Angeles Times* in 2012 revealing the lack of diversity among Academy Award voters; in fact, 94% of Academy voters were White and 77% were male. Accordingly, it is no surprise that if the decision makers of what is deemed appropriate for film and television and worthy of the profession's accolades are largely male, what we see on screen will also reflect this pattern. The report highlighted that roles in film and television are more difficult to obtain for middle-aged and older women; where women do have roles, they tend to have fewer lines yet "show more skin" than their male counterparts. These issues are not confined to the United States. In the U.K., both the BBC Trust Annual Report (2015) and a subsequent government green paper on the future of the BBC (Department for Culture, Media, & Sport, 2015) reported a need to reflect the diversity of the television viewing population by developing a more balanced representation in terms of gender and ethnicity on screen. In 2015, a number of leading actresses from the U.S. and UK were united in speaking out about sexism in the film and television industry, notably in a year that saw the making of the film *Suffragette* (Kavanaugh, 2015), which charted some of the violent struggles in the fight for women's right to vote in the UK. Meryl Streep, one of Hollywood's most successful actors, who took the role of Emmiline Pankhurst in the film, discussed in an interview with BBC Radio 4 how women are excluded from film distribution and financing and are routinely paid less than men. Other leading actors, including Emma Watson, Jennifer Lawrence, Emma Thompson, Maggie Gyllenhaal, and Helen Mirren, have been equally forthright in bringing to light the gender pay gap in the media industry and sexism in film and television, including a persistent ageism in relation to female performers. The chapters that focus on the film and television industry, therefore, constitute an important social *and* academic endeavor, developing evidence and understanding of deeply embedded gendered assumptions and how these might be challenged and held accountable in an industry that has huge everyday influence across generations.

Drs. Helen Rodgers, Liz Yeomans, and Sallyann Halliday's chapter, "The 'Gogglebox' and Gender: An Interdiscursive Analysis of Television Representations and Professional Femininities," opens this section. The chapter offers insights into the experiences of women working or studying in three professions (public relations, psychology/criminology, and government/ politics) by exploring how these professions are represented in television programs. The authors argue that television representations of professional roles reflects a range of "isms," including sexism, racism, and ageism, which play an important role in (re)constructing and (re)negotiating gendered professional identities. Drawing on cultural studies, the chapter utilizes the "circuit of culture" framework (du Gay, Hall, Janes, Madsen, Mackay, & Negus, 1997, 2013) and critical discourse analysis to explore the experiences of women at differing stages of their careers in public relations, psychology/criminology, and government/politics. Themes of regulation, professional identity, early career influences, media influences in relation to television, and a concern to respond to pressures regarding appearance, looks, and media scrutiny are explored.

The chapter by Dr. Kimberly Yost, "Mediating the Future: Women Political Leaders in Science Fiction Television," explores representations of women leaders in science fiction television series. Yost suggests that expectations of legitimate political authority are gendered. In this chapter, the author examines how science fiction television enables reflection on current reality and contemporary social relations. The scenarios in science fiction narratives are argued to require particular forms of leadership, which may have implications for current perceptions of women political leaders. The chapter goes on to explore the masculine-coded leadership qualities seen in representations of Colonial President Laura Roslin of *Battlestar Galactica* and Prime Minister Harriet Jones of *Doctor Who*, before considering President

Allison Taylor of *24* and Samantha Willis of *Survivors*. Taylor and Willis are argued to be represented more tentatively and uncertainly, suggesting a disconnect between the women and the requirements of the position they hold. The author suggests that subtle forms of prejudice and disapproval of women leaders emerging can be seen in these latter representations.

Dr. Shana Matamala and Stephanie Abrahim begin their chapter, "The Runway-Ready Ringleader and Other Media Myths: An Analysis of Common Television and Film Stereotypes of Women Leaders," by contemplating the extent to which screen images influence individual perceptions of oneself and other women. They question whether these images outweigh other influences, including those of the family and our educational experiences. To undertake a critical examination of the myths and stereotypes perpetuated by the media, Matamala and Abrahim conducted a theoretical thematic analysis of U.S. film and television from the 1950s to the present day. Following several stages of analysis, three main stereotypes were identified: the communal caretaker, the devil woman, and the runway-ready ringleader. Matamala and Abrahim discuss each of these stereotypes in turn, identifying representative characters from film and television for each. One of the most interesting findings from the study, they argue, is the "repackaging" of the communal caretaker stereotype. While in the 1950s it was the housewife who was stereotyped in this way, recently the communal caretaker myth is told more often through the bumbling father, such as Homer from *The Simpsons*. Such characters are portrayed as unable to perform relatively simple household tasks, traditionally associated with women, thereby perpetuating the communal caretaker role for women.

The chapter entitled "Working in Shondaland: Representations of African American Women in Leadership," by Drs. Carrie Wilson-Brown and Samantha Szczur, examines popular American programs produced by Shondaland, the production company of Shonda Rhimes, a successful African American businesswoman. As Shondaland attracts millions of viewers within and beyond the U.S., the authors sought to interrogate representations of African American women who feature as lead roles in programs, including *Grey's Anatomy* (Dr. Miranda Bailey), *Scandal* (Olivia Pope), and *How to Get Away with Murder* (Annalise Keating). Drawing on critical organizational communication and critical media scholarship, Wilson-Brown and Szczur examine how race and sex interweave in the media representations of the lead African American female characters, illustrating how the characters demonstrate and reflect challenges that African American women in leadership positions encounter. Wilson-Brown and Szczur alert us to how gender and race expectations influence and shape the work and lives of African American women—not least, they note, in Rhimes's casting and writing despite claims from Rhimes that these are colorblind processes. Wilson-Brown and Szczur highlight how Rhimes's programs reflect the political economy of the televisual entertainment industry, including ~~who~~ or what can or cannot attain success. Importantly, the authors point to how the strong representation of African American women in leadership roles is accompanied by what they call a discourse that promotes a *benign* (lack of) racial politics, signaling that, while African American women are enabled to be seen occupying positions of influence, this must be done in a way that is not viewed as radical or disruptive and does not unsettle audiences or wider stakeholders.

The final chapter of the volume, by Dr. Alexia Panayiotou, is entitled "The Margin as a Space of Resistance: Transforming Gendered Leadership Through Popular Film." Beginning from the premise that popular culture influences how and what we learn about leaders, Panayiotou examines popular Hollywood films from the last 30 years to explore how executive women are portrayed in organizational spaces. In order to question the power that space has in organizations, the chapter draws on the theoretical lens of Butler's (1990) concept of "gender performativity." This approach illustrates that gender is not something we *are*, that is a fixed identity, but is something we *do*, which, in turn, may be prescribed by hegemonic discourses.

Following a search on IMDbPro focusing on identifying full-length English-language films produced during the last 30 years (1985–2014), Panayiotou conducted an in-depth examination of five films: *Baby Boom* (Meyers, Block, & Shyer, 1987), *Working Girl* (Wick & Nichols, 1988), *Disclosure* (Crichton & Levinson, 1994), *What Women Want* (Cartsonis, Davey, Matthews, Meyers, Williams, & Meyers, 2000), and *The Devil Wears Prada* (Finerman & Frankel, 2006). As she observes, although the search encompasses a lengthy time period, films in which women were portrayed in a central executive role, with a storyline that evolved in a corporate work space, are notably limited. While a preliminary analysis of the films suggests the perpetuation of a traditional sex stereotype, the chapter concludes by offering some hope regarding the subversive, and educational, power of popular film. Panayiotou identifies a new strong plot that challenges old stereotypes.

CONCLUSION

Collectively, the chapters in this volume reflect the beginning of a rich, diverse, emergent strand of academic research to examine relationships between the media in its multiple forms and women's leadership. Illuminating the positioning of women leaders and professionals as both complex and problematic, these chapters offer an important agenda for management and organization scholars. The chapters attest to the need to describe and make visible women's (mis)representations in the media, yet also draw attention to the importance of situating their (mis)representations in the broader social, economic, historical, cultural, and political context as a means to gain insight into their development and evolution. As a rich and diverse site of research, examination of the media calls for a broad methodological repertoire. The chapters in this book draw from multiple sources, including the development of thematic analysis to illuminate stereotypes (Matamala & Abrahim), the use of critical discourse analysis to understand professional women's experience (Rodgers et al.), a rhetorical analysis of the covers of *Time* magazine (French & Webster), and an interrogation of the power dynamics manifested in the media's practice of nicknaming women leaders (Pullen & Taksa).

This volume is a first step in stimulating further research that poses critical questions concerning gendered and sexualized representations of women leaders in textual and visual forms and considers the media's influence on gender equality and social justice. We hope the chapters offer fruitful avenues for future research to continue the momentum of challenging gendered media representations of women leaders and professionals.

REFERENCES

Acker, J. (1990). Hierarchies, jobs, bodies: A theory of gendered organizations. *Gender & Society, 4*(2), 139–158. doi: 10.1177/089124390004002002

BBC. (2015). *Annual Report and Accounts.* Retrieved from http://www.bbc.co.uk/aboutthebbc/insidethebbc/howwework/reports/ara

Butler, J. (1990). *Gender trouble: Feminism and the subversion of identity.* New York, NY: Routledge.

Cartsonis, S., Davey, B., Matthews, G., Meyers, N., Williams, M. (Producers), & Meyers, N. (Director). (2000). *What women want* [Motion picture]. United States: Paramount Pictures.

Crichton, M., Levinson, B. (Producers), & Levinson, B. (Director). (1994). *Disclosure* [Motion picture]. United States: Warner Bros.

Czarniawska, B., & Rhodes, C. (2006). Strong plots, popular culture in management practice and theory. In P. Gagliardi & B. Czarniawska (Eds.), *Management education and humanities* (pp. 195–218). London, UK: Edward Elgar.

Department for Culture, Media & Sport. (2015, July 16). *Government begins debate on the future of the BBC.* Retrieved from https://www.gov.uk/government/news/government-begins-debate-on-the-future-of-bbc

Du Gay, P., Hall, S., Janes, L., Madsen, A. K., Mackay, H., & Negus, K. (1997). *Doing cultural studies: The story of the Sony Walkman.* London, UK: Sage.

Du Gay, P., Hall, S., Janes, L., Madsen, A. K., Mackay, H., & Negus, K. (2013). *Doing cultural studies: The story of the Sony Walkman* (2nd ed.). London, UK: Sage.

Finerman, W. (Producer), & Frankel, D. (Director). (2006). *The devil wears Prada* [Motion picture]. USA: 20th Century Fox.

Hellgren, B., Löwstedt, J., Puttonen, L., Tienari, J., Vaara, E., & Werr, A. (2002). How issues become (re)constructed in the media: Discursive practices in the AstraZeneca merger. *British Journal of Management, 13*(2), 123–140. doi: 10.1111/1467-8551.00227

Jamieson, K. H. (1995). *Beyond the double bind: Women and leadership.* New York, NY: Oxford University Press.

Kanter, R. M. (1983). *Men and women of the corporation* (2nd ed.). New York, NY: Basic Books.

Kavanaugh, R. (Producer), & Gavron, S. (Director). (2015). *Suffragette* [Motion picture]. UK: Pathé.

Macharia, S. (2015). *Who makes the news? Global Media Monitoring Project.* Toronto, ON: World Association for Christian Communication. Retrieved from http://cdn.agilitycms.com/who-makes-the-news/Imported/reports_2015/global/gmmp_global_report_en.pdf

Macharia, S., O'Connor, D., & Ndangam, L. (2010, September). *Who makes the news? Global Media Monitoring Project.* Toronto: World Association for Christian Communication. Retrieved from http://www.genderclearinghouse.org/upload/Assets/Documents/pdf/gmmp_global_report_en.pdf

Mavin, S. (2008). Queen bees, wannabees and afraid to bees: No more 'best enemies' for women in management? *British Journal of Management. 19*(S1), S75–S84. doi: 10.1111/j.1467-8551.2008.00573.x

Mavin, S., Bryans, P., & Cuningham, R. (2010). Fed-up with Blair's babes, Gordon's gals, Cameron's cuties, Nick's nymphets. Challenging gendered media representations of women political leaders. *Gender in Management: An International Journal, 25*(7), 550–569. doi: 10.1108/17542411011081365

Mavin, S., & Grandy, G. (2013). Doing gender well and differently in dirty work: The case of exotic dancing. *Gender, Work & Organization, 20*(3), 232–251. doi: 10.1111/j.1468-0432.2011.00567.x

Mazza. C., & Alvarez, J. L. (2000). Haute couture and Pret-à- porter: The popular press and the diffusion of management practices. *Organization Studies, 21*(3), 567–588. doi: 10.1177/0170840600213004

Meyers, N., & Block, B. A. (Producers), & Shyer, C. (Director). (1987). *Baby boom* [Motion picture]. United States: United Artists.

Muzio, D., & Tomlinson, J. (2012). Editorial: Researching gender, inclusion and diversity in contemporary professions and professional organizations. *Gender, Work & Organization, 19*(5), 455–466. doi:10.1111/j.1468-0432.2012.00608.x

Pantti, M. (2005). Masculine tears, feminine tears—and crocodile tears. Mourning Olof Palme and Anna Lindh in Finnish newspapers. *Journalism, 6*(3), 357–377. doi: 10.1177/1464884905054065

Ranta, E. (2012, January 7). Torveloita ja tyrkkyjä—tässäkö se lasikatto on? [Village idiots and self-promoters—is this where the glass ceiling is?] *Taloussanomat.* Retrieved from http://www.taloussanomat.fi/tyo-ja-koulutus/2012/01/07/torveloita-ja-tyrkkyja-tassako-se-lasikatto-on/201120096/139?&n=12#comments

Stead, V., & Elliott, C. (2009). *Women's leadership.* London, UK: Palgrave Macmillan.

Tienari, J., Holgersson, C., Meriläinen, S., & Höök, P. (2009). Gender, management and market discourse: The case of gender quotas in the Swedish and Finnish media. *Gender, Work & Organization, 16*(4), 501–521. doi: 10.1111/j.1468-0432.2009.00453.x

Vinnicombe, S. Doldor, E., Sealy, R., Pryce, P., & Turner, C. (2015). *The female FTSE Board Report 2015. Putting the UK Progress into a Global Perspective.* Cranfield, UK: Cranfield School of Management. Retrieved from http://www.som.cranfield.ac.uk/som/dinamic-content/research/ftse/FemaleFTSEReportMarch2015.pdf

Walby, S. (1986). *Patriarchy at work: Patriarchal and capitalist relations in employment, 1800–1984. Feminist perspectives..* Cambridge, UK: Polity.

Wick, D. (Producer), & Nichols, M. (Director). (1988). *Working girl* [Motion picture]. United States: 20th Century Fox.

Women's Media Center. (2015). *The status of women in the U.S. media 2015.* Retrieved from http://www.womensmediacenter.com/pages/2015-statistics

PART I

WOMEN EXECUTIVES

CHAPTER 1

IS SHE REALLY INTO IT?

The Media as Misleading in Its Portrayals of Female Executives' Work–Family (Im)Balance

**Maura J. Mills, Leanne M. Tortez,
and Maria E. Gallego-Pace**
Hofstra University

From well-respected print news outlets to television to movies, mainstream media has always played a key role in how women are perceived and, correspondingly, stereotyped. This is no less true when it comes to women in leadership and executive-level positions. Such a directional impact is suggested by the transmission model (Carey, 2008; Kelan, 2013), whereby media input influences how female leaders are perceived by society, which, in turn, informs the opportunities available to them and the identities they assume. This model serves as the foundation for the majority of media research (Jensen, 2002) and has recently been enhanced (Craig, 2013) to stress the importance of a meta-theoretical perspective of the transmission model, which emphasizes cultural and societal shifts, as is evident in the examples and arguments used throughout this chapter. This chapter also aligns with van Zoonen's (1994)

Gender, Media, and Organization, pages 19–35
Copyright © 2016 by Information Age Publishing
19

emphasis on the role played by the transmission model in regard to media portrayals of women specifically, highlighting the need for the aforementioned cultural and societal considerations.

In line with the transmission model and its more recent societal and cultural framing, it stands that female leaders' (mis)representation by the media is detrimental to societal perceptions of the female leader (e.g., see Sung, 2013, for findings from the television show *The Apprentice*) and, therefore, her professional progression. Overall, the fact that female leaders are often misrepresented in the media comes as no surprise, considering that leadership is traditionally viewed as a masculine domain (see Heilman & Haynes, 2008, for a discussion of negative perceptions of incumbents in opposite-gender-typed roles). However, the nature of the media coverage that female leaders receive is substantially understudied as well as slanted in perspective. For instance, a key stereotype that has been levied against female leaders is in regard to their family commitments, and it is a multifaceted assumption (Mills, 2015). Specifically, the media often portrays female employees as having familial commitments outside of work that limit their dedication to (and therefore competence at) their jobs in ways that are not presumed to be the case for male employees. While this assumption is often made of all female employees, its deleterious effects arguably echo more intensively for women in leadership positions. This is particularly true considering that employees in such high-level roles are (a) more visible, and (b) subject to less rigid work–family boundaries than are non-leader employees (Grotto, 2015), which increases the likelihood that leaders will experience work infringing upon family demands.

Further, when female leaders are given press, such coverage often involves mention of their familial commitments at a rate disproportionately higher than similar comments are made regarding male leaders (Macharia, O'Connor, & Ndangam, 2010). In line with the transmission model, such coverage—whether intentionally or otherwise—implies that female leaders are (or should be) primarily family-oriented, therefore perpetuating the stereotype that these women compromise their commitment to and/or competence at their jobs in ways that male leaders do not (Campus, 2013). Given the dramatic ramifications that such misrepresentations can yield at both the organizational and societal levels, attention to this aspect of female leaders' misrepresentation in the media is crucial to a comprehensive understanding of the larger context of gender equality and social justice at the executive levels of organizations. As such, this chapter exposes the work–family-related misperceptions of female leaders by the media and discusses the adverse ways that both women and organizations are influenced by these misrepresentations as seen through the transmission model. In an attempt to combat the fallout from such misrepresentations, we also propose ways that researchers and practitioners alike can best attend to this issue in the modern workplace, wherein the leadership gender gap continues to tip (albeit slowly) toward more equal representation.

(UN)INTENTIONAL SUBTERFUGE?

Some may even go so far as to suggest that such gendered criticism of leaders by the media uses the transmission model to pigeon-hole women back into traditionally gendered (familial) roles (Wood, 1994). This is similarly the case when the media highlights female leaders who have been pushed over the proverbial *glass cliff*—for example, they have been set up for failure in a high-level position or project that is unlikely to succeed due to external contingencies (e.g., Ryan & Haslam, 2005). Bershidsky (2014) notes that while more women are brought in during times of crisis, when change is not immediate (i.e., failure), they are dismissed and the "safe" White male is brought in and credited with turning things around; this is known as the *savior effect* (Cook & Glass, 2013). Further, while both men and women brought into such precarious positions often fail due to unfavorable external contingencies, female leaders face disproportionally more publicity regarding such an outcome than do male leaders (The Economist, 2014). Such was the case for Carly Fiorina, former CEO of Hewlett-Packard, who saw the technology company through a merger/acquisition during a time of great uncertainty within the industry, only to be fired shortly thereafter and widely criticized in the media for the layoffs that accompanied the merger—as they often do (Cooney, 2015). Such misrepresentations thwart the progress of female leaders (Catalyst, 2007; Hu, 2015) as they not only fight against traditional corporate challenges (regardless of gender) but also bear the burden of additional challenges that come with the gendered stereotypes regarding female leaders' work–family balance/conflict.

Interestingly, the media's family-related backlash against female leaders that is discussed herein is not limited to women with families (understood here to be spouse/children).[1] Perhaps because society so inherently associates women with the familial roles of wife and mother, female leaders who do not hold such roles are also questioned about them—namely, why they have *not* assumed those responsibilities. In this way, then, the female leader is entrenched in a "damned if you do, damned if you don't" predicament from which she cannot emerge without critique. For instance, former United States Secretary of State Condoleezza Rice was repeatedly questioned about her relationship status (single), her ideal "fairytale wedding," whether she was "high-maintenance" and, in general, was expected to justify her (assumedly unfeminine) singledom (DePaulo, 2011). Notably, this would likely have (and historically has) gone unquestioned in a male leader not entrenched in the same societal expectations. Such media enthrallment (and judgment) of the unmarried female leader was perhaps best epitomized by Piers Morgan when interviewing Dr. Rice on his late night show. Referring to his upcoming segment, Morgan used this lead: "When we come back, Condoleezza Rice talks about her dream job, and *more importantly*, her dream man" (DePaulo, 2011, para. 4, emphasis by DePaulo).

Regardless of whether or not any given female leader has a traditional family, and regardless of whether the ensuing media-driven subterfuge is intentional or unintentional, the media is an extremely powerful influence in terms of how female leaders are viewed (Bhatt, Payne, Feldt, & Litzenberger, 2013; Wood, 1994). As the transmission model evidences, this is true not only in regard to the media's role in communicating information but also in its ability to influence the beliefs, attitudes, and behaviors of society. As such, when the media portrays female leaders in a negative light (Bligh, Schlehofer, Casad, & Gaffney, 2012) or in a certain stereotypical way with regard to their work–family commitments (and in which domain such commitments should or could weigh more heavily), it becomes easy for society to perceive the same and to adopt (or reinforce) those views and stereotypes as their own.

THE OTHER EXTREME

In fact, female leaders may feel as though they must go to the opposite extreme (disassociating themselves from the family domain at work) in order to prevent that stereotypical perception from being levied against them. For example, Newton-Small (2014) noted that many women running for political office try to avoid mention of their families because they do not want to be perceived as "too soft" (in an interesting comparison, male candidates often flaunt their families in an effort to make them seem more relatable). Another recent example of this is the self-proclaimed dictatorial managerial style of Katharine Zaleski, former manager at *The Huffington Post* and *The Washington Post*, and now-president of PowerToFly, a company designed with the intent of facilitating women's success in the work domain by allowing for workplace flexibility. However, Zaleski (2015) noted that this mission stands in stark contrast to her prior dealings with female subordinates, which were characterized by her insensitivity to the challenges faced by employed parents—often in an attempt to bolster perceptions of her own commitment to her work. When Zaleski became a parent herself, she looked to the media for examples of successful working mothers in high-level positions and came away disheartened. After reading everything from Sandberg's (2013) *Lean In* to Slaughter's (2012) widely-read article "Why Women Still Can't Have It All," Zaleski felt discouraged at the possibility that she saw as lying before her—that of "put[ting] up with the choices made by a male-dominated work culture if [she] want[ed] to succeed" (2015, para. 10). Sadly, she ultimately determined that her only means of success in both domains was to quit her job and start her own company—an admirable step into proactive molding of one's environment that speaks to Craig's (2013) meta-theoretical perspective of the transmission model as being more adaptive than its traditional view of a one-way street (Coleman, 2008). Was that likely the only solution? Probably not. But the fact that the media led her to believe that to be the case is itself revealing about the state of (mis)representation of female leaders in the media.

Another prime instance of an unfortunate extreme is the 2013 action of Marissa Mayer, president and CEO of Yahoo!, who decided to put an end to the company's remote work policy (Kennedy, 2013)—a type of policy that is typically regarded as a strategy to facilitate effective management of both the work and home domains. With that announcement, however, came an immediate backlash from the media, accompanied by extensive analysis of her actions and her reasoning, and critique of her own usage of the company's remote work policy after the birth of her child in a previous year (Weinberger, 2013). It is difficult to imagine that the same harsh critique and, more so, dive into personal life would have come of a male CEO making the same policy changes. In fact, multiple male CEOs, including Hubert Joly of Best Buy and Brian Moynihan of Bank of America, instituted similar policy changes during the same time frame (Schulte, 2013) that, by comparison, went largely unnoticed by the media.

MULTIFACETED MEDIA BACKLASH

This media backlash, however, is again multifaceted. Not only does it draw attention to female leaders' actions in more profound ways than those of male leaders, but it also backs the female leader into the proverbial corner. That is, in line with the aforementioned examples (Newton-Small, 2014; Zaleski, 2015), female leaders may feel the need to take a harsh stand on such issues in an attempt to convince others that they are serious businesswomen as opposed to being overly concerned with familial commitments and related flexibility needs. In this way, female leaders are forced to walk a fine line in juggling the soft skills and communal attributes that they are stereotypically expected to have, while still maintaining the decisive and driven attributes that a stereotypically strong leader engenders. The catch-22 is that by stepping too far in that direction, the female leader falls victim to the influence of the role congruity theory of prejudice (Eagly & Karau,

2002). Specifically, by failing to display the gender role-prescribed behaviors and attitudes (e.g., communal, caring, soft) presented in the media via the transmission model, she stands out as challenging the stereotype with which others are comfortable, thereby standing in opposition to their innermost schemas that help them organize their world and others' places in it.

Such opposition to gender stereotypes also leads to further negative backlash from subordinates, colleagues, and the media alike, who often equate likability with competence for female leaders in a way that is not done for male leaders (the femininity-competence double bind) (see Campus, 2013; Jamieson, 1995). That is, the former are deemed "irritable," "bossy," or even "the b-word" (see Ezzedeen, 2013 for examples of depictions in movies such as *The Devil Wears Prada*). For instance, Jill Abramson, the *New York Times'* first female executive editor, was continuously criticized for being too "pushy" and was ultimately fired in May 2014 (Khazan, 2014), and Carly Fiorina, the aforementioned former CEO of Hewlett-Packard, who has been criticized for her leadership style of focusing too sharply on the bottom line (something that male leaders do regularly, with little if any media backlash), rather than for moving the technology company "from lagging... to leading in every product category" (Cooney, 2015, para. 8). Men behaving in the same way, however, are more often lauded with descriptors such as "driven," "ambitious," "decisive," or "a strong leader." Such stereotypes endure in the mainstream media—and therefore in the culture as per the transmission model—despite having been called into question repeatedly by research in recent years (e.g., Koenig, Eagly, Mitchell & Ristikari, 2011).

THE DOUBLE-EDGED SWORD

The media all too commonly levies such negative descriptors upon successful female leaders while at the same time accusing them of being overly involved with family in ways that male leaders are not. One of the most notable recent examples of this, in line with the transmission model, is the media's handling of Hillary Clinton's campaign for U.S. President in 2016. Oft criticized in the media for her pantsuits (dubbed too masculine and lacking the "glam" factor; see Stevens, 2007, for a discussion of the trivialization effect), she has more recently been the victim of media debates about her commitment to the presidential role due to, of all things, her daughter's recent pregnancy. The media outwardly wondered whether Clinton would be too emotionally overwhelmed by her new role as a grandmother to commit to the presidency and to serve competently in that role if she wins it. Indeed, Pruden (2013) suggested, "life at the hearth with [her husband] and the dogs would be more rewarding" for a woman of 69; Pruden added, while "not particularly old for a man... a woman in public life is getting past her sell-by date at 69" (para. 10).

Interestingly, another viewpoint of the double-edge might suggest that if Clinton were to succeed in a presidential bid, her commitment to her (grand) parental role may be brought into question, as suggested by Edwards (2014). Since many see it as unnatural or unlikely for women to succeed in both domains, it may be assumed that her success in one role would only be possible because of a lack of attention to her other role—a perversion of Hobfoll's (1989) conservation of resources theory that would seem ludicrous if suggested of men. In fact, male leaders are often perceived as more trustworthy and stable employees when they are married with children than when they are not, even receiving what has come to be called the *fatherhood bonus* insofar as others' perceptions of their work-related competence are concerned, as well as actual monetary benefit (Correll, Benard, & Paik, 2007).

Even the thought of the same family-centered concerns raised about Clinton being levied about a potential male leader seems outlandish. This is especially true considering that the familial role in question is not even a parental role, but a grandparental one. Because Clinton's only child is grown, backlash about a heavy workload affecting her parenting does not seem applicable but, rather, this serves as evidence of how far the media is willing to go to find a reason why this female leader may be unfit for the position. Plenty of past (male) presidents have been grandparents (many with grandchildren actually *residing in* the White House), but that fact has not been raised as a concern about their dedication to either role. Indeed, in addition to questioning female leaders' job competence due to their having a family, the media often does the same when they *do not* have a family, thereby further illustrating the double bind. For instance, when Elena Kagan (in her 50s, single, and childless) was nominated as a Supreme Court Justice in 2010, a reporter questioned her competence at handling workplace issues, considering that she had never had children (Holson, 2010). The fact that such questions are even asked of female leaders is itself an indication of the media's gendered stereotypes concerning both leaders and women, as well as the media's influence via the transmission model on societal perceptions of women's dominant characteristics and important values (van Zoonen, 1991). Such questions are rarely asked of, and such concerns are rarely raised regarding, the male leader, as he is simply assumed to be primarily committed to his work rather than torn between work and family and perhaps only quasi-committed to (or competent at) either—the latter being the media-fueled assumption often made of female leaders.

THE HARM EXTENDS BEYOND WOMEN LEADERS

It may be easy to assume that the only real victims of these media misperceptions are female leaders, in particular those targeted by name but also those who may be assumed guilty by association (gender). However, such an assumption would be alarmingly misinformed. In fact, the failure of the media to normalize women as capable in the simultaneous roles of leaders and family members is harmful not only to women, but also to society as a whole as well as to organizations.

At the most obvious level, such misperceptions are harmful to women in the ways mentioned previously, as well as by sending destructive messages to girls, young women, and other aspiring female leaders, as explicated below. Negative media messages concerning women as well as an overall dearth of coverage of female leaders (not to mention the small percentage of women in such roles) sends the message to nonleader women and girls that leadership positions are largely unobtainable. Indeed, Bhatt et al. (2013) emphasized that the shortage of positive portrayals of female leaders in the media is particularly detrimental to young girls, as their aspirations and beliefs concerning gender are still forming and are thus largely impressionable. As an example of this, Zeilinger (2012) noted that the 2008 U.S. presidential campaign was especially harmful to young women in their formative years, as it depicted Hillary Clinton and Sarah Palin less as legitimate candidates and more as "sexist dichotomies" (para. 6), criticizing both for attempting to lead as well as for failing to meet expected standards of femininity.

Further, such misperceptions also limit same-sex mentoring opportunities available to women who transcend such negative effects of the media coverage and persist in their goals of a leadership role (Hoobler, Lemmon, & Wayne, 2011). Women may also experience stereotype threat[2] as they continuously see their gender represented in less than favorable ways in the media (Ezzedeen, 2013). Indeed, Davies, Spencer, and Steele (2005) found that women exposed to gender-stereotypic commercials strongly preferred a follower role versus a leadership role in a subsequent task. Conversely, women exposed to media images depicting other women in counterstereotypical and powerful roles have been found to have more positive self-perceptions as well as greater leadership aspirations (Simon & Hoyt, 2012).

Specifically in regard to family demands, an unfortunate number of media messages suggest to women that they should feel guilty if they outsource some home or family demands (e.g., daycare) to others (Korabik, 2015). Perhaps worse are the media and society's reactions when women outsourcing these demands do *not* feel guilty about doing so, resulting in society's perception of those women as selfish and thereby making them feel as though they should feel even guiltier (for not only "shirking" demands, but for doing so "cold-heartedly" and without "remorse"). With regard to career, such media messages—whether intentionally or otherwise—send these women the message that career power means having their family life and family-related decisions unfairly scrutinized and being judged by a harsher yardstick than their male counterparts will likely be judged. As such, a subset of these women will decide—perhaps even subconsciously—that one (albeit extreme) way to avoid this negative attention and judgment is by not advancing to positions of power at all. Unfortunately, in that way, such media messages via the transmission model can thwart women's success in powerful corporate positions even before it has begun.

On a larger scale, these types of media messages are also detrimental to society as a whole, as the media's tendency to give a gender-biased view of female leaders may result in unfair favoritism of the male leader at the organizational level when it comes to both administrative decision-making as well as to corporate culture as a whole. For example, such misperceptions can result, whether directly or indirectly, in a failure to see women as competent (or to hold higher competence standards for women than for men, who may be assumed competent as opposed to fighting an uphill battle) and in a devaluation of their performance. In turn, then, it can also indirectly lead to discriminatory treatment of women in organizations, including preventing them from attaining leadership positions at a rate similar to men (or at a minimum making it harder for them to do so).

MOVING FORWARD

Of prime importance in remedying these issues is a forward-focused agenda targeting these concerns from an informed perspective and taking action to remedy them in the workplace. This is best derived from evaluating existing research and using those findings to implement improved practices throughout the media as well as in corporations.

Existing Research Must Drive Further Inquiry

Women

In an attempt to begin filling the potholes that riddle the road paved for female leaders, more research must examine the contextual factors that are of greatest help to women in attaining (and succeeding in) leadership positions. For instance, many female leaders express the need for a trusted social support network, including seasoned female leaders as mentors (Ragins, Townsend, & Mattis, 1998). Recently, Cheung and Halpern (2010) conducted a review of qualitative research targeting female leaders who are successful in both work and family domains (as defined by leaders' own satisfaction with and perceptions of the interplay between these life roles). They found that success was facilitated by moving beyond the passive receipt of media messages inherent in the transmission model by redefining the two roles to fit their personal needs (versus the societal/

media expectation of what those roles should look like and how they should be fulfilled), as well as outsourcing some societally prescribed "motherly duties" to others (spouse, family, friends, or paid workers). Future research can further expand on such recommendations by including even more factors for facilitating success and evaluating their influence quantitatively.

Media

Further, while many sources comment on the adverse effects of the media on female leaders, this area is particularly underrepresented in the research domain. Such underrepresentation was highlighted by a recent content analysis of gender roles in the media (Collins, 2011), which determined that female leaders were underrepresented across a wide range of media and that the consequences for such underrepresentation, while not yet fully known, could be widely detrimental. A worldwide, longitudinal research effort known as the Global Media Monitoring Project (Macharia et al., 2015) is attempting to highlight this inequity as a first step toward rectifying it, noting that gender bias exists from multiple media perspectives, including percentage of men versus women identified by their family status (5% versus 19%, respectively), as well as the news topics in which men versus women were mentioned (men were mentioned in 70–90% of the news stories about professional businesspeople, compared to women's mention in 10–30% of those stories). With these findings in mind, we suggest that a stronger research emphasis on the role played by the media in yielding further information about female leaders and their work–family challenges would be useful in determining any potential differential relationships or identifying potential causes of deleterious effects. For instance, such research could shed light on what types of media outlets (i.e., newspaper, internet, television, etc.) and what kinds of foci (i.e., women as incompetent, sexist language/imagery, etc.) may have the most detrimental effects, and under what conditions. Determining such information is the necessary first step to rectifying the problem. Likewise, another critical issue to consider is that, given that men make most of the decisions in the media (Bhatt et al., 2013), research should look at the differential impact of media decisions made by men versus women on female leaders' portrayals in the media. Likewise, consideration should be given to examining how the broader editorial context may influence content decision making in a gender-biased manner. These considerations could further shed light on the source of the problem in order to better understand the issue and determine the most effective approach to remedying it.

Corporations

Hopefully by now most companies recognize the myriad benefits that can come with having women in leadership roles. Increasingly known as the female advantage (Helgesen, 1990), having women in positions of leadership increases the likelihood that companies will benefit from transformational and other underutilized yet highly effective leadership styles that capitalize on intermediary and interpersonal skills (Eagly & Carli, 2003). Krishnan and Park (2005) found a significant positive relationship between the proportion of women in top leadership and company performance, and Rosener (1990) suggested that women's use of a nontraditional leadership style "can increase an organization's chances of surviving in an uncertain world" (para. 3). As such, hopefully corporate leaders are asking themselves how they can foster an environment that supports women's career development and rise up the corporate ladder. Considering the transmission model's suggestion that media portrayals influence the perception of women by key organizational stakeholders (and others) and therefore influence the opportunities made available to them within the organization, research must examine the organizational elements (e.g., culture, support, recruitment/selection) that are conducive to attracting and retaining both male and female leaders equally. Corporate leaders can use the results of such research as a sort of organizational culture checklist to ensure that they are fostering an environment that does not constrain one gender more than the other and, in fact, supports both in their quest for greater responsibility and influence within the organization.

Action Steps in Practice

Media

As long as female leaders are misrepresented in the lens of the media, the types of issues discussed heretofore will continue to be prevalent. However, such a slanted outcome need not be the case interminably. In fact, the media can leverage its power to contribute toward the solution, as opposed to contributing to the problem. Key in doing so, however, is the media beginning to focus more on women's abilities and potential—both in leadership roles and in other professional domains—and less on women's familial status. Such a focus on female leaders as simply leaders, not as failed in their societal/parental/gender roles, not as unique or novel because of their "success against the odds," would facilitate the normalization of women in leadership roles and their success in that domain. Indeed, it is (long past) time for the media to step forward as a positive force in the fight to end sexism and promote equality. A prime example of media being used in this way is the motion picture *Miss Representation* (Siebel Newsom & Constanzo, 2011), which brought into the limelight key issues in this domain. In this regard, part of the solution may come from fighting media with media; we must recognize that just as the media holds the potential to do great harm, it likewise holds the potential to do great good. Indeed, a recent study found that positive media coverage has the potential to counteract the "competent but cold" stereotype regarding female political leaders (Schlehofer, Casad, Bligh, & Grotto, 2011) and no doubt similar findings are possible beyond the political domain.

Corporations

That said, the media's talk is of limited significance without associated follow-through, and walking that talk should be the responsibility of today's corporations and leaders. It is incumbent upon them to

1. set and adhere to policies and procedures that support women and men equally within all levels of organizational hierarchy (Sprung, Toumbeva, & Matthews, 2015), including ensuring that female leaders are treated equitably to men not only on the journey to the top but also while in those high-level positions (e.g., see Grant & Sandberg, 2015, on women leaders doing office housework)
2. hire and promote based upon skill and ability with a cautious eye toward selection criteria such as "fit," which can work against women moving into (male-dominated) top tiers
3. facilitate an equality-focused organizational culture
4. ensure that such a culture is promoted in practice—not just in lip-service—by managers throughout the organization in their dealings with employees at all levels and of both genders.

Indeed, individual managers' buy-in is key to the success of such corporate endeavors, as is evident in Tracy and Rivera's (2010) findings that male managers' personal values (e.g., their wives staying home to care for their children) translate into workplace decisions (e.g., not enacting work–life policies). However, it is not just male managers with whom we are concerned. Indeed, female managers are not immune to working against their own gender's scaling of the corporate ladder (recall the aforementioned example of Zaleski, who admitted to years of undermining female employees due to misplaced and assumed familial reasons). Either way, such findings serve as an important reminder that even high-level organizational change needs to start at an individual level.

CONCLUSION

Chief among concerns regarding how female leaders are misrepresented in the media is in regard to work–family considerations. As seen through the lens of the meta-theoretical transmission model, the media all too often makes and disseminates assumptions that (a) women with familial obligations are not competent enough to succeed in leadership roles; and (b) such multiple roles (family, work/leader roles) might compromise the female leader's work performance in ways that are not believed to be of concern regarding male leaders.

It is our hope that this chapter has illuminated some of the core work–family (mis)perceptions of female leaders that are so often levied by the media and subsequently incorporated into company culture as well as societal stereotypes. We also hope to have offered some actionable steps for research and practice in order to begin to progressively overcome these detrimental (mis)perceptions.

NOTES

1. We recognize that family responsibilities often stretch beyond one's spouse and children. However, because these are the familial roles for which women are most typically assumed to be responsible, they are the family referent used herein.
2. Stereotype threat, as termed by Steele and Aronson (1995), describes individuals' risk of unintentionally conforming to negative stereotypes about one's group.

REFERENCES

Bershidsky, L. (2014, April 29). Why women CEOs get fired more often. *Bloomberg View*. Para 3. Retrieved from http://www.bloombergview.com/articles/2014-04-29/why-women-ceos-get-fired-more-often

Bhatt, M., Payne, R., Feldt, G., & Litzenberger, A. (2013). *Leadership fictions: Gender, leadership and the media*. Los Angeles, CA: FEM Inc. and Take the Lead. Retrieved from http://www.taketheleadwomen.com/wp-content/uploads/2013/03/TTL_Leadership-Fictions.pdf

Bligh, M. C., Schlehofer, M. M., Casad, B. J., & Gaffney, A. M. (2012). Competent enough, but would you vote for her? Gender stereotypes and media influences on perceptions of women politicians. *Journal of Applied Social Psychology, 42*(3), 560–597. doi: 10.1111/j.1559-1816.2011.00781.x

Campus, D. (2013). *Women political leaders and the media*. New York, NY: Palgrave Macmillan.

Carey, J. W. (2008). *Communication as culture, revised edition: Essays on media and society*. New York, NY: Routledge.

Catalyst. (2007). *The double-bind dilemma for women in leadership: Damned if you do, doomed if you don't*. Retrieved from http://www.catalyst.org/system/files/The_Double_Bind_Dilemma_for_Women_in_Leadership_Damned_if_You_Do_Doomed_if_You_Dont.pdf

Cheung, F. M., & Halpern, D. F. (2010). Women at the top: Powerful leaders define success as work + family in a culture of gender. *American Psychologist, 65*(3), 182–193. doi: 10.1037/a0017309

Coleman, R. (2008). The becoming of bodies: Girls, media effects and body image. *Feminist Media Studies, 8*(2), 163–179. doi: 10.1080/14680770801980547

Collins, R. L. (2011). Content analysis of gender roles in media: Where are we now and where should we go? *Sex Roles, 64*(3), 290–298. doi: 10.1007/s11199-010-9929-5

Cook, A., & Glass, C. (2013). Above the glass ceiling: When are women and racial/ethnic minorities promoted to CEO? *Strategic Management Journal, 35*(7), 1080–1089. doi: 10.1002/smj.2161

Cooney, D. (2015, July 15). Background check: Why was Carly Fiorina fired from HP? *NBC News.* Retrieved from http://www.nbcnews.com/meet-the-press/why-was-carly-fiorina-fired-n356731

Correll, S. J., Benard, S., & Paik, I. (2007). Getting a job: Is there a motherhood penalty? *American Journal of Sociology, 112*(5), 1297–1339. doi: 10.1086/511799

Craig, R. T. (2013). Communication theory and social change. *Communication & Social Change, 1*(1), 5–18. doi: 10.4471/csc.2013.01

Davies, P., Spencer, S., & Steele, C. (2005). Clearing the air: Identity safety moderates the effects of stereotype threat on women's leadership aspirations. *Journal of Personality and Social Psychology, 88*(2), 276–287. doi: 10.1037/0022-3514.88.2.276

DePaulo, B. (2011, January 24). Does Piers Morgan ask why Condi Rice is single? Let me count the ways. *Huffington Post.* Retrieved from http://www.huffingtonpost.com/bella-depaulo/does-piers-morgan-ask-why_b_812416.html

Eagly, A. H., & Carli, L. L. (2003). The female leadership advantage: An evaluation of the evidence. *The Leadership Quarterly, 14*(6), 807–834. doi: 10.1016/j.leaqua.2003.09.004

Eagly, A. H., & Karau, S. J. (2002). Role congruity theory of prejudice toward female leaders. *Psychological Review, 109*(3), 573–598. doi: 10.1037/0033-295X.109.3.573

Edwards, H. S. (2014, May). Nana for president. *Washington Monthly.* Retrieved from http://www.washingtonmonthly.com/magazine/march_april_may_2014/ten_miles_square/nana_for_president049284.php

Ezzedeen, S. R. (2013). The portrayal of professional and managerial women in North American films: Good news or bad news for your executive pipeline? *Organizational Dynamics, 42*(4), 248–256.

Global Media Monitoring Project (2015, November). *Who makes the news?* Retrieved from http://cdn.agilitycms.com/who-makes-the-news/Imported/reports_2015/global/gmmp_global_report_en.pdf

Grant, A., & Sandberg, S. (2015, February). Madam C.E.O., get me a coffee. *New York Times,* p. SR2. Retrieved from http://www.nytimes.com/2015/02/08/opinion/sunday/sheryl-sandberg-and-adam-grant-on-women-doing-office-housework.html?_r=0

Grotto, A. R. (2015). On-demand: When work intrudes upon employees' personal time—does gender matter? In M. J. Mills (Ed.), *Gender and the work–family experience: An intersection of two domains* (pp. 201–223). New York, NY: Springer.

Helgesen, S. (1990). *The female advantage: Women's ways of leadership.* New York, NY: Doubleday.

Heilman, M. E., & Haynes, M. C. (2008). Subjectivity in the appraisal process: A facilitator of gender bias in work settings. In E. Borgida & S. Fiske (Eds.), *Beyond common sense: Psychological science in the court room* (pp. 127–155). Mahwah, NJ: Lawrence Erlbaum.

Hobfoll, S. E. (1989). Conservation of resources: A new attempt at conceptualizing stress. *American Psychologist, 44*(3), 513–524. doi: 10.1037/0003-066X.44.3.513

Holson, L. M. (2010, May 14). Then comes the marriage question. *The New York Times.* Retrieved from http://www.nytimes.com/2010/05/16/fashion/16noticed.html

Hoobler, J. M., Lemmon, G., & Wayne, S. J. (2011). Women's underrepresentation in upper management: New insights on a persistent problem. *Organizational Dynamics, 40,* 151–156. doi: 10.1016/j.orgdyn.2011.04.001

Hu, N. (2015, March 21). If we want equality, then we must stop perpetuating gender roles. *Harvard Political Review.* Retrieved from http://harvardpolitics.com/harvard/want-equality-must-stop-perpetuating-gender-roles/

Jamieson, K. H. (1995). *Beyond the double bind: Women and leadership.* New York, NY: Oxford University Press.

Jensen, K. B. (2002). The state of convergence in media and communication research. In K. Jensen, *A Handbook of media and communication research* (pp. 1–12). New York, NY: Routledge.

Kelan, E. (2013). The becoming of business bodies: Gender, appearance, and leadership development. *Management Learning, 44*(1), 45–61. doi: 10.1177/1350507612469009

Kennedy, L. (2013, March 5). Yahoo's Marissa Mayer is in a lose-lose battle. *Huffington Post.* Retrieved from http://www.huffingtonpost.com/babypost/yahoos-marissa-mayer-is-i_b_2784199.html

Khazan, O. (2014, May 14). Jill Abramson and the 'narrow band' of acceptable female behavior. *The Atlantic.* Retrieved from http://www.theatlantic.com/business/archive/2014/05/jill-abramson-and-the-narrow-band-of-acceptable-female-behavior/370916/

Koenig, A., Eagly, A., Mitchell, A., & Ristikari, T. (2011). Are leader stereotypes masculine? A meta-analysis of three research paradigms. *Psychological Bulletin, 137*(4), 616–642. doi: 0.1037/a0023557

Korabik, K. (2015). The intersection of gender and work–family guilt. In M. J. Mills (Ed.), *Gender and the work–family experience: An intersection of two domains* (pp. 141–157). New York, NY: Springer.

Krishnan, H. A., & Park, D. (2005). A few good women—on top management teams. *Journal of Business Research, 58*(12), 1712–1720. doi: 10.1016/j.jbusres.2004.09.003

Macharia, S., O'Connor, D., & Ndangam, L. (2010). *Who makes the news? Global Media Monitoring Project.* Toronto, ON: World Association for Christian Communication. Retrieved from http://cdn.agilitycms.com/who-makes-the-news/Imported/reports_2010/global/gmmp_global_report_en.pdf

Mills, M. J. (2015). *Gender and the work–family experience: An intersection of two domains.* New York, NY: Springer.

Newton-Small, J. (2014, September 29). The pros and cons of 'President Grandma.' *Time*. Retrieved from http://time.com/category/uncategorized/page/3151/?__rmid=read-daily-even-if-it-is-for-j-464078189.html

Pruden, W. (2013, September 24). Hillary's roots give her away. *The Washington Times*. Retrieved from http://www.jewishworldreview.com/cols/pruden092413.php3

Ragins, B. R., Townsend, B., & Mattis, M. (1998). Gender gap in the executive suite: CEOs and female executives report on breaking the glass ceiling. *Academy of Management Executive, 12*(1), 28–42.

Rosener, J. (1990). Ways women lead. *Harvard Business Review, 68*(6), 119–125. Retrieved from https://hbr.org/1990/11/ways-women-lead

Ryan, M. K., & Haslam, S. A. (2005). The glass cliff: Evidence that women are over-represented in precarious leadership positions. *British Journal of Management, 16*(2), 81–90. doi: 10.1111/j.1467-8551.2005.00433.x

Sandberg, S. (2013). *Lean in: Women, work, and the will to lead*. New York, NY: Alfred A. Knopf.

Schlehofer, M. M., Casad, B. J., Bligh, M. C., & Grotto, A. R. (2011). Navigating public prejudices: The impact of media and attitudes on high-profile female political leaders. *Sex Roles, 65*(1), 69–82. doi: 10.1007/s11199-011-9965-9

Schulte, B. (2013, April 11). 'Queen bee' CEOs get scrutiny and flak while 'king wasps' get a free pass. *Washington Post*. Retrieved from https://www.washingtonpost.com/lifestyle/style/queen-bee-ceos-get-scrutiny-and-flak-while-king-wasps-get-a-free-pass/2013/04/11/89d40d76-9acc-11e2-9a79-eb5280c81c63_story.html

Siebel Newsom, J., & Costanzo, J. [Producers] & Siebel-Newsom, J. [Director]. (2011). *Miss Representation* [Motion picture]. U.S.A.: Girls' Club Entertainment.

Simon, S., & Hoyt, C. L. (2012). Exploring the effect of media images on women's leadership self-perceptions and aspirations. *Group Processes & Intergroup Relations, 16*(2), 232–245. doi: 10.1177/1368430212451176

Slaughter, A. (2012, July/August). Why women still can't have it all. *The Atlantic*, 85–102. Retrieved from http://www.theatlantic.com/magazine/archive/2012/07/why-women-still-cant-have-it-all/309020/

Sprung, J. M., Toumbeva, T. H., & Matthews, R. A. (2015). Family-friendly organizational policies, practices, and benefits through the gender lens. In M. J. Mills (Ed.), *Gender and the work–family experience: An intersection of two domains* (pp. 227–249). New York, NY: Springer.

Steele, C. M., & Aronson, J. (1995). Stereotype threat and the intellectual test performance of African Americans. *Journal of Personality and Social Psychology, 69*(5), 797–811. doi: 10.1037/0022-3514.69.5.797

Stevens, A. (2007). *Women, power, and politics*. New York, NY: Palgrave.

Sung, C. C. M. (2013). Media representations of gender and leadership: From a discourse perspective. *Brno Studies in English, 39*(1), 89–105. Retrieved from http://connection.ebscohost.com/c/articles/88432602/language-gender-us-reality-tv-show-analysis-leadership-discourse-single-sex-interactions

The Economist. (2014, May 3). *The glass precipice: Why female bosses fail more often than male ones*. Retrieved from http://www.economist.com/news/business/21601554-why-female-bosses-fail-more-often-male-ones-glass-precipice

Tracy, S. J., & Rivera, K. D. (2010). Endorsing equity and applauding stay-at-home moms: How male voices on work-life reveal aversive sexism and flickers of transformation. *Management Communication Quarterly, 24*(1), 3–43. doi: 10.1177/0893318909352248

van Zoonen, L. (1991). Feminist perspectives on the media. In J. Curran & M. Gurevitch (Eds.), *Mass media and society* (pp. 33–54). London, UK: Edward Arnold.

van Zoonen, L. (1994). *Feminist Media Studies.* London, UK: Sage.

Weinberger, D. (2013, March 2). What Mayer misses on work–life balance. *CNN.* Retrieved from http://edition.cnn.com/2013/03/02/opinion/weinberger -work-from-home/

Wood, J. T. (1994). *Gendered lives.* Belmont, CA: Wadsworth.

Zaleski, K. (2015, March 3). Female company president: "I'm sorry to all the mothers I worked with." *Fortune.* Retrieved from http://fortune.com/2015/03/03/ female-company-president-im-sorry-to-all-the-mothers-i-used-to-work-with/

Zeilinger, J. (2012, July 16). Why millennial women do not want to lead. *Forbes.* Retrieved from http://www.forbes.com/sites/deniserestauri/2012/07/16/ why-millennial-women-do-not-want-to-lead/

CHAPTER 2

WHO'S THAT GIRL?

The (Mis)Representation of Female Corporate Leaders in *Time*

Sandra L. French and Lisa Baker Webster
Radford University

Many media studies have been conducted focusing on the power of the media to shape cultural opinions. Real (1977) stated that

> Mass-mediated culture has the power
>
> (a) To shape behavior and beliefs.
> (b) To determine aesthetic taste in cultural and artistic matters.
> (c) To maintain or modify the arrangement of society; and through all of these,
> (d) To play a part in ordering or disordering personal, group, or international life. (p. 4)

Several scholars have examined how women are underrepresented, or misrepresented, in television programs, newspapers and magazines, photographs, and advertising. Many analyses have been conducted regarding

Gender, Media, and Organization, pages 37–48
Copyright © 2016 by Information Age Publishing
37

media content, looking inside the pages and on the covers of various publications, with several disturbing findings as a result, establishing solid evidence that women and men are treated differently in the media.

Miller (1975), examining the content of news photographs, found 81% of photographs in the *Washington Post* and the *Los Angeles Times* were of males, while one-fourth of the women featured in the *Post* were brides. Johnson and Christ (1988) analyzed the covers of *Time* magazine from 1923–1987, determining that women were pictured on only 14% of the covers. The Johnson and Christ (1988) study examined women covers using the criteria of age, nationality, citizenship, and occupation. Of those covers, the largest occupation featured was artist/entertainer, while women holding positions of leadership in government or business accounted for only 7.5% of covers within this 64-year time period. Their subsequent study, published in 1995, of international women featured on *Time*'s cover during the same period included 126 women, only one of whom was a business executive (Johnson & Christ, 1995). Also in 1995, the Global Media Monitoring Project (GMMP) began providing longitudinal data on gender representations in world media in five-year increments, studying women's presence in relation to men, gender bias and stereotyping in news media content. Their most recently released data from 2010 indicate that women in professional business occupations are underrepresented, accounting for only 27% of media coverage in the United States of business persons, executive managers, and entrepreneurs (Macharia, O'Connor, & Ndangam, 2010). In 2013, Grandy conducted a quantitative analysis of women's visibility in U.S. and Canadian business magazines, analyzing one year of publications of the top three U.S. and the top three Canadian business magazines. She discovered that over one year's time, only four women appeared on the cover of either *Bloomberg Businessweek*, *Forbes*, or *Fortune* magazine, or merely 13.3% of the 30 covers.

The rhetorical analysis presented in this chapter examines media construction of female corporate leaders as portrayed on the covers of *Time* magazine. A weekly news magazine in publication since 1923, *Time* boasts a U.S. readership of over 17 million (TIME Media Kit, 2015). According to *Time*'s media kit, their readership is 48% female, and thus it seems wise to see what portion of their audience does or does not see itself reflected in the publication (TIME Media Kit, 2015). We chose to focus on *Time* not only because of its wide range of stories in business, politics, and contemporary culture, but also its historical tendency to feature a single person on its cover. Writing for the *Huffington Post*, Vagianos (2014) examined U.S. magazine covers that feature female leaders and highlights the top 23 magazine covers that she believes to have depicted those leaders in a positive manner, with *Time* and *Newsweek* having the most notable covers.

In 1976, *Time* compiled a gallery of 2,810 of its covers, ranging from 1923–1975, in book form, arguing in its introduction that

The faces on *Time* have been the faces of the world. The makers of peace and war, the prophets, merchants, and creators, the rebels and kings, the heroes of the age or of the moment. . . . For *Time* believes that history is made by men and women, no matter how strong the forces and movements that carry them along. (*Time* editors, 1976, p. 56)

Thus an examination of *Time* covers provides a window into not only current thinking, but longitudinal trends regarding the newsworthiness of women and their accomplishments.

Women on the cover of *Time* date back to 1923, when Eleanora Duse, an Italian actress, was the first female to be featured. While most of the women appearing on the cover during *Time*'s early years were entertainers or political spouses, *Time* also included such historical female figures as golfer Edith Cummings in 1924 and social movement leader Carrie Chapman Catt in 1926. An examination of *Time* magazine covers provides a primary lens through which to view representations of working women who have been featured in this way. To "land" a cover is an indication that one has captured the public's imagination in significant ways. Consequently, our content analysis of *Time* covers is a window into what, and how, working women have been portrayed as newsworthy.

It is impossible to conduct an analysis of women corporate leaders without addressing issues regarding the perception of appropriate gender roles. According to a 2009 landmark study conducted by *Time* and the Rockefeller Foundation that examined how individual Americans were responding to current gender issues; it was observed

that men and women were in broad agreement about what matters most to them; gone is the notion that women's rise comes at men's expense. As the Old Economy dissolves and pressures on working parents grow, they share their fears about what this means for their children and their frustration with institutions that refuse to admit how much has changed. In the new age, the battles we fight together are the ones that define us. (Gibbs, 2009, para. 3)

As more women are earning professional degrees and obtaining leadership positions within organizations, their increased representation should be visible in these media sources, given that mass media is a reflection of the reality in which we live. The persuasive effect of the media can be seen in our everyday lives. It is estimated that we come into contact with hundreds of media messages daily. The media has taken an assertive role in shaping our perception of events, as Klenke (1996) noted: "The media, like leaders, transmit values and culture. The role of mass communication in shaping views of ourselves and the world around us has been widely recognized" (pp. 110–111). The mass media determines not only what issues are important, but strongly influences what the public thinks about. According to Klenke, the term *pseudo-charisma* is often used to refer to "the media's manufacture of charismatic leaders through selective coverage. We can observe daily the manipulation of propaganda techniques and use of opinion polls to create an image of leadership" (p. 115). Such research suggests that media play a powerful role in the creation and acceptance of leaders in our culture.

The latest statistics show that women are still vastly underrepresented in positions of corporate leadership. Among Standard and Poor 500 companies, women currently hold just one-quarter of executive and senior leadership positions, not quite one-fifth of board seats, and only 4% are CEOs (Bernstein, 2015). Visual images help construct one's public media persona, increasing the likelihood they will be recognized by the public at large. Therefore, how and where women are photographed and how often their pictures appear in well-known publications is a reflection of women's perceived contributions to leadership in business. While male leaders such as Steve Jobs of Apple or Mark Zuckerberg of Facebook are often featured on the covers of leading magazines and are easily identifiable, with such a small percentage of females holding corporate leadership positions, can the same be said for these female counterparts? If the few female leaders are rarely visually featured in the media, how can they become role models for future female entrepreneurs? In providing an analysis of how often female corporate leaders appear on the cover of *Time* magazine and the text, if any, that accompanies their pictorial image, we see the relative value placed on women corporate leadership in society and can discuss any gains made in women's corporate leadership as evidenced by a larger percentage of coverage over time.

In addition to the small number of females assuming corporate leadership roles, recent research has also indicated a trend of "large numbers of highly qualified women dropping out of mainstream careers" (Canas & Sondak, 2011, p. 90). While many explanations such as childcare or eldercare could be cited for this pattern, many women revealed that they left because their jobs were not satisfying, they were understimulated, or there was a lack of opportunity for advancement at these organizations. Women have also identified the absence of female mentors in the workplace as contributing to feelings of isolation and loneliness.

Another reason for the "opting out" of talented women could be the lack of positive female leaders reflected in the media. Because we are a mass-mediated society, whenever we watch TV, read a magazine, or listen to a news report, we are constantly receiving messages about what a female leader should be. Political leaders such as Hillary Clinton, Angela Merkel, and Sarah Palin are often critiqued on their hairstyles and clothes. Marissa Mayer, current president and CEO of Yahoo!, was criticized for her short maternity leave. Movies such as *Horrible Bosses* (2011), *The Proposal* (2009), and *The Devil Wears Prada* (2006), portray female bosses as unfulfilled in their personal life and bitter, irrational, and overly harsh in their managerial style. With such stereotypical images being frequently depicted in the mainstream media, women may be subtly discouraged from even pursuing leadership roles.

In "Framing Feminism," Lind and Aravena (2013) studied the use of the terms *woman* or *women* and *feminist/s/ism* in the news and public affairs programs. Woman or women was used more than 40 times as often as the term feminist/s/ism on such news programs as ABC, CNN, NPR, and PBS. How the media frames these words is important because such use enlightens the audience about feminist concerns and the feminist perspective, presents feminism as something that does not happen often in the private sphere, and communicates that feminism is not relevant to the majority of citizens. When feminism is used by the media, it is often associated with such areas as politics, business, media, and the arts. Feminists are seen as not quite regular or normal. The message is clear that *real* women have homes and engage in regular day-to-day work. Real women would not appear on the cover of magazines. Constructing the message that feminists are unconventional and scarce not only disempowers feminism but also discourages other women from attempting similar forms of success. *Time* magazine was also guilty of contributing to the mixed messages projected to the public over the women's movement. Rhode (1995) criticized *Time's* coverage of this important topic, stating: "*Time's* coverage failed to mention the movement's substantive achievements or grassroots organizing efforts and capped it all with a ludicrous cartoon" (p. 693). Since media helps shape our understanding of people, events, and policy, an analysis of *Time* magazine's images of working women uncovers the framing of how women corporate leaders are represented or misrepresented.

Even after several decades of female forays into business, politics, and other previously male-dominated arenas, Shugart (2003) argued, "Traditional gender constructs long have been a staple of the mass media, which in turn are a primary, if not the primary, means by which those constructs are reified and articulated to the public today" (p. 1). Many times, the representation of female leaders in the mass media may actually discourage any role identification by other women:

> When women do hold positions of authority and propose fundamental political, economic, or social changes, the media frequently call them into question, both as women and as leaders. In the media, such questioning is typically very public, very emotional and often very "dirty" in nature. (Klenke, 1996, p. 118)

A study conducted by researchers at Catalyst (Sabattini, 2007), a leading research and advisory firm that helps companies expand opportunities for women at work, cites gender stereotyping as a major culprit in the corporate women's leadership gap. While women leaders still struggle with issues of achievement and gendered social expectations, leadership opportunities in business, politics, and public life have expanded for those with the skills and savvy to negotiate what Kathleen Hall Jamieson described as "double binds" (1995), in which she depicts women's leadership efforts as a series of double binds from which women had to extricate themselves before reaching their potential. Jamieson's work details five specific double binds acting as constraints on women exercising leadership: womb/brain, silence/shame, sameness/difference, femininity/competence, and aging/invisibility. While all five are useful constructs for discussing the portrayal of women's leadership in media, we focus here on the two we found most evident during our research—Jamieson's femininity/competence bind and the sameness/difference bind.

Jamieson's binds were studied by French and Holden (2012), who examined the roles the womb/brain and femininity/competence binds played in media coverage of Hillary Clinton and Sarah Palin. Our chapter offers an analysis of media portrayals of women corporate leaders using Jamieson's landmark double binds from her groundbreaking book as our guide. By providing a rhetorical analysis and a demonstration of longitudinal trends in the portrayal of women's corporate leadership, we offer an assessment of the gendered construction of women leaders as portrayed in a key U.S. news publication, *Time*.

METHOD

Our examination of *Time* covers was a four-step process. First, we began by creating a spreadsheet listing all covers on which women appear. Women were then categorized as *specific* or *generic*. A specific cover was defined as a woman who was mentioned by name somewhere on the cover—for example, Hillary Clinton or Janet Yellen. Generic female covers were defined as instances where women were intended to be representative of a larger group, such as *working mothers* or *female veterans*. Since this volume deals specifically with how women leaders are represented in the media, only specific covers were analyzed. At this stage it was noted whether or not a cover included a single image of one woman or a composite photograph of several women. As long as the women were named specifically on the cover, the image was included in our analysis; however, *Time's* special issues, which tend to feature a composite of dozens of people, such as the "100 Most Influential People" issues, are not included in these findings.

After identifying the specific covers, at the third stage, only covers featuring a female organizational leader were analyzed. Additionally, we addressed the fact that it is possible for a woman leader to be featured on the cover for a reason other than her leadership: for example, if she (or her spouse) was involved in a scandal of some kind. In these cases, we used how the headline on the cover referred to the woman to help determine whether or not the article centered on the woman "as leader." We recognize that this method limited the number of covers available for analysis; however, we find found this to be important news in and of itself. As of December 2014, men have appeared on the cover 4,292 times, women only 763 times. Of the 763 covers featuring specific women, only six include women corporate leaders. Consistent with the previous study conducted by Johnson and Christ (1988), the bulk of covers including women fell into the occupation of entertainers, specifically actresses and opera singers. The fourth and final stage of analysis involved an examination of the cover photos and headlines, looking for evidence of Jamieson's double binds. In particular, we found that the layout and design of the covers illustrated Jamieson's femininity/competence bind and the sameness/difference bind.

DISCUSSION

The six corporate female leaders featured on the cover of *Time* from 1923–2014 and included in our analysis are Elizabeth Arden (1946), the Wallaces (1951), Alicia Patterson (1954), Sheryl Sandberg (2013), Janet Yellen (2014), and Mary Barra (2014). Industries represented by these six women range from makeup to publishing, from Facebook to General Motors, and the Federal Reserve. From 1954 to 2013, almost 60 years, not a single female corporate leader was pictured on *Time's* cover. During the decades in which women fought for the equal rights amendment, through the "have it all" decade of the 1980s, not a single business woman was featured on the cover. A full 50%, three of the six covers that featured women in corporate leadership, appeared in 2013–2014.

In analyzing the photographs, four of the six covers are head or portrait shots; only Sheryl Sandberg and Mary Barra are featured in a long or body shot. In both long shots, the women have their arms crossed in front of them. In all six covers, women's jewelry is visible and each woman is clearly wearing makeup. In two of the six covers, the woman is looking off to the side; the remaining four have photographs in which the female is looking to the center, presumably directing out at the audience. Lila Wallace is the only woman without a solo cover; she is featured with her husband. It should be noted that the headline for this couple, the co-founders of *Reader's Digest,* is "The Dewitt Wallaces"—as if his name should suffice to introduce them both to the world. The couple is not standing side by side; rather, Lila is behind her husband, clearly in the background of the picture.

Femininity/Competence Bind

According to Jamieson (1995), the femininity/competence double bind is undergirded by an assumption that feminine women are neither mature nor decisive. Women must negotiate this bind by demonstrating a mythical and unattainable balance of feminine characteristics and masculine toughness. Jamieson cited Margaret Thatcher as an example of a woman who felt the constriction of this bind, choosing to lower the pitch of her voice to adopt a more masculine sound, as "the deeper male voice, however, has long been assumed as the norm for exercise of leadership" (1995, p. 121). While we are not analyzing speeches here, we might similarly assume that the preferred standard clothing for leadership is the business suit. In our analysis of these six covers, we see a longitudinal change in the negotiation of business attire. While the Elizabeth Arden cover is a very tight portrait shot, stopping just below the shoulders, it is clear she is wearing a suit, as is Alicia Patterson. As the founder and editor of *Newsday*, which became one of the most successful daily postwar newspapers in the 1940s, Patterson was clearly leading in a man's world, and while her portrait has her in a suit, she is also wearing a white blouse with a bow: a clear attempt to negotiate the femininity/competence bind.

While the picture of the Wallaces makes it impossible to determine with certainty whether Lila Wallace is wearing a dress or a suit, her position in the photograph behind and slightly off-center to her husband is indicative of a submissive, more traditionally feminine posture. Moving from the 1950s into the 21st century, we see our first instance of a picture and headline combination that underscores the longevity of this dilemma for female leaders. Sheryl Sandberg, COO of Facebook, is featured on the March 18, 2013, cover. She is the first female corporate leader to appear in a full body shot wearing a dress, and the dress is somewhat form-fitting with a V-shaped neckline. Clearly Sandberg is not trying to look like a man in this photograph. Perhaps we are putting this double bind behind us? Then, we read the headline, pasted across the front of the picture: "Don't hate her because she's successful." And with that phraseology, *Time* assumes a societal backlash against this woman's accolades, further solidifying the continued existence of the femininity/competence bind.

Sandberg's dress, with high heels to match, is a vibrant red. A 2015 *Inc.* magazine web article, "13 Women Who've Redefined Power Dressing," cited the head of the Scottish National Party, Nicola Sturgeon, stating, "Red is a power color" (Henry, 2015, para. 2). Sandberg herself is cited in the article, stating that she doesn't like to get too "fashiony" (para. 10). Thus we see the negotiation of the femininity/competence bind; I must appear powerful, but not so powerful that men find me threatening.

In 2014, the two women corporate leaders featured on *Time's* cover—Janet Yellen and Mary Barra—also evidence the femininity/competence bind. With Janet Yellen, we return to the head shot. However, in this cover, Yellen is wearing neither a suit nor a dress but, instead, a sweater twinset in deep purple, complete with gold buttons and black trim. Her facial appearance is somewhat stern; she is looking away from the camera with a serious expression. Could the clothing be an attempt to soften her image? Help negotiate societal expectations? Then, in October 2014, Mary Barra appeared on the cover. As the CEO of General Motors, Barra is leading GM at a critical time in the car automotive company's history, and she must guide GM through a recall of 30 million vehicles and pending litigation. In Barra's cover, we see a return to the business suit, in this case a black pantsuit, with some ornamental gold jewelry at the chest. Barra is straight-faced, looking center toward the camera (and reader). Each image portrays an attempt to navigate a mythical perfect balance between femininity and competence.

Sameness/Difference Bind

Closely related to the femininity/competence bind is the sameness/difference bind. According to Jamieson (1995), "[W]omen are subordinate whether they claim to be different from men or the same" (p. 16). This bind suggests that the de facto professional standard is male-defined and male-centered. Once compared to this standard, whether from a perspective of sameness or difference, women are judged inferior. In order to analyze the presence of the sameness/difference bind, we must first explore the male characteristics that form the culturally accepted standard of the business professional. Stereotypically male characteristics such as power, domination, seriousness, and strength combine to form our cultural lens of business professionalism.

In our six covers, each woman is photographed in such a way as to portray seriousness and strength. Not one woman is smiling in these photographs, nor do any show their teeth. All have tight-lipped, determined looks on their faces. We argue this lack of emotion is an attempt to mask their femininity. A study by Rodgers, Kenix, and Thorson (2007) examined the emotional portrayals of individuals in news photographs of a major U.S. daily newspaper. The findings highlight that women are most often photographed as happy or smiling. When female organizational leaders are depicted as showing little emotion, it may be an attempt to create distance from the cultural perception of women as warm and friendly and, therefore, not as serious as their masculine counterparts.

Four out of our six covers depict women wearing suits. The suit has long been described as the primary attire for business and management personnel. In her study of the power suit in politics, Flicker (2013) argued, "The pantsuit has become established as the 'suit for women' and represents a submissive adaptation to the male dress code—the suit—which still represents White male hegemony in the global sphere" (p. 216). Several of the women studied here are wearing feminized versions of a suit, noting Alicia Patterson's white blouse with a bow at the neck, and Elizabeth Arden's clearly visible pearls at the neckline. Only Sheryl Sandberg is wearing a dress but, as already mentioned, in the power color red.

Of the six covers, five covers also contained other symbols of masculinity suggesting that these women are not representative of the typical female. On the Elizabeth Arden cover, she is pictured with two racehorses, something that was (and still is) a male-dominated field. As previously mentioned, Lila Wallace is photographed behind Dewitt Wallace, which sends a subliminal message that it is the female standing behind her man, and she is there more for his support than to make any real contributions. Words can also have an association with male characteristics. Sheryl Sandberg has the word "successful," Janet Yellen has the words "trillion dollars," and Mary Barra has the word "mechanic" in blue type on her cover. By having these words associated with the female leaders, it is somehow trying to legitimize who they are and why they are on the cover of the magazine. This analysis shows that women are caught in a communicative lose/lose bind of how leadership can be visually represented in their person. Women constantly walk a tightrope of balancing inclusion and exclusion; dress too differently from a man and risk being perceived as one who cannot handle what is, de facto, a man's job, or dress too much like a man and garner criticism and backlash for discarding the unique characteristics of womanhood. The result is the same: women are still judged by masculine standards of what leadership *looks like*.

CONCLUSION

Despite the range of industries and time periods represented by our six female corporate leaders, they all must visually craft a perception of leadership capability while negotiating the common catch-22 of balancing their femininity with their competence and their similarity and difference when compared to culturally accepted gender stereotypes. These binds intersect with one another and are not easily untangled. Women's attempts to navigate these binds are apparent in visual communication through choice of clothing, makeup, and camera angle. Perhaps the most alarming finding of this preliminary research is the fact that through an examination of 91 years of publication, only six female corporate leaders were featured on *Time* magazine covers, demonstrating that women professionals are drastically underrepresented by a publication that claims to serve them. There was little need to discuss such issues as diversity or ageism because the number was so low. If we are to encourage the next generation of female leaders to enter the corporate world, there is a need for role models or mentors for them to see.

For future analysis, to include a wider range of women who appear on the cover of *Time*, we identified several female covers of women featured for their expertise in politics, art, sports, and entertainment. By opening up the analysis to a wider range of women, more longitudinal trends could be examined.

We close this chapter by offering a few final thoughts on the implications of who is featured on the cover of *Time*. Time Warner publishes 140 magazines, including *Time, Life, Sports Illustrated, Fortune, Parenting*, and *Entertainment Weekly*. If promoting a more consistent and positive image of female leaders was truly a top priority in our mass-mediated culture, the ability to do so lies with those who are controlling the media. However, from a business standpoint, if female leaders on the cover of magazines do not sell, it is the publisher who is at a financial loss. According to a report from *AdWeek*, the June 16 issue of *People* featuring Hillary Clinton was the worst-selling of 2014 with 503,890 copies sold, while the magazine's best-selling issue featured Robin Williams after his death in late August (Fuller, 2014). Further examination is warranted to see *why* such magazines with female leaders and trendsetters on the cover tend to sell fewer copies. With only six female corporate leaders featured in 91 years of news covers, could it be that not only are some of these women misrepresented but might we also say that *Time* has missed representing women's leadership contributions to business?

REFERENCES

Bernstein, A. (2015). *Why are we so hard on female CEOs?* Retrieved from https://hbr. org/2015/05/why-are-we-so-hard-on-female-ceos

Brener, R. (Producer), & Gordon, S. (Director). (2011). *Horrible bosses* [Motion Picture]. United States: New Line Productions.

Bullock, S. (Producer), & Fletcher, A. (Director). (2009). *The proposal* [Motion Picture]. United States: Touchstone Pictures.

Canas, K. A., & Sondak, H. (2011). *Opportunities and challenges of workplace diversity: Theory, cases, and exercises* (2nd ed.). Upper Saddle River, NJ: Prentice Hall.

Caracciolo Jr, J. (Producer), & Frankel, D. (Director). (2006). *The devil wears prada* [Motion Picture]. United States: Twentieth Century Fox Film Corporation.

Flicker, E. (2013). Fashionable (dis-)order in politics: Gender, power and the dilemma of the suit. *International Journal of Media & Cultural Politics, 9*(2), 201–219. doi: 10.1386/macp.9.2.183_1

French, S. L., & Holden, T. Q. (2012). Positive organizational behavior: A buffer for bad news. *Business Communication Quarterly, 75*(2), 208–220. doi: 10.1177/1080569912441823

Fuller, J. (2014, December 16). *People* Magazine's worst selling issue this year? The one with Hillary Clinton on the cover. *The Washington Post.* Retrieved from http://www.washingtonpost.com/blogs/the-fix/wp/2014/12/16/people-magazines-worst-selling-issue-this-year-the-one-with-hillary-clinton-on-the-cover/

Gibbs, N. (2009, October 14). What women want now. *Time*. Retrieved from http://content.time.com/time/specials/packages/article/0,28804,1930277_1930145_1930309,00.html

Grandy, K. (2013). The glossy ceiling: Coverage of women in Canadian and American business magazines. *Journal of Magazine & New Media Research, 14*(1), 1–20. Retrieved from http://aejmcmagazine.arizona.edu/Journal/Summer2013/Grandy.pdf

Henry, Z. (2015). 13 women redefining how to dress for success. *Inc*. Retrieved from http://www.inc.com/zoe-henry/13-women-rocking-power-dressing.html

Jamieson, K. H. (1995). *Beyond the double bind: Women and leadership*. New York, NY: Oxford University Press.

Johnson, S., & Christ, W. (1988). Women through *Time*: Who gets covered? *Journalism Quarterly, 65*(4), 889–897. doi: 10.1177/107769908806500408

Johnson, S., & Christ, W. (1995). The representation of women: The news magazine cover as an international cultural artifact. In D. A. Newsom, & B. J. Carrell (Eds.), *Silent voices* (pp. 215–235). Lanham, MD: University Press of America.

Klenke, K. (1996). *Women and leadership: A contextual perspective*. New York, NY: Springer.

Lind, R., & Aravena, C. (2013). Framing feminism. In R. Lind (Ed.), *Race/gender/class/media 3.0* (pp. 140–148). Upper Saddle River, NJ: Pearson.

Macharia, S., O'Connor, D., & Ndangam, L. (2010). *Who makes the news? Global Media Monitoring Project*. Toronto, ON: World Association for Christian Communication. Retrieved from http://cdn.agilitycms.com/who-makes-the-news/Imported/reports_2010/global/gmmp_global_report_en.pdf

Miller, S. H. (1975). The content of news photos: Women's and men's roles. *Journalism & Mass Communication Quarterly, 52*(1), 70–75. doi: 10.1177/107769907505200112

Real, M. R. (1977). *Mass-mediated culture*. Englewood Cliff, NJ: Prentice-Hall.

Rhode, D. (1995). Media images, feminist issues. *Signs: Journal of Women in Culture and Society, 20*(3), 685–709. Retrieved from http://www.jstor.org/stable/3174839

Rodgers, S., Kenix, L. J., & Thorson, E. (2007). Stereotypical portrayals of emotionality in news photos. *Mass Communication and Society 10*(1), 119–138. doi: 10.1080/15205430709337007

Sabattini, L. (2007). The double-bind dilemma for women in leadership: Damned if you do, doomed if you don't. *Catalyst*. Retrieved from http://www.catalyst.org/system/files/The_Double_Bind_Dilemma_for_Women_in_Leadership_Damned_if_You_Do_Doomed_if_You_Dont.pdf

Shugart, H. A. (2003). She shoots, she scores: Mediated constructions of contemporary female athletes in coverage of the 1999 U.S. women's soccer team. *Western Journal of Communication, 67*(1), 1–31. doi: 10.1080/10570310309374756

Time editors. (1976). *Faces in the news: A gallery of 2810 time cover painting and photographs*. New York, NY: Time, Inc.

TIME Media Kit. (2015). Print audience. *Time, Inc*. Retrieved from http://www.timemediakit.com/audience/

Vagianos, A. (2014, January 27). 23 magazine covers that got it right when depicting powerful women. *The Huffington Post*. Retrieved from http://www.huffingtonpost.com/2014/01/27/magazine-covers-powerful-women_n_4673808.html

CHAPTER 3

A FAIRYTALE CAREER

Media Representations of Australia's First Female Banking CEO

Helena Liu
University of Technology Sydney

Leadership is a highly gendered phenomenon. The prevalent underrepresentation of women in executive leadership positions and ongoing challenges for the few who occupy those positions reflect an abiding association between leadership and men and masculinities (Alvesson & Billing, 2009). Mainstream theorizing, development, and practice have traditionally defined leadership in masculine terms, romanticizing paternalism and conquest (Collinson & Hearn, 1994; Kerfoot & Knights, 1993). Consequently, female leaders often find themselves in a "double bind" (Jamieson, 1995), in which they are expected to simultaneously enact stereotypical notions of masculinity to persuade their competence and stereotypical notions of femininity to maintain their likeability (Hall & Donaghue, 2012).

Although the ways in which women are marginalized and subordinated by prevailing gender norms are well-documented (Calás & Smirnich, 2006; Collinson & Hearn, 1996; Eagly & Carli, 2007; Gherardi, 1996; Haslam &

Gender, Media, and Organization, pages 49–62

Ryan, 2009; Hearn, Sheppard, Tancred-Sheriff, & Burrell, 1989), relatively less is known about how women co-construct their leadership with the media. As a key platform on which social meanings are produced, disseminated, and consumed, the media plays a powerful role in supporting or subverting gender norms in the representation of leaders (Liu, Cutcher, & Grant, 2015). This chapter examines how gender norms inform the visual and verbal media representations of Gail Kelly from her appointment to Westpac Banking Corporation in 2008, where she became the first (and so far only) woman to lead a major Australian bank through the Global Financial Crisis (GFC) until 2010.

In doing so, the chapter aims to contribute to existing understandings of leadership by demonstrating how the media co-constructed a gendered image of a high-profile female CEO. It also highlights the important role of context, where gender norms intersect with the GFC and the history of the banking sector to mediate representations of leadership. By delineating how one female CEO sought to present herself in the media through interviews and photographs and how she was subsequently framed by the media, the chapter can potentially illustrate how women in leadership positions engage with media producers in ways that have greater potential to resist oppressive gender norms.

This chapter begins with the background to the study, including an overview of Kelly's career and the history of Westpac. It will then outline the methods of analysis. The findings in relation to Kelly's media representation will then be detailed, starting with her appointment through to the GFC.

BACKGROUND

Gail Kelly was born in Pretoria, South Africa, and began her career as a high school teacher. She later undertook an accelerated development program at South Africa's Nedcor Bank, starting as a teller then rising to head of human resources (Brammall, 2006). In 1997, Kelly immigrated to Australia with her family, eventually taking citizenship in 2001 (Light, 2009). She first arrived at the Commonwealth Bank of Australia before she was offered the role of Head of Business Banking at St. George Bank, Australia's then fifth-largest bank, where she later became CEO upon the sudden death of Ed O'Neal in 2001 (Brammall, 2006). During her time at St. George, Kelly oversaw five years of increased profitability, ending her tenure with the bank having doubled its assets and net profit after tax. Kelly became the first incumbent CEO to be recruited by a rival Australian bank (Johnston & Swift, 2007).

Founded in 1817, Westpac was Australia's first bank. Following deregulation in Australia during the 1980s, the bank experienced a decade of rapid expansion through the aggressive acquisition of smaller banks (Westpac Banking Corporation, 2010). However, Westpac suffered during the 1990s financial crisis, reporting the largest loss, at the time, for an Australian corporation—$1.6 billion in 1992 (Westpac Banking Corporation, 2010). In 1993, Westpac appointed Robert "Bob" Joss, the former vice-chairman of Wells Fargo, to turn around the ailing bank (Potter, 1993). Part of Joss's strategy involved acquisitions in Australia and New Zealand (Allard, 1995). His six-year tenure was considered highly successful, during which he was said to have transformed the company's operations and culture (Korporaal, 2008). When Joss resigned in 1999, he was replaced by David Morgan, an internal candidate. Morgan headed the company under what was generally considered a steady and conservative leadership until his retirement in 2008 (Verrender, 2008). Kelly succeeded Morgan until her own retirement in 2015.

Despite deregulation and privatization during the 1980s, Australia has one of the most concentrated banking sectors in the world. This is, in part, due to the enforcement of the Four Pillars policy preventing the four major banks (known collectively as the Big Four) from merging with one another, but enabling them to dominate the market through mergers with and acquisitions of smaller banks. At Kelly's retirement in February 2015, Westpac stood as Australia's second-largest bank in terms of market capitalization valued at $109.94 billion (MarketWatch, 2015).

MEDIA DISCOURSE ANALYSIS

The analysis of media texts in this chapter follows the methodological tradition of discourse analysis: a qualitative, constructionist approach concerned with how language-in-use constitutes social reality (Grant, Hardy, & Putnam, 2011). Discursive analyses of leadership have become increasingly adopted as they offer a contextually grounded approach to examining how leadership is co-created between social agents (Fairhurst & Uhl-Bien, 2012; Liu, 2010). For this study, I focus on Kelly's *construction* in the Australian print media. The media plays a key role in circulating the shared meanings that constitute our culture. The capacity for the media to privilege certain information, omit other information, and construe and constrain meaning through the representation of certain interpretations as *true*, makes the media a powerful agent in the social construction of leadership (Fairclough, 1989).

In the last 60 years, the media has seen a persistent shift toward *designing* as opposed to *writing* texts (Kress, Leite-García, & van Leeuwen, 1997). In the media reporting of leaders, visual portraits contribute considerably to meaning making. Discursive studies of leadership that have embraced visuals include Guthey and Jackson (2005), who demonstrated how CEO portraits construct corporate identity, and Sinclair (2012), who showed how embodied performances of leadership are enacted through portraits. Liu and Baker (2014; 2016) have also explored how visuals contribute to classed and racialized constructions of philanthropists in the media. As such, I not only focused on the verbal representations of Kelly but also took into consideration how her portraits shaped her construction as a leader.

For this study, media data about Kelly were collected from the announcement of her appointment at Westpac in August 2007 until June 2010 by means of *Factiva*, a media database, owned by Dow Jones, that aggregates full-text articles and transcripts internationally from the mid-1980s. The wide inclusion of media outlets and available timeframe of articles made *Factiva* a suitable choice for data collection, and, in total, 136 were collected across 16 major national and state/territory publications with 81 (60%) of these articles sourced in their original visual form via a microfilm database.

Analysis of the media data began by building an event history database (Poole & Van de Ven, 1990), which involved sorting the articles in chronological order to ascertain convergences in the way Kelly, Westpac, and the wider context were constructed in the media at the time. This process allowed the key events in Kelly's tenure to be broadly mapped out by identifying the occurrences in the media data that resulted in a shift in how she was represented—for instance, when Kelly made significant announcements of bank decisions that prompted renewed media attention and appraisals.

Following this, the articles were coded for references to leadership, comprising attributes, strategy, purpose, and context. This broad inclusion of leadership constructs reflected the diverse theoretical renderings of leadership as individual, processual, and contextually embedded phenomena (Grint, 2000, 2005), while also capturing the ways in which Kelly and the media constructed her leadership in the data. Additionally, the visual forms of articles were coded in terms of layout, including the use of graphic elements (e.g., photographs, cartoons, and figures), relative saliencies of headlines, pull quotes and captions, and framing devices (Gardner & Avolio, 1998; Kress & van Leeuwen, 1996). During this stage of analysis, it became apparent that gender stereotypes pervaded the media characterizations of Kelly. While I acknowledge that concepts of masculinity and femininity can reinforce gender binaries that do not represent the plurality and complexity of human experience, data were coded for masculine and feminine leadership styles in order to reflect the ways in which binary constructions were reproduced by the Australian media.

APPOINTMENT TO WESTPAC

Kelly was announced as the CEO of Westpac in August 2007 at the same time the first reports of the GFC appeared in the Australian media. The timing of her appointment reflects the "glass cliff" phenomenon, which suggests that women are more likely to be appointed to positions of leadership when organizations are facing a crisis (Haslam & Ryan, 2009; Ryan & Haslam, 2007). In the context of historical public distrust towards the major banks, the media by and large heralded Kelly's gender as a welcome change from the traditional image of a banker. A feminized image of Kelly suffused the media, with intense focus on Kelly's family and physical appearance. Few articles failed to mention her husband and four children, including triplets, while articles such as the one by Hannon (2008) described Kelly as "52, with her short blonde hair, blazing smile and smart, solid-color pantsuits" arriving at "an industry which is regularly painted as being populated by pinstripe-suited greedy and rapacious bankers" (p. B3).

Kelly's visibility as a CEO was utilized by the media as symbolic of the interests of all women, framing her as a female champion and ideal: "The embodiment of the woman who has it all, a strong 25-year marriage, happy children and a soaring corporate career" (Devine, 2003, p. 46) and who "goes out of her way to show that a woman can have a home, children and a career" (Murphy, 2008, p. 1). The centrality of Kelly's roles as a wife and mother of four to her leadership was enhanced by narratives of her career at St. George Bank through an almost exclusive focus on her improvements in either family-friendly policies or customer satisfaction: "At St. George, where she has been chief executive for the past 5½ years, she has not only doubled the bank's assets, profits and share price, she has introduced a series of innovative family friendly policies for its 8500 staff" (Korporaal, 2007, p. 5), and "[St. George] still stands head and shoulders above its major competitors when it comes to customer satisfaction" (Brammall, 2006, p. 90). Kelly's relationship with her followers was also stressed: "She doubled profits and delivered share price gains that beat the Big Four with a focus on customer service. The first woman to run one of Australia's 10 largest companies is remembered at St. George for attending staff birthday celebrations" (Larter, 2007, para. 1).

Kelly's leadership identity thus rests on assumptions of femininity as inherently caring and nurturing. Kelly supported this characterization herself, citing "people orientation" and "customer satisfaction" as her ideological causes as a leader. In comparing Westpac with her predecessor's bank in the U.S., Wells Fargo, she described, "They have a model which we so passionately believe in which is focusing on people and focusing on customers—driving deep relationships with customers and earning all of our customers' business" (Korporaal, 2008, p. 33). By emphasizing such causes in her leadership, Kelly framed herself as selflessly devoted to people-oriented agendas, rather than personal goals and achievements. Kelly's framing is consistent with Hall and Donaghue's (2012) analysis of the media coverage of Australia's first female prime minister that suggested a female leader is more likely to be accepted as ambitious if her ambitions are constructed for a collective, rather than for herself.

Alluding to the iconic dragon logo of her former bank, St. George, the media extended the fantasy imagery to describe her "fairytale" career (Murphy, 2008, p. 1). This included depictions of Kelly as the protective knight, powerful sovereign, damsel, and even the dragon: "[Kelly] has thrown down the gauntlet to her competitors to put the focus back on the customer" (Hannon, 2008, p. B3); "[W]hile St. George may have been secretly hoping to attract a white knight, it had already embraced one in the shape of Kelly herself. . . . The investment community can only step back and admire the persuasive power of a damsel out to impress" (John, 2008a, p. 19); "St. George Bank . . . doubled its assets under her reign" (Overington, 2009, p. 3); and "Mrs Kelly has certainly breathed fire into the world of banking" ("Dragon lady's fire moves mountains," 2008, p. 136). By drawing on a pantheon of archetypal fairytale roles, the media melded traditional masculinist ideals of leadership such as strength, power, and conquest with allusions to bedtime stories from the sphere of her family life.

Visual representations of Kelly supported her feminized construction as a warm and relational leader. Portraits commonly cast her with others engaged in an amicable handshake or cheerful laughter, while emphasizing her feminine appearance through her brightly colored outfits and glittering jewelry. Figure 3.1, for example, shows Kelly with Westpac chairman Ted Evans in a lounge engaged in a relaxed and friendly conversation.

Figure 3.1 Ted Evans and Gail Kelly from *The Australian*, 17 May 2008 (Korporaal, 2008, p. 33)

She leans forward with her palms laid open on her lap, projecting warmth and openness. Kelly's relationship with Evans in particular is highlighted through the patterns and vectors in the photograph, where the repeating polka dot pattern of Kelly's suit and Evans' tie and the shape of the cushion between them accentuate their connection.

EMERGENCE OF THE GFC

Shortly following the first month of Kelly's appointment to Westpac in February 2008, the GFC began to be reported with increasing alarm in the Australian media. Following the collapse of banks in the U.S. and UK, Australian banks were met with growing scrutiny and concern that they might meet the same fate. In articles about Kelly, the GFC was framed as a fragile and uncertain situation: "The financial crisis that began with U.S. housing has spread rapidly around the world is not over, and the ripples are only starting to be felt here" (Knight, 2008, p. 21).

Initially, the media maintained confidence for Westpac with Kelly at the helm, suggesting that she had the appropriately cautious approach to handle the GFC. For example, Westpac was described as a "top-tier organization best equipped to deal with the shocks reverberating through the financial world" (Verrender, 2008, p. 21) and Kelly's approach framed as, "[T]he new game is risk management first and keeping the house in order while customers are served" (Durie, 2008b, p. 28) and where, "judging by her cautious optimism and Westpac's own figures, the odds seem to be favoring the view of [heading] off a more painful downturn" (John, 2008c, p. 22). Such appraisals of Kelly reflect trait and behavioral theories of leadership that have suggested women possess unique skills that help them navigate through crises (Ryan & Haslam, 2007). Women have been said to be more risk-averse (Nelson, 2015), while bearing greater ability to balance risk and cope with failure (Ryan, Haslam, & Postmes, 2007). Although recent research has called into question these generalized, essentialist statements about women (Nelson, 2015), they persist in stereotypical assumptions about women's suitability to lead during crises (Haslam & Ryan, 2009; Ryan & Haslam, 2007).

At the onset of the GFC, Westpac moved quickly to propose a merger with St. George. As soon as the merger began, media portrayals of Kelly shifted. Westpac was characterized as a growing empire, appropriating Kelly's former depiction as a sovereign. For example: "When Kelly gets her old empire at St. George back under her new wings, she will be boss of the biggest bank" (Durie, 2008a, p. 44); and "Westpac is getting its hands on a solid, well-run competitor which will help its chief executive (and ex-Dragon boss) Gail Kelly to overhaul the less customer friendly parts of her empire" (John, 2008b, p. 28). The articles predominantly described the merger with St. George as a predatory move on the part of the larger bank and cautioned about Westpac's growing dominance in the banking sector.

As the media characterized the merger between Westpac and St. George as an aggressive strategy, they also came to interpret Kelly's behavior as contradictory to her hitherto feminized image. McCullough (2008) suggested that the merger contravened Kelly's idealization as a gentle and nurturing mother: "In the face of her keen family life, some more unkind critics say the sudden move by her new employer Westpac on St. George is akin to a mother eating her children" (p. 73). There were indications in the data that Kelly attempted to overturn the media backlash. She employed family metaphors when persuading the strategic advantages of the acquisition: "Having a range of brands as part of the family, we will be able to be quite strategic in different sorts of ideas" (Korporaal, 2008, p. 33). However, Kelly's depiction of the bank as a family was not widely adopted by the media and thus failed to gain traction in counteracting the constructions of her "aggressive" leadership.

Kelly was met with more criticism in the media in December 2009, as the GFC progressed, when she became the first major bank CEO to announce the decision to increase lending rates by 45 basis points, almost double the Reserve Bank's official rate increase of 25 basis points. She emphasized the care and concern that went into her decision: "These are difficult decisions. We take an awful lot of time and a great deal of thought to make these decisions, but it was made against this backdrop" (Johnston, 2009, p. 1), but when none of the other Australian banks increased their rates as high as Westpac, the media depicted Kelly as greedy and rapacious—the very archetype of a banker that she was expected to subvert.

Kelly's decision was framed as "flint-hearted" (Penberthy, 2009, p. 22) and an "opportunistic move" ("Westpac dives at a rate rise," 2009, p. 20) that "[reinforced] the bastard bank mythology" (Syvret, 2010, p. 2). It was again described as contradicting her feminized identity as a mother: "It sits oddly with the kind of rhetoric we saw from Gail Kelly upon her appointment as CEO, where she talked at length about her family-minded approach to work" (Penberthy, 2009, p. 22). In particular, media articles explained this change by dichotomizing Kelly's leadership identity between the exterior and interior and, respectively, what is "fake" and "real" (Tracy & Trethewey, 2005). Johnston and Lee (2009), for example, claimed that "the shine has finally worn off her personal brand" (p. 1), as though her real self has been exposed from beneath her fake surface.

The media utilized cartoons to further signify this dichotomy, such as that of Figure 3.2, in which Kelly is depicted at a home loan application interview with a couple. A thought bubble on the left shows that the couple is picturing Kelly dressed as Santa Claus and handing out money in a compassionate and charitable characterization, while Kelly in the thought bubble on the right is

Figure 3.2 Gail Kelly from *Sydney Morning Herald*, 10 December 2009 ("The fruit of Westpac's approach to interest rates," 2009, p. 20)

imagining fleecing a sheep. This cartoon acknowledges the established media construction of Kelly as caring and nurturing, yet reconstructs that image as a figment of the public's imagination. References to Kelly's family that had initially pervaded her media portrayals disappeared during this period.

Despite the widespread negative portrayals of Kelly in the media during the height of the financial crisis, media representations of her started to improve from May 2010. As the media began to report on the economic recovery, Kelly received media attention when she announced an initiative to contribute to superannuation for employees on unpaid parental leave in June 2010, claiming it was "her own unpaid leave" that inspired this policy (Vasek, 2010, p. 3). The media praised this initiative as a sign of her continued commitment to her family-friendly causes: "In a rare insight into her role as a mother of four and a corporate boss, Mrs Kelly said it was important for companies to ensure women were given the opportunity to rise through management ranks and balance family life" (Johnston, 2010, p. 2). Subsequently, references to Kelly's roles as a mother and wife once again returned to her media representations, restoring her feminized, though favorable image.

CONCLUSION

In examining the media representations of Gail Kelly, Australia's first female CEO of a major bank, this chapter has contributed to our understandings of leadership by showing the ways in which the media and Kelly co-constructed a highly gendered leadership image. In the context of historical public distrust towards the banking leaders, Kelly's gender initially offered a welcome point of difference. At her celebrated appointment to Westpac, Kelly openly shared stories of her family life to support her portrayal in the media as a caring and nurturing mother of four. Media discourses embraced her feminized persona yet disrupted the gender binary through the playful use of fairytale imagery that combined feminine portrayals of her as a damsel with strong and protective characterizations of her as also a knight and sovereign.

However, Kelly's female advantage proved to be limited during the GFC (Ross-Smith & Huppatz, 2010) as the media nevertheless held to stereotypical, essentialist notions of gender. When Westpac merged with Kelly's former bank, St. George, in May 2008 and increased interest rates in December 2009, these decisive actions were seen as contravening Kelly's feminized persona. As a result, Kelly experienced a media backlash during the GFC, where her fairytale characterizations were reframed to suggest she was aggressively and selfishly expanding her empire. Kelly was caught in the gender double bind (Hall & Donaghue, 2012), where her leadership during crisis was perceived as out of line with her previously celebrated femininity. Only when the GFC subsided in Australia was Kelly able to restore her feminized persona by promoting family-friendly policies.

In addition, the chapter has demonstrated that media representations of leadership are both verbally and visually constructed. Before the onset of the GFC, Kelly was predominantly photographed with White men, whose presence served to accentuate Kelly's relational image as well as signal to their support and endorsement of her leadership. Brightly colored outfits and jewelry also played a significant role in Kelly's portraits to visually signify her difference from a grey, conservative banker. During the GFC, existing depictions of Kelly's likeable image were challenged through the use of cartoons that dichotomized her identity between what was fake and exaggerated negative portrayals of what was real (Tracy & Trethewey, 2005).

Finally, the analysis highlights the importance of context, where the GFC, the history of the banking sector, and wider gender norms shaped ideas of the desirable qualities of a banking leader. Thus, while femaleness was initially valorized for breaking from the "bastard bank mythology" (Syvret, 2010, p. 2), Kelly's gender ultimately contradicted abiding masculinist ideals of leadership that limited the scope of her appropriate behavior, particularly during a period of crisis.

In closing, Kelly's case highlights that the gains that have been made in female representation in positions of senior leadership cannot be read in isolation from the systemic inequality rooted and reproduced in gender norms. The media in particular remains a powerful agent in keeping these gender stereotypes and structures intact. However, female leaders do not passively endure gender norms, but through their visibility, they hold the potential to disrupt them. This chapter has demonstrated that the discursive co-construction of leadership in the media is an ongoing, negotiated process. Kelly's example offers one way in which a female CEO might influence her media representation as a capable leader by committing to feminine agendas and collective ambitions. Although in some ways this reinforced stereotypical, essentialist notions of femininity, Kelly's case showed that it is possible to subvert the gender binary in the media through hybrid gender identities that combined a celebrated feminized persona with masculinist leadership ideals (Connell, 2010). Alternatively, leaders may choose to do gender differently by embodying otherwise ambiguous and fluid gender identities through the narratives they share and photographs they pose for in the media that challenge limiting gender norms.

REFERENCES

Allard, T. (1995, November 3). Westpac gets itchy feet. *The Sydney Morning Herald*, p. 35.

Alvesson, M., & Billing, Y. D. (2009). *Understanding gender and organizations* (2nd ed.). London, UK: Sage.

Brammall, B. (2006, May 27). In the sweet spot. *Sun Herald*, p. 90.

Calás, M. B., & Smircich, L. (2006). From the "woman's point of view" ten years later: Towards a feminist organization studies. In S. R. Clegg, C. Hardy, & W. R. Nord (Eds.), *The Sage handbook of organization studies* (2nd ed., pp. 284–346). London, UK: Sage.

Collinson, D. L., & Hearn, J. (1994). Naming men as men: Implications for work, organization and management. *Gender, Work & Organization, 1*(1), 2–22. doi: 10.1111/j.1468-0432.1994.tb00002.x

Collinson, D. L., & Hearn, J. (Eds.). (1996). *Men as managers, managers as men: Critical perspectives on men, masculinities, and managements.* London, UK: Sage.

Connell, C. (2010). Doing, undoing, or redoing gender? Learning from the workplace experiences of transpeople. *Gender & Society, 24*(1), 31–55. doi: 10.1177/0891243209356429

Devine, M. (2003, November 30). $10bn business and four kids: One woman's balancing act. *Sun Herald*, p. 46.

Dragon lady's fire moves mountains. (2008, May 17). *The Gold Coast Bulletin*, p. 136.

Durie, J. (2008a, October 8). Happy days aren't here again. *The Australian*, p. 44.

Durie, J. (2008b, October 31). Kelly's gang ready to make mark. *The Australian*, p. 28.

Eagly, A. H., & Carli, L. L. (2007). Women and the labyrinth of leadership. *Harvard Business Review, 85*(9), 62–71. Retrieved from https://hbr.org/2007/09/women-and-the-labyrinth-of-leadership

Fairclough, N. (1989). *Language and power.* London, UK: Longman.

Fairhurst, G. T., & Uhl-Bien, M. (2012). Organizational discourse analysis (ODA): Examining leadership as a relational process. *The Leadership Quarterly, 23*(6), 1043–1062. doi: 10.1016/j.leaqua.2012.10.005

Gardner, W. L., & Avolio, B. J. (1998). The charismatic relationship: A dramaturgical perspective. *Academy of Management Review, 23*(1), 32–58. doi: 10.5465/AMR.1998.192958

Gherardi, S. (1996). Gendered organizational cultures: Narratives of women travellers in a male world. *Gender, Work & Organization, 3*(4), 187–201. doi: 10.1111/j.1468-0432.1996.tb00059.x

Grant, D., Hardy, C., & Putnam, L. (2011). *Organizational discourse studies* (3 vol. set). Thousand Oaks, CA: Sage.

Grint, K. (2000). *The arts of leadership.* New York, NY: Oxford University Press.

Grint, K. (2005). *Leadership: Limits and possibilities.* Basingstoke, UK: Palgrave Macmillan.

Guthey, E., & Jackson, B. (2005). CEO portraits and the authenticity paradox. *Journal of Management Studies, 42*(5), 1057–1082. doi: 10.1111/j.1467-6486.2005.00532.x

Hall, L. J., & Donaghue, N. (2012). "Nice girls don't carry knives": Constructions of ambition in media coverage of Australia's first female prime minister. *British Journal of Social Psychology, 52*(4), 631–647. doi: 10.1111/j.2044-8309.2012.02114.x

Hannon, K. (2008, May 17). Custom-made in her image. *The Canberra Times,* p. B3.

Haslam, S. A., & Ryan, M. K. (2009). The road to the glass cliff: Differences in the perceived suitability of men and women for leadership positions in succeeding and failing organizations. *The Leadership Quarterly, 19*(5), 530–546. doi: 10.1016/j.leaqua.2008.07.011

Hearn, J., Sheppard, D. L., Tancred-Sheriff, P., & Burrell, G. (Eds.). (1989). *The sexuality of organization.* London, UK: Sage.

Jamieson, K. H. (1995). *Beyond the double bind: Women and leadership.* New York, NY: Oxford University Press.

John, D. (2008a, September 9). Lady luck smiles on Westpac bid. *The Sydney Morning Herald,* p. 19.

John, D. (2008b, October 30). The dragon could have survived the onslaught on its own. *The Sydney Morning Herald,* p. 28.

John, D. (2008c, October 31). Cautious Kelly bets on avoiding the worst. *The Sydney Morning Herald,* p. 22.

Johnston, E. (2009, December 8). We'll all pay more to borrow: Kelly defends rate rise. *The Sydney Morning Herald,* p. 1.

Johnston, E. (2010, April 14). Kelly's leaps and bounds. *The Age,* p. 2.

Johnston, E., & Lee, J. (2009, December 12). Backlash: Gail Kelly's big stumble. *The Sydney Morning Herald,* p. 1.

Johnston, E., & Swift, B. (2007, August 17). St. George's Kelly to take reins at Westpac. *The Australian Financial Review,* p. 1.

Kerfoot, D., & Knights, D. (1993). Management, masculinity and manipulation: From paternalism to corporate strategy in financial services in Britain. *Journal of Management Studies, 30*(4), 659–677. doi: 10.1111/j.1467-6486.1993.tb00320.x

Knight, E. (2008, October 31). Too soon for any pats on back. *The Sydney Morning Herald,* p. 21.

Korporaal, G. (2007, August 18). New Westpac chief promises culture shift. *The Australian*, p. 5.

Korporaal, G. (2008, May 17). Evans satisfied he chose the right woman for the job. *The Australian*, p. 33.

Kress, G., Leite-García, R., & van Leeuwen, T. (1997). Discourse semiotics. In T. A. van Dijk (Ed.), *Discourse as structure and process. Discourse studies: A multidisciplinary introduction* (Vol. 1, pp. 257–291). London, U.K.: Sage.

Kress, G., & van Leeuwen, T. (1996). *Reading images: The grammar of visual design.* London, UK: Routledge.

Larter, P. (2007, October 30). Gail Kelly. *The Bulletin, 125*(44).

Light, D. (2009, June 1). A talent for banking. *Money*, p. 16.

Liu, H. (2010). When leaders fail: A typology of failures and framing strategies. *Management Communication Quarterly, 24*(2), 232–259. doi: 10.1177/0893318909359085

Liu, H., & Baker, C. (2014). White knights: Leadership as the heroicisation of whiteness. *Leadership*, 1–29. http://doi.org/10.1177/1742715014565127

Liu, H. & Baker, C. (2016). Ordinary aristocrats: The discursive construction of philanthropists as ethical leaders. *Journal of Business Ethics, 133*(2), 261–277. doi: 10.1007/s10551-014-2394-2

Liu, H., Cutcher, L., & Grant, D. (2015). Doing authenticity: The gendered construction of authentic leadership. *Gender, Work & Organization, 22*(3), 237–255. doi: 10.1111/gwao.12073

MarketWatch. (2015). WBC Stock Charts. Retrieved from http://www.marketwatch.com/investing/stock/wbc/charts?CountryCode=AU

McCullough, J. (2008, May 17). A dragon in her sights—Westpac's CEO keeps cool under pressure. *The Courier-Mail*, p. 73.

Murphy, D. (2008, May 13). How Kelly slew the dragon. *The Sydney Morning Herald*, p. 1.

Nelson, J. A. (2015). Are women really more risk-averse than men? A re-analysis of the literature using expanded methods. *Journal of Economic Surveys, 29*(3), 566–585. doi: 10.1111/joes.12069

Overington, C. (2009, August 21). Westpac's Kelly tops Clinton in power poll. *The Australian*, p. 3.

Penberthy, D. (2009, December 11). Gail Kelly's corporate gluttony has exposed the presumption women bring a heart-warming otherness. *The Advertiser*, p. 22.

Poole, M. S., & Van de Ven, A. H. (1990). Methods for studying innovation development in the Minnesota Innovation Research Program. *Organization Science, 1*(3), 313–335. doi: 10.1287/orsc.1.3.313

Potter, B. (1993, January 25). At, last, a new Westpac chief. *The Age*, p. 1.

Ross-Smith, A., & Huppatz, K. (2010). Management, women and gender capital. *Gender, Work and Organization, 17*(5), 547–566. doi: 10.1111/j.1468-0432.2010.00523.x

Ryan, M. K., & Haslam, S. A. (2007). The glass cliff: Exploring the dynamics surrounding the appointment of women to precarious leadership positions. *Academy of Management Review, 32*(2), 549–572. doi: 10.5465/AMR.2007.24351856

Ryan, M. K., Haslam, S. A., & Postmes, T. (2007). Reactions to the glass cliff: Gender differences in the explanations for the precariousness of women's leadership positions. *Journal of Organizational Change Management, 20*(2), 182–197. doi: 10.1108/09534810710724748

Sinclair, A. (2012). Leading with body. In E. Jeanes, D. Knights, & P. Yancey Martin (Eds.), *Handbook of gender, work and organization* (pp. 117–130). Chichester, UK: Wiley.

Syvret, P. (2010, March 24). Westpac tactic puts its IQ into question. *The Courier-Mail*, p. 2.

The fruit of Westpac's approach to interest rates. (2009, December 10). *The Sydney Morning Herald*, p. 20.

Tracy, S. J., & Trethewey, A. (2005). Fracturing the real-self–fake-self dichotomy: Moving toward "crystallized" organizational discourses and identities. *Communication Theory, 15*(2), 168–195. doi: 10.1111/j.1468-2885.2005.tb00331.x

Vasek, L. (2010, June 30). Westpac to fatten up parents' super funds. *The Australian*, p. 3.

Verrender, I. (2008, May 6). Happy Dragon has little to smile about. *The Sydney Morning Herald*, p. 21.

Westpac Banking Corporation. (2010). Company overview. Retrieved from http://www.westpac.com.au/about-westpac/the-westpac-group/company-overview/

Westpac dives at a rate rise. (2009, December 2). *The Advertiser*, p. 20.

CHAPTER 4

PULLING A CHAIR UP TO THE TABLE

A Critical Analysis of the "Lean In" Self-Help Movement and Its Implications for Individual Women and Women's Equality at Work

Judith A. Clair and Caela McCann
Boston College

Over the last several years, Sheryl Sandberg, COO of Facebook, has rolled out a "lean in" movement, which seeks to inspire women to individually and collectively lean in to their careers and leadership as a path to addressing persistent gender inequality in the workplace. Sandberg's message has struck a deep chord, and there is weighty evidence of the impact it is having on public and private discourse concerning gender inequality and women at work. Her 2013 book, *Lean In: Women, Work and the Will to Lead*, sold 140,000 copies in its first week of publication (Post Staff Report, 2013), and it has topped bestseller lists including Amazon.com and *The New York Times*. At the time of this chapter's writing (2015), Sandberg had also generated

Gender, Media, and Organization, pages 63–76
Copyright © 2016 by Information Age Publishing
All rights of reproduction in any form reserved.

a large virtual community in the form of 21,097 discussion groups called "Lean In Circles," across 97 countries (leanin.org, 2015). Additionally, a talk delivered at TEDWomen by Sandberg on "Why We Have Too Few Women Leaders" (Sandberg, 2010) had over five million views. In the wake of *Lean In: Women, Work and the Will to Lead*, many new self-help books on the art of how to navigate one's life in the context of work and leadership have appeared. For example, Katty Kay and Clair Shipman weighed in with *The Confidence Code* (2014), Kirsten Gillibrand published her memoir *Off the Sidelines* (2014), Arianna Huffington urged readers to *Thrive* (2014), and former Nasty Gal CEO Sophia Amoruso instructed women in how to be a *#GIRLBOSS* (Amoruso, 2014). Almost all of these books reference the book *Lean In*, apparently seeking to ride its coattails, and Sheryl Sandberg herself publically recommends many of them on their front or back covers. Finally, a wide range of op-eds and critiques with provocative titles and prominent commentators—"Yes, You Can" (Slaughter, 2013), "Pompom Girl for Feminism" (Dowd, 2013), "Dig Deep Beyond Lean In" (hooks, 2013), "I Leaned In: Why Sheryl Sandberg's 'Circles' Actually Help" (Bennett, 2013)—demonstrate the resonance of Sandberg's message, the range of reactions, and the heatedness of the debate about whether her approach is the best solution.

In light of this evidence, it is centrally important that one read between the lines (Simonds, 1992) of the Lean In movement. Here we do so, positioning the movement as a form of self-help produced predominately by women for women, and employ a discursive approach that includes an analysis of visual as well as written forms to unpack its message, appeal, and influence. Our analysis draws from a systematic review of all of the elements of the Lean In movement, from video, to the books, to leanin.org. We additionally draw from extensive op-eds and critical publications appearing since the writing of the book *Lean In*, starting in 2013 (see Table 4.1, which lists a selection of our primary sources).

Through our analysis, we seek to make two primary contributions to scholarship on women and work. First, while organizational scholars often study the social and structural context surrounding working women which shapes their self-perceptions, career choices, and hopes for the future (e.g., Ridgeway, 2011), the role of self-help as part of the social context influencing employees is almost never considered (for exceptions, see Clark & Salaman, 1998; Kenny & Bell, 2014). Consequently, we hope to motivate scholars to further investigate the self-help genre as a central component of the social context surrounding working women, given that the genre is widely consumed by such women (Simonds, 1992). Second, the self-help genre also "offers a rich source of materials for tracing changing notions of the self" (McGee, 2005, p. 17). Thus, we additionally hope to shed light on what the vast appeal of the lean in movement says about how modern

TABLE 4.1   Illustrative Examples of Published Critiques of Sandberg's *Lean In* Book and Movement

Title	Author	Periodical	Publication Date
How to Succeed in Business	Applebaum, Anne	New York Review of Books	June 6, 2013
I Leaned In: Why Sheryl Sandberg's Circles Actually Help	Bennett, Jessica	New York Magazine	March 7, 2013
Recline!	Brooks, Rosa	Foreign Policy	February 21, 2014
Why you Should Lean In to Sheryl Sandberg's New Book	Chang, Alexandra	Wired	March 11, 2013
On the Sheryl Sandberg Backlash	Chittal, Nisha	Huffington Post	February 25, 2013
Lean In: Not Much of a Manifesto, but Still a Win for Women	Corrigan, Maureen	NPR	March 12, 2013
Lean In, Trickle Down: The False Promise of Sheryl Sandberg's Theory of Change	Covert, Bryce	Forbes.com	February 25, 2013
Pompom Girl for Feminism	Dowd, Maureen	New York Times	February 23, 2013
Facebook Feminism, Like It or Not	Faludi, Susan	Baffler	Issue No. 23
Exclusive: First Look at Sheryl Sandberg's New Book	Gara, Tom	Wall Street Journal	February 5, 2013
The Absurd Backlash Against Sheryl Sandberg's Lean In	Goldberg, Michelle	Daily Beast	March 1, 2013
Sheryl Sandberg: The Facebook Boss on a Self-Help Mission	Harris, Paul	Guardian	February 23, 2013
Maybe You Should Read the Book: The Sheryl Sandberg Backlash	Holmes, Anna	New Yorker	March 4, 2013
Dig Deep: Beyond Lean In	hooks, bell	Feminist Wire	October 28, 2013
Feminism's Tipping Point: Who Wins from Leaning In?	Losse, Kate	Dissent Magazine	March 26, 2013
Lessons From Facebook's Sheryl Sandberg on How to Succeed in Business by Really Trying	Poczter, Sharon	Forbes.com	February 11, 2013
Why Women Still Can't Have It All	Slaughter, Anne Marie	Atlantic	July/August 2012
Yes, You Can	Slaughter, Anne Marie	New York Times	March 7, 2013
Review: Sheryl Sandberg's Lean In is Full of Good Intentions, but Rife with Contradictions	Schultz, Connie	Washington Post	March 1, 2013
The Uselessness of Hating Sheryl Sandberg	Traister, Rebecca	New Republic	February 27, 2014
Leaning In to New Ideas	Wilson, Marie C.	Huffington Post	March 8, 2013

women's self-views and hopes for their futures have started to shift as we ascend further into the 21st century.

Our chapter is organized into four sections. First, we briefly review the Lean In movement. Then, we position the Lean In movement within the self-help genre. Next, we ask: Why is the Lean In message so appealing to so many? Finally, we consider: What is the larger significance of Sandberg's Lean In movement?

SHERYL SANDBERG'S LEAN IN MOVEMENT

Sheryl Sandberg initially approached the topic of gender inequality cautiously through several public speeches, but her efforts quickly built into the so-called Lean In movement. In 2010, Sandberg gave her first lecture on gender inequality at a TEDWomen conference titled "Why We Have Too Few Women Leaders." In the talk, Sandberg made the case that women face many institutional and cultural barriers that hold them back from career and leadership advancement. Sandberg emphasized in her speech the importance of focusing on how women can take personal responsibility to improve their situation (Sandberg, 2010). Some scholars and public commentators have critiqued Sandberg's focus on women's personal responsibility, seeing individuals' efforts as futile in light of institutional and cultural structures that ultimately result in persistent gender inequities (e.g., hooks, 2013). Nonetheless, Sandberg trains her lens on a message emphasizing self-determination (Deci & Ryan, 2008) and instructs women to take responsibility by sitting at the table, making one's partner a real partner, and not leaving (the workforce) before one needs to leave. Follow these three steps and, during her TEDWomen talk, Sandberg asserted, the world would become a more equal place, a world "where women [run] half our countries and companies and men [run] half our homes" (2010, 14:15).

Sandberg followed her TEDWomen talk with a Barnard College commencement speech in 2011 that revisited and built on these ideas. Addressing an all-woman graduating class, and recognizing that gender equality in the workplace was unlikely to be achieved in her generation, Sandberg (2011, 5:55–7:50) entreated:

> You are the promise for a more equal world. You are our hope.... You are going to lean way into your career.... You are going to pick your field and ride it all the way to the top.... If all young women start to lean in, we can close the ambition gap right here, right now, if every single one of you leans in.

Sandberg's Lean In movement formally began in 2013 with the publication of *Lean In: Women, Work, and the Will to Lead*; through her online forum, leanin.org, which offers "women ongoing inspiration and support to help them achieve their goals" (leanin.org, 2015); and via "Lean In Circles," which are self-led discussions among circle members, often on college campuses and in professional settings, with the mission to encourage women to lean into their careers. Soon after, Sandberg published *Lean In for College Graduates*, in which her appeal and advice were translated for the direct use of co-eds (Sandberg, 2014). Sandberg also continued to provide written commentary on the website leanin.org and in other forums, such as a *New York Times* "Women at Work" column co-authored with University of Pennsylvania Professor Adam Grant (e.g., Sandberg & Grant, 2015a, 2015b). As Kantor (2013, para. 2) commented in *The New York Times*, the Lean In movement "attempts a Friedan-like feat: a national discussion of the gender-problem-that-has-no-name, this time in the workplace, and a movement to address it."

LEAN IN AS A SELF-HELP GENRE

Our analysis shows that the Lean In movement fits comfortably within the self-help genre, which is comprised of oral and written discourse that seeks to appeal to individuals' needs and desires for self-invention and self-transformation (McGee, 2005; Neville, 2013). Ultimately, the message of the self-help genre reflects a dominant cultural narrative, especially in the United States, that any person is capable of achieving individual success if they just work hard enough (Biggart, 1983; Simonds, 1992). "The figure of the self-made man—and more recently that of the self-made woman—comforts and consoles us, suggesting that vast material, social, and personal success are available to anyone who is willing to work long and hard enough" (McGee, 2005, p. 11). Similarly, the Lean In movement offers women a set of practices that, if applied, seemingly will provide them with transformative opportunities for career success and leadership advancement.

In particular, the Lean In movement is consistent with a female-centric self-help genre. Female-centric self-help directly tackles women's social and personal problems (Hazleden, 2011; Simonds, 1992), such as a lack of confidence, the need to ask more in negotiations with others, and tricky relationships with other women (e.g., Babcock & Laschever, 2007; Crowley & Elster, 2012; Kay & Shipman, 2014). In the case of the Lean In movement, Sandberg offers women inspiration and advice specifically targeting women's attitudes and behaviors at work that have traditionally held them back from advancement.

Many parallels have been drawn between the women's movement of the 1960s–1980s aroused by Betty Friedan's *Feminine Mystique* (1963) and Sandberg's Lean In movement. As noted in *Time* magazine: "It's probably not an overstatement to say Sandberg is embarking on the most ambitious mission to reboot feminism and reframe discussions of gender since the launch of *Ms.* magazine in 1971" (Luscombe, 2013, para. 4).

However, Sandberg's Lean In movement is different in critical ways from the earlier feminist movement. Women's participation in this feminist movement arose organically in individual and collective response to consciousness-raising around the "problem that had no name"—that middle-aged women had grown discontented with their lives as homemakers—as discussed in *The Feminine Mystique*. Conversely, Sandberg's intended audience appears to be primarily young, well-educated, pre-professional, and newly professional women, and Sandberg herself is orchestrating the movement.

It must also be noted that Sandberg's Lean In movement also has an unusual twist compared to traditional social movement doctrines. Rather than emphasizing collective action for gender equity through consciousness raising, collective strategizing, political action, and public demonstrations of solidarity (e.g., Taylor, 1996), the Lean In movement calls for individual efforts toward a singular goal (to lean in). The premise appears to be that if women individually lean in, together their collective push will result in more women as institutional leaders who will, in turn, generate greater gender equality because larger numbers of women at the top will promote institutional change.

EXPLAINING THE APPEAL OF THE LEAN IN MOVEMENT

We believe that two features of the Lean In movement create a strong appetite for Sandberg's message. First, we believe that a major appeal of the Lean In movement is its modern format, which is reflective of young women's tastes for consuming self-help. Second, we believe that the content of Sandberg's message offers advice that appeals to motivated young women who are looking to autonomously and ambitiously pursue professional success.

Appealing Format

How a message is offered in terms of its packaging, not just its content, greatly influences the appeal to individuals' desires and notions of the self (Zukin & McGuire, 2004). The Lean In movement offers a format that, we assert, resonates in various ways with modern women's needs and desires around how they consume new information, products, and services and, in turn, how they see themselves.

To explain this attraction, it is necessary to first discuss traditional formats of the self-help genre. Historically, the self-help genre took the form of the self-help book. Readers widely consumed self-help books including *I'm OK, You're OK* (Harris, 1969); *How to Win Friends and Influence People* (Carnegie, 1981); *Men Are From Mars, Women Are From Venus* (Gray, 1992); *Seven Habits of Highly Effective People* (Covey, 1996); *Who Moved My Cheese: An Amazing Way to Deal with Change in Your Work and in Your Life* (Johnson, 2002); and *The Secret* (Byrne, 2006). The arrival of vastly popular TV talk shows starting in the late 1960s meant that by the 1990s, people were also watching self-help on shows such as Oprah Winfrey and Martha Stewart.

In the mid-1990s, the self-help environment again shifted as the Internet revolutionized culture and commerce, providing information disseminated through near-instant forms of communication and social bonding. The Lean In movement is rooted in this technologically savvy landscape, which reflects how modern women incorporate the Internet and social media into their lives (Hochschild, 2003; Simonds, 1996), and we believe that this alignment drives some of its appeal. Young women now entering the workforce have grown up sharing and seeking help on themes that the prior generation viewed as private matters—relationships, self-image, career, sexuality—on the pages of Facebook and Twitter, and they have observed (and participated with) others doing so, as well. These activities take place alongside advertisements and pop-ups, blurring the line between the commercial and the personal. Consistent with this new form, in addition to her book, Sandberg provides her website as well as inspiration through short articles such as "Speaking While Female" (Sandberg & Grant, 2015a) that conform to the bite-sized pieces of information women consume on LinkedIn and Facebook newsfeeds. Only a click away from the messages and appeals on leanin.org, women can brand themselves with travel mugs and T-shirts with the Lean In logo. Today, women can (and often do) literally inscribe on their bodies and in their Twitter feeds and blogs their allegiance to the Lean In movement and its ideals.

Beyond its technological approach, visitors to leanin.org find positive stories of how others leaned in, from journalists to artists, military personnel to filmmakers, businesspersons to authors and engineers. The stories told are genuine and often profound; for instance, Cheryl La Sonde, a domestic violence safe house manager, starts her story by stating: "I am a survivor of domestic violence" (La Sonde). In the education section of leanin.org, successful professionals and academics, mostly women, provide advice in an engaging and down-to-earth manner in short videos on topics such as creating a level playing field, negotiating effectively, and communicating with confidence. Through the videos, the viewer is also given tangible sources of virtual community with other women from around the globe that deliver inspiration and hope.

Finally, we believe that Sandberg's physical presentation also plays a key role in the attractiveness of the Lean In movement to young women.

Sandberg manages to present herself as simultaneously strong, humble, self-doubting, a feminist, a mother, wildly successful in a male-dominated profession, and aggressively committed to gender equity change. We believe that young women are drawn to her, as she serves as a critically important feminist alternative to an older generation of activist women with whom they may no longer identify. The attraction of young women is indicated by the wide adoption of Lean In Circles on college campuses across the U.S. and globally.

Appealing Message

Beyond its modern format and visual rhetoric, we assert that the content of the movement's message is deeply appealing to the young women it seeks to influence. Research demonstrates that gender inequality in the workplace remains a critical problem (Catalyst, 2014). Though women are well represented among middle-level managers in Fortune 500 organizations, they rarely serve in the most influential positions at the apex of corporate hierarchies and boards of major corporations (Catalyst, 2014). They are especially underrepresented in certain professions and industries such as engineering (Catalyst, 2013a) and high tech (Catalyst, 2013b). The Lean In message tackles an especially thorny problem faced by working women—that they work in unequal cultural and institutional structures (Ridgeway, 2011) but nonetheless must manage their work and career trajectory as best they can.

It does so by providing young women with a message they want to and are ready to hear: It's time to take personal responsibility, to lean into your own career success despite the fact that institutional and cultural inequality remains a problem. As discussed by Chase (1995), not all women want to engage in collective protest and activism to achieve gender equity; rather, their primary commitment is to the professional work itself. Similarly, the Lean In movement appeals to women's sense of responsibility for their own career success and provides a ready response to women's restlessness in the face of negative messages about gender equity in the workplace.

THE LARGER SIGNIFICANCE OF THE LEAN IN MOVEMENT

Will the Lean In movement have lasting significance? We can only speculate about whether it will have a meaningful impact on women's experiences at work. On the one hand, the Lean In movement has been roundly censured as deeply ineffectual and flawed (e.g., Faludi, 2013; hooks, 2013). Conversely, even with these criticisms, we believe that critics underestimate the transformational potential of the Lean In movement.

Like the self-help genre more broadly, critics recognize that a major flaw in the Lean In movement is its tendency to psychologize and medicalize women's difficulties in the workplace. Critics assert that inequality for women in the workplace does not originate from women themselves; it results from negative messages in the culture and structural inequities women face in their lives (e.g., Ridgeway, 2011). Change must first take place in the social and structural systems (hooks, 2013; Ridgeway, 2011).

Nonetheless, Sandberg motivates women to assert agency in their lives. Self-determination theory (Ryan & Deci, 2008) proposes that when an individual engages in self-help that provides a sense of greater control, agency, and mastery over one's life, the person experiences enhanced self-determination. Heightened self-determination, in turn, fosters wellness and healthy functioning (Deci & Ryan, 2008).

Further, we believe that critics underestimate the power of individual actions, such as leaning in, to create social change. Scholarly research on institutions demonstrates that microactions at the level of the individual can start to shift cultural norms and institutional structures (Creed & Scully, 2000). Drawing from this line of research, Sandberg's revolution is perhaps best understood as a type of tempered radicalism (Meyerson, 2001; Meyerson & Scully, 1995), in which change in organizations related to social justice concerns is made through individuals engaging in small pushes and pulls from within the organization rather than through organized solidarity among groups seeking radical change from the outside (Meyerson & Scully, 1995). In this way, "identity deployment" can be a force for social change within oppressive institutional structures (Creed & Scully, 2000). When employees reveal a stigmatized invisible identity at work, educate colleagues on one's experiences of marginality, or push for the adoption of new organizational policies, they start to shift cultural norms and institutional policies (e.g., Clair, Beatty, & MacLean, 2005; Creed & Scully, 2000).

Another criticism is that Sandberg has virtually excluded the feminist dynasty from the conversation. For example, hooks (2013) has pointed out that she offered a definition of feminism in *Feminist Theory from Margin to Center* (hooks, 2000b) and then again in *Feminism is For Everybody* (hooks, 2000a), which Sandberg seems to have overlooked. Faludi (2013) similarly suggests that Sandberg ignored her attempts to engage with her around the faults of the Lean In movement. For both hooks and Faludi, Sandberg's oversight is an indictment of her message's credibility, and it cannot possibly be taken seriously given its failure to recognize and build upon the feminist discourse that precedes it.

A close read of feminist ideology signals that, while Sandberg's movement is not well aligned with second-wave feminism's focus on group protest and a radical overturning of corporate structures that perpetuate inequality (e.g., hooks, 2013), it is nonetheless reflective of the ideology of third-wave feminism. Third-wave feminism emerged in the 1990s and is characterized by close ties to commercialization (Goodkind, 2009), with an emphasis on "individual initiative, rejection of group identity and in some cases spurning the label 'feminist,' as [women] seek power in their professional and personal lives" (Iannello, 2010, p. 70). Sandberg's own message, to lean in, resonates closely with this modern form.

Finally, there are two undeniable successes of the Lean In movement that should be recognized. First, there is no doubt that Sandberg has generated one of the most active public conversations and debates about women in the workplace in decades, as demonstrated in Table 4.1. There is no doubt that the conversation has had a profound impact on understandings of women, work and leadership.

Second, the Lean In movement bridges shared interests across generational divides, bringing together women who have ascended to leadership and those women who aspire to do so. For us, the Lean In movement has served as the basis of conversation between professor (Judy) and student (Caela), as well as woman to woman. Often, our opinions have aligned more clearly with our respective generations—Judy calling for a greater focus on institutional change than Sandberg addresses, and Caela hesitantly approaching the topic and title of feminist. We have often disagreed regarding the accuracy of Sandberg's claims and the benefits and disadvantages of her approach. No matter, the Lean In movement has encouraged a conversation that might have otherwise gone unspoken. Although the true influence of the Lean In movement cannot yet be determined, at the very least, Sandberg is pulling a chair up to the table to discuss women's inequality and female engagement in the professional world—a conversation long overdue.

REFERENCES

Amoruso, S. (2014). *#GIRLBOSS.* New York, NY: Penguin.

Applebaum, A. (2013). *How to Succeed in Business. New York Review of Books.* Retrieved from http://www.nybooks.com/articles/2013/06/06/sheryl-sandberg-how-succeed-business/

Babcock, L., & Laschever, S. (2007). *Women don't ask: The high cost of avoiding negotiation—and positive strategies for change.* New York, NY: Bantam.

Bennett, J. (2013). I leaned in: Why Sheryl Sandberg's 'circles' actually help. *The Cut.* Retrieved from http://nymag.com/thecut/2013/03/what-i-learned-at-the-lean-in-sandbergs-right.html#

Biggart, N. W. (1983). Rationality, meaning and self-management: Success manuals 1950–1980. *Social Problems, 30*(3), 298–311. doi: 10.2307/800355

Brooks, R. (2014). *Recline! Foreign Policy.* Retrieved from http://foreignpolicy.com/2014/02/21/recline/

Byrne, R. (2006). *The secret.* New York, NY: Atria Books.

Carnegie, D. (1981). *How to win friends and influence people.* New York, NY: Pocket Books.

Catalyst. (2013a). *Quick take: Women in the sciences.* [Graphic illustration of women's share in the labour force by science occupation and sex in Canada in 2006]. Retrieved from http://www.catalyst.org/knowledge/women-sciences

Catalyst. (2013b). *Quick take: Women in high tech, globally.* [Graphic illustration of women and men employed in select high tech occupations in the U.S., 2012]. Retrieved from http://www.catalyst.org/knowledge/women-high-tech-globally

Catalyst. (2014). *Quick take: Women in the United States.* [Graphic illustration of women's share of the U.S. labor force (percent)]. Retrieved from http://www.catalyst.org/knowledge/women-united-states

Chang, A. (2013). Why you Should Lean In to Sheryl Sandberg's New Book. *Wired.* Retrieved from: http://www.wired.com/2013/03/lean-in-to-sheryl-sandbergs-book/

Chase. S. E. (1995). *Ambiguous empowerment: The work narratives of women superintendents.* Amherst, MA: Amherst College Press.

Chittal, N. (2013). On the Sheryl Sandberg Backlash. *Huffington Post.* Retrieved from http://www.huffingtonpost.com/nisha-chittal/sheryl-sandberg_b_2755348.html

Clair, J. A., Beatty, J. E., & MacLean, T. L. (2005). Out of sight but not out of mind: Managing invisible social identities in the workplace. *Academy of Management Review, 30*(1), 78–95. doi: 10.5465/AMR.2005.15281431

Clark, T., & Salaman, G. (1998). Management gurus narratives and the construction of managerial identity. *Journal of Management Studies, 35*(2), 137–161. doi: 10.1111/1467-6486.00088

Corrigan, M. (2013). Lean In: Not much of a manifesto, but still a win for women. *NPR.* Retrieved from: http://www.npr.org/2013/03/12/174016175/lean-in-not-much-of-a-manifesto-but-still-a-win-for-women

Covert, B. (2013). Lean In, trickle down: The false promise of Sheryl Sandberg's theory of change. *Forbes.* Retrieved from http://www.forbes.com/sites/brycecovert/2013/02/25/lean-in-trickle-down-the-false-promise-of-sheryl-sandbergs-theory-of-change/#49e5445c2228

Covey, S. (1996). *Seven habits of highly effective people.* New York, NY: Free Press.

Creed, D. W. E., & Scully, M. A. (2000). Songs of ourselves: Employees' deployment of social identity in workplace encounters. *Journal of Management Inquiry, 9*(4), 391–412. doi: 10.1177/105649260000900410

Crowley, K., & Elster, K. (2012). *Mean girls at work: How to stay professional when things get personal.* New York, NY: McGraw-Hill.

Deci, E. L., & Ryan, R. M. (2008). Self-determination theory: A macrotheory of human motivation, development, and health. *Canadian Psychology, 49*(3), 182–185. doi: 10.1037/a0012801

Dowd, M. (2013, February 24). Pompom girl for feminism. *New York Times.* Retrieved from http://www.nytimes.com/2013/02/24/opinion/sunday/dowd-pompom-girl-for-feminism.html?_r=0

Faludi, S. (2013). Facebook feminism: Like it or not. *The Baffler, 23.* Retrieved from http://www.thebaffler.com/ salvos/facebook-feminism-like-it-or-not

Friedan, B. (1963). *The feminine mystique.* New York, NY: W.W. Norton.

Gara, T. (2013). Exclusive: First look at Sheryl Sandberg's new book. *Wall Street Journal.* Retreived from http://blogs.wsj.com/corporate-intelligence/2013/02/05/sheryl-sandbergs-fight/

Goldberg, M. (2013). The absurd backlash against Sheryl Sandberg's Lean In. *Daily Beast.* Retrieved from http://www.thedailybeast.com/articles/2013/03/01/the-absurd-backlash-against-sheryl-sandberg-s-lean-in.html

Gillibrand, K. (2014). *Off the sidelines: Raise your voice, change the world.* New York, NY: Random House.

Goodkind, S. (2009). "You can be anything you want, but you have to believe in it": Commercialized feminism in gender-specific programs for girls. *Signs: Journal of Women in Culture and Society, 34(2),* 397–422. doi: 10.1086/591086

Gray, J. (1992). *Men are from Mars, women are from Venus.* New York, NY: HarperCollins.

Harris, P. (2013). Sheryl Sandberg: The Facebook boss on a self-help mission. *The Guardian.* Retrieved from http://www.theguardian.com/theobserver/2013/feb/24/sheryl-sandberg-facebook-boss-mission-lean

Harris, T. (1969). *I'm ok, you're ok.* New York, NY: HarperCollins Publishers.

Hazleden, R. (2011). Dragon-slayers and jealous rats: The gendered self in contemporary self-help manuals. *Cultural Studies Review, 17(1),* 270–295. doi: 10.5130/csr.v17i1.1723

Hochschild, A. R. (2003). *The commercialization of intimate life: notes from home and work.* Berkeley, CA: University of California Press.

Holmes, A. (2013). Maybe you should read the book: The Sheryl Sandberg backlash. *New Yorker.* Retrieved from http://www.newyorker.com/books/page-turner/maybe-you-should-read-the-book-the-sheryl-sandberg-backlash

hooks, b. (2000a). *Feminism is for everybody.* Brooklyn, NY: South End Press.

hooks, b. (2000b). *Feminist theory from margin to center.* Brooklyn, NY: South End Press.

hooks, b. (2013). Dig deep beyond lean in. *The Feminist Wire.* Retrieved from http://thefeministwire.com /2013/10/17973/

Huffington, A. (2014). *Thrive.* New York, NY: Harmony.

Iannello, K. P. (2010). Women's leadership and third-wave feminism. In K. O'Connor (Ed.), *Gender and women's leadership: A reference handbook* (pp. 70–77). Thousand Oaks, CA: Sage.

Johnson, S. (2002). *Who moved my cheese?: An amazing way to deal with change in your work and in your life.* New York, NY: Penguin Books.

Kantor, J. (2013, February 22). A titan's how-to on breaking the glass ceiling. *New York Times.* Retrieved from http://www.nytimes.com/2013/02/22/us/sheryl-sandberg-lean-in-author-hopes-to-spur-movement.html

Kay, K., & Shipman, C. (2014). *The confidence code.* New York, NY: Harper Collins.

Kenny, K., & Bell, E. (2014). Irony as discipline: Self-help and gender in the knowledge economy. *Social Politics: International Studies in Gender, State and Society, 21(4),* 562–584. doi: 10.1093/sp/jxu012

La Sonde, C. (n.d.). *Domestic violence safe house manager.* Retrieved from http://www.leanin.org/stories/cheryl-lasonde

Leanin.org. (2015). *Lean in circles.* Retrieved from www.leanin.org

Losse, K. (2013). Feminism's tipping point: Who wins from Leaning In? *Dissent Magazine*. Retrieved from https://www.dissentmagazine.org/online_articles/feminisms-tipping-point-who-wins-from-leaning-in

Luscombe, B. (2013, March 7). Confidence women: Facebook's Sheryl Sandberg is on a mission to change the balance of power. Why she just might pull it off. *Time*. Retrieved from http://ideas.time.com/2013/03/07/confidence-woman/

McGee, M. (2005). *Self-help inc*. London, UK: Oxford University Press.

Meyerson, D. E. (2001). *Tempered radicals: How individuals use difference to inspire change at work*. Cambridge MA: Harvard Business School Press.

Meyerson, D. E., & Scully, M. (1995). Crossroads tempered radicalism and the politics of ambivalence and change. *Organization Science, 6*(5), 585–600. doi: 10.1287/orsc.6.5.585

Neville, P. (2013). Helping self-help books: Toward a new research agenda. *Interactions: Studies in Communication and Culture, 3*(3), 361–379. doi: 10.1386/iscc.3.3.361_1

Poczter, S. (2013). Lessons from Facebook's Sheryl Sandberg on how to succeed in business by really trying. *Forbes*. Retrieved from http://www.forbes.com/sites/sharonpoczter/2013/02/11/lessons-from-facebooks-sheryl-sandberg-on-how-to-succeed-in-business-by-really-trying/

Ridgeway, C. (2011). *Framed by gender: How gender inequality persists in the modern world*. New York, NY: Oxford University Press.

Ryan, R. M., & Deci, E. L. (2000). Intrinsic and extrinsic motivations: Classic definitions and new directions. *Contemporary Educational Psychology, 25*(1), 54–67. doi: 10.1006/ceps.1999.1020

Sandberg, S. (2010). *Why we have too few women leaders* [Video file]. Retrieved from http://www.ted.com/talks/sheryl_sandberg_why_we_have_too_few_women_leaders?language=en

Sandberg, S. (2011). *Barnard commencement speech*. [Video file]. Retrieved from https://www.youtube. com/watch?v=AdvXCKFNqTY

Sandberg, S. (2013). *Lean in: Women, work, and the will to lead*. New York, NY: Alfred A. Knopf.

Sandberg, S. (2014). *Lean in for college graduates*. New York, NY: Alfred A. Knopf.

Sandberg, S., & Grant, A. (2015a, January 1). Speaking while female. *New York Times*. Retrieved from http://www.nytimes.com/2015/01/11/opinion/sunday/speaking-while-female.html

Sandberg, S., & Grant, A. (2015b, March 8). How men and succeed in the boardroom and the bedroom. *New York Times*. Retrieved from http://www.nytimes.com/2015/03/08/opinion/sunday/sheryl-sandberg-adam-grant-how-men-can-succeed-in-the-boardroom-and-the-bedroom.html

Schultz, C. (2013). Review: Sheryl Sandberg's Lean In is full of good intentions, but rife with contradictions. *New Republic*. Retrieved from https://www.washingtonpost.com/opinions/review-sheryl-sandbergs-lean-in-is-full-of-good-intentions-but-rife-with-contradictions/2013/03/01/3380c00e-7f9a-11e2-a350-49866afab584_story.html

Simonds, W. (1992). *Women and the self-help culture: Reading between the lines*. New Brunswick, NJ: Rutgers University Print.

Simonds, W. (1996). All consuming selves: Self-help literature and women's identities. In D. Grodin, & T. R. Lindlof (Eds.), *Constructing the self in a mediated world* (pp. 15–30). Thousand Oaks, CA: Sage.

Slaughter, A. (2012). Why women still can't have it all. *Atlantic.* Retrieved from http://www.theatlantic.com/magazine/archive/2012/07/why-women -still-cant-have-it-all/309020/

Slaughter, A. M. (2013, March 10). Yes, you can. *New York Times.* Retrieved from http://www.nytimes.com/2013/03/10/books/review/sheryl-sandbergs-lean-in.html?_r=0

Taylor, V. (1996). *Rock-a-by-baby: Feminism, self-help, and post-partum depression.* New York, NY: Routledge.

Traister, R. (2014). The uselessness of hating Sheryl Sandberg. *New Republic.* Retrieved from https://newrepublic.com/article/116794/rosa-brooks-hates-sheryl-sandberg-and-misses-point

Wilson, M. (2013). Leaning In to new ideas. *Huffington Post.* Retrieved from http://www.huffingtonpost.com/marie-c-wilson/sheryl-sandberg-lean-in_b_2838451.html

Zukin, S., & Maguire, J. S. (2004). Consumers and consumption. *Annual Review of Sociology, 30,* 173–197. doi: 10.1146/annurev.soc.30.012703.110553

CHAPTER 5

"THERE'S NEVER BEEN A BETTER TIME TO BE A WOMAN"

The Discursive Effects of Women on Boards' Research Reports

Scarlett E. Brown
King's College London

Elisabeth K. Kelan
Cranfield University

The relative absence of women directors on corporate boards has received a great deal of media attention in recent years; however, the effect of these media portrayals has had little academic analysis (De Anca & Gabaldon, 2014; Terjesen, Sealy, & Singh, 2009). This oversight is problematic, as how leaders are represented can have a powerful influence over the cultural discourses surrounding business and leadership (Kelan, 2013). Research that examines representations of leaders and boards of directors in business

Gender, Media, and Organization, pages 77–92

media (Bernardi, Bean, & Weippert, 2002; Guthey & Jackson, 2005; Kelan, 2013), company annual reports (Benschop & Meihuizen, 2002), and in press coverage (McGregor, 2000) demonstrates how these representations matter, particularly from a gender perspective. Regarding women on boards (WoB), the media has the potential to support the drive for increasing gender diversity on boards by raising awareness concerning the value of board gender parity and championing women board directors (De Anca & Gabaldon, 2014). The media may also reproduce gendered expectations regarding women leaders (Eagly & Carli, 2003), for instance, by presenting women directors homogeneously as more risk-averse (Roberts, 2015) rather than as individuals and directors in their own right.

WoB has also been examined by a wealth of research institutes, consultancies, policymakers, think tanks, and businesses (Seierstad, Warner-Søderholm, Torchia, & Huse, 2015), many of which produce research reports,[1] often in collaboration with academics (see, for example: McKinsey & Company, 2007, 2008; Sealy & Doherty, 2012; Sealy & Vinnicombe, 2012, 2013; Struber, 2012; Vinnicombe, Doldor, & Turner, 2014; Vinnicombe, Doldor, Sealy, Pryce, & Turner, 2015). The advantages of these collaborations to both parties are clear: financial sponsorship can be hugely beneficial to academics, and the knowledge created can be applied in practical contexts to benefit companies and influence policymakers (Mason, 2015). Additionally, these reports are a specific and tangible way for researchers to show that their work has impact, "taking academic work and turning it into knowledge that is useful and used by business, government, and society more broadly" (Mason, 2015. p. 1). In relation to WoB, these research reports have been highly influential in increasing the number of women being appointed (Seierstad et al., 2015). Despite this, little analysis has been conducted into how they visually or discursively represent women directors and what effects this may have (De Anca & Gabaldon, 2014). Given their high circulation in business media and that they are thought of as being highly influential (Mason, 2015), these reports can be considered media portrayals in their own right; analysis needs to be conducted into how these reports shape the WoB agenda beyond simply recruiting more women to boards.

This chapter addresses the lack of analysis of research reports by presenting findings from academic research into the experiences of men and women seeking non-executive director (NED) roles on corporate boards in the UK. We start by discussing relevant literature, in particular examining the business case for women that has become de rigueur in discussions around board diversity in the UK (Prügl, 2012; Roberts, 2015; Seierstad et al., 2015) and underpins many of these research reports. Second, we discuss the methodology of the research. We then outline indicative findings showing how men and women draw on the findings of WoB research reports as a way of making sense of their experiences of seeking NED roles, engendering a belief that it is easier for women to get onto boards than it is men and a belief that it is easier for those with accountancy qualifications. Finally, we offer some brief conclusions and indications for further research.

WOMEN ON BOARDS—RESEARCH AND THE MEDIA

In the last decade WoB has received a great deal of attention in the academic community and been studied across academic disciplines (Huse, Hoskisson, Zattoni, & Viganò, 2011; Seierstad et al., 2015; Terjesen et al., 2009). In addition to academic scholarship, the issue is also examined by other research organizations, consultancies, think tanks, and businesses (Davies, 2011; Hedley May, 2014; Korn Ferry, 2013; McKinsey & Company, 2007, 2008, 2010; Sealy & Doherty, 2012; Struber, 2012; Vinnicombe et al., 2014; Vinnicombe et al., 2015). These studies aim to increase the number of WoB by drawing attention to women's relative absence from the boardroom and emphasizing the business case for board gender parity (Huse et al., 2011). In the UK, the reports are often produced in collaboration with academics. For example, the Cranfield University Female FTSE reports are written by academics, financially sponsored by large corporations, supported by diversity organizations, and receive a great deal of coverage in the national press. While acknowledging the irony, a recent research report produced by the Chartered Association of Business Schools argues that the Female FTSE reports have had a huge influence over the subsequent increase in the proportion of women directors (Mason, 2014). Their high reputation within the business elite and in academia and society more widely (Mason, 2014; Seierstad et al., 2015) means that they can be thought of as media representations in their own right and are key stakeholders in shaping the political and business agenda.

Academic research that seeks to build a business case for gender-diverse boards has largely drawn from readily available, subscription-based data, such as BoardEx,[2] to examine the effect of appointing women to boards. These commonly highlight a positive relationship between the appointment of women and various measures of board or company success, such as financial performance, return on investments, higher firm value, greater innovation, board productivity, and organizational effectiveness (Post & Byron, 2015; see Terjesen et al., 2009 for an overview). While this research is abundant and often convincing, it must be acknowledged that these findings are rarely able to demonstrate a direct causal relationship between the appointment of women and board success. Board success is notoriously difficult to define and measure, and the business case research is a field "plagued with endogeneity" (Schwartz-Ziv, 2011, p. 2).

The business case for WoB is a key theme in much of the business literature and media coverage, communicating an overall assertion that women on
boards are "not just the right thing, but the 'bright' thing" (Brown, Brown, &
Anastasopoulos, 2002, p. 1). Research reports, such as the McKinsey *Women
Matter* series (McKinsey & Company, 2007; 2008; 2010) or the Credit Suisse
Research Institute (Struber, 2012), draw on elements of the business case
to advocate the need to improve the gender diversity of boards; this also
formed the basis of the UK's response to the lack of WoB. When, in 2003,
Norway brought in a gender quota (requiring all boards over a certain size to
have at least 40% representation of both men and women), other countries
were pushed for a response of how they would be tackling the WoB issue.
In the UK this led to the production of the *Women on Boards* report (Davies,
2011)—commonly referred to as the Davies' report[3]—a governmental white
paper that called on business leaders to meet a voluntary target of 25% for
women's board representation by 2015—this has now been met. Seierstad
and colleagues (2015) argue that in the UK the Davies' report (2011) and
subsequent Female FTSE reports were a key driver for change, where the
number of women on FTSE100 boards rose from 12.5% in 2011 to 25% in
2015 (Seierstad et al., 2015; Vinnicombe et al., 2015).

Unlike Norway, where much of the debate centered on justice-based reasoning for board diversity, the UK Davies' report and subsequent discussions have emphasized the business case. The report, for instance, states:

> There is a strong business case for balanced boards. Inclusive and diverse
> boards are more likely to be effective boards, better able to understand their
> customers and stakeholders and to benefit from fresh perspectives, new ideas,
> vigorous challenge and broad experience. This in turn leads to better deci-
> sion making. (Davies, 2011, p. 7)

Lord Davies presented the business case for appointing women, emphasizing how it will benefit the board and companies and referencing a "growing body of evidence" (Davies, 2011, p. 7) that draws a positive relationship
between women directors and financial performance (Joy, Carter, Wagner,
& Narayanan, 2007; McKinsey & Company, 2007). The equality, social justice, or critical standpoints that are included in much of the academic research are sidelined in favor of this perspective. This is made even more
evident in the following quotation from Vince Cable, MP, who was the UK
Business Secretary at the time the Davies's report was published. In a BBC
interview discussing WoB, he stated, "This is not about equality, this is about
good governance and good business" (Seierstad et al., 2015, p. 12). This
dismissal of equality in favor of utilitarian, business-focused arguments is
typical of the media coverage of women on boards in the UK.

In addition to the expectation that having women on boards will yield
positive business outputs, a range of media coverage (and, to a lesser extent,

academic research) has put forward a case for increased numbers of women directors that valorizes so-called feminine traits and the potential for change they offer. Roberts (2015) argued that the global financial crisis in 2008 was a pivotal moment for the women in leadership and WoB debate, allowing for the "(re)emergence of the business case for gender equality" (p. 124). There developed a "women-as-saviors" case for female leadership, where the appointment or promotion of women was viewed as key to economic recovery, largely reliant on stereotypical, gendered assumptions that they are more risk-averse than men. Christine Lagarde, managing director of the International Monetary Fund (IMF) infamously quipped that "if Lehman Brothers had been Lehman Sisters, today's economic crisis clearly would look quite different" (Lagarde, 2010, p. 1), a perspective that is often cited in media outputs (Prügl, 2012; Roberts, 2015). This reproduces the notion that women can moderate the excessively risky and testosterone-driven behavior of men, simply with their presence (McDowell, 2011; Prügl, 2012). While research has drawn a connection between testosterone and success in risky industries (Coates & Herbert, 2008), little association has been found between gender diversity and less risk (Adams & Ragunathan, 2013). This perspective therefore has the potential for opening discursive space for criticism of the financial markets (Roberts, 2015), but it places high expectations on women directors to engender cultural change in the boardroom and draws on essentialized notions of men and women.

Paradoxically, WoB research has taken up the subject of women in banking and financial industries in a different way. Rather than emphasizing women's potential with regard to risk aversion or feminine leadership qualities, financial qualifications are seen as a way for women to demonstrate their credibility on the same terms as men in the boardroom. In the report *Women in Finance: A Springboard to Corporate Board Positions?* conducted by academics and sponsored by a major research council in conjunction with the Association of Chartered Certified Accountants (ACCA), Sealy and Doherty (2012) state:

> Female board members felt [financial qualifications] gave them credibility to be perceived as *not so different from the men*, enabling them to be judged in the same terms, giving them perceived legitimacy and a common language. Finance was described as the language of the board and having it gave women access to the conversation. The language of finance also helps to break down some persistent stereotypes about women's competence and emotional nature. (p. 5–6, emphasis added)

From this perspective, women are encouraged to demonstrate their qualification for the boardroom by accentuating their *similarities* with men rather than their differences (Noon, 2007) and by deliberately challenging women's presumed emotional nature. This draws on a different aspect of the business case, one that views women as an underutilized pool of (gender-neutral) talent, rather than privileging women's qualities or traits. Boards are encouraged to "fish in a bigger pond" (Treanor, 2012, para. 9), because getting more women into business is a way of tackling the "talent shortage"[4] (McKinsey & Company, 2007, p. 10).

Increased public focus on WoB and the business case in the UK has led to a cultural shift and a need for women directors that has, arguably, made women highly desirable for board roles; positive discrimination towards women is expected, rather than debated (Noon, 2007). However, there are tensions in how WoB are represented: simultaneously as women with gendered, feminine traits, and also as gender-neutral actors who are able to justify their legitimacy on the same grounds as men. While these representations are contradictory, there is little research that examines how they affect aspirant directors' perceptions of who should be on boards or how they make sense of the appointment process in light of these reports. Given that the media has a powerful role to play in how leaders are perceived, particularly women leaders (Kelan, 2013), it is critical that these discursive effects be understood.

METHODOLOGY

The chapter draws upon in-depth, qualitative interviews with 15 men and 15 women seeking NED roles on FTSE 100 or FTSE 250[5] boards, between January 2013 and November 2014. The candidates were interviewed three times[6] over this period, leading to 86 interviews. This longitudinal focus reveals how candidates made sense of the recruitment and selection processes, recognizing that appointment to the board can take many months and that candidates' perceptions can change over time. The interviews were conducted face-to-face,[7] audio-recorded, and professionally transcribed,[8] and then proofread and analyzed by the first author. They were first analyzed by hand and then entered into the qualitative data analysis software *Dedoose*, which collated similar themes together. This chapter draws on occasions where the women participants referred explicitly or implicitly to research reports about WoB.

Following thematic coding we used discourse analysis (DA) (Potter & Wetherell, 1987) to examine the candidates' language and how this discursively creates meaning, allowing candidates to make sense of their experiences (Potter & Wetherell, 1987). We also utilized aspects of narrative analysis (NA)—in particular the work on *sensemaking* (Brown, Stacey, & Nadhakumar, 2008). Both DA and NA have at their center a concern with how people make sense of their experiences, what interpretative repertoires (Potter & Wetherell, 1987) or units of sense-making (Edley, 2001) they draw upon to do so, and how the use of these structures discursively creates meaning. The combination of DA and NA forms a narrative-discursive (ND) method (Taylor, 2015; Taylor & Littleton, 2006), which is particularly appropriate for longitudinal research due to its focus on how accounts can be enduring or repeated over time. Using ND, we examine the pool of resources (Taylor, 2015) that individuals use to explain their experiences and pay particular attention to what contributes to this pool together with occasions where resources are repeatedly used. Research reports, we argue, form part of these discursive resources.

While not explicitly concerned with the representativeness of the sample, the candidates come from a wide selection of career backgrounds. This helps ensure that emerging results are not simply symptomatic of differences between industries, given that traditionally male-dominated businesses tend to have fewer WoB (Vinnicombe et al., 2015). This was also useful in studying WoB research reports, as many produced in recent years are industry-specific reports encouraging the appointment of candidates from, for instance, digital (Korn Ferry, 2013), legal (Hedley May, 2014), or finance (Sealy & Doherty, 2012) fields.

THERE'S NEVER BEEN A BETTER TIME TO BE A WOMAN

In making sense of their experiences, all 30 aspirant directors discussed the recent focus in the UK on board diversity and WoB in the media. For women, this often formed part of their motivation for seeking board roles. For example, Pamela[9] and Catrin told us:

> I always wanted to be a NED, and everyone I've talked to, they are saying … there has never been a better time for women to do this. With all the pressure on companies, I should use this window. (Pamela)

> I suppose I felt that if I can't get a NED now, I'll never get one. Because there's got to be some advantages of being a woman and at the moment there is an advantage. Since the Davies report, I just think it's much harder if you're a man than a woman because if you're trying to balance your board then it's going to be much more natural to take a woman than a man. (Catrin)

Almost all women candidates said something similar to these statements. Many referenced the Davies report, Female FTSE, or the recent focus on WoB in the media and felt that it had opened up the boardroom to women. The Davies report was seen to have such a significant impact on the world of NED search that many of the women, similar to Catrin above, suggested that it was now much harder for men to get roles, as women were in such high demand.

This "woman's advantage" interpretive repertoire—the belief that it is easier for women than men—was also evident in men's accounts in relation to the difficulty they face in seeking NED roles. Alex and Raymond told us:

> One very well-known city headhunter, female, said to me, "If you wore a skirt, I'd get you to any board room you want, any day." But at the minute there's a flood of women being recruited, there was that big push, there was the Davies report and was other committees and reports and things that came out...and it was predominantly significantly female-focused recruitment at that time. (Alex)

> Well, I think at the moment, I mean...let's be very open about it. If you are a female director and you've got experience of China, you can write your own check at the moment...because boards haven't got those experiences. (Raymond)

As with the women, nearly all of the men drew on the "woman's advantage" repertoire and discussed this in relation to the recent pressure being placed upon boards to diversify. Alex, as well as attributing this to the Davies report, suggests that headhunters adopt this discourse: This indicates the strength of the Davies report and associated media in shaping the culture towards WoB, through influencing both organizations and individual behaviors and attitudes. It also offers some insight into how networks of individuals who have a stake in the WoB agenda may draw upon and reinforce the idea that women have an advantage. For Alex and Raymond, this is one way that they make sense of the difficulties they face gaining board roles.

It is important to highlight two aspects of the way the women's advantage discourse is deployed. First is its resonance, even in the face of contradictory evidence: Although the number of women being appointed has increased since the Davies report, the majority (70%) of FTSE 100 and FTSE 250 board roles went to men in this period, a situation that is highlighted in the Davies report and subsequent research reports (Davies, 2011; Sealy & Vinnicombe, 2012, 2013; Vinnicombe et al., 2014, 2015). The accounts suggest that candidates perceive these reports as evidence of the success for WoB when, in fact, the increase in women's appointments to boards from less than 10% to 30% demonstrates evidence of a persistent preference for men. The discursive effect is not reflective of factual reality but still forms part of their sensemaking.

Second, we note how the women's advantage discourse contrasts to the female advantage discourse (Eagly & Carli, 2003, p. 807) that underpins the business case for women directors. Given there has been a huge focus on the business case in the UK and this has been instrumental in getting businesses and chairs to commit to appointing women, it is notable that the female advantage is not in any of the aspirant directors' accounts. Women rarely put themselves forward as *female* leaders, and there was little or no mention of what specific skills women might bring to the boardroom. Instead, women's advantage relates solely to boards' need to fulfill a diversity agenda. On one hand, we find the absence of the business case or female advantage (Eagly & Carli, 2003) discourses encouraging, particularly given their reliance on essentialist perspectives of gender and expectations that women display female leadership (Eagly & Carli, 2003). On the other, the strength of the women's advantage discourse only in relation to meeting a diversity target may imply a backlash against positive discrimination towards women (Noon, 2007), or it may belittle the value of women who are appointed.

BEING AN ACCOUNTANT

A further research report that several interviewees discussed was the ACCA report mentioned above (Sealy & Doherty, 2012), which argues that financial qualifications—such as the accountancy qualifications that ACCA provide—could act as a "springboard" (p. 1) for women into board positions. Although it was not covered in the national press, the report was launched at a networking event that many of the interviewees attended, and it circulated through NED networks. It was discussed by candidates in relation to their experiences and their perceptions of what boards are looking for. Philippa, for instance, told us:

> I was in the last two for a FTSE 350 and the headhunter said, "Oh well, you aren't an accountant," but it was apparently close between me and the other lady.... I never got feedback to say it was because I wasn't an accountant and that was why I didn't get it. But... I did see, did you see? Some... a paper, the ACCA have done some research. (Philippa)

Although Philippa has a broad range of financial, board-relevant experience, on several occasions she attributes lack of success in part to her not being an accountant. The use of "but" in the statement, "I never got feedback to say it was because I was not an accountant, *but*..." implies that it *was* due to her not being an accountant; she sets up the potential discrediting factor—not getting feedback—and then utilizes the ACCA paper as support for her belief that it was due to the lack of accountancy qualification. This "counter-dispositional" discursive device (Whittle & Mueller, 2011)—providing the alternative explanation to demonstrate she has considered it, and then dismissing it—provides a repertoire to make sense of not being appointed. We cannot know if this actually was a factor in her not gaining the role—and as discursive researchers we take people's constructions as the topic of study, rather than presuming they relate to a necessary truth about what happened (Potter & Wetherell, 1987; Whittle & Mueller, 2011)—this suggests that the research reports resonate with candidates when they corroborate their perceptions of what they need to be or do to be successful. Similar to the women's advantage discourse discussed earlier, this discourse draws on many sources: the headhunter's comment and the ACCA report are both offered as a way of making sense of her failure to get the role.

In a later interview, Philippa raises the ACCA research again in relation to her perception of what constitutes an "ideal" board candidate.[10]

> From your experience and the interviews you've had so far, do you think there is an ideal board candidate? Do you have a sense of what they are looking for; what you need to be?
>
> There is, there definitely is. . . . Well, when you talk about audit committee there is, I don't know how much I'm making . . . how insecure I feel about it. . . . But I do feel . . . the fact that I'm not an accountant, not a qualified accountant . . . well like in the ACCA research, it is financial qualifications. Now I can see . . . for some board appointments, like to be the chair of an audit committee of a FTSE 100 and not be an accountant—I can see there's risk in that. But like . . . with the job I did get, it honestly didn't matter, and I don't think it matters for all boards. So I think there is a little bit of a preconceived—"This is what it looks like, if we want the person to chair the audit committee" thing. (Philippa)

This second account also elucidates the importance of the ACCA research as a source of understanding. Overall, Philippa criticizes the preconceived, narrow perspective that candidates need to have financial qualifications—a perspective she sees as being perpetuated by the ACCA report. This criticism is part of a wider discourse present in many candidates' accounts: boards and headhunters are highly restrictive in whom they are looking for, and it is based on very narrow criteria. As Philippa goes on to explain, this is challenged by candidates gaining roles without fitting the narrow definition of an ideal board member; however, this casts Philippa being appointed to a board role *without* accountancy qualifications as an exception to a wider rule, which the report reinforces. While the overall aim of the report is to encourage women from a broad range of finance backgrounds to seek board roles, this would suggest the report is being taken as evidence that accountancy qualifications are *necessary* for board roles, reproducing the very discourses they are at least partly attempting to challenge.

CONCLUDING THOUGHTS:
REPRESENTING WOMEN DIRECTORS

WoB research reports are, almost without exception, underpinned by a motivation to increase the number of WoB. The Davies report and Female FTSE reports encourage businesses to diversify their boards; similarly, the

ACCA report highlights the value of financial qualifications in making women suited to NED roles. They form part of the cultural discourse of WoB, which has been integral to pushing the agenda forward (Seierstad et al., 2015). While this is a positive development considering women's continued underrepresentation, these findings imply contradictions between the intentions of the WoB reports and how aspirant directors interpret them.

Both men and women in the research saw the high impact of the cultural discourse around WoB as evidence that it is now easier for women to gain board positions than men, drawing on a women's advantage interpretative repertoire. For the women, it is part of their motivation, while men use it to account for the difficulty they face getting roles. While it is perceived as easier for women to achieve board roles than it previously has been, the candidates rarely acknowledge that the majority of boardroom roles still go to men (Sealy & Vinnicombe, 2013; Vinnicombe et al., 2014, 2015); there is no evidence it is actually easier for women than men. Similarly, they do not adopt the business case or "female advantage" (Eagly & Carli, 2003) discourses to explain this preference despite it being a key part of the rhetoric being put forward by the media. Candidates also mention other research reports to show how powerful some discourses perpetuated by these reports can be. In this case, the ACCA report perpetuates the belief that accountancy qualifications are a key kind of human capital desired on boards, despite candidates being successful without them. In both cases discussed here, the interviewees are presenting research reports as representative of fact or truth, and they persist even when contradicted by candidates' own experience.

Although part of a much wider discussion, these findings raise a question as to what contributes to the legitimacy of the research reports and durability of discourses. It may in part be due to the authors of the reports: Mervyn Davies has held senior roles in government and in business (Medland, 2013), and the Female FTSE and ACCA reports represent collaborations between academic researchers and powerful political and business actors—indeed it is this collaboration that makes their impact on the WoB issue so substantial (Seierstad et al., 2015). This collaboration between academia and business also presents issues. As Benschop and Meihuizen (2002) noted in relation to company annual reports, factual information is being displayed, but it must also necessarily represent the authors and/or organization in a positive light, which affects the way they are written. Such reports therefore occupy an interesting location between public accountability and the personal interests of the organization or author(s). Similarly, complex findings can become oversimplified, both in translation from academic research into research reports and in how they are interpreted by audiences. This highlights the risk of losing the nuance or independence that academic research provides.

This chapter does not seek to denigrate the influence of such reports on the WoB agenda or question the value of disseminating academic research to a wider field; indeed, it is arguably the duty of academics to ensure that research reaches and influences those whom it examines. Rather, these findings indicate a need to examine the discursive effects of research reports beyond simply increasing the numbers of WoB. When research presents snapshot quantitative data concerning the current situation—for instance, the number of women on boards, or directors with accountancy qualifications—this may contribute to maintenance of the status quo if these reports not only mirror reality but also shape perception. Given the number of WoB reports that have been produced in recent years (we have covered several in this chapter, but it is by no means a comprehensive list), it is important that we acknowledge how they shape who seeks to be appointed and who is appointed to corporate board roles (De Anca & Gabaldon, 2014). These research reports need to be examined as a form of media in their own right, with the potential to have powerful, discursive effects. We have highlighted this, here, based on interview data, but future research in this area would benefit from examining this issue from multiple perspectives, integrating interviews with consumers alongside interviews with producers of the reports, and analysis of the texts themselves.

NOTES

1. These are often referred to by academics as "practitioner reports" as they are primarily aimed at diversity practitioners rather than academic audiences. This does not apply as neatly for WoB research, as there are no practitioners as such and candidates commonly referred to them as "reports." For the sake of ease, we use "research reports" throughout the chapter.
2. BoardEx is an online consolidation of the public domain information of boards of directors and senior management of publicly quoted and large private companies. It is available at http://corp.boardex.com/about-boardex/
3. We should also note the irony here: a report about women on boards, based on research conducted by women, has become known by the man who commissioned it.
4. The "talent shortage" perspective is also, arguably, a myth perpetuated by those whom it benefits, such as executive search firms (Faulconbridge, Beaverstock, Hall, & Hewitson, 2009).
5. FTSE 100 and FTSE 250 together make up the 350 companies with the largest share value, as listed on the London Stock Exchange.
6. The design of the research intended to interview candidates three times over this period. Due to candidates' schedules, this resulted in 25 being interviewed three times, and four twice.
7. Some were conducted over the telephone, although all candidates met with the interviewer at least once.

8. The transcription system is an adapted and simplified version of the Jefferson system: (.)—a short notable pause; (0.9)—an exactly timed longer pause (more than 5 seconds, here 9 seconds); (inaud)—inaudible; ((text)) —annotation of nonverbal activity or supplemental information; (...) material deliberately omitted; ".. —direct speech reported by interviewee; wor- — abrupt halt or interruption of word; wo:rd—extreme stretching of preceding sound, prolongation of a sound; = —break and subsequent continuation of a single utterance; HAHA—loud laughter; HEHE—laughter; TEXT—strong emphasis or loud volume; ^Text^—speech delivered quieter than usual for the speaker; >text—speech delivered more slowly than usual for the speaker; [...]—start and end point of overlapping talk.

9. All names are pseudonyms.

10. The "ideal" board member was one of the research themes that formed the basis of the interviews.

ACKNOWLEDGMENTS

This research was funded through an Economic and Social Research Council Collaborative (CASE) Studentship: A collaboration between King's College London and Sapphire Partners.

REFERENCES

Adams, R., & Ragunathan, V. (2013). Lehman sisters. Asian Bureau of Finance and Economic Research Working Papers. Retrieved from http://abfer.org/working-papers.html

Benschop, Y., & Meihuizen, E. (2002). Keeping up gendered appearances: Representations of gender in financial annual reports. *Accounting, Organizations and Society, 21*(11), 611–636. doi:10.1016/S0361-3682(01)00049-6

Bernardi, R., Bean, D., & Weippert, K. (2002). Signaling gender diversity through annual report pictures. *Accounting, Auditing & Accountability Journal, 15*(4), 609–616. doi: http://dx.doi.org/10.1108/09513570210441440

Brown, A. D., Stacey, P., & Nandhakumar, J. (2008). Making sense of sensemaking narratives. *Human Relations, 61*(8), 1035–1062. doi:10.1177/0018726708094858

Brown, D., Brown, I., & Anastasopoulos, V. (2002). *Women on boards: Not just the right thing... but the "bright" thing.* The Conference Board of Canada. Retrieved from http://www.utsc.utoronto.ca/~phanira/WebResearchMethods/women-en-bod&fp-conference%20board.pdf

Coates, J. M., & Herbert, J. (2008). Endogenous steroids and financial risk taking on a London trading floor. *Proceedings of the National Academy of Sciences USA.* Retrieved from http://www.pnas.org/content/105/16/6167.full.pdf+html?sid=923de3de-1794-448b-be58-5019925c299b

Davies, M. (2011, February). *Women on boards: February 2011.* Retrieved from https://www.gov.uk/government/uploads/system/uploads/attachment_data/file/31480/11-745-women-on-boards.pdf

De Anca, C., & Gabaldon, P. (2014). Female directors and the media: Stereotypes of board members. *Gender in Management: An International Journal, 29*(6), 334–351. doi: http://dx.doi.org/10.1108/GM-07-2013-0079

Eagly, A. H., & Carli, L. L. (2003). The female leadership advantage: An evaluation of the evidence. *The Leadership Quarterly, 14*(6), 807–834. doi:10.1016/j.leaqua.2003.09.004

Edley, N. (2001). Analysing masculinity: Interpretative repertoires, ideological dilemmas and subject positions. In M. Wetherell, S. Taylor, & S. Yates (Eds.), *Discourse as data: A guide for analysis* (pp. 189–228). London, UK: Sage.

Faulconbridge, J., Beaverstock, J., Hall, S., & Hewitson, A. (2009). The 'war for talent': The gatekeeper role of executive search firms in elite labour markets, *GeoForum, 40*(5), 800–808. doi:10.1016/j.geoforum.2009.02.001

Guthey, E., & Jackson, B. (2005). CEO portraits and the authenticity paradox. *Journal of Management Studies, 42*(5), 1057–1082. doi: 10.1111/j.1467-6486.2005.00532.x

Hedley May. (2014). *Lawyers on boards—Where are they?* Hedley May Thought Leadership. Retrieved from http://www.hedleymay.com/Thoughtleadership/Lawyers_on_Boards.pdf

Huse, M., Hoskisson, R., Zattoni, A., & Viganò, R. (2011). New perspectives on board research: Changing the research agenda. *Journal of Management and Governance, 15*(1), 5–28. doi: 10.1007/s10997-009-9122-9

Joy, L., Carter, N. M., Wagner, H. M., & Narayanan, S. (2007). The bottom line: Corporate performance and women's representation on boards. *Catalyst.* Retrieved from http://www.catalyst.org/system/files/The_Bottom_Line_Corporate_Performance_and_Womens_Representation_on_Boards.pdf

Kelan, E. (2013). The becoming of business bodies: Gender, appearance, and leadership development. *Management Learning, 44*(1), 45–61. doi: 10.1177/1350507612469009

Korn Ferry. (2013). *The Digital Board: Appointing non-executive directors for the internet economy.* Korn Ferry Institute. Retrieved from http://www.kornferryinstitute.com/sites/all/files/documents/briefings-magazine-download/The_Digital-Board_Final.pdf

Lagarde, C. (2010, May 11). What if it had been Lehman Sisters? *DealBook.* Retrieved from http://dealbook.nytimes.com/2010/05/11/lagarde-what-if-it-had-been-lehman-sisters/?_r=0

Mason, R. (2015). The impact of business school research: Economic and social benefits. *Chartered Association of Business Schools.* Retrieved from http://charteredabs.org/wp-content/uploads/2015/03/Chartered-ABS-Impact-Case-Studies-Publication-2015.pdf

McDowell, L. (2011). *Capital culture: Gender at work in the city.* New York, NY: Wiley.

McGregor, J. (2000). Stereotypes and symbolic annihilation: Press constructions of women at the top. *Women in Management Review, 15*(5/6), 290–295. doi: http://dx.doi.org/10.1108/09649420010343186

McKinsey & Company. (2007). Gender diversity, a corporate performance driver. *Women Matter, 1.* Retrieved from http://www.mckinsey.com/features/women_matter

McKinsey & Company. (2008). Female leadership, a competitive edge for the future. *Women Matter, 2.* Retrieved from http://www.mckinsey.com/features/women_matter

McKinsey & Company. (2010). Women at the top of corporations: Making it happen. *Women Matter, 4.* Retrieved from http://www.mckinsey.com/features/women_matter

Medland, D. (2013, October 17th). Lord Davies: How he leapt outside his comfort zone. *Financial Times.* Retrieved from http://www.ft.com/cms/s/0/36d8d182-2786-11e3-8feb-0044feab7de.html#axzz3uzJTmN00

Noon, M. (2007). The fatal flaws of diversity and the business case for ethnic minorities. *Work, Employment and Society, 21*(4), 773–784. doi: 10.1177/0950017007082886

Post, C., & Byron, K. (2015). Women on boards and firm financial performance: A meta-analysis. *Academy of Management Journal, 58*(5), 1546–1571. doi:10.5465/amj.2013.0319

Potter, J., & Wetherell, M. (1987). *Discourse and social psychology: Beyond attitudes and behaviour.* London, UK: Sage.

Prügl, E. (2012). "If Lehman brothers had been Lehman sisters…": Gender and myth in the aftermath of the financial crisis. *International Political Sociology, 6*(1), 21–35. doi: 10.1111/j.1749-5687.2011.00149.x

Roberts, A. (2015). The political economy of "transnational business feminism": Problematising the corporate-led gender equality agenda. *International Feminist Journal of Politics, 17*(2), 1–23. doi: 10.1080/14616742.2013.849968

Schwartz-Ziv, M. (2011). Are all welcome a-board: Does the gender of directors matter? (Working Paper). The Hebrew University of Jerusalem and Harvard. Retrieved from http://www.hks.harvard.edu/m-rcbg/Events/schwartz%20ziv.pdf

Sealy, R., & Doherty, N. (2012). *Women in finance: A springboard to corporate board positions?* The Association of Chartered Certified Accountants (ACCA). Retrieved from http://www.accaglobal.com/content/dam/acca/global/PDF-technical/human-capital/pol-tp-cgs.pdf

Sealy, R., & Vinnicombe, S. (2012). *The female FTSE board report 2012: Milestone or millstone?* Cranfield, UK: Cranfield School of Management. Retrieved from http://www.som.cranfield.ac.uk/som/dinamic-content/research/documents/2012femalftse.pdf

Sealy, R., & Vinnicombe, S. (2013). *The female FTSE board report 2013: False dawn of progress for women on boards?* Cranfield, UK: Cranfield School of Management. Retrieved from http://www.som.cranfield.ac.uk/som/dinamic-content/media/Research/Research%20Centres/CICWL/FTSEReport2013.pdf

Seierstad, C., Warner-Søderholm, G., Torchia, M., & Huse, M. (2015). Increasing the number of women on boards: The role of actors and processes. *Journal of Business Ethics.* Online early. doi: 10.1007/s10551-015-2715-0

Struber, M. (2012). *Gender diversity and corporate performance.* Credit Suisse Research Institute. Retrieved from http://publications.credit-suisse.com/

Taylor, S. (2015). Discursive and psychosocial? Theorising a complex contemporary subject. *Qualitative Research in Psychology, 12*(1), 8–21. doi: 10.1080/14780887.2014.958340

Taylor, S., & Littleton, K. (2006). Biographies in talk: A narrative-discursive research approach. *Qualitative Sociology Review, 2*(1), 22–38. Retrieved from http://www.qualitativesociologyreview.org/ENG/Volume3/abstracts.php#art2

Terjesen, S., Sealy, R., & Singh, V. (2009). Women directors on corporate boards: A review and research agenda. *Corporate governance: an international review, 17*(3), 320–337. doi: 10.1111/j.1467-8683.2009.00742.x

Treanor, J. (2012, November 30). Women in the boardroom: Vince Cable urges top firms to diversify boards. *The Guardian.* Retrieved from http://www.theguardian.com/lifeandstyle/2012/nov/30/vince-cable-ftse-100-women-in-boardroom

Vinnicombe, S., Doldor, E., & Turner, C. (2014). *The female FTSE board report 2014: Crossing the finish line.* Cranfield, UK: Cranfield School of Management. Retrieved from http://www.som.cranfield.ac.uk/som/dinamic-content/research/ftse/The%20Female%20FTSE%20Board%20Report%202014.pdf

Vinnicombe, S., Doldor, E., Sealy, R., Pryce, P., & Turner, C. (2015). *The Female FTSE Board Report 2015: Putting the UK progress into a global perspective.* Cranfield, UK: Cranfield School of Management. Retrieved from http://www.som.cranfield.ac.uk/som/dinamic-content/research/ftse/FemaleFTSEReportMarch2015.pdf

Whittle, A., & Mueller, F. (2011). Bankers in the dock: Moral storytelling in action. *Human Relations, 32*(2), 187–210. doi: 10.1177/0170840610394308

PART II

WOMEN PROFESSIONALS AND LEADERS

CHAPTER 6

DRESS AND THE FEMALE PROFESSIONAL

A Case Study of *Working Woman*

Ann Rippin
University of Bristol

Harriet Shortt
University of the West of England

Samantha Warren
Cardiff University

Women and their clothes have always been a serious matter (Hollander, 1993). Using a visual social semiotic approach (van Leeuwen, 2005), in this chapter we undertake a rich viewing of 1980s cultural texts to explore the performative heritage of gender through the adoption of clothes, make-up, and accessories. This is a timely investigation because today's 40-something women leaders and managers were socialized into their understandings of being professional women as a result of the proliferation of print, television, and film images in the 1980s (see for example, *Baby Boom*, 1987;

Gender, Media, and Organization, pages 95–110
Copyright © 2016 by Information Age Publishing
All rights of reproduction in any form reserved.

Working Girl, 1988). Through these images, women were instructed in the arts of tackling men's dominance in the workplace through the adoption of shoulder pads, big hair, and sharp suits. They are now playing out these roles as managers in an increasingly surveillance-oriented world due to the growth of the Internet, social media, and readily available digital image technologies. These media enable a (damaging) hyper-visible and obsessive focus on women professionals' appearance; for example, politicians in the press are assessed on their fashion sense before their ministerial skills and abilities (Greenslade, 2014). At the same time, self-help texts for female professionals continue to be full of advice stressing how women should look the part if they want to succeed (Kenny & Bell, 2011).

Picking up on this self-help genre, our analysis uses a sample of style-advice features in *Working Woman* magazine, published in the mid-1980s and specifically aimed at the aspiring female professionals of that era. We contend that the 1980s, which were a period of upheaval in organizations as a consequence of the 1970s' oil crises, the beginnings of deregulation, and—significantly here—the influx of women into the workplace, became a setting where performance became paramount. Women knew that they had to look the part but were not sure how that might be achieved. They accessed magazines such as *Working Woman* for guidance. Through an analysis of the images and text in these articles, we attend to the detail of how women's dress became a proxy for feminist power through tailoring detail in costume, hair/make-up, and props. We show how early gendered socialization might play out in women's later professional lives as leaders and managers, in order to contribute to the debate around post-feminist charges that sexism in the workplace—particularly on the grounds of appearance—may no longer be an issue (Lewis, 2014; Walters, 2011).

DRESSING FOR SUCCESS

Although in our opinion still underresearched, dress, clothing, and bodily appearance have been recognized as part of the symbolic landscape of organizational life for some time (e.g., Rafaeli, Dutton, Harquail, & Mackie-Lewis, 1997) and are growing in importance as organizations have increasingly drawn on the aesthetic labor of their employees as extensions of corporate brand and in the name of customer service (Nickson & Warhurst, 2007). Aesthetic labor impacts on men and women differently; however, organizationally encouraged (or required) grooming and packaging of female employees has been an extension of management strategy more commonplace for women than for men (Caven, Lawley, & Baker, 2013). What underlies such endeavors—and the significance of organizational dress more generally—is the fact that clothing in all societies functions as a form of "writing on the body" that communicates identities, culture, and belief systems (Dant, 1999). We suggest that life in organizations is no different in this regard and, indeed, that given the economic stakes involved, organizations are arenas where the operation of dress as a potential signifier and/or mode of differentiation and discrimination is particularly salient.

Feminist organizational theorists have long put forward the view that work organizations—and especially management—are masculine spheres masquerading under the guise of gender neutrality (Acker, 1990). This encoding of management as male is materialized through implicit and explicit expectations about what constitutes an appropriate managerial body. For example, Waring and Waring (2009) noted how the traditionally masculine traits of "strength, stamina, power and control" (p. 361) are seen as desirable attributes among city workers, and Meriläinen, Tienari, and Valtonen (2015) commented that executive search consultants' conceptualizations of the "ideal body" for senior leadership roles "filters out most female bodies already at the outset" (p. 17). If male bodies are seen as an organizational ideal, it stands to reason, then, that masculine-style dress is what we would also expect to see as the norm among white-collar workers. Indeed, the phrase itself, with its allusion to the "white collar" of a man's shirt, is telling in this regard. The masculine norm of business dress is not a benign characteristic, however. In the mid-1980s (around the time *Working Woman* magazine was in print), Forsythe, Drake, and Cox (1985) found that otherwise identical female job applicants had a higher chance of being hired if they wore masculine business clothes, and, although we might hope that this finding is a thing of the past, recent studies have also shown how graduate entrants to the labor market still associate formal business dress (read: variations on the male suit) with how to feel like and communicate one's professional seriousness (Cardon & Okoro, 2009).

Against this backdrop of (male) business dress as norm, professional women's attire attracts far more attention than that of their male counterparts. As Mavin, Bryans, and Cunningham (2010) forcefully documented, media representations contribute significantly to the *doing* of gender in popular culture in ways that hyperinflate the significance of women's appearance rather than their skills and attributes. These authors note, for example: "Appear too feminine and the media will not take you seriously. Appear too masculine or too neutral and your appearance will be picked over and ridiculed and you will be described as too dowdy to be considered fit for power" (p. 558).

Somewhat depressingly, advice to women to make the most of their sexualized appearance at work has even garnered support from academic researchers. Hakim's (2010) concept of "erotic capital" included dress, make-up, and adornments as the fifth element of what she controversially saw as a legitimate source of competitive advantage in the workplace (and other arenas) for women in particular because, as she contended, "they work harder at personal presentation" (p. 504) than men.

What we aim to show in this chapter is that these concerns exercised earlier generations of professional women at a time when they were entering the workplace in greater numbers. The choice of formal work wear for women was never innocent. Rather, women understood that dress functioned as a kind of armor at work, a resource to be deployed in the corporate arena (Hollander, 1994). Although these questions have always been thorny and anxiety-provoking issues for women, we concentrate on just over one year, 1984–1985, when women's expectations of corporate success were high (Slaughter, 1984), but the minefield of what to wear at work was still primed. The readership looked to *Working Woman* for answers and reassurance; in this chapter, we consider the advice they received and ponder its continuing relevance today.

METHODOLOGY AND SAMPLE

Our approach to this research rests on the well-established observation that the media is a powerful force in shaping social attitudes: for example, the influence of lifestyle magazines in affecting young women's self-esteem and body image (Grabe, Ward, & Hyde, 2008) and the role of popular culture texts as an important source of cultural transmission and reinforcement (Parker, 2014). The source materials for our analysis are the issues of *Working Woman* that carried a series of articles that ran for just over a year between November 1984 and December 1985. *Working Woman* was a serious magazine seemingly intended as inspiration, a reference guide, and an advice manual for aspiring female professionals. Serendipitously, the magazines were unearthed during Harriet's parents' house move around the time of the call for chapters for this volume and constitute a found sample, a snapshot of a moment in time when professional identity at work was potentially open to change and when women, theoretically, could have developed an entirely new way of dressing at work. At that time, because of women's entry into the workforce in new positions of authority, they arguably had more say in how they dressed for their new status. The majority of articles tackle important and worthy issues including pension planning, dealing with discrimination, and sexual harassment. However, while browsing through these issues, we were struck by the blend of what we saw as the deadly serious remit of the magazine in its capacity as handbook to the corporate fray, and the either infantilized frivolity—grown women portrayed either as china dolls or mischievous little girls—or warrior-like aesthetic of the numerous images and style features also contained within the editions. One of the advertisements, for example, in the second issue of the magazine, features a coat that could easily fit as a costume in *Game of Thrones*, complete with a leather gun flap over the left shoulder. This led us to consider the power of the media in sending seemingly contradictory messages to the fledgling female professional that simultaneously enlightened and (one assumes) empowered her while, at the same time, either reducing her power to traditional notions of femininity or reinforcing the need to be masculine through its style advice (Kenny & Bell, 2011).

We employed two levels of visual methods in analyzing the magazines. First, we employed a rich viewing (e.g., van Leeuwen, 2005) of the photographs displayed as part of the 18 style advice features we surveyed in a social-semiotic analysis, drawing on the accompanying text and our combined knowledge of the cultural context of economic and organizational conditions in the 1980s in the UK. Because our concern was to look at the way working women were encouraged to consider the impression they were making at work—as a performance—we considered feature articles on clothes, hair, cosmetics, and accessories. These we see as analogous to the theatrical trappings of costume, make-up, and props, and they are, therefore, an appropriate theatrical as well as empirically significant framework. We each coded a sample of magazines and then jointly discussed the development of categories and emerging themes across the images.

Second, we employed a visual method in sharpening the underlying meanings of the themes. To accentuate the key points our analyses had generated, Ann hand drew a series of stylized sketches based on specific images from the magazines, chosen to exemplify a particular element. Drawing has often been discussed as a research method for teasing out research subjects' subjective and emotional experiences around their workplace lives (e.g., Stiles, 2014; Taussig, 2011), but its power as an analytical device stems from the idea that the hand-drawn sketch is more commonly used as a working-through of possible forms and associated meanings by the researcher herself. As William Kentridge (2014), the celebrated American artist, suggested, "[A]ll drawing works with the precept of the paper as membrane between us and the world" (p. 19). Drawing allows us to manifest more than words and photographs can. It can at once show both a whole and an interpretation of that whole; as Berger succinctly expressed, "[D]rawing is an autobiographical record of one's discovery of an event, seen, remembered and imagined" (2007, p. 3). Drawing the fashions is a way of abstracting their essence and of recording their most striking features that are communicated from sensory impressions to the retina through to the brain and then on to communicate that experience to the viewer. Drawings, therefore, go some way to mitigating the mismatched perceptions that a verbal description alone might give rise to. And, of course, fashion drawing and illustration has a long and honorable tradition in women's consumption of popular culture, which makes it an especially appropriate method for this discussion.

With this in mind, a selection of Ann's drawings are reproduced and act as a valuable mode of dissemination of the power of the original magazine images' composition and features, but stripped bare of their more entertaining semiotic associations that cloud the key messages we want to convey. This method also has the useful function of side-stepping the permissions issues that arise from reproducing original media images, especially given that tracing copyright holders for a 30-year old, out-of-print magazine proved problematic.

THE CASE DATA—*WORKING WOMAN* MAGAZINE (1984–1985)

Clothes

During a period when women are not only entering the workplace, but doing so in positions of increasing seniority at the time of publication (Crompton, 1997), there is a palpable sense of anxiety and a desire to manage confusion in *Working Woman*. No real template for how women were supposed to dress in order to command respect in managerial roles was available, and so that template had to be invented. What is striking is that the silhouette shown almost exclusively in the fashion pages of the magazine under the fashion editorship of Kathryn Samuel is an exaggeratedly masculine one, to the point where it is satirized in an article in the May 1985 issue. This article, titled "You Are What You Wear" (Green, 1985), shows a series of cartoon-style images of stereotyped dressers with a text outlining the effect they produce, which women are expected to want to avoid. "Madame boss" parodies the 1985 look very crisply: "Extra Straight Skirt, Extra Wide Shoulders" and "Something Soft Near the Face and carry a briefcase rather than a handbag" (p. 58). The look is challenged in 1984, when Samuel predicted a more traditionally feminine turn in business dressing: "That mannish style of tailoring which has monopolised the look of shirts and coats for countless winters is facing a decidedly feminine challenge. For tailoring is going soft and shapely" (Samuel, 1984, p. 52). Samuel went on to outline the new look:

> Jackets that previously denied the existence of the female anatomy now lovingly outline the curve of a bosom or a waist. The shoulder line, although still broad and padded, has lost its sharp edge to become softly rounded onto a sleeve that is gathered gently and tapers to the wrist. The skirt you wear with your shapely jacket accentuates the image. Pencil slim skirts have risen to fashionable heights that hover just on the knee. (p. 52)

Figure 6.1

By the following year, however, the aggressive masculine outline was back. Samuel's (1984) message about soft and shapely accentuation of the female form above, was also severely undercut by the accompanying fashion shoot in which the model is shown dropping her papers and giggling like a little girl (Figure 6.1).

The mannish silhouette against which Samuel (1985a) reacted so strongly is illustrated graphically a year later, suggesting that it remained influential on the working woman's buying patterns. In the article, "Get Knitted," she showcased the extraordinarily stylized V body shape achieved through massive shoulder pads and tapering skirts with dark tights and shoes. This image (Figure 6.2) calls to mind the ideal physique of the warrior, broad chested to intimidate the enemy, the V pointing to the genitals to indicate the source of vitality and virility, plus the absence of broader, female hips.

The aim of the sweater dress is to replace the two-piece suit. The knitted outfits are soft and giving rather than stiff and unbending, and so traditional gender binaries are in play here, although the battle-ready body is still a must as we are informed that softness must not give way to bulges, and a good-quality wool is required to avoid this happening. There are conflicting messages here. Readers are counseled to look like the conventional

Figure 6.2

stereotype of the warrior in their silhouettes, but to soften that look with lovely soft, yielding fabrics like high-quality wool, and to stand out through the use of bold colors such as red, black, yellow, and fuchsia. This approach is consonant with the association of men with dark suits since the Victorian era, and the chromophobia that still operates in many large organizations where black, navy, and charcoal grey are considered suitable for business wear (Batchelor, 2000; Harvey, 1997; Hollander, 1994; Rippin, 2015). Color, in contrast, is the province of women (Hollander, 1993).

This confusion is epitomized by what happens at the neckline. The bodily sexuality of the woman has to be carefully managed, but there is no positive way to do this, particularly when it comes to breasts. As we have seen, the exaggerated V silhouette camouflages the curves of the female body,

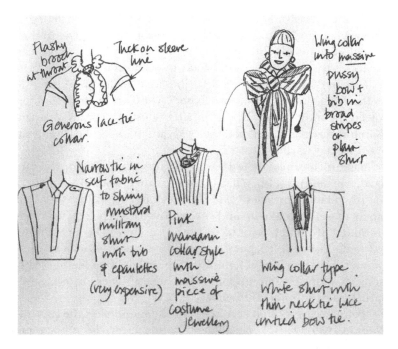

Figure 6.3

but the neckline risks admitting women's breasts back into the workplace. A variety of strategies are deployed throughout the issues of the magazine, and they come together particularly in an article on what to wear under your masculine suit. The plain white shirt is problematic for women. Samuel (1985c) wrote, "[D]o you wish you hadn't diluted the image [of the business suit] to reveal a dull cotton stripe that would probably look better on a man?" (p. 66). The perennial problem is what to wear instead of the phallic man's necktie (Figure 6.3).

Generally speaking, necklines are filled with scarves, soft bows, and ornate costume jewelry clamping a neckline shut. There is no hint of cleavage in any of the photoshoots except the one that accompanies the story on underwear (Samuel, 1985b). Covering up is the answer to dealing with sexuality in the workplace.

Accessories

The articles in *Working Woman* are clear that accessories are a key part of impression management. Clifton-Mogg (1985) stated unequivocally: "We are all—like it or not—judged on the first impressions we make at work as well as at home" (p. 50). For this reason, as the title of the article suggests, a working woman needs "only the best." Accessories must give off the air of professionalism and so a solid silver pen is preferable to a chewed Bic biro™. The key accessory is the briefcase, which is, according to Mason (1984), a "power accessory" (p. 22) that she describes as a "delicious phrase." Mason satirizes the conventional man's briefcase: "A stiff and formal-looking atta-ché projects the most power. Not surprising: it usually comes with armored corners, reinforced walls and six-digit locks, and it looks like a weapon to be used in commuter warfare" (p. 22).

The image of business as warfare, with the male warrior as standard, is rejected, but still present. What the less warlike woman wants is "softer leathers" or "pliable canvasses" (Mason, 1984, p. 22), which can accommo-date papers as well as make-up and "even groceries" (p. 22). The message, again, is mixed. If women want to be powerful, they need the stiff, formal, armored weapon in the corporate melee or battleground. On the other hand, women want markers of femininity in soft, yielding leather. The com-promise is to adopt chromophobic colors again: black, brown, and grey. Red, or fuchsia, is adopted at their own risk.

The second accessory that receives specific attention is the pair of spec-tacles (Smith, 1985). This article about choosing spectacles is fascinating be-cause it mixes information concerning the gender stereotypes of the time with technical information about the materials from which spectacles are made, dire warnings about finding a good optician in a time of deregulation, and a personal narrative of a spectacle wearer. Thus, the stereotype of the working woman is that she is intellectual bluestocking, career conscious, and image wary. Additionally she is "[m]otivated, management-trained, eats All Bran and *wears specs*" (Smith, 1985, p. 62, emphasis in original). However, Smith told readers that they must wear their specs with "flamboyance, style and humour" (p. 62), which is curious advice for women trying to establish their credibility. Georgina, the case example of a woman with a passion for and wardrobe of spectacles, is seen in the huge glasses fashionable at the time, and although she is commended for her wit in her choice of specs, she is also shown copying men's clothes in a very standard way (Figure 6.4). Again, the messages are contradictory and confused, requiring women to be serious, somber, and business-like, while projecting humor and lightness.

Make-Up

Throughout the run of the magazine from 1984–1985 there is a good deal of advice about cosmetics and hair styling. One article in particular is fascinating in its serious approach to the hazards of corporate life, advising on hair products to use "if the electricity generated by heavy duty office

Figure 6.4

carpets in cold weather make your hair stand on end" (Smith, 1984, p. 31).
Apparently danger can come at the working woman even in the innocent
activity of walking through the office. There is a certain briskness about the
advice given on make-up. The emphasis is on grooming the body and particularly the face with make-up viewed as a necessity to be applied quickly and
touched up as needed, and not an element of personal adornment to be
enjoyed. This is a vital element of self-presentation. There is a kind of grim
determination in Garratt's (1985) article, "Putting Your Best Face Forward,"
in her argument that in order women to be confident, they need to be well-
groomed. The woman in Garratt's case study, who undergoes a professional
makeover, is Marie-Claude Cousin, "a vastly experienced international marketing manager, with good, though not stunning looks" (p. 37). The message here is stark: Grooming for the corporate world is serious business with
no time for false praise. Honest appraisal is the order of the day and the
committed businesswoman needs to sort herself out unflinchingly.

DISCUSSION

Several themes emerge from a study of the text and images in this suite of
magazine articles. The first is that this area of corporate life is fraught with
anxiety. Proctor's (1985) article on professional wardrobe advisors highlights this perspective. The fashion consultant "is someone who will take
the hassle out of deciding what to wear. Someone who will come to your

home, rummage through your wardrobe and weed out any *disasters lurking in its depths*" (p. 53, emphasis added).

Babette Monteil, one of the featured consultants, is recommended by psychiatrists to women "who have lost touch with their looks and need help to regain their confidence" (Proctor, 1985, p. 53). There is a great deal at stake here, and self-esteem is shaky in the corporate theatre of anxiety. Getting it right, performing well, and showing well, matter. In one article, Esta Charkham, a client who is a TV producer, stated clearly, "I use clothes to play the game" (Proctor, 1985, p. 54). In the same article, one client, a director of consumer marketing for a huge multinational PR company, needs "clothes as a form of armor." As she put it, "I need clothes to give me clout" (p. 54).

The anxiety is further raised by the lack of clarity in the rules women are expected to follow. There is a constant tension between looking professional, which is largely constructed as looking masculine, and being true to the self, which presents as feminine. The satirical article mentioned above, "You Are What You Wear" (Green, 1985) begins with the statement:

> You may think you are merely choosing a new shirt/dress/blouse. You are, in fact, saying something about yourself just as clearly as if you were signaling the message in semaphore or tapping it out in Morse....Your clothes, your whole style of self-presentation add up to an advertisement for the woman within...and we all know about the need to be legal, decent, honest, and truthful. Are you sure you still want that purple satin shirt? (p. 58)

The article is intended to be humorous, but it has a sinister tone with the potential to unnerve women so out of touch with their looks that they consult a psychiatrist. And the types that Green lampoons include all the options open to women. There is the *Lesser Dresser, Madame Boss, The Flaunter, The Vamp, All Woman,* and *Mode Mad.* All options are heavily criticized: the ultrafeminine, the rebel in any sense, the colorful extrovert, the fashion victim, and the antifashionista, as well as the power dresser and the overtly sexual vamp. There is no safe alternative, no middle ground. You, the working woman, are always subject to negative scrutiny under the male gaze.

Indeed, the female body in general needs to be controlled and sanitized. Sweat is a particular anxiety. While it is not confined to women as a concern, there is still a hint of the maxim: "Horses sweat, men perspire, ladies merely glow" about the attention given to this manifestation of women's leaky bodies (the topic of menstruation is conspicuously absent from the magazine). There is advice on antiperspirants, as well as drastic recourse to surgery in having sweat glands sealed. The wearing of linen suits on hot summer days is one of the more feasible measures suggested.

Finally, it is noticeable that the performance never stops, including when one travels for work. The only place where the mask is allowed to slip is in the exclusively nonwork area of holidays, and the home, although the latter is in the article on what to wear under the business suit (Samuel, 1985b).

CONCLUSION

The concerns that appear in *Working Woman* at the outset of women's managerial and professional aspirations after the second wave feminism of the 1970s are still at play in contemporary organizations, despite what Lewis (2014) referred to as "a postfeminist climate where women's belief that they are equal means that ongoing sources of inequality are ignored, rendered invisible and have become increasingly difficult to name" (p. 1846). One of these sources—identified in this chapter—is the issue of the female body as deviation from the standard male norm. Women still have to manage their sexuality in the workplace carefully, and part of this identity project is mediated through what they wear and how they comport themselves (Kenny & Bell, 2011). Women must be at once asexual and all woman. Women continue to be anxious about managing their fluid and leaky bodies, in the form of lumps and bumps under their power dresses, or their blood, sweat, and tears.

McRobbie (2009) suggested that we should not be surprised by the failure of women's magazines to offer women real alternatives to a visual identity shaped by phallocractic hegemony. Although her work in the early 1990s saw potential for women's magazines to champion a feminist agenda, writing some 20 years later, she noted that "the idea of feminist content disappeared and was replaced by aggressive individualism, by a hedonistic female phallicism...and by obsession with consumer culture" (McRobbie, 2009, p. 5). Rampant consumer capitalism and the need to sell magazines in the face of increasing competition from the Internet go some way in explaining why women's magazines sold out in this way. But magazines still must have caught onto a cultural zeitgeist among young women for circulation to remain high. It is surely no coincidence that third-wave feminism also emerged in the mid-1990s, championing the liberal rights of women to act and behave as they chose in order to "reclaim a type of traditional femininity from both patriarchy and [second-wave] feminism" (Lewis, 2014, p. 1849). Under third-wave feminism, the stay-at-home Mom, or the immaculately made-up, highly sexualized vamp is as empowering a female identity position as the successful politician or aerospace engineer. Traditional feminine guises are not markers of male dominance *so long as they are adopted by choice*. As McRobbie (2009) nicely put it, "wearing spindly stilettos and 'pencil' skirts...does not in fact mean entrapment (as feminists would once have seen it) since it is now a matter of choice rather than obligation" (p. 65).

These ideas, resting on the rise of genetic "explanations" (Walters, 2011, p. 144) for biological sexual difference, naturalize certain behaviors as female traits and "the taken-for-granted status of feminism in all facets of life such that the expectation of equality is now unremarkable" (Lewis 2014, p. 1850). Women have made great strides in entering—and excelling in—education, employment, and the political sphere, and, therefore, from the perspective of third-wave feminism, how women choose to live their lives, act, and—particularly in our case—dress, is a matter of individual personal choice and not oppression even if it reinforces hitherto stereotypical versions of femininity.

Of course, women's magazines are an example par excellence of how this discourse of choice is amplified. Positioned as a new source of female-derived authority, ever-more complex and bizarre demands on women to conform to a particular type of feminine identity, leach through the style advice features and glossy pages of contemporary magazines (and their online counterparts). As we have seen in the *Working Woman* features discussed above, consumerist style advice comes in a form that is "cajoling and also encouraging" (McRobbie, 2009, p. 62) and offers ideas that are "both progressive but also consummately and reassuringly feminine" (p. 57). Yet this "fashion-beauty complex" (p. 63) remains an embodiment of heteronormative, phallocentric, male desire and the extent to which it is chosen "willingly" needs to be set against the possibility that it is a "biopolitical [practice] of new governmentality" (p. 60). It is (depressingly) no surprise that professional women are subject to assessments of their appearance and fashion sense above their skills and abilities (Greenslade, 2014), trivializing their achievements, efficacy, and the extent to which they should be taken seriously. Indeed, women continue to be instructed in the arts of looking the part in managerial self-help texts in ways men are not (Kenny & Bell, 2011). The onslaught of these idealized images, particularly given the ease with which photographs can be manipulated in digital form, makes it even harder to recognize if women are making these choices freely and willingly. Constant immersion in visual media makes it harder than ever to distinguish between free choice and false consciousness.

In our survey of *Working Woman* magazine, then, we have briefly traced the genealogy of these concerns and shown how perennial they are in terms of women's struggle to manage and maintain identities as professional workers. As McRobbie's (2009) analysis leads us to expect, women are still forced to choose between being pseudo-men, homologues, or sex objects to reduce their threat to a male-dominated public sphere, despite making considerable advances into positions of power. They are still held in the constraints and forced choices of the male gaze—except that this now appears as a self-imposed, empowering female norm. What saddened us, as authors and women, is that 30 years ago, when women were finally beginning to reach coveted powerful positions in organizations, there was a brief open moment when women—and more appositely women's magazines—could rewrite the norms of gendered organizational scripts, but failed to do so. Instead we saw the beginnings of McRobbie's (2009) idea of the "postfeminist masquerade" (p. 59) that allowed the subliminal power of the patriarchy to quietly but firmly close the alternative wardrobe door.

REFERENCES

Acker, J. (1990). Hierarchies, jobs, bodies: A theory of gendered organizations. *Gender & Society, 4*(2), 139–158. doi: 10.1177/089124390004002002

Baby Boom. (1987). United Artists, USA.

Batchelor, D. (2000). *Chromophobia.* London, UK: Reaktion Books.

Berger, J. (2007). John Berger: Life drawing. In J. Savage (Ed.), *Berger on drawing* (pp. 1–10). London, UK: Occasional Press.

Cardon, P. W., & Okoro, E. A. (2009). Professional characteristics communicated by formal verses casual workplace attire. *Business Communication Quarterly, 72*(3), 355–260. doi: 10.1177/1080569909340682

Caven, V., Lawley, S., & Baker, J. (2013). Performance, gender and sexualised work: Beyond management control, beyond legislation? A case study of work in a recruitment company. *Equality, Diversity and Inclusion, 32*(5), 475–490. doi: 10.1108/EDI-08-2011-0051

Clifton-Mogg, C. (1985, May). Only the best. *Working Woman,* 50–51.

Crompton, R. (1997). *Women and work in modern Britain.* Oxford, UK: Oxford University Press.

Dant, T. (1999). *Material culture in the social world.* London, UK: McGraw Hill.

Forsyth, S., Drake, M., & Cox, C. E. (1985). Influence of applicant's dress on interviewer's selection decision. *Journal of Applied Psychology, 70*(2), 374–378.

Garratt, P. (1985, August). Putting your best face forward. *Working Woman,* 36–38.

Grabe, S., Ward, L. M., & Hyde, J. (2008). The role of the media in body image concerns among women: A meta-analysis of experimental and correlational studies. *Psychological Bulletin, 134*(3), 460–476. doi: 10.1037/0033-2909.134.3.460

Green, F. (1985). You are what you wear. *Working Woman,* May, 58–59.

Greenslade, R. (2014). *Daily Mail* goes back in time to analyse female MPs as sex objects. Retrieved from http://www.theguardian.com/media/greenslade/2014/jul/16/dailymail-women

Hakim, C, (2010). Erotic capital. *European Sociological Review, 26*(5), 499–518. doi: 10.1093/esr/jcq014

Harvey, J. (1997). *Men in black.* London, U.K.: Reaktion Books.

Hollander, A. (1993). *Seeing through clothes.* Berkeley, CA: University of California Press.

Hollander, A. (1994). *Sex and suits: The evolution of modern dress.* New York, NY: Kodansha International.

Kenny, K., & Bell, E. (2011). Representing the successful managerial body. In E. Jeanes, D. Knights, & P. Yancey Martin (Eds.), *Handbook of gender, work, and organization* (pp. 163–176). London, UK: Wiley-Blackwell.

Kentridge, W. (2014). *Six drawing lessons.* Cambridge, MA: Harvard University Press.

Lewis, P. (2014). Postfeminism, femininities, and organization studies: Exploring a new agenda. *Organization Studies, 35*(12), 1845–1866. doi: 10.1177/0170840614539315

Mason, A. (1984, November). Special cases. *Working Woman*, 22–23.

Mavin, S., Bryans, P., & Cunningham, R. (2010). Fed-up with Blair's babes, Gordon's gals, Cameron's cuties, Nick's nymphets: Challenging gendered media representations of women political leaders. *Gender in Management: An International Journal, 25*(7), 550–569. doi: 10.1108/17542411011081365

McRobbie, A. (2009). *The aftermath of feminism: Gender, culture, and social change.* London, UK: Sage.

Meriläinen, S., Tienari, J., & Valtonen, A. (2015). Headhunters and the "ideal" executive body. *Organization, 22*(1), 3–22. doi: 10.1177/1350508413496578

Nickson, C., & Warhurst, D. (2007). Employee experience of aesthetic labour in retail and hospitality. *Work, Employment, and Society, 21*(1), 103–120. doi: 10.1177/0950017007073622

Parker, M. (2014). (Seeing) organizing in popular culture: Discipline and method. In E. Bell, S. Warren, & J. Schroeder (Eds.), *The Routledge companion to visual organization* (pp. 379–390). Abingdon, UK: Routledge.

Proctor, J. (1985, September). Style Counsel. *Working Woman*, 52–57.

Rafaeli, A., Dutton, J., Harquail, C. V., & Mackie-Lewis, S. (1997). Navigating by attire: The use of dress by female administrative employees. *Academy of Management Journal, 40*(1), 19–45. Retrieved from http://www.jstor.org/stable/257019

Rippin, A. (2015). Feminine writing: Text as dolls, drag, and ventriloquism. *Gender, Work and Organization, 22*(2), 112–128. doi: 10.1111/gwao.12080

Samuel, K. (1984). Going soft. *Working Woman*, October, 52–57.

Samuel, K. (1985a, November). Get knitted. *Working Woman*, 52–57.

Samuel, K. (1985b, February). A soft touch. *Working Woman*, 66–71.

Samuel, K. (1985c, August). Topping shirts. *Working Woman*, 66–71.

Slaughter, A. (1984, August). Don't fence us in. *Working Woman*, 5.

Smith, N. (1984, November). Brushing up. *Working Woman*, 31–34.

Smith, N. (1985, February). Spectacular. *Working Woman*, 62–65.

Stiles, D. (2014). Drawing as a method of organizational analysis. In E. Bell, S. Warren, & J. Schroeder (Eds.), *The Routledge companion to visual organization* (pp. 227–242). Abingdon, U.K.: Routledge.

Taussig, M. (2011). *I swear I saw this.* Chicago, IL: University of Chicago Press.

van Leeuwen, T. (2005). *Introducing social semiotics.* London, UK: Routledge

Walters, N. (2011). *Living dolls: The return of sexism.* London, UK: Virago.

Waring, A., & Waring, J. (2009). Looking the part: Embodying the discourse of organizational professionalism in the city. *Current Sociology, 57*(3), 344–364. doi: 10.1177/0011392108101587

Working Girl. (1988). Twentieth Century Fox, USA.

CHAPTER 7

IN THE NAME OF THE OTHER

Nicknaming and Gendered Misrepresentation/s of Women Leaders

Alison Pullen and Lucy Taksa
Macquarie University

The underrepresentation of, progress of, and barriers for women leaders are well established, especially for women in male-dominated organizations and institutions. Discrimination, bias, tokenism, lack of quality mentoring, and exclusion from social and informational networks are very real for women. Given such experiences, women leaders' agentic identity work often includes hyperfemininity (Billing & Alvesson, 2000), acting as honorary men (Collinson & Hearn, 1996), "managing like a man" (Wajcman, 1998), or being construed as androgynous (Korabik, 1990). The possibilities available for many women leaders are constructed and constrained by women leaders' images in the mass media. These media images reinforce stereotypes of women/femininity as *in relation* to the dominant male leadership norm. Given the cultural production of women's leadership in the mass media, in this chapter we focus on an elite group of first leaders in politics (whom we refer to as "Firsts") to show the ways in which these exceptional

Gender, Media, and Organization, pages 111–132
Copyright © 2016 by Information Age Publishing

women are represented in the mass media. These women advanced beyond the norms of the gendered organization by becoming the first in their country's history to take on a senior leadership position in a long legacy of male occupants. From our initial analysis we observed that when these Firsts were represented in the media they were always given nicknames. We note that while men and women are given nicknames, nicknaming, as we discuss below, is a gendered strategy that reinforces male leaders' masculinity and success, with women leaders being undermined. Examining Firsts demonstrates the ways in which nicknaming is invoked to represent and misrepresent women leaders and women's leadership, thereby challenging the advancement of women into the male dominant arena of politics.

Leadership is masculine at symbolic and material levels (Calás & Smirich, 1991), and the ideal leader is disembodied and rational (Ford, 2006; Pullen & Vachhani, 2013) and silently male. Leadership reinforces male identities and sustains asymmetrical gender relations (Collinson & Hearn, 1996; Ford, 2006). Media constructions work through the hegemonic infrastructure of the media and leadership to cast, position, and re-inscribe Firsts as the other despite their phenomenal success. Masculinity has long been associated with rationality, measurement, objectivity, control, individualism, and competitiveness, while femininity is associated with caring, nurturing, empathy, relationships, and sharing (e.g., Fletcher, 2004). The cultural construction of femininity around body and emotions, and of masculinity around disembodiment and rationality, reinforces leadership as the domain of men and masculinity. When women leaders are represented within this gendered cultural construction as the other, men are represented and legitimated as "natural" and women as disruptive, infectious, and dangerous. It is important that leadership identities are read within their specific social, cultural, and political discourses (Ford, Learmonth, & Harding, 2008) and are evidenced in media texts and the language in use. One discursive deployment is nicknaming, which reinforces gendered stereotypes in the mass media. In her early research on management, corporate power, and gender, Kanter (1977) outlined four stereotypical roles that professional women were assigned or adopted: the seductress or sex object, mother, pet, and iron maiden. According to Ryan (2013), these roles have continued to be reinforced, which we argue is evident in the nicknames applied to women in the mass media.

This chapter takes nicknaming as a discursive strategy to explore women's mis/representation in mass media, specifically print media and Internet media technologies, which in our case were print and internet newspapers. These technologies reach large audiences, and we can therefore deduce that mass media has the capacity to culturally produce women leaders internationally. In this way, mass media shapes and marks women's leadership roles and images, the stereotypes surrounding women's leadership that other women are influenced by, and, eventually, the perceived success of women leaders. In this chapter we focus on the dominant nickname identified in the mass media of Firsts: the Iron Lady. The Iron Lady nickname is analyzed to expose the ways in which women leaders are always seen *in relation* to their male counterparts. In simple terms, women cannot be, they can only be *in relation* to men. As such, nicknaming as a discursive strategy marks the ways in which we read women in the mass media and the ways in women become known in life and history. The power of mass media cannot be underestimated, and nicknaming as a gendered strategy illustrates the tensions between masculinity and femininity in representing women as leaders. This chapter is structured as follows: First, we give a brief overview of nicknaming and reveal it as a gendered communication practice, highlighting the ways in which women are constructed as other; second, we explain the media analysis process before going on to discuss our media data. In the third section we suggest that women's leadership as *in relation* to men's leadership is problematic because women's deferral to men undermines women as leaders and their leadership. We also propose that nicknaming reinforces culturally produced stereotypes that are deeply entrenched in mass media generally and require undoing if women are to advance on their own terms, rather than always *in relation* to men. Finally, we conclude with some brief suggestions for further research.

NICKNAMING: A GENDERED STRATEGY

Nicknaming is a global phenomenon and emerges in masculine organizational contexts (Collinson, 1988; Taksa, 2005). As numerous scholars have pointed out, nicknaming is a gendered mode of communication that reflects and reinforces beliefs and attitudes about gender categories (de Klerk & Bosch, 1996; Phillips, 1990: Taksa, 2012a; Weatherall, 2002). Hence, by exploring gendered nicknaming processes we recognize the rendering of women leaders as other/ed. The word "nickname" comes from the Middle English "an eke name," which means "another name" and is "in opposition to some other naming conventions" (McDowell, 1981, p. 1). Nicknames and nicknaming practices have been studied across a wide number of disciplines, including anthropology, ethnography, folklore, history, geography, linguistics, sociology, psychology, indigenous political, educational, legal, and organizational and management studies (Breen, 1982; McDowell, 1981; Schindler, 2002; Taksa, 2012a, 2012b; Weatherall, 2002; Wood, 1998). Such scholarship has indicated that nicknaming functions differently across cultures, often as a source of insult and humor; a means of exercising collective control and/or power; imposing social pressure; enforcing and maintaining social boundaries and identities; reinforcing social and moral norms; contributing to social cohesion, accommodation, and adjustment;

and enhancing solidarity and providing a deterrent to deviance (Breen, 1982; Saunders, 1990).

For this chapter, we focus on different types of names and naming practices as "they set up relationships of similarity and difference" (de Pina-Cabral, 1984, p. 149). As Battestini (1991, p. 106) noted, "To name an object or a phenomenon is to erase part of its mystery; to classify it in an overall system is to familiarize it; to establish correspondences based on differences, similarities, and analogies." We will demonstrate that the specific types of nicknames applied to women leaders positions them *in relation* to men because what is left unknown, mysterious, is dangerous. De Klerk and Bosch (1996, p. 539) argued, nicknaming can "be regarded as an accurate...barometer of societal attitudes to the gender groups" because they perpetuate gender-related stereotypes. In a similar vein, Phillips (1990) noted that male nicknames were linked to strength and hardness, while female nicknames were associated with "beauty, pleasantness, kindness, and goodness" (p. 286). In his study of Navanogal in west-central Spain, Brandes noted that "the only women who" possessed "personalised nicknames" were "those with names which mock deviation from the ideal feminine role" (1975, p. 146). Additionally, Brandes reiterated the point made by Pitt-Rivers (1961) that derogatory names are "one of the most effective community mechanisms for the maintenance of social control" (p. 146). Nicknaming also relates to the physical body, as Schindler (2002) highlighted: "[E]ven the nicknames that were coined to reflect aspects of personal appearance...often occupy a metaphorical status" (p. 61). By uniting "affective and informative references, subjective and objective elements of communication," such nicknames set "the tone of social intercourse" (Schindler, 2002, p. 56). Leading women have been nicknamed "iron maiden" (Kanter, 1977, p. 235) and "Iron Lady" (Klenke, 1996, p. 221; Kunin, 2008, pp. 117–118) , "the Beast of Belsen" (Taksa, 2012a, p. 27), "rottweiler with lipstick" (Beck & Davis, 2005, p. 282), "the perfumed steamroller" (Elliott, 2010), and "pit bull with lipstick" (Carlin & Winfrey, 2009, p. 338). In effect, "nicknames are speaking social relations" (Schindler, 2002, p. 84) that "display a fundamental ambivalence toward the behavior they depict" (McDowell, 1981, p. 12). From this perspective, various kinds of gender-ambiguous, monstrous, ugly, or grotesque nicknames given to women can be seen to operate in a similar manner to sick jokes. According to Sev'er and Ungar (1997), who adopt a power perspective on humor, such jokes "serve as coping mechanisms for dealing with bothersome issues such as sexuality" and reflect "men's struggle to deal with their anxiety about the changing role of women," which reveal "power imbalances between men and women." Manifestations of "[p]ower imbalances under the auspices of...gender-based humour," they argue, can be "seen as reinforcing old belief systems, blocking social change, and preserving inequality...between men and women, which in turn helps to solidify and perpetuate that power disparity" (Sev'er & Ungar, 1997, p. 88).

MEDIA ANALYSIS OF FIRST WOMEN

The gendered mis/representations of women leaders are culturally sustained in the press. Mass media "reflect and/or shape dominant ideologies" (Klenke, 1996, p. 114), and our use of newspapers, magazines, and encyclopedia are indicative of the power of mass media technologies to construct and maintain stereotypes surrounding women leaders. Analyzing nicknaming in mass media is a way to reveal the ways in which female leaders are discursively and materially represented. Nicknaming creates an awareness of the ways in which language perpetuates cultural norms that continue to mark women as other. After identifying 20 first leaders globally between 1945 and the present day, we observed that the dominant nickname used for these women was Iron Lady. Due to the depth of material that we surfaced on the Iron Lady, we concentrated our analysis on exploring the tensions between the masculine term "iron" and the feminine term "lady." In this chapter, we focus on 14 Firsts who were identified as leaders in global politics, starting with Barbara Castle, a British Labour Party politician from 1945 to 1979, (see Table 7.1 for full information).

During our analysis, we identified all instances of nicknaming in the press in the period 1945–2015 for the 14 first leaders that we selected to discuss for this chapter. We quickly discovered that the nicknames assigned to very diverse women leaders was remarkably consistent in our database, which comprised 107 media accounts, as well as encyclopedia entries. These media accounts spanned local newspapers, such as the *London Evening Post* and *New York Times*, which used the Iron Lady in their press sources; national press such as the *Australian Broadcasting Commission*, Israel's *Haaretz*, *Russia Today*; and international media sources, such as *Business Week* and *The Economist*, which crossed national boundaries. We read the ways in which Firsts were portrayed in the media as women and leaders *in relation* to the nicknames, and in some cases the ways in which Firsts talked about themselves in media interviews. Both authors analyzed the data separately and then compared our analyses.

The analytical discussion that follows represents dominant themes emerging from the data and our joint reflections on the meanings associated with the nicknames in use. However, it was clear that in all of the data on Firsts' nicknames that the nicknames were personal and in many cases pejorative; for example, Madeleine Albright was referred to as "an unparalleled serpent" (Groer, 2010, para. 1) and a "hawk" (Chernyshev, 2012, para. 1). Additionally, personality characteristics and nicknames were sometimes conjoined, as in the case of "the 'Iron Lady' of Pakistan" Benazir Bhutto, who was described as being steadfast and persevering (Bangash, 2011, para. 1). These nicknames can be read to suggest that because they are out of place in the traditionally male domain of politics, women are intruders. The

TABLE 7.1 First Leaders

Name	Role	Country	Service period	Nickname/s
Barbara Castle	Labour Party British Politician	UK	Member of Parliament for Blackburn 1945–1979	The Iron Lady; Red Queen
Margaret Thatcher	Prime Minister of Britain	UK	1979–1990	The Iron Lady; bitch
Helen Clark	Prime Minister of New Zealand	New Zealand	1999–2008	The Iron Lady; ditch the bitch
Julia Gillard	Prime Minister of Australia	Australia	2010–2013	Aussie Margaret Thatcher; the new Iron Lady; Kentucky Fried Quail
Edith Cresson	Prime Minister of France	France	1991–1992	Mitterand's Iron Lady; the perfumed one
Angela Merkel	Chancellor of Germany	Germany	2005–present	Germany's Iron-curtain Lady; Iron Mädchen; Iron Girl; The Iron Frau
Dalia Grybauskaite	President of Lithuania	Lithuania	2009–present	Iron Lady; Steel Magnolia
Golda Meir	Prime Minister of Israel	Israel	1969–1974	Iron Lady; Mother of a nation
Benazir Butto	Prime Minister of Pakistan	Pakistan	1988–1990 and 1993–1996	Iron Lady of Pakistan
Indira Ghandi	Prime Minister of India	India	1980–1984	India's Iron Lady
Dilma Vana Rousseff	President of Brazil	Brazil	2011–present	Iron Lady
Vaira Vike-Freiberga	President of Latvia	Latvia	1999–2001	Baltic Iron Lady
Madeline Albright	America's first female Secretary of State	U.S.	1997–2001	Titanium Lady
Ellen Johnson-Sirleaf	First democratically elected Liberian President	Africa	2005–present	Africa's Iron Lady

nicknames used combine traditionally masculine with traditionally female language and imagery. We propose that this nicknaming reinforces "worn-out assumptions and beliefs about women's ability to lead" (Klenke, 1996, p. xiii). As described more fully in the following section, despite being exceptional women leaders—Firsts in politics in their own countries—they are typically represented in the media as women first and leaders second.

"The Iron Lady": Leadership as Will, Strength, and Feminine

Our analysis of the media accounts of 14 Firsts highlighted that the Iron Lady was the most dominant nickname. As pioneers in male-dominant educational, political, and business contexts who managed to break into male territories, these Firsts were marked as exceptional and different. This difference, their otherness from the same (Pullen & Simpson, 2009)—the male and masculine—were enhanced by the nicknames that reinforce their sex role as women breaking through male and masculine social cultural norms. The relationship between the masculine "iron" and the feminine "lady" merits further exploration across a range of Firsts to identify how the nickname has been used to convey a gendered representation in relationship to leadership.

The first Iron Lady in the UK was Barbara Castle, who "single-handedly broke the glass ceiling in British politics becoming the first woman" British Labour Party Politician in 1945 (Suroor, 2002, para. 3). Having joined the Labour Party in the 1930s when women "were confined to the party kitchen, making tea for the male grandees" (Suroor, 2002, para. 3), she became "[a]n uncompromising campaigner for women's rights" throughout her political career (Suroor, 2002, para. 3). Castle served as a Member of Parliament (MP) for Blackburn from 1945–1979 and was appointed a life peer in 1990 with the title Baroness Castle of Blackburn. In an article entitled "U.K. loses its first Iron Lady," Suroor (2002) commented that she "was first labelled Britain's Iron Lady, almost 30 years before the Tories got their own Iron Lady in Margaret Thatcher" (para. 4). Castle was referred to as "Labour's Red Queen" (Perkins, 2002, para. 1), and depicted as "fiery" and provoking "passions" (Hewitt, 2008, para. 1). Soon before she died in 2002, Gordon Brown, then Chancellor of the Exchequer (a senior position in the British Parliament), called her his "mentor and tormentor" (Suroor, 2002, para. 2), implying respect for her and her knowledge, and frustration at her style of command.

During her political life, Castle battled with "empires of men" (Perkins, 2010, para. 19). On becoming Minister in 1964, she was referred to as the PM Harold Wilson's "little minister" (Suroor, 2002, para. 5). She was consistently showered with personal abuse and ridiculed by interviewers, with comments like: "'You're a woman. And you can't even drive' as a typical introductory remark" (Perkins, 2010, para. 6). Perkins (2010) also notes that Castle was "marked out by her slightness and above all by her flaming red hair" (para. 12). The nickname Red Queen referred symbolically to her leadership of the Labour Party, traditionally associated with left-leaning causes and her hair colour.

As will be evident *in relation* to the other Firsts, over the decades, women's physical characteristics have been marked out in ways never ascribed to men: "Her personal charms won her admirers: her passionate advocacy of the causes of the left guaranteed her criticism" ("Labour stalwart Castle dies," 2002, para. 3). The Iron Lady nickname came from descriptions of Castle as possessing a "radical and independent spirit" (para. 3) and being a "formidable champion" (para. 6), "courageous, determined, tireless and principled" (para. 7) and "outspoken" (para. 18). Lord Callaghan paid tribute to "her tenacity and her sheer hard work," noting that "she was always a fighter," as well as for "her tenacity and her sheer hard work" (paras. 9–10). Of herself, Castle referred to the "anger" and "fury" that kept her in politics (2002, para. 15) well into her eighties. These characteristics were captured in the nickname the Iron Lady—but always a lady.

Interestingly for our analysis of nicknaming of women leaders, the Iron Lady depicts masculinity associated with industrial strength and the endurance of Castle's leadership style and activism. However, as Jones (2000, para. 9) noted: "She also won a bigger share of the national purse for the National Health Service and equal pay for women. She always championed her own gender, but not at the cost of sacrificing her femininity." Here we get direct insight that regardless of her political success and effective leadership, her womanhood and femininity were always present in media representations. Furthermore, as indicated by "Lady" (Suroor, 2002, para. 4) and "Queen" (Perkins, 2002, para. 1), her femininity was in keeping with traditional and respectable femininity.

The iconic Iron Lady was Margaret Thatcher. Baroness Thatcher was a controversial figure in British politics and was known for her authoritarian leadership style. While a student at Oxford University, in 1946 she was Chair of the Oxford University Conservative Association ("Margaret Thatcher Biography," n.d.). The film *The Iron Lady* (Jones & Lloyd, 2011), which depicted her life history, emphasized Thatcher's great tenacity in running for parliament. Thatcher devoted herself to her role as a politician, despite being a parent to twins and, as such, her credibility as a good woman and mother was questioned. Some of her speeches have contributed to well recognized dictums, such as, "If you want something said, ask a man. If you want something done, ask a woman" (Hui, 2013, para. 2) and "Every Prime Minister needs a Willie" ("UK Politics—Whitelaw," 1999, para. 5). As the first female prime minister of Britain, Thatcher was controversial and was said to have built the myth of the Iron Lady. She was fearless and determined, believing in the "nation" and herself as the savior of the nation after post-war prosperity. However, hate attacks came from working-class Britain when she was labeled the heartless "milk-snatcher" (Vallely, 2013, para. 3) after she stopped the provision of free milk for school children, and for her role in the closure of mining and other heavy industry that forced high unemployment in working-class communities. As Vallely (2013) noted: "No British prime minister of the last century has created greater myths than Margaret Thatcher. And yet there are huge chasms between myths and the Mrs" (para. 1). Upon her resignation and subsequent death, people sang the song from the musical *Wizard of Oz*, "Ding Dong, the Witch is Dead" (para. 4), signaling what was perceived by some to be her cold, hard, unemotional pursuit of her political causes. Further, other epithets used in parliament were "Attila the Hen," "ditch the bitch," and some male MPs associated her voice with a "perfumed fart" (Vallely, 2013, para. 5). These hateful nicknames were always associated with her femaleness. French President Francois Mitterrand once described Thatcher as having the "eyes of Caligula and the mouth of Marilyn Monroe" (Volkery, 2013, para. 2). The tensions between the malicious eyes of this Roman emperor and the seductive talk of a sex icon highlight the associated tensions between excessive masculinity and femininity. U.S. President Ronald Reagan referred to her affectionately as "England's Best Man" (Volkery, 2013, para. 2). However, the Iron Lady nickname was given to her in 1976 by the Soviet newspaper *Red Star* after Thatcher stated: "The Russians are bent on world domination" (Volkery, 2013, para. 4). Her "unbending dominatrix" (para. 4) role and her handbag became part of her caricature. Styled to perfection with the same clothes and hair, this marked an unquestioning steadfast loyalty to her politics and her leadership of Britain, despite criticism.

Helen Clark, a Labor politician and prime minister of New Zealand for three successive terms (1999–2008), was known for appointing an extraordinarily diverse cabinet, including 11 women and four Maori men and women ("Helen Clark," 2016). After her years of service as prime minister, in 2009 Clark became the first woman administrator of the United Nations Development Program. Also nicknamed the Iron Lady, with a reputation for a "no-nonsense" approach and "strong" leadership, Clark described the experience of women in top leadership positions in an interview with Peacock (2014) by commenting: "Once you're at the top, everyone wants to knock you off, but not because you're a woman" (para. 6) (2014).

Although Clark denied having experienced sexism, according to Peacock, Clark did encounter her fair share of prejudice, including being told that the seat she was running for was a "working man's seat" and other forms of "petty criticisms" including that people didn't like her hair, the colour of her jacket or the tone of her voice—insults that arguably would not be directed at male politicians. (2014, para. 7)

In addition, in her last unsuccessful election her opponents "urged voters to 'ditch the bitch'" (Martinson, 2014, para. 5). We argue that these same criticisms and such language would not be directed at men.

Clark also told Peacock (2014, para. 16) that she "avoided sexist treatment" by becoming "known as somebody not to mess with" (in this regard she commented: "The media formed a view of me that I was pretty strong, so it would be a brave person who is going to question a decision I made, I didn't muck around" [para. 16]). This iron strength and "sticking to your will" (Peacock, 2014, para. 17) infuses the leadership style adopted by both Helen Clark and Margaret Thatcher, in terms of decision-making and its associated rationality. Also in this interview with Peacock, Clark referred to the "insufferable attacks" (Peacock, 2014, para. 10) and vitriolic sexist abuse of Julia Gillard, prime minister (PM) of Australia (2010–2013), noting that such attacks had never been leveled at a male politician.

Gillard came to power after "a bloodless coup" (Rodgers, 2010, para. 1) at a meeting of the Federal Labor Parliamentary Party deposed Prime Minister Kevin Rudd. Subsequently, she was ousted in a similar fashion. Gillard spent her tenure as PM downplaying her sex, stating publicly that while she was the only redhead to become PM, she "did not set out to crash my head against any glass ceilings" (Summers, 2010, para. 1).

The abuse of Gillard was very public and personal, including being called a "Kentucky Fried Quail" with "small breasts and huge thighs" (Peacock, 2014, para. 8) and "a big red box" on the official dinner menu at a Federal Conservative Opposition fundraiser (Wilson, 2013, para. 1). Her "deliberately barren" (Summers, 2010, para. 13) status was a source of much public interest. Gillard was called the Iron Lady initially by Andrew Bolt (2009), an Australian radio disc jockey who specializes in offensive and controversial commentary, when she was still Deputy Prime Minister, and she was quickly dubbed the "Aussie Margaret Thatcher."

Bolt's (2009) newspaper article "Julia Gillard gets down and dirty as the new Iron Lady" invokes getting down to business but also could be read as "getting down" sexually or even submissively. By the time Gillard became Prime Minister, Dale's (2010) article "Julia Gillard's body language says she's the new iron lady" reveals the media's preoccupation with her leadership, as was made particularly evident in Dale's comment: "The firmness of Ms Gillard's hands suggests a real mark of solidity" (inset para.). For communications expert Michael Kelly (para. 1), Gillard's body language was comparable to that of the "formidable Margaret Thatcher" (para. 1). As Kelly saw it, "The firmness of Ms Gillard's hands suggests a real mark of solidity. She seems to be quite stiff with her hands, like she's trying to give others around her the impression that she's very firm and passionate about what she's saying" (para. 1). Moreover, he thought that her "mixture of passion and energy" (para. 1) enabled her to come "across as a very strong and powerful leader" (para. 1), whose "humour and ability to make 'little digs' at herself" (para. 1), were praiseworthy. This humor was deemed important to the PM's leadership position because "If she didn't do that, she might come across as a bit too hard-edged" (para. 1). In contrast to Mr. Abbott (the then-Opposition Leader), Gillard was described as dressing "like a leader and like a strong business woman" (Kelly, in Dale, 2010), which endorsed her professionalism and composure. In subsequent years, journalists continued to associate Gillard with the masculine qualities of iron. In 2012, the political editor of a conservative newspaper titled an article on Gillard, "Julia must show mettle while iron's hot" (Shanahan, 2012), while another journalist commented that "Gillard's backers are fond of using the Iron Lady tag for their boss to demonstrate grit and conviction" (Benson, 2012, para. 9).

Our analysis indicates that Julia Gillard is the first of the Firsts whose Iron Lady nickname was contested. Cooke (2010, p. 2) observed: "This is the legacy of the Iron Lady. This is the mould that Julia Gillard should do everything in her power to avoid" and journalist Paul Kelly (2010) commented: "Despite the right turn, Gillard is no Iron Lady" (para. 3). Although he noted that "Gillard may be as tough as Margaret Thatcher" (para. 3), Kelly thought that Gillard's beliefs were "far distant from the Iron Lady" (para. 3). In fact, he argued that Gillard was "formidable because her personality radiates two qualities: She is competent and she is compassionate" (para. 3). In this statement, competence was/is clearly being associated with the masculine rationality of managers (Ford, 2006) and being feminine was/is equated with compassion, consistent with the gendered binary and associated stereotypes between masculinity and femininity.

Other notable Iron Lady nicknaming is evident in media accounts of Edith Cresson, the first woman prime minister of France (1991–1992) after being a successful businesswoman. In May 1991, Cresson was named Mitterand's Iron Lady. While being known for her bluntness, energy, and stubbornness, she was assessed and held accountable *in relation* to her male colleagues. Upon her appointment as prime minister (PM), Cresson received misogynist remarks about her sex, which was then parodied when a popular television show featured two puppet characters, one sexy and the other servile. In that depiction, women's sexuality and servitude were combined rather than the often passive servile characteristics of women to men and the agentic sexual agency of women to secure men.

During Cresson's term as PM, she fueled controversy and became increasingly unpopular, particularly given her outspokenness. For example,

Cresson was quoted as saying: "To get the country moving it is necessary to let off some bombs. I shall commence the bombardment" (Rowlatt, 1999, para. 14). Cresson was also called the "perfumed one" (para. 17) by farmers. Marking Cresson as "one" singles her out, and combined with "perfumed" marks her out by smell. Cresson is therefore marked as different, a woman out of place in the male bastion of French politics. Yet, in Cresson fashion, she retaliated by calling them woman-haters. This First leader disrupted the status quo of the political arena and was removed from office after one year.

Angela Merkel, "Germany's iron-curtain lady" ("Germany's iron-curtain lady," 2005) or "Iron Mädchen"—girl in English (Elkins, 2005). Germany's Iron Frau (Paterson, 2010) has received much attention related to her leadership style. Heralded as independent, especially in regard to her personal relationships with men and husbands, and often marked by lack of presence: "Iron Lady Angela Merkel vanishes amid trouble home and abroad" and the leader of Europe's biggest economy "distinguished by her absence" (Boyes, 2010, para. 1). Merkel, who is widely regarded as the most influential leader in Europe (Elkins, 2005), was, nevertheless, described in highly personalized terms by journalist Ruth Elkins (2005, para. 10):

> Men tend to underestimate the dumpy, childless Ossi divorcee. Despite the obvious similarities, she is not a Teutonic Margaret Thatcher. She may be tough, but she has an immediate personal affability. "Das Mädchen" is a girl's girl and has surrounded herself with female advisors. . . . She is a proponent of women's rights and often complains loudly about the glass ceiling restricting women in the workplace.

The initial use of the German term *Das Mädchen* in the early days of her political career discursively positioned Merkel as subordinate. Later, in 2010 when her leadership style was being questioned, she was criticized for being tired and searching for a second wind. The problem, according to Boyes (2010), related to

> . . . two components to her leadership. The first was what might be called situational leadership . . . Leadership-on-demand. The second ingredient to Merkel-management is a certain furtiveness. She observes very carefully the formation of a German national interest—her concern for the past six months has been to position a German at the helm. of the European Central Bank—and then pounces. (Boyes, 2010, para. 5)

While Boyes thought that the style of Merkle's government was "ideally suited to her temperament," he argued that it had "to be changed" because it was "no longer effective" (Boyes, 2010, para. 5).

Despite recognition of her achievements, Merkel's leadership has consistently been scrutinized and criticized, as occurred during the Eurozone crisis, when the media questioned Merkel's leadership with headlines such as: "Eurozone tarnishes Germany's 'Iron Lady'" (Jones, 2011). Despite Merkel's no-nonsense approach, Dos Santos's (2013) article, "Germany's Modest Mutti Merkel is no Iron Lady Thatcher," distinguished her from Thatcher by noting: "Merkel's anti-ego approach made her an unlikely icon of our times" (para. 11). Merkel's leadership of the country is not about her; she downplays herself and, as such, is seen as "Mutti" (mummy) by millions. Her softer leadership style is read as endorsing the caring feminine values of leadership.

Dalia Grybauskaite, the first female President of Lithuania (2009–present), also has a reputation as an Iron Lady ("Lithuania elects first female president," 2009, para. 4) or a "Steel Magnolia" ("Lithuania's new president," 2009, title). In this imagery, the hard, strong core is packaged with the floral magnolia, which has emphasized Grybauskaite's femininity, while recognizing her skills as a "black belt in karate" (para. 4) and her early childhood sporting achievements. Golda Meir, Prime Minister of Israel ("Israel elects first female leader," 1969), was also referred to as an Iron Lady (Butt, 1998, para. 1), most recently in the title of an article celebrating her 117th birthday (Yadid, 2015). Her transgression of traditional gendered norms was aptly summed up by David Ben-Gurion, who described her as "the best man in government" (Butt, 1998, para. 1). In her life we also witness the transgression of the domestic, private sphere of home for her political leadership. Although she stayed at home during the 1920s to raise her two children, it was said that "there was nothing of a housewife in Golda Meir" (Butt, 1998, para. 6). As Shlaim described her (2008, para. 2):

> Even at the height of her power, "Golda" . . . looked like a kindly Jewish grandmother, with her craggy face, baggy suits, orthopaedic shoes and old-fashioned handbag, but this homely exterior masked a pugnacious personality, a burning ambition, monumental egocentrism and an iron will.

Meir was not the "type of woman . . . who . . . let her husband narrow her horizons" (Butt, 1998, para. 7).

Benazir Butto, Prime Minister of Pakistan (1988–1990 and 1993–1996), had a leadership style that was depicted as stubborn and authoritative. In 2011, Bangash (2011) paid tribute to Butto's "steadfastness, perseverance, loyalty and commitment . . . qualities which indeed made her the 'Iron Lady' of Pakistan" (para. 1). She was also specifically labeled as an "inspiring feminist" (para. 5). Similarly, Indira Ghandi became known as "The Iron Lady of India" (Thelikorala, 2011). Dilma Vana Rousseff, the first woman to be elected president of Brazil (in 2010) had been nicknamed Iron Lady five years earlier, when she became chief of staff to then-president Luiz Inácio Lula da Silva (Rohter, 2005) because of her "brusque manner and short temper" (Rousseff, 2014). Vaira Vike-Freiberga, the Latvian President, was nicknamed the "Baltic Iron Lady" because she "is not afraid to speak her mind" (Bilefsky, 2005, para. 4) and bears "an eerie resemblance to former Prime Minister Margaret Thatcher of Britain," "with her helmet of carefully coifed auburn hair" (Bilefsky, 2005, para. 7). The comparison, according to Behr in an article entitled: "Tea with the Iron Lady," was based on her "tough-mindedness and knack for biting one-liners" (Behr, n.d.). Madeline Albright, America's first female secretary of state, attracted a variety of nicknames, such as "Titanium Lady" (Bridge, 2010), Russia's foe and Serbia's butcher, whose approach to diplomacy with the Russian Federation was described as: "[t]o pressure, severely criticize, but still cooperate" and who would be "remembered as a harsh 'lady with a brooch'" (Chernyshev, 2012, paras. 18–19).

Ellen Johnson-Sirleaf, the first democratically elected Liberian president (2005–present), who erased her country's crushing debt and received a Nobel Peace Prize for her work to secure women's rights (which the prize committee described as fundamental to advancing world peace) was called "Africa's Iron Lady" (Boyes, 2011; McClanahan, 2011) "due to her strong will and political persistence" (Davies, 2009, para. 3), particularly in opposing Charles Taylor in the 1997 presidential elections during Liberia's brutal civil war.

What becomes apparent with all of these First Women is that they had difficult tasks to confront, and their successful endurance was reinforced by being associated with the qualities of metal so aptly reflected in the Iron Lady nickname. The nickname Iron Lady cements their leadership position and success, yet it also serves to undermine it insofar as the association of strong and successful leadership with masculine leadership serves to raise questions about their ability to be themselves as women (Ladkin & Taylor, 2010). This subversion of First Women's leadership becomes most powerful when the personal is invoked, whether it is the color of their hair, their status as a mother, or the shape of their thighs. The ways these women are represented in the media are central to the cultural production of their leadership and the continuation of their career, politics, business, and activism.

IN RELATION: THE CULTURAL PRODUCTION OF WOMEN'S LEADERSHIP THROUGH NICKNAMING

As we have seen above, women as leaders and women's leadership is culturally produced through the mass media and their associated technologies. Especially evident are the ways in which women leaders are represented *in relation* to men leaders and the ways in which women's leadership is read *in relation* to men's leadership. We have suggested that one discursive strategy—nicknaming—perpetuates women leaders as other. Nicknaming therefore reproduces women as marginal, subordinate, and present, but only *in relation* to men's existence in leadership. In simple terms, men leaders exist while women leaders can only ever be present.

To summarize, leadership is reinforced through the media, and "excellent leadership is exercised and enacted as an expression of socially constructed institutions and culturally grounded values" (Holmberg & Åkerblom, 2001, p. 83). Our analysis of Firsts highlighted the media construction of women leaders, even when they are recognized as being exceptional, tends to represent them through nicknames that are historically and culturally gendered. The media accounts of them and their leadership styles highlight that the dominant nickname for female political leaders was the Iron Lady. The only exceptions to being referred to as the Iron Lady were when women were depicted *in relation* to their sexuality and/or attractiveness to others. The Iron Lady enabled women to be contained, managed, and controlled. When women are read as being sexual and attractive to men, women are given more agency, freedom, and individuality compared to the Iron Ladies. Bodies matter to leadership (Sinclair, 2005), and women's bodies and the ways in which they are read by others are important to their success as effective leadership. To illustrate, when bodies age such as in the case of Ghandi, their leadership effectiveness is questioned. Women's bodies are used by those who create the nicknames to classify and categorize women; nicknames are conduits in the exercise of power and control over women by men. As we have witnessed in this chapter, nicknaming (e.g., the Iron Lady) positions them in the name of the other. The use of this nickname aligns the feminine and consumes and subsumes it within the masculine. Therefore, for women leaders, the feminine is co-opted within the dominant discourses of leadership, which are masculine. In the case of the Iron Lady, the industrial products of iron rationalize the feminine, which seems otherwise untamed. Women leaders as other are arrested to render them controlled, to be subordinated, and to be kept in their place (Gherardi, 1995) and to be made inferior. The embodied/emotional feminine must be assigned *in relation* to the norm/the rational and, as we have discussed, the use of nicknaming as a discursive strategy assists with the cultural construction of leadership within the cultural and political contexts. The cultural production of women leaders as other and the nicknames and stereotypes produced and reproduced contribute to women's perception of themselves and other women's leadership potential and effectiveness. The perpetuation of othering in leadership practice contributes to symbolic and material discrimination in organizations and institutions.

The use of nicknames renders women *in relation* to their male counterparts all the way from career history, election, office, to exit. Firsts only exist *in relation*—the feminine *in relation* to the dominant masculine. The Iron Lady nickname illustrates the "aesthetic ambivalence associated with women embodying the role of 'leader'" (Ladkin, 2010, p. 95). When presenting as forceful and effective leaders, they are unpopular, albeit sometimes respected, and when popular they are consigned to traditional feminine (maternal) roles. Their success as leaders depends on their leadership being consumed by the masculine ideal of leadership—strength and the like. Women become rationalized. Höpfl and Matilal (2007) argued that when women threaten the organizational symbolic order, perhaps as they enter leadership, "organizations seek to subject women to the therapeutic imperative of rationality as the price of membership and of 'success'" (p. 198). Leadership requires women to address subordination, conforming in one way or other to the masculine organization, and, as we have seen, nicknaming gives women's subordination another hit.

In this chapter we have established that First Women in leadership positions and their leadership practices are not discussed on their own terms, but always *in relation* to the men who went before them. Furthermore, while women have made great progress into senior leadership positions, as our sample of exceptional Firsts has shown, much more is required from society at large and organizations in particular to undo the stereotypes associated with nicknames cast on women leaders. Developing women leaders requires us to rethink the ways in which the feminine—in practice and theory—always sits alongside the masculine. We suggest also that elite roles such as the highest level of political leadership produce specific barriers for women, including overcoming the cultural production of gendered stereotypes. It would be beneficial for future research to focus on (a) the ways in which specific gendered economies employ and produce particular nicknames; (b) the processes through which nicknaming further produces inequality; and (c) how women leaders identify with and resist the mass production of their gendered lives through representation in the mass media. We limited our research and discussion to exceptional women in politics to explore dominant nicknames; however, further exploration of the relationship between nicknaming—and sexuality, race, and age, in particular—would warrant further study.

It seems that while women are making huge inroads into senior leadership roles, there is much work to be done to enable women leaders to exist on their own terms—not assigned *in relation* to their male counterparts. One way forward is questioning the discursive regimes inherent in organizations. We explored nicknaming to show how power is exercised in and through mass media technologies and which, because of the intention to reach mass audiences via mass communication, produces images of women leaders that are not progressive to women's advancement in leadership in the future and, indeed, are symbolically and materially detrimental to many women leaders who are continually marked *in relation* to men.

REFERENCES

Bangash, Y. K. (2011, October 24). A tribute to Pakistan's iron lady. *Tribune*. Retrieved from http://tribune.com.pk/story/280841/a-tribute-to-pakistans-iron-lady/

Battestini, S. P. X. (1991). Reading signs of identity and alterity—history, semiotics and a Nigerian case. *African Studies Review, 34*(1), 99–116. doi: 10.2307/524257

Beck, D., & Davis, E. (2005). EEO in senior management: Women executives in Westpac. *Asia Pacific Journal of Human Resources, 43*(3), 273–288. doi: 10.1177/1038411105055063

Behr, R. (n.d.). Tea with the iron lady. *Baltics Worldwide*. Retrieved from http://www.balticsworldwide.com/vike-freiberga_tea.htm

Benson, S. (2012, July 27). Aussie iron lady will die fighting. *Daily Telegraph*. Retrieved from http://www.dailytelegraph.com.au

Bilefsky, D. (2005, 15 December). 'Baltic Iron Lady' stands up to the Kremlin. *Global Security News*. Retrieved from http://globalsecuritynews.com/Russia/Bilefsky-Dan/Baltic-Iron-Lady-stands-up-to-the-Kremlin

Billing, D. Y., & Alvesson, M (2000). Questioning the notion of feminine leadership: A critical perspective on the gender labelling of leadership. *Gender, Work & Organization, 7*(3), 144–157. doi: 10.1111/1468-0432.00103

Bolt, A. (2009, June 19). Julia Gillard gets down and dirty as the new iron lady. *Herald Sun*. Retrieved from http://www.heraldsun.com.au/news/julia-gillard-gets-down-and-dirty-as-the-new-iron-lady/story-e6frf7jo-1225737432183

Boyes, R. (2010, January 25). Iron lady Angela Merkel vanishes amid trouble home and abroad. *Times Online*. Retrieved from http://www.thetimes.co.uk/tto/news/world/agenda/article1840406.ece

Boyes, R. (2011, October 8). Peace shattered as Africa's iron lady shares Nobel Prize ahead of election. *The Australian*. Retrieved from http://www.theaustralian.com.au/news/world/peace-shattered-as-africas-iron-lady-shares-nobel-prize-ahead-of-election/story-e6frg6so-1226161800645

Brandes, S. H. (1975). The structural and demographic implications of nicknames in Navanogal, Spain. *American Ethnologist, 2*(1), 139–148. doi: 10.1525/ae.1975.2.1.02a00080

Breen, R. (1982). Naming practices in Western Ireland. *Man New Series, 17*(4), 701–713. doi: 10.2307/2802041

Bridge, R. (2010, October 27). Cold comfort as "titanium lady" Madeleine Albright visits Moscow. *Russia Today*. Retrieved from https://www.rt.com/usa/madeleine-albright-visits-moscow/

Butt, G. (1998, April 21). Golda Meir. *BBC News*. Retrieved from http://news.bbc.co.uk/1/hi/events/israel_at_50/profiles/81288.stm

Calás, M. B., & Smircich, L. (1991). Voicing seduction to silence leadership. *Organization Studies, 12*(4), 567–601. doi: 10.1177/017084069101200406

Carlin, D. B., & Winfrey, K. L. (2009). Have you come a long way, baby? Hillary Clinton, Sarah Palin, and sexism in 2008 campaign coverage. *Communication Studies, 60*(4), 326–343. doi: 10.1080/10510970903109904

Chernyshev, P. (2012, May 17). Madeleine Albright: Russia's foe and Serbia's butcher. *Pravda*. Retrieved from: http://www.pravdareport.com/society/stories/17-05-2012/121151-madeleine_albright-0/

Collinson, D. L. (1988). Engineering humour: Masculinity, joking and conflict in shop-floor relations. *Organization Studies, 9*(2), 181–199. doi: 10.1177/017084068800900203

Collinson, D., & Hearn, J. (Eds.). (1996). *Men as managers, managers as men: Critical perspectives on men, masculinities and managements*. London, UK: Sage.

Cooke, G. (2010, July 26). Preserve us from an Aussie Iron Lady. *ON LINE opinion*. Retrieved from http://www.onlineopinion.com.au/view.asp?article=10735

Dale, A. (2010, July 9). Julia Gillard's body language says she's the new iron lady. *Daily Telegraph*. Retrieved from http://www.dailytelegraph.com.au/news/national/julia-gillards-body-says-shes-the-new-iron-lady/story-e6freuzr-1225889591705

Davies, D. (2009, April 8). The "remarkable life" of Liberia's "iron lady." *NPR*. Retrieved from http://www.npr.org/templates/story/story.php?storyId=102865779

de Klerk, V., & Bosch, B. (1996). Nicknames as sex-role stereotypes. *Sex Roles, 35*(9–10), 525–28. doi: 10.1007/BF01548251

de Pina-Cabral, J. (1984). Nicknames and the experience of community. *Man, New Series, 19*(1), 148–150. ISSN: 00251496

Dos Santos, N. (2013, September 26). Germany's modest mutti Merkel is no iron lady Thatcher. *CNN*. Retrieved from http://www.cnn.com/2013/09/26/business/angela-merkel-is-no-maggie-thatcher/index.html

Elkins, R. (2005, June 19). Angela Merkel: Iron mädchen. *Independent*. Retrieved from http://www.independent.co.uk/news/people/profiles/angela-merkel-iron-maumldchen-494602.html

Elliott, T. (2010, May 15). A media star gets a whiff of reality. *Sydney Morning Herald*. Retrieved from http://www.smh.com.au/entertainment/books/a-media-star-gets-a-whiff-of-reality-20100514-v3l1.html

Fletcher, J. K. (2004). The paradox of postheroic leadership: An essay on gender, power, and transformational change. *Leadership Quarterly, 15*(5), 647–661. doi: 10.1016/j.leaqua.2004.07.004 (*AN: 14650048*)

Ford, J. (2006). Discourses of leadership: Gender, identity and contradiction in a U.K. public sector organization. *Leadership, 2*(1), 77–99. doi: 10.1177/1742715006060654

Ford, J., Learmonth, M., & Harding, N. (2008). *Leadership as identity*. Basingstoke, UK: Palgrave Macmillan.

Germany's iron-curtain lady. (2005, May 31). *Economist*. Retrieved from http://www.economist.com/node/4010748

Gherardi, S. (1995). *Gender, symbolism and organizational cultures*. London, UK: Sage.

Groer, A. (2010, June 15). Madeleine Albright's diplomatic jewelry: Read my pins. *Smithsonian, Politics Daily*. Retrieved from http://www.politicsdaily.com/2010/06/15/madeleine-albrights-diplomatic-jewelry-read-my-pins-at-smith/

Helen Clark. (2016). *Encyclopaedia Britannica*. Retrieved from http://www.britannica.com/biography/Helen-Clark

Hewitt, P. (2008, September 19). Labour's greatest hero: Barbara Castle. *Guardian*. Retrieved from http://www.theguardian.com/commentisfree/2008/sep/19/labourconference.labour

Holmberg, I., & Åkerblom, S. (2001). The production of outstanding leadership—an analysis of leadership images in the Swedish media. *Scandinavian Journal of Management, 17*(1), 67–85. doi: 10.1016/S0956-5221(00)00033-6

Höpfl, H., & Matilal, S. (2007). "The lady vanishes": Some thoughts on women and leadership. *Journal of Organizational Change Management, 20*(2), 198–208. doi: 10.1108/09534810710724757

Hui, A. (2013, April 8). Thatcherisms: If you want something said, ask a man; if you want something done, ask a woman. *Globe and Mail*. Retrieved from: http://www.theglobeandmail.com/news/world/thatcherisms-if-you-want-something-said-ask-a-man-if-you-want-something-done-ask-a-woman/article10841341/

Israel elects first female leader. (1969, March 7). *BBC News*. Retrieved from http://news.bbc.co.uk/onthisday/hi/dates/stories/march/7/newsid_4205000/4205843.stm

Jones, B. (2011, August 17). Eurozone crisis tarnishes Germany's "iron lady." *CNN*. Retrieved from http://edition.cnn.com/2011/BUSINESS/08/17/germany.merkel.popularity/

Jones, C. (2000, September 29). Barbara Castle: Scaling the ramparts. *BBC News*. Retrieved from http://news.bbc.co.uk/1/hi/uk_politics/946997.stm

Jones, D. (Producer) & Lloyd, P. (Director). (2011). *The Iron Lady* [Motion picture]. UK: Pathe.

Kanter, R. M. (1977). *Men and women of the corporation*. New York, NY: Basic Books.

Kelly, P. (2010, August 14). Gillard leans to the left. *Australian*. Retrieved from http://www.theaustralian.com.au/national-affairs/opinion/gillard-leans-to-the-left/story-e6frgd0x-1225905084394

Klenke, K. (1996). *Women and leadership: A contextual perspective*. New York, NY: Springer.

Korabik, K. (1990). Androgyny and leadership style. *Journal of Business Ethics, 9*(4–5), 283–292. doi: 10.1007/BF00380328

Kunin, M. M. (2008). *Pearls, politics, and power: How women can win and lead*. White River Junction, VT: Chelsea Green Publishing.

Labour stalwart Castle dies. (2002, May 4). *BBC News*. Retrieved from http://news.bbc.co.uk/1/hi/uk_politics/1967159.stm

Ladkin, D. (2010). *Rethinking leadership: A new look at old leadership questions*. New horizons in leadership studies. Cheltenham, UK: Edward Elgar.

Lithuania elects first female president. (2009, May 18). *ABC*. Retrieved from http://www.abc.net.au/news/2009-05-18/lithuania-elects-first-female-president/1686180

Lithuania's new president Steel magnolia: Dalia Grybauskaite is tough—and she needs to be. (2009, May 21). *Economist*. Retrieved from http://www.economist.com/node/13702731

Margaret Thatcher Biography. (n.d.). *bio*. Retrieved from http://www.biography.com/people/margaret-thatcher-9504796

Martinson, J. (2014, January 28). Will Helen Clark be the first woman to run the UN? *Guardian.* Retrieved from http://www.theguardian.com/lifeandstyle/2014/jan/27/will-helen-clark-be-first-woman-to-run-united-nations

McClanahan, P. (2011, April 12). Africa's "iron lady" revitalizes Liberia. *Christian Science Monitor.* Retrieved from http://www.csmonitor.com/World/Africa/2011/0412/Africa-s-Iron-Lady-revitalizes-Liberia

McDowell, J. H. (1981). Toward a semiotics of nicknaming, the Kamsá example. *Journal of American Folklore, 94*(371), 1–18. doi: 10.2307/540773

Paterson, T (2010, 12 April). The iron Frau: Angela Merkel. Independent. Retrieved from http://www.independent.co.uk/news/world/europe/the-iron-frau-angela-merkel-1941814.html

Peacock, L. (2014, January 22). New Zealand's former woman PM: Margaret Thatcher set the tone for women in politics. *Telegraph.* Retrieved from http://www.telegraph.co.uk/women/womens-politics/10587999/Margaret-Thatcher-set-the-tone-for-women-in-politics-says-woman-Prime-Minister-of-New-Zealand.html

Perkins, A. (2002, May 4). Baroness Castle of Blackburn. *Guardian.* Retrieved from http://www.theguardian.com/news/2002/may/04/guardianobituaries.obituaries

Perkins, A. (2010, September 3). How Barbara Castle broke the glass ceiling of politics. *BBC News.* Retrieved from http://www.bbc.co.uk/news/uk-politics-11149803

Phillips, B. S. (1990). Nicknames and sex role stereotypes. *Sex Roles, 23*(5), 281–289. doi 10.1007/BF00290049

Pitt-Rivers, J. A. (1961). *The people of the Sierra.* Chicago, IL: Phoenix.

Pullen, A., & Simpson, R. (2009). Managing difference in feminized work: Men, otherness and social practice. *Human Relations, 62*(4), 561–587. doi: 10.1177/0018726708101989

Pullen, A., & Vachhani, S. (2013). The materiality of leadership. [Special issue]. *Leadership, 9*(3), 315–319. doi: 10.1177/1742715013486038

Rodgers, E. (2010, June 24). Gillard ousts Rudd in bloodless coup. *ABC.* Retrieved from http://www.abc.net.au/news/2010-06-24/gillard-ousts-rudd-in-bloodless-coup/879136

Rohter, L. (2005, June 22). World briefing. Americas: Brazil: "Iron lady" is new chief of staff. *New York Times.* Retrieved from http://query.nytimes.com/gst/fullpage.html?res=9C00E1DD1E3BF931A15755C0A9639C8B63

Rousseff, D. (2014, October 27). Brazil's Iron Lady. *BBC News.* Retrieved from http://www.bbc.com/news/world-latin-america-11446466

Rowlatt, J. (1999, March 16). Cresson: The careless commissioner. *BBC News.* Retrieved from http://news.bbc.co.uk/1/hi/world/europe/255053.stm

Ryan, K. (2013). The media's war on women: Gendered coverage of female candidates. *Xavier Journal of Politics, 4*(1), 13–25. Retrieved from http://www.xavier.edu/xjop/documents/XJOPVol4No1Ryan.pdf

Saunders, G. R. (1990). Review of *Aggression and community: Paradoxes of Andalusian culture* by David D. Gilmore. *Ethnohistory, 37*(3), 349–351. doi: 10.2307/482472

Schindler, N. (2002). *Rebellion, community and custom in early modern Germany.* Cambridge, UK: Cambridge University Press.

Sev'er, A., & Ungar, S. (1997). No laughing matter: Boundaries of gender-based humour in the classroom. *The Journal of Higher Education, 68*(1), 87–105. AN: 9706264408

Shlaim, A. (2008). The face that launched a thousand MiGs, *Guardian.* Retrieved from http://www.theguardian.com/books/2008/aug/16/biography.politics

Shanahan, D. (2012, February 28). Julia must show mettle while iron's hot. *Australian.* Retrieved from http://www.theaustralian.com.au/opinion/columnists/julia-must-show-mettle-while-irons-hot/story-e6frg75f-1226283279695

Sinclair, A. (2005). Body possibilities in leadership. *Leadership, 1*(4), 387–406.

Summers, A. (2010, June 25). Historic moment, but barriers remain for half the population. *Age.* Retrieved from http://www.smh.com.au/federal-politics/political-opinion/historic-moment-but-barriers-remain-for-half-the-population-20100624-z3bp.html

Suroor, H. (2002, May 5). U.K. loses its first iron lady. *Hindu.* Retrieved from http://www.thehindu.com/2002/05/05/stories/2002050500511400.htm

Taksa, L. (2005). About as popular as a dose of clap: Steam, diesel and masculinity at the New South Wales Eveleigh railway workshops. *Journal of Transport History* (UK), *26*, 79–97. AN 18543771

Taksa, L. (2012a). Naming bodies at work: Considering the gendered and emotional dimensions of nicknaming. *International Journal of Work Organisation and Emotion, 5*(1), 26–40. doi: http://dx.doi.org/10.1504/IJWOE.2012.048590

Taksa, L. (2012b). Naming, condoning, and shaming: Interpreting employee assessments of behaviour and misbehavior in the workplace. In A. Barnes & L. Taksa (Eds.), *Rethinking misbehavior and resistance,* (pp. 57–84). Bingley, U.K.: Emerald.

Thelikorala, S. (2011, November 20). Indira Gandhi: Iron lady of India. *Sunday Times.* Retrieved from http://www.sundaytimes.lk/111120/Timestwo/int015.html

UK Politics—Whitelaw: The archetypal Tory. (1999, July 1). *BBC News.* Retrieved from http://news.bbc.co.uk/2/hi/uk_news/politics/382770.stm

Vallely, P. (2013, April 9). How Margaret Thatcher built the myth of the iron lady. *Independent.* Retrieved from http://www.independent.co.uk/news/uk/politics/how-margaret-thatcher-built-the-myth-of-the-iron-lady-8565103.html

Volkery, C. (2013, April 8). The iron lady: Margaret Thatcher dies at 87. *Spiegel Online.* Retrieved from http://www.spiegel.de/international/europe/former-british-prime-minister-margaret-thatcher-dies-at-87-a-893188.html

Wajcman, J. (1998). *Managing like a man: Women and men in corporate management.* London, UK: John Wiley & Sons.

Weatherall, A. (2002). *Gender, language, and discourse.* Hove, UK: Routledge.

Winneker, C. (2006, January 18). Iron Frau shows her mettle with Putin. *Politico.* Retrieved from http://www.politico.eu/article/iron-frau-shows-her-mettle-with-putin/

Wilson, L. (2013, June 12). Australian PM Julia Gillard hits out at rival party's dig at her small breasts and huge thighs on fundraiser menu. *Metro.* Retrieved from http://metro.co.uk/2013/06/12/australian-pm-julia-gillard-hits-out-at-rival-partys-dig-at-her-small-breasts-and-huge-thighs-on-fundraiser-menu-3838163/

Wood, M. (1998). Nineteenth century bureaucratic constructions of Indigenous identities in NSW. In N. Peterson & W. Sanders (Eds.), *Citizenship and Indigenous Australians: Changing conceptions and possibilities* (pp. 35–54). Cambridge, UK: Cambridge University Press.

Yadid, J. (2015, May 3). Israel's iron lady unfiltered: 17 Golda Meir quotes on her 117th birthday. *Haaretz*. Retrieved from http://www.haaretz.com/israel-news/.premium-1.654218

CHAPTER 8

CAVEMAN MERITOCRACY

Misrepresenting Women Managers Online

Janne Tienari
Aalto University

Pasi Ahonen
University of Essex

Women are strong in those fields for which evolution has prepared them. It's different in male fields. . . . Women are very emotional and short-term in their thinking. . . . Making sensible decisions is so-so, basically just lottery.

—Asterix [pseud.], comment on Ranta, 2012, 7.1.2012, 16.51[1]

The online comment above was posted in response to a feature article published in a web-based Finnish business newspaper, *Taloussanomat* (Ranta, 2012). The article itself drew attention to the reasons why women seldom make it to the upper echelons of companies in Finland. It built on a Chamber of Commerce report published some months earlier that examined women's representation in top management and on corporate boards of directors (Turunen, 2012). The text, supportive of women in management

Gender, Media, and Organization, pages 133–151
Copyright © 2016 by Information Age Publishing
All rights of reproduction in any form reserved.

and written in an upbeat and playful style, attracted a large number of on-line comments that were often belittling and abusive of women managers.

In this chapter, we provide a close reading of the comments on the *Taloussanomat* article to analyze gendered online media constructions and audience dynamics in the online business press context. In total, there were 236 online comments, which is a relatively high number for an article published in *Taloussanomat*. This suggests that the article not only attracted attention but also drove readers to take an active role in the media debate. The case reveals that (misogynist) misrepresentations of women are commonplace in Finland, despite its distinctly gender-egalitarian image, a tradition of policies that enhance gender equality, and a long history of women's full-time participation in the labor market. Along with the other Nordic countries, Finland regularly features among the countries with the smallest gender gap in the annual studies by the World Economic Forum (2014). Hence, our example puts into sharp relief the ways in which online environments enable reproduction of gender stereotypes, myths, and outright vitriol that are constitutive of anti-women discourse and misogyny even in societies that are seemingly egalitarian.

We propose the term *caveman meritocracy*[2] as shorthand to characterize the logic that dominates the commentary on the media article. It builds on what we call *caveman talk*, a register[3] (Halliday & Hasan, 2013) of text in which gender differences are essentialized as deeply natural, primordial relations between men and women. These essential differences are presented in a dismissive tone that emphasizes their seemingly self-evident status in an aggressive manner. The mode of caveman talk is not one of engagement; it is declarative, as if stating undisputed and generally accepted facts. Caveman meritocracy thereby evokes a seemingly meritocratic system where men prevail for natural reasons. This language or talk not only frames management as a distinctly gendered (in this case, masculine) activity but also draws upon notions of nature and evolution to claim that women are unsuitable for positions of responsibility and leadership. However, online media also allow for other discourses or registers to surface, ones that challenge the masculinist worldview. In this chapter, we elucidate caveman talk and how it serves to (re)construct a particular gendered idea of meritocracy and consider its consequences for understanding gender, management, and online media.

GENDER, MANAGEMENT, AND ONLINE MEDIA

It is well established that the media are active in forming frames of reference in relation to gender (Macdonald, 1995, 2003). The media both reflect and construct social reality. While media serve to circulate and reproduce established understandings and taken-for-granted assumptions concerning the roles and positions of men and women in society, gender discourses in the media are also open to contestation and change. This also applies to the question of gender and management. Extant research tells us that the media is a key site where gender is *done* in and for management (Deutsch, 2007; Kelan, 2010; Tienari, Holgersson, Meriläinen, & Höök, 2009; Tienari, Meriläinen, & Lang, 2004; cf. West & Zimmerman, 1987). It routinely portrays men and women differently as corporate managers (Krefting, 2002; Lämsä & Tiensuu, 2002) and as political leaders (Mavin, Bryans, & Cunningham, 2010). The male norm in management is perpetuated, and women are compared to an elusive masculine ideal.

At the same time, media discourses are also subject to contestation and change in the sense that media texts and the comments they engender are not crafted and consumed in a vacuum. Established understandings and taken-for-granted assumptions can be challenged, and practices of crafting and consuming media texts are subject to scrutiny (Coleman & Ross, 2010; Hellgren, Löwstedt, Puttonen, Tienari, Vaara, & Werr, 2002; Talbot, 2007). The media can bring alternative meanings based on different assumptions to the fore, challenge the status quo, and work to reduce hierarchical perceived gender differences. They can downplay, set aside, or ignore binary gender differences, or at least draw attention to gender imbalances in organizations (Tienari et al., 2009).

While extant research on gender and management in the media tends to focus on journalistic texts (Achtenhagen & Welter, 2011; Ahl & Marlow, 2012; Tienari et al., 2009), our primary focus in this chapter is on the *comments* that an article written by a journalist attracted. Online comments are a relatively new form of media text, and they do not conform to journalistic conventions. They also differ from traditional letters to the editor in that they are not selected or edited by journalists or printed in the newspapers themselves. They only exist online and as seemingly unfiltered audience engagement with and reactions to the journalistic content rather than as a part of it. Online comments are, in many ways, interventions of social media discourses and practices into the journalistic sphere, interventions that journalists themselves find quite vexing and problematic due to their often aggressive tone and unconstructive nature (Marchionni, 2014). Such commentary on newspaper articles has only recently begun to attract scholarly attention, focusing on questions such as civility and incivility of language in online comments, the influence and consequences of anonymity online, and the role that online comments play in the public debate mediated by newspapers (Canter, 2012; Gervais, 2014; Hmielowski, Hutchens & Cicchirillo, 2014; Santana, 2014).

An emerging area of interest is the treatment and representation of women and women's issues on online forums and in social media more generally (Binns, 2012; Herring, Job-Sluder, Scheckler, & Barab, 2002; Jane, 2012, 2014, 2015; Mantilla, 2013; Megarry, 2014). These studies draw attention to the vitriolic, misogynist, sexualizing, and openly violent nature of comments that women daring to take space online receive. These kinds of analyses have not yet, however, made their way to management, organization, or leadership studies. This chapter is an attempt to begin the discussion of these issues in the contemporary interconnected global economy where new media play an increasingly influential role. We ask the question: What do online comments that media texts engender tell us about gender and management today?

The emergence of online commentary in web-based newspapers is a development that brings together traditional forms of media texts, journalistic content, and the practices of new media. Newspapers see online comments as a key means with which to engage their audiences who, to an increasing extent, expect that they are able to make their voice heard in connection with news and feature articles. In the ever-expanding mediascape (Appadurai, 1990) enabled and driven by new technologies, newspapers are seeking ways to remain relevant and to foster and even enhance public debate by making available new forms of engagement and debate between journalists and members of the public (Canter, 2012; Santana, 2014). While these aims are highly laudable, realities on the ground are often quite different. Despite the facility of online comments, media still tends to function in accordance with its traditional monodirectional model; online commentary tends to take place between members of the public as journalists are notably reluctant to engage with commentators (Canter, 2012).

Civility, or lack thereof, is an important question when it comes to public debate and the role of the media. Journalistic media texts are, by and large, civil. This is because civility is seen as a fundamental value of public debate that media see themselves as fostering (Wessler & Schultz, 2009). Civility—that is, treating others with courtesy or at least refraining from personal attacks, stereotyping, hate speech, vitriol, and the like—is generally seen as a crucial aspect of constructive, persuasive, public debate in the media. Without it, the debate quickly becomes an impoverished mud-slinging contest between the small number of those who are prone to engage in such activities while most potential participants withdraw their contributions (Gervais, 2014; Rowe, 2014; Santana, 2014). In online comments, however, incivility and abusive rhetoric are prevalent and at times even dominant (Gervais, 2014; Marchionni, 2014; Megarry, 2014).

In the comments on newspaper articles, then, broader trends in online culture are evident. Online language use is often less concerned with social graces and conventions of courtesy or politeness, let alone so-called political correctness. *Flaming* (making intentionally offensive and contradictory comments) and *trolling* (intentionally misunderstanding or misrepresenting aspects of a debate to draw unaware discussion participants into useless and endless debates simply for the fun of it) make their appearance in newspaper comments (Buckels, Trapnell & Paulhus, 2014; Cole, 2015; Jane, 2012, 2014, 2015). Online discussions are sharper, more intolerant, and more inflammatory than discussions where discussants are in the presence of each other (Santana, 2014). These characteristics of online commenting are also likely to give rise to reinforced misrepresentations of women managers because the medium prompts more direct and abusive communication than would be socially acceptable in face-to-face interactions or in texts written by professional journalists. As such, we argue that studying journalistic media texts and online comments offers a way of approaching the ways in which gender is done in everyday life (Gherardi, 1994). Our Finnish example illustrates this in a pointed way.

REPRESENTING WOMEN MANAGERS IN A BUSINESS NEWSPAPER

A feature article titled "Village Idiots and Self-Promoters—Is This Where the Glass Ceiling Is?" was published in *Taloussanomat* on January 7, 2012 (Ranta, 2012). The article was written by a woman journalist, and it framed the issue of the lack of women in top management positions in an upbeat, light-hearted manner, as the headline above evinces. The article was crafted from interviews with two top managers (a man and a woman) and an ex-manager (woman). Women managers were given a voice in the text through extensive quotations. Men's domination in management roles, the scarcity and weakness of women's networks, gendered family and childcare issues, and structural impediments in business were briefly repeated as the main reasons for the small number of top women managers in Finland. The crux of the article, however, was in highlighting the differences between men and women in how they approach management challenges. Women's skills as managers were flagged: "Women's ability to analyze things is excellent. Women are great as managers—as long as they do not burn themselves out," a female manager in the article argued (Ranta, 2012, para. 11).

The article, however, did not aim to dismantle or challenge the idea of the salience of gender as a factor in management. In fact, it relied on generalizing differences between the sexes and on forging essential(ist) links between gender-based differences and management behavior. Women managers stood out and in good stead, the article implied, by virtue of being female. Addressing the apparently obvious question of whether women are competitive first and foremost among each other, one of the women managers interviewed stressed that "I don't think that women are nasty to each other." In fact, she observed that "all my female bosses have been better than the men," and concluded that "I guess the fact that you are in the minority brings about a sense of solidarity" (Ranta, 2012, para. 24).

The language in the article deployed gendered generalizations and essentialism to drive home the point that women can be and are effective managers and leaders. The choice of words and expressions—beginning with the provocative title—suggests that the *Taloussanomat* article was written in a deliberately pointed way to trigger reactions and discussion. It was unapologetically albeit entertainingly on the side of women managers as it spoke for women's special skills and encouraged women themselves to be more active in taking up challenges and in managing their careers. What is particularly interesting to us here is how the article gave rise to a frenzy of comments by readers and how, in the comments, the gender egalitarian society reveals a more vicious side and the civility of the media discourse begins to crumble.

ONLINE COMMENTS RUN AMOK

Readers can comment on articles published in the online newspaper *Taloussanomat* (taloussanomat.fi) with a few clicks. The comments themselves can be *liked* (clicking on an image to give a thumbs up) or *disliked* (given a thumbs down). Anonymous comments are allowed, but users are reminded of comment etiquette before they post. *Taloussanomat* underlines that commentators are legally responsible for their comments, and that it reserves the right to remove any comments from the website. Even heated discussion is acceptable, we are told, as long as the comments do not break the law or breach norms of common decency.[4] According to the etiquette, comments that are abusive to specific individuals or groups are not tolerated.

The article "Village Idiots and Self-Promoters—Is This Where the Glass Ceiling Is?" attracted a total of 236 comments in four days between January 7 and 11, 2012. Most comments were made during the first 24 hours; some 30 comments were made thereafter, and only two comments were made on January 11. No comments were made after that date, which underlines the temporary and opportunistic nature of online commentary. Online comments on articles do not readily result in prolonged, in-depth public debates. Most of the commenting, then, followed the publication of the article very closely.

The comments cannot easily be considered to form a discussion or a debate, as many commentators were content to make statements that did not relate to other comments. Some comments, in turn, referenced other comments but did not relate to the theme of women managers in any way; they engaged with other commentators but not with the topic of the article. Overall, the discourse was fragmented, incomplete, and lacking coherence;

a centrifugal antenarrative assemblage of texts heading in a number of directions (Boje, 2001, 2007).

We focused on the 170 comments that directly or indirectly refer to women managers or at least to gender in broader terms. It is worth noting that many of the comments did not follow the newspaper's comment etiquette; they were, arguably, directly abusive and/or offensive (to women as a group).[5] Given the anonymity of the comments, we do not have any definite data on the gender composition of the commentators or knowledge of who they were. We assume that the readership of *Taloussanomat* consists of people who have some kind of connection to business organizations or an interest in reading business news. What we do know is that 30 commentators used a male pseudonym, and an additional 53 commentators indicated in their comments that they were men. There were 21 female pseudonyms, and an additional 20 commentators indicated that they were women. The rest of the comments and their pseudonyms, if any, were more ambiguous. We strongly suspect that the great majority of the remaining commentators were men, given the tone, style, and content of the comments.

What is notable is that in this instance the *Taloussanomat* article did not attract many internet trolls, commentators whose sole aim is to skew a discussion for personal amusement with outlandish, irrelevant, and often offensive interjections. Few comments matched the kinds of entries that literature identifies as trolling (Binns, 2012; Buckels et al., 2014). Excessively violent or hateful comments—*e-bile* to use Jane's (2012, 2014, 2015) terminology—were also rare. We identified six e-bile comments, and they all seemed to be from the same source. What we considered to be e-bile were comments such as "Well-educated whores want to be part of highly advanced technology Finland; . . . bitches belong where they are told with their menstrual pains and hormonal imbalances, to give birth. Period."

We analyzed the comments in sequence, preserving their temporal order, and also retained the relationship of the comments with follow-up comments. We ranked the texts for relevance (that is, whether and how directly they referred to the article they were ostensibly commenting on) and categorized relevant comments in terms of their register, the tenor, and mode in which they discussed the issue of women managers. It is notable that 66 comments were not related in any discernable way to the topic of women managers, and we excluded these texts from further analysis. Out of the remaining 170 comments, we classified 50 as instances of discourse where gender differences were directly described as deriving from an ostensibly natural order of things, a primordial essence that determines the roles for the sexes. We refer to this as *caveman talk* because it assumes that women are inherently inferior to men in management and in life in general. In this talk type, we identified four recurring themes:

1. Women as excessively controlling micromanagers
2. Women as unreliable backstabbers
3. Women as emotionally distant and supercilious managers
4. Women as womanist conspirators

These themes constitute a discourse—albeit a fragmented one—wherein women are represented in degrading ways and essential *primordial character-istics* are attached to women managers.

Another distinct category of texts (22 comments) rested explicitly on irrefutable meritocracy: Those who deserve top positions reach them. The logic in this category of texts is self-explanatory and self-fulfilling: Those at the top are the most competent and the most competent end up at the top. Finally, and in opposition to caveman talk in particular, 26 comments in our sample challenged the idea of essential gender differences, criticizing the views expressed by other commentators or even the uncomplicated understanding of gender of the original article (11 comments we classified as anti-caveman talk as they challenged the views expressed directly as sexist and incorrect, while 15 comments made acerbic remarks about caveman talk).[6] It is noteworthy that the challenging of caveman talk was mostly done by reversing the gender hierarchy of and using essentializing language to argue that women as a group make better managers. Although few, there were some comments that could be considered to be feminist, pointing out the problems with both essentialized gender assumptions as well as the pitfalls of so-called meritocracies.

CAVEMAN MERITOCRACY

The dominant register of the online comments on women managers in response to the *Taloussanomat* article was caveman talk. These were comments where women's inferiority to men as managers and/or human beings was presented as self-evident, a result of essential differences between men and women. Women managers were called *bitches, fuck-ups, petty bosses, nerdy girls*, and mere *extras*. In our materials, one of the first themes to recur in the comments was women's alleged essential tendency towards excessive control and micromanagement:

> A woman wants to keep control of everything and does not trust her subordinates. Male subordinates get picked on by woman managers and they are under constant surveillance. (7.1.2012, 19:03)

> Who wants to have a "bitch" as their boss who ... starts to micromanage minutiae and avoids making big decisions? (7.1.2012, 8:02)

These kinds of comments claim that women lack a sense of the big picture and with it a fundamental leadership trait that is a sense of judgment and proportion. In these characterizations, women emerge not as incompetent or hapless as managers but rather excessively controlling bureaucrats, incapable of making big decisions. Women are administrators, not leaders. Moreover, under the micromanagement of women, the working environment suffers:

> The unfortunate truth about women as managers is that the work climate deteriorates and job autonomy is lost. Women want to keep all strings in their own hands; they don't trust their subordinates. (7.1.2012, 19:03)

> The truth is that as managers women are prone to neurotic behavior, cracking under pressure. They are not prudent, they pick fights. They don't take responsibility and they let others do the work. Rather than seeing all their negative traits as causing the problems, they blame men, the society, glass ceilings etc. They are free-riders. I'm just wondering whether we can ever see a generation of women who'd take a look in the mirror, develop themselves in order to become a genuine alternative to men managers, and offer a constructive perspective to management. (7.1.2012, 11:48)

A second recurring theme in the comments depicted women as back-stabbers:

> My only female boss was bureaucratic, uptight, untrustworthy, and negative. Some of my male bosses have been fantastic, some have been jerks. But not one of them has stabbed me in the back. (7.1.2012, 17:31)

Women managers, the comments assert, cannot be trusted. The claims often relied on the discursive practice of professing the evidence of experience (Scott, 1991). According to this logic, the evidence was plainly visible and therefore as irrefutable as it was damning; it was based on direct contact with women managers, or at least *a* woman manager.

The third recurring theme in the comments was the reversal of gender socialization and familial responsibility discourses. Sarcastic comments drawing on this logic represented women managers as uncaring, unwilling to consider familial responsibilities, and lacking the ability to provide emotional support:

> I've always had male bosses who have been affable and supportive, the kind of people you can go to and talk about your problems. My one female boss was really rigid and the work climate was awful. It's really nice to go and try and convince a childless career rocket why I forgot to punch myself out when I had to go and take my kid to the doctor's. (7.1.2012, 17:36)

> Based on my experience, I don't think women are better as managers. The only woman I ever had as a boss had absolutely no clue about technology,

production, and business, and she had none of that famous emotional intelligence. (7.1.2012, 23:55)

Men managers emerge here as enlightened leaders while women managers lack emotional intelligence and empathy. Women managers are caught in a double bind of not matching male criteria of success but not living up to the nurturing female stereotype either (Gherardi, 1994). A further twist in the reversal logic is representing other women as a woman manager's worst enemy:

> I don't share huber's [*sic,* Satu Huber is one of the woman managers interviewed in the article] view of women as good managers. When I worked in . . . insurance, I only came across selfish, back-stabbing women managers who were full of themselves. I have never experienced the same from male bosses. A woman is a wolf to another woman, also in working life. (7.1.2012, 7:38)

Through such comments, men managers are represented as the true egalitarians or meritocrats, more able to treat everyone with respect and integrity. Women managers explicitly lack those qualities. Women are represented as hard-nosed, sharp-elbowed careerists to whom other people are either obstacles or means to further personal advancement. Hence, the masculine symbolic order shapes and constrains women managers' social relations with other women (Mavin, Grandy, & Williams, 2014).

While some comments claim that women lack any ability to work together with other women, in other comments women's networks and support systems were treated as highly suspicious attempts to gain unfair advantage in an otherwise meritocratic system. The fourth recurring theme in the comments—and in sharp contrast to the above—was the conspiratorial, women-preferring woman manager:

> Women's career development comes to an end due to the fact that women think themselves better than men because they are women. Women form cliques and networks only amongst themselves. (7.1.2012, 10:48)

In these comments, women seeking solidarity and empowerment through connecting with other women are represented as exclusionary and conspiratorial. Gender quotas, whose purpose is to right historical wrongs and current day imbalances, are presented as evidence of women's natural superciliousness, sense of entitlement, and selfishness:

> Women want all kinds of quotas for themselves because they think they are better by nature. This is where women succumb to their own selfishness. When women don't succeed by these means, they accuse men of discrimination. (7.1.2012, 10:48)

What we call caveman talk, then, presents men as the inherently more capable gender and whatever women do, be it focusing on their own career or attempts to join forces with other women, it is represented not only as a weakness and a failing but also as antimeritocratic. This sentiment leads some commentators to be directly dismissive of women as managers, as professionals, and as human beings. The woman journalist who wrote the *Taloussanomat* article became a case in point:

> Women are clearly at a lower level. You can see that in the competence of the writer of the story. Not even the most basic principles of journalism were followed. (7.1.2012 12:20)

If the kind of caveman talk that we outline above relies on steep, primordial differences between the genders, another strong strand of this talk, in some 30 comments, specifically refuted the idea that the lack of women in top positions in organizations was an indication of any discrimination. These comments pick up the idea of competition but frame it even more explicitly in terms of meritocracy: Those who deserve the top positions reach them. True equality, these commentators hold, is achieved through noninterference in the prevailing conditions.

> We're only in the second week of the new year, and what do we see: feminists whining again. It's all men's fault when women are not competent enough. No-one stops women from establishing their own publicly listed companies! Do that if you think you are as competent as men. Don't be martyrs and whine about quotas and equality! (7.1.2012 11:17)

Comments like these were typical contributions: Expertise, not gender, is and should be the deciding factor in reaching top positions in organizations. In these comments, gender divisions are depicted as natural and a result of personal choices and initiative. The commentators do not discuss any kind of structural or historical disadvantages in women reaching top jobs. The reasoning is that they have not achieved top positions because of the lack of individual effort or required personal traits. Some commentators identifying themselves as women shared this view:

> Many women think too much of themselves. This is my woman's opinion. I've succeeded by just being myself. I haven't taken notice of sexism. I haven't whined. I've concentrated on the job at hand. Also, I try to avoid female colleagues who are all the time concerned about what others think of them. How can someone like that focus on what's really important? (7.1.2012, 21:45)

Success is presented as a personal and personality question. In this comment the self-identified woman manager emphasizes the importance of *being herself* at the same time as it is important to ignore sexism and focus on the task at hand. It is a personal failure if one loses focus on organizational goals or lets side issues, such as sexism, affect them. The very final comment in the thread, made on January 11, sums up the danger of being identified as a woman manager. It captures the attitude behind caveman talk:

> A woman is an E X T R A. Forever and always. (11.1.2012, 20:43)

CHALLENGING CAVEMAN TALK

Alongside what we call caveman meritocracy—and caveman talk that brings it into being—attempts at representing women managers in other ways were also made in the online comments. Women's special qualities were presented as an asset, echoing the sentiment of the *Taloussanomat* article. This discourse also involved derogatory remarks about men. These interventions were, however, relatively rare in comparison to occurrences of caveman talk. Only in a handful of comments were women depicted as professionals who have specific individual skills and competences—just like men. In contrast, many essentializing comments reiterated women's special management qualities as they were presented in the *Taloussanomat* article:

> Research has established that women are stronger in logical thinking. Research has also established that women can multitask. This is an important management trait. (7.1.2012 16:25)

> Women have a higher work ethic. So there is a bit of pressure and the poor boys are not fond of it. Challenging male authority on a wider scale is a blow to their self-esteem. (7.1.2012, 16:18)

> I've noticed that men only see others' mistakes and not their own. They bolster their self-esteem with technical knowledge and they are unable to see the big picture.... Women *dare* to question established ways of working and to report problems.... Women make things run smoother and more openly. (7.1.2012, 14:43)

All these comments confront caveman talk while relying on similarly essentialist logic. Apart from a few comments that pointed to the need to break out of traditional gender roles and chauvinism, much of the discourse of women's special management qualities reproduced established assumptions about women's qualities as managers, only in more positive ways. It elevated women on the basis of the same generalizations that were used to degrade them.

Finally, a small number of comments reflected on the tone and content of the comments themselves and drew parallels between them and the world of work at large:

What's behind all this are men who hate women. You only need to read these comments to understand that there are a great many men like that. They think that a woman's place is in the kitchen, between a fist and the cooker,[7] and their job is to serve men. These men do not want women in leadership positions because they think they'll lose out. It is still a man's world, and it is not going to change when attitudes are this old-fashioned and chauvinistic. (8.1.2012, 5:05)

The references to meritocracy in the online commentary are presumably based on the assumption that gender equality has already been achieved, which pervades Finnish society (Korvajärvi, 2002). However, despite its egalitarian image, Finnish society is deeply divided along gender lines, to which the comment above seems to refer. Firstly, the Finnish labor market is notably gender segregated (Kolehmainen, 2002). Vertical segregation makes it very difficult for women to reach top positions, for example in business organizations and higher education. Horizontal segregation, in turn, segments the job market into *women's jobs* and *men's jobs*. The former tend to be devalued both in sociocultural and economic terms. Secondly, Finnish women tend to do a double shift—they work full-time outside the home while still doing most of the housework and reproductive labor (Nätti, Anttila, & Väisänen, 2005).

DISCUSSION AND CONCLUSIONS

In this chapter, we provided a close reading of online comments that an article in the business press engendered and considered what they tell us about gender and management today. We took issue with misrepresentations of women managers. We argue that the dominant register in the comments is what we refer to as caveman talk. It is often dismissive of women as managers and as human beings, and represents women and men as fundamentally different creatures. The online comments make the masculine norm in management not only explicit but seek to legitimize it as an inalienable truth: a natural order of things.

We need to keep in mind that the comments do not exist in a vacuum or take some kind of natural and organic form. They are, literally, *comments* on a media article. The focal article, then, needs to be considered as a frame that gives the comments both the space the comments occupy and the direction they take (e.g., Macdonald, 1995, 2003). The article framed the issue in an intentionally provocative manner. The title itself created a rather unflattering image of male managers, representing gender differences as sharp and significant, even essential. While the media article was supportive of women managers in a somewhat essentialist manner while still retaining journalistic factuality, the online comments actively degraded women.

The alleged characteristics of women managers were mocked; their female traits ridiculed; their behaviors, whether ostensibly feminine or masculine, derided; and their assumed weaknesses exaggerated.

Importantly, *women* appeared as a monolithic group, characterized and apparently limited by their essential and inferior qualities. They emerged from the depictions in the comments through *lack*. There is no logic or consistency to the caveman talk in terms of claims made—women are, for example, depicted both as being in cahoots with each other and unable to work with each other—but the consistent and essential representation of women managers through a lack that either has primordial origins or at least becomes evident through competition (and assumes the form of *battle of the sexes*) is what organizes caveman talk. In this logic, the current organizational realities and the lack of women managers are a natural outcome of meritocracy, competition, and the evolutionary traits of each sex.

The assumption that competence is something objectively measurable and observable (Tienari et al., 2004; Tienari et al., 2009), at least post facto, allows for the logical extension that because there are not more women in top management, women are in one way or another unsuited for the positions. The notion of competence draws from and adheres to masculine ideals and expectations that are difficult if not impossible for women to fully meet (Kerfoot & Knights, 1998; Ross-Smith & Kornberger, 2004; Tienari et al., 2009). The commentary reflects the fact that women in management face what Gherardi (1994) called "dual presence" where they are simultaneously expected to be like men (to adhere to masculine norms in management) and be different from them (to bring something extra to management by virtue of being women).

In summary, we argue that the notion of caveman meritocracy captures the content and form of the discourse that builds on male supremacy in management as an undisputable fact and does so in an aggressive way by means of exaggerations and generalizations that misrepresent women managers as professionals and as human beings. Caveman talk is, we argue, a mundane form of epistemic violence constitutive of anti-women sentiments and misogyny (still) prevalent in the seemingly egalitarian societal context of Finland. The sentiments that caveman talk expresses are something that would be mostly hidden from public view without the internet and the discursive practices of social media (cf., Gherardi, 1994). Our analysis adds to extant research a hitherto unexplored dimension, or perhaps an extension, of media analysis, the discourse on gender and management in the nowadays prevalent comment sections of online newspapers. This liminal textual space, where the discursive practices of social media uneasily meet those of journalism and where the exchange of views—of sorts—takes place adjacent to, although not within, the recognized confines of mediated public debate, is increasingly important and warrants further and closer research attention.

At the same time, caveman talk is a product of the specific conditions of possibility that social media and network culture create and enable. Its character is produced by these conditions. Online commenting often unfolds in gushes of emotional outrage before it dies down and the commentators move on to commenting on something else. As in new media more generally, time, space, and context become blurred as the commenting can be done in all kinds of circumstances without the other participants knowing about these conditions of content production. A spur-of-the-moment thought becomes public and permanent when the commentator presses *enter*.

Finally, we are not suggesting that caveman talk represents a truer social discourse than do more civil forms of public debate. Rather, we propose that it forms a mode of operating and a register of text that has found a conducive environment on the Internet (Canter, 2012; Cole, 2015; Gervais, 2014; Hmielowski et al., 2014). It forms a character and part of the culture of that space and thereby makes that particular space accessible and available in specific ways, to specific kinds of actors and particular kinds of opinions and ideologies. In this way, the online space is no different from any other space, but it is governed by its own relations of power and it has its own forms of language and expression. This chapter is a modest attempt at making this visible for the purposes of studying gender, management, and the media.

NOTES

1. Below we will identify the comments by their time stamp as it is the clearest way of identifying the comments, many of which were anonymous. The time stamp for Asterix's comment is 7.1.2012 16:51.
2. By deploying the notion of caveman meritocracy, we do not mean to suggest that prehistoric cultures were necessarily patriarchal or male-dominated. The reference point is in the present, among the present-day "Neanderthals," men and women who claim evolutionary justifications for their gender constructs, behaviors, and prejudices.
3. Halliday and Hasan (2013, p. 23) define *register* as "the set of meanings, the configuration of semantic patterns, that are typically drawn upon under the specified conditions, along with the words and structures that are used in the realization of these meanings."
4. *Taloussanomat* seems to assume that a universal definition for common decency exists, whereas we see this to be a contested notion. Our analysis indicates that it is contextual and open for debate. Questioning and breaching norms of common decency is a notion that is at the heart of new media and their culture of immediate and seemingly unmediated engagement. The issue of incivility in online media is of increasing importance and attention.
5. Offensive comments were not removed. More than three years later, as we wrote this in April 2015, the 236 comments were still available online.

6. The remaining 72 comments in our sample, while linked to the issue at hand, were repetitions (reposts of a comment already posted at least once), brief factual additions, clarifications, or comments on comments that added little in terms of substance. These texts were excluded from further analysis. The detailed textual analysis was carried out on a total of 98 comments.

7. The Finnish saying, "a woman's place is between a fist and a cooker," is paraphrased here. The gist of the saying is that women are supposed to obey and serve their husbands and, by extension, men in general. Although the saying may originally be misogynist, it nowadays is used more to flag outdated ideas of gender relations, as is the case here.

REFERENCES

Achtenhagen, L., & Welter, F. (2011). Surfing on the ironing board: The representation of women's entrepreneurship in German newspapers. *Entrepreneurship and Regional Growth, 23*(9–10), 763–786. doi: 10.1080/08985626.2010.520338

Ahl, H., & Marlow, S. (2012). Exploring the dynamics of gender, feminism and entrepreneurship: Advancing debate to escape a dead end? *Organization, 19*(5), 543–562. doi: 10.1177/1350508412448695

Appadurai, A. (1990). Disjuncture and difference in the global cultural economy. In M. Featherstone (Ed.), *Global culture* (pp. 295–310). London, UK: Sage.

Binns, A. (2012). Don't feed the trolls!: Managing troublemakers in magazines' online communities. *Journalism Practice, 6*(4), 547–562. doi: 10.1080/17512786.2011.648988

Boje, D. M. (2001). *Narrative methods for organizational and communication research.* London, UK: Sage.

Boje, D. M. (2007). The antenarrative cultural turn in narrative studies. In M. Zachry & C. Thralls (Eds.), *Communicative practices in workplaces and the professions: Cultural perspectives on the regulation of discourse and organizations* (pp. 219–238). Amityville, NY: Baywood.

Buckels, E. E., Trapnell, P. D., & Paulhus, D. L. (2014). Trolls just want to have fun. *Personality and Individual Differences, 67*, 97–102. doi: 10.1016/j.paid.2014.01.016

Canter, L. (2012). The misconception of online comment threads: Content and control on local newspaper websites. *Journalism Practice, 7*(5), 604–619. doi: 10.1080/17512786.2012.740172

Cole, K. K. (2015). "It's like she's eager to be verbally abused": Twitter, trolls, and (en)gendering disciplinary rhetoric. *Feminist Media Studies, 15*(2), 356–358. doi: 10.1080/14680777.2015.1008750

Coleman, S., & Ross, K. (2010). *The media and the public: "Them" and "us" in media discourse.* Chichester, UK: Wiley-Blackwell.

Deutsch, F. M. (2007). Undoing gender. *Gender & Society, 21*(1), 106–127. doi: 10.1177/0891243206293577

Gervais, B. T. (2014). Incivility online: Affective and behavioral reactions to uncivil political posts in a web-based experiment. *Journal of Information Technology & Politics, 12*(2), 1–19. doi: 10.1080/19331681.2014.997416

Gherardi, S. (1994). The gender we think, the gender we do in our every-day organizational lives. *Human Relations, 47*(6), 591–610. doi: 10.1177/001872679404700602

Halliday, M. A. K., & Hasan, R. (2013). *Cohesion in English.* English language series. Abingdon, UK: Routledge.

Hellgren, B., Löwstedt, J., Puttonen, L., Tienari, J., Vaara, E., & Werr, A. (2002). How issues become (re)constructed in the media: Discursive practices in the AstraZeneca merger. *British Journal of Management, 13*(2), 123–140. doi: 0.1111/1467-8551.00227

Herring, S., Job-Sluder, K., Scheckler, R., & Barab, S. (2002). Searching for safety online: Managing "trolling" in a feminist forum. *The Information Society, 18*(5), 371–384. doi: 10.1080/01972240290108186

Hmielowski, J. D., Hutchens, M. J., & Cicchirillo, V. J. (2014). Living in an age of online incivility: Examining the conditional indirect effects of online discussion on political flaming. *Information, Communication & Society, 17*(10), 1196–1211. doi: 10.1080/1369118X.2014.899609

Jane, E. A. (2012). "Your a ugly, whorish, slut": Understanding e-bile. *Feminist Media Studies, 14*(4), 531–546. doi: 10.1080/14680777.2012.741073

Jane, E. A. (2014). "Back to the kitchen, cunt": Speaking the unspeakable about online misogyny. *Continuum, 28*(4), 558–570. doi: 10.1080/10304312.2014.924479

Jane, E. A. (2015). Flaming? What flaming? The pitfalls and potentials of research-ing online hostility. *Ethics and Information Technology, 17*(1), 65–87. doi: 10.1007/s10676-015-9362-0

Kelan, E. (2010). Gender logic and (un)doing gender at work. *Gender, Work and Organization, 17*(2), 174–194. doi: 10.1111/j.1468-0432.2009.00459.x

Kerfoot, D., & Knights, D. (1998). Managing masculinity in contemporary or-ganizational life: A managerial project. *Organization, 5*(1), 7–26. doi: 10.1177/135050849851002

Kolehmainen, S. (2002). Koulutus, sukupuoli ja työnjako [Education, gender and the distribution of labour]. *Sosiologia, 39*(3), 200–214. Retrieved from http://urn.fi/URN:NBN:fi:ELE-885827

Korvajärvi (2002). Gender-neutral gender and denial of difference. In B. Czar-niawska, & H. Höpfl (Eds.), *Casting the other. The production and maintenance of inequalities in work organizations* (pp. 119–137). London, U.K.: Routledge.

Krefting, L. (2002). Re-presenting women executives: Valorization and devaloriza-tion in U.S. business press. *Women in Management Review, 17*(3–4), 104–119 doi: 10.1108/09649420210425255.

Lämsä, A-M., & Tiensuu, T. (2002). Representations of the woman leader in Finnish business media articles. *Business Ethics: A European Review, 11*(4), 363–374. doi: 10.1111/1467-8608.00296

Macdonald, M. (1995). *Representing women: Myths of femininity in the popular media.* London, UK: Arnold.

Macdonald, M. (2003). *Exploring media discourse.* London, UK: Arnold.

Mantilla, K. (2013). Gendertrolling: Misogyny adapts to new media. *Feminist Studies, 39*(2), 563–570. doi: 10.2307/23719068

Marchionni, D. (2014). Online story commenting. *Journalism Practice, 9*(2), 230–249. doi: 10.1080/17512786.2014.938943

Mavin, S., Bryans, P., & Cunningham, R. (2010). Fed-up with Blair's babes, Gordon's gals, Cameron's cuties, Nick's nymphets: Challenging gendered media representations of women political leaders. *Gender in Management: An International Journal, 25*(7), 550–569. doi: 10.1108/17542411011081365

Mavin, S., Grandy, G., & Williams, J. (2014). Experiences of women elite leaders doing gender: Intra-gender micro-violence between women. *British Journal of Management, 25*(3), 439–455. doi: 10.1111/1467-8551.12057

Megarry, J. (2014). Online incivility or sexual harassment? Conceptualising women's experiences in the digital age. *Women's Studies International Forum, 47*(Part A), 46–55. doi: 10.1016/j.wsif.2014.07.012

Nätti, J., Anttila, T., & Väisänen, M. (2005). Tietotyö, työaika ja ajankäyttö kotitaloudessa. [IT work, working time, and time use in households]. In H. Pääkkönen (Ed.), *Perheiden ajankäyttö* (pp. 43–66). Helsinki, FI: Tilastokeskus.

Ranta, E. (2012, January 7). Torveloita ja tyrkkyjä—tässäkö se lasikatto on? [Village idiots and self-promoters—is this where the glass ceiling is?]. *Taloussanomat.* Retrieved from http://www.taloussanomat.fi/tyo-ja-koulutus/2012/01/07/torveloita-ja-tyrkkyja-tassako-se-lasikatto-on/201120096/139?&n=12#comments

Ross-Smith, A., & Kornberger, M. (2004). Gendered rationality? A genealogical exploration of the philosophical and sociological conceptions of rationality, masculinity and organization. *Gender, Work & Organization, 11*(3), 280–305. doi: 10.1111/j.1468-0432.2004.00232.x

Rowe, I. (2014). Civility 2.0: A comparative analysis of incivility in online political discussion. *Information, Communication & Society, 18*(2), 121–138. doi: 10.1080/1369118X.2014.940365

Santana, A. D. (2014). Virtuous or vitriolic: The effect of anonymity on civility in online newspaper reader comment boards. *Journalism Practice, 8*(1), 18–33. doi: 10.1080/17512786.2013.813194

Scott, J. W. (1991). The evidence of experience. *Critical Inquiry, 17*(4), 773–797.

Talbot, M. (2007). *Media discourse: Representation and interaction.* Edinburgh, UK: Edinburgh University Press.

Tienari, J., Holgersson, C., Meriläinen, S., & Höök, P. (2009). Gender, management and market discourse: The case of gender quotas in the Swedish and Finnish media. *Gender, Work & Organization, 16*(4), 501–521. Doi: 10.1111/j.1468-0432.2009.00453.x

Tienari, J., Meriläinen, S., & Lang, G. (2004). "Naiskiintiöt" mediassa: Ikkuna suomalaiseen työelämän tasa-arvokeskusteluun ["Quotas for women" in the media: A window on the debate on work life equality in Finland]. *Työelämän Tutkimus, 2–3,* 84–95.

Turunen, R. (2012). *Pätevä johtaja paperilla—diskursseja pätevyyden sukupuolittuneisuudesta mediassa* [Competent manager on paper—discourses on the gendering of competence in the media]. (Master's thesis). Aalto University School of Business, Helsinki, Finland.

Wessler, H., & Schultz, T. (2009). Can the mass media deliberate?: Insights from print media and political talk shows. In R. Butsch (Ed.), *Media and public spheres* (pp. 15–27). Basingstoke, UK: Palgrave Macmillan.

West, C., & Zimmerman, D. H. (1987). Doing gender. *Gender & Society, 1*(2), 125–151. doi: 10.1177/0891243287001002002

World Economic Forum. (2014). *The Global Gender Gap Report 2014.* Retrieved from http://reports.weforum.org/global-gender-gap-report-2014/

CHAPTER 9

WYNNE SOME, LOSE SOME

An Intersectional Approach
to Media Prejudice
Against Canadian Women Politicians

Rita A. Gardiner
The University of Western Ontario

How can an intersectional analysis, coupled with an Arendtian phenomenological investigation, add conceptual richness to current theorizing concerning women politicians and media prejudice? I suggest that the dual lens of intersectionality and Arendtian phenomenology illustrates how prejudice is multifaceted and works to privilege some bodies over others. This privileging involves not only political action but also political speech. Specifically, I consider the effects of media prejudice on the success and failure of two political campaigns. The first politician I discuss is Canada's first openly gay premier, Kathleen Wynne. The second politician is Olivia Chow, the initial frontrunner to replace the former mayor of Toronto, Rob Ford. When we consider these women's campaigns through an intersectional lens, interesting facts emerge. It appears that Wynne's lesbian identity did not affect her campaign as much as Chow's ethnic identity did.

Gender, Media, and Organization, pages 153–166
Copyright © 2016 by Information Age Publishing
All rights of reproduction in any form reserved.

Indeed, ethnic prejudice in the media was a major factor in Chow's defeat (Honderich, 2014; Mallick, 2014). Focusing on gender alone, therefore, may be insufficient to explain why some women politicians are successful or suffer defeat. As such, the present inquiry adds to current literature that critiques media bias against women politicians by showing how media and political prejudice is multifaceted (Adcock, 2010; Bligh & Kohles, 2008; Mavin, Bryans, & Cunningham, 2010; Ross & Comrie, 2011).

A secondary aim of this chapter is to tease out some problems with political rhetoric. My premise is that rhetoric functions to privilege a certain kind of political posturing. As a result, those who do not perform rhetoric well will be less likely to obtain leadership positions in the political arena. If we want broader political representation, we must consider how dominant political discourses encourage a particular style of politics to prevail.

I begin by outlining how an intersectional analysis, coupled with a phenomenological inquiry, sheds light on media prejudice and the reinforcement of certain cultural norms. Next, I examine how media prejudice influenced two political campaigns. Then, using an Arendtian lens, I examine the place of *truth* in present-day politics to gain insight into prejudice. The political theorist Hannah Arendt knew first-hand how the media could tarnish a person's reputation. Her book on Adolf Eichmann created a media stir when she presented the controversial claim that evil, such as his, was banal. Nonetheless, it is not Arendt's reputation that I am concerned with here. Rather, I concentrate on her exploration of the antipathy between truth and politics. I will return to this point in due course. For now, I want to discuss how using intersectionality, together with Arendtian phenomenology, offers methodological and theoretical insights into how prejudice works.

INTERSECTIONALITY AND ARENDTIAN
PHENOMENOLOGY—COMBINING THEORY AND PRAXIS

An intersectional lens reveals that our identities are complex and variable (Von Wahl, 2011). As such, intersectionality provides both a methodological and theoretical framework to consider how diverse identity factors influence political leaders. As a methodological tool, intersectionality can enable us to assess a situation from different perspectives. It complements an Arendtian phenomenological approach because both uniqueness and plurality are taken into account (Gardiner, 2015). In Arendtian terms, uniqueness refers to the fact that each of us has a specific way of seeing the world, which derives from our particular life experiences as well as our intersectional identity. Plurality refers to the manner in which we live with others. Both concepts are foundational to Arendt's phenomenological approach. Combining these two approaches helps illuminate the ways in which prejudice shores up institutional and gender hierarchies.

Using this dual lens as a way to think about theory and praxis alerts us to the problems with some theorizing concerning women and politics, namely that women leaders will do politics in a similar manner. In some instances, gender may be the most salient factor in making a decision; in other situations, it may be a person's class or ethnicity that comes to the forefront (Eagly, 2005). Hence, too much focus on a politician's gender may obscure the relevance of other identity characteristics with respect to their political outlook.

If we consider the actions of political leaders through an intersectional lens, we may gain more understanding. For instance, German Chancellor Angela Merkel's political actions are not always in alignment with gender-friendly policies (Von Wahl, 2011). Her scientific background, Protestant upbringing, and previous political experience are all factors in Merkel's political decision making. Where Merkel has made a radical gendered change in German politics is in her cabinet. Six out of 14 members of her cabinet are female, more than in previous administrations (Von Wahl, 2011). Having more female voices in political leadership positions may help to broaden the conversations that take place. Increased gender parity may also offer potential for diverse perspectives. Such diversity may, for example, encourage environmental and family-friendly policies, as in Norway (Adler, 1996). As such, having more women around the table can help to change the dominant political climate.

Although some researchers claim that political conversations alter when there is greater gender equity (Adler, 2015), electing women does not always equate to policy change (Genovese & Steckenrider, 2013). Being a woman, in and of itself, does not mean a politician has a predisposition to female-friendly policies. This belief confuses the politics of representation with the politics of presence (Phillips, 1995). Hence, we must be cautious when claiming that female politicians advance women-friendly policies. An obvious example here is how Margaret Thatcher had no interest in advancing women's issues (Jones, 2015). In short, electing women politicians does not mean they will work for gender justice.

In fact, gender justice needs to be connected with social justice if we are to obtain greater diversity in political perspectives. In the next section, there is an examination of two political leaders and the media coverage they received in their campaigns. Using an intersectional lens offers insight into how media, as well as wider societal prejudice, works to privilege some bodies over others.

PORTRAIT OF A LEADER

Kathleen Wynne is a politician with firm roots in Ontario. Born in Toronto in 1953, she has lived most of her life in the province. Before coming out as a lesbian at age 37, Wynne was married and a mother of three children. She started out in politics at a grass-roots level, serving as a school trustee before running for provincial office. Elected in 2003, Wynne was Minister of Education and, later, Minister of Aboriginal Affairs under the premiership of Dalton McGuinty. However, his Liberal government became increasingly unpopular due to media allegations of corruption and mismanagement at the highest level, eventually forcing McGuinty to resign. In his place, Wynne was elected leader of her party, becoming, by default, Ontario's premier.

At first, the media saw Wynne as little more than a caretaker leader, while the Liberals searched for someone more suitable. When women are caretaker leaders, it can have a negative effect on their careers (Ryan, Haslam, & Postes, 2007), but this was not so in Wynne's case. One reason may be due to her decision to do something relatively unusual in politics. In a televised leader's campaign debate, she took responsibility for the mistakes of the previous government, apologizing to the people of Ontario. The media's condemnation of her apology was swift. Apologizing showed that Wynne was a weak leader, thus proving her unsuitability to govern the province. However, the people of Ontario thought otherwise. From trailing in the polls, Wynne and her team won the election easily. She became Canada's first openly gay premier and Ontario's first woman premier in 2013.

Throughout her campaign, Wynne appeared as a strong leader with a vision (her banner picture on twitter shows her jogging, reiterating this notion of strength). Wynne liked to state that she is a "policy wonk," a term that conjures up a gender-neutral or even somewhat masculine identity. In fact, Wynne often downplayed her gender and emphasized her analytic skills. This may well be a smart political tactic on her part, since voters regard dominant political traits as masculine (Bligh & Kohles, 2008; Dunaway, Lawrence, Rose, & Weber, 2013). For women to succeed in senior political roles, their actions must fit within particular stereotypes of good leaders. Such stereotypes are often masculinized (Mavin, Bryans, & Cunningham, 2010).

In a portrayal of Wynne in *Toronto Life*, the headline read "Because Kathleen Wynne Is One of Us" (Preville, 2013). What being "one of us" seems to imply is that Wynne, a grandmother of three, was no threat to the dominant gender or ethnic hierarchy. By embracing Wynne as one of us this allowed her to be open about her lesbian identity. In electoral speeches, Wynne expressed her belief that the people of Ontario do not judge their political leaders on race, color, or sexual orientation. Wynne's political rhetoric allowed her to tackle prejudice head on by asserting that Ontarians are not prejudiced. In Wynne's case, this strategy has been successful. Conversely, when we examine Olivia Chow's bid for political leadership, we see how ethnic and gender prejudice played a critical role in her campaign defeat (Honderich, 2014; Mallick, 2014).

PORTRAIT OF A LOSER

Both friends and foes regard Olivia Chow as a politician with high ethical standards. Even journalists who disagree with Chow's left-leaning politics state that she is a well-intentioned individual (Blanchford, 2014). Consequently, when Chow announced she was running for the position of mayor of Toronto, the news was initially treated positively. After all, the question of ethical leadership was going to play an important role in the mayoral race, given that many Torontonians were looking for a different style of leader than that of the previous incumbent, Rob Ford. His activities transformed Ford into an international media star and his city into something of a joke. The nickname *Toronto the Good* no longer seemed an appropriate nickname for Canada's largest metropolis. Many Torontonians were angry with the mayor's antics and wanted radical change. At first, Chow seemed the perfect choice to succeed the disgraced former mayor and bring a more self-controlled and ethical style of leadership back to the city.

Born in Hong Kong, Chow speaks fluent Mandarin, an asset in a city comprised of a multiplicity of ethnicities. In 1970, when she was 13, her family immigrated to Canada. In her autobiography, published just prior to the campaign, Chow was candid about her father's abusive nature and how her childhood was affected negatively by his violence against her brother and her mother. However, she described herself as "the golden girl" and not the victim of her father's brutality. Similar to many immigrants to Canada, Chow and her family took a while to adjust to their new situation. Her parents found it hard to find work, and the family lived in difficult financial circumstances, very different from their life in Hong Kong (Chow, 2014). Chow's knowledge of what it was like to be a stranger in a new land, together with her personal experience of family violence, shaped her politics. The political causes Chow espouses are social justice issues such as child poverty, sexual violence, homelessness, and immigration reform.

Chow knows municipal politics well, having served as a Toronto City Councilor for 14 years. Prior to her mayoral bid, Chow was a federal Member of Parliament for the downtown riding of Toronto-Spadina. Further, her husband, Jack Layton, was one of Canada's most popular politicians and led his Federal New Democratic Party to Official Opposition status shortly before his death in 2011. Chow and Layton were a powerful political couple in Canada. Their home was often used as a venue for launching political campaigns (Chow, 2014). One journalist described Chow as "the Hillary Clinton of Toronto politics" (Doolittle, 2014, para. 3). Additionally, *NOW* magazine voted her Best City Councilor seven times and the most popular Toronto politician in 2010 (Chow, 2014). Thus, she had widespread support going into the mayoral campaign.

Nevertheless, Chow's political fortunes turned out different from what was predicted. Her luck started to dissipate within a few months of the campaign. In December 2013, she announced she had a mild form of Ramsay Hunt syndrome. This syndrome results in a temporary facial disorder, thus affecting her ability to smile. Photographs of Chow began appearing in the media where she appeared to be scowling at the camera—and there were more serious problems to come. In debates, media reports suggested that Chow was not quick enough with her responses (Moore, 2014), neither was she aggressive when provoked by others in debate. Her lack of aggression was perceived as negative. Moreover, her ethnic identity, not a factor earlier in her campaign, began to receive critical media attention (Honderich, 2014). Two days before the election, a *Toronto Sun* cartoon depicted Chow in a Chairman Mao suit, with slit eyes, holding on to her former husband's coat-tails. Although many expressed outrage at this offensive cartoon, it serves to indicate some of the offensive media treatment she received. This negative treatment by the media was not new for Chow. As a councilor, she was labeled Chow-Cescu (in reference to the ex-dictator Nicolae Ceausescu of Romania) by the same newspaper. In a city that prides itself on its acceptance of minorities, something different was emerging. Prejudice that was once covert was now overt.

Viewing Chow's campaign through an intersectional lens reveals how media prejudice affects women politicians in different ways. In her case, both ethnic and gender prejudice played a role in her political upset (Mallick, 2014). Visible minorities may face additional prejudice in political campaigns. An intersectional analysis sheds light on how media prejudice may influence political success or failure (Kulich, Ryan, & Haslam, 2014).

THE POLITICS OF APPEARANCE

A gendered analysis is, however, useful in understanding media prejudice against women politicians, perhaps nowhere more so than the way that the media report on politicians' appearance (Mavin et al., 2010). In the case of these two politicians, we see how much media commentary focused on Chow's feminine appearance. Not only did the media report on what kind of clothes she wore, but also her penchant for bright colors (Chow likes to wear yellow). There are also insinuations that Chow's cultural sensitivity was politically motivated. A headline in *Toronto Life* reads "Costume Drama: Olivia Chow's Many Vote-Courting Fashion Statements" (Jervis, 2014). Rather than Chow's wearing of cultural dress being a mark of respect for other cultures, this media reporter suggested it was a calculated strategy.

Chow presents in a more feminine way than Wynne, who prefers to wear business suits. In the past, reporters commented on the severity of Wynne's appearance and how her business suits are similar to Hillary Clinton's pant-suits. Since becoming premier, her image has received more media atten-tion (Blizzard, 2013). The most common mention of Wynne's appearance during the campaign concerned the way her spectacles made her look like a schoolmarm. Indeed, the media now refers to Wynne as "Premier School-marm" (Benzie, 2013, para. 1). What we see from media reporting on these two women politicians is that appearance matters, but in different ways (Mavin et al., 2010).

The media still judges women politicians by different criteria than men. One such criterion is through a woman's personal relationship with a male leader (Adcock, 2010; Bargel, Fassin, & Latté, 2013). As previously stated, some media reports suggest that Chow's political rise was not due to merit, but to her relationship with a powerful man. The underlying supposition is that her marital alliance helped her gain political prominence. This type of media prejudice reaffirms traditional gender prejudices by downplaying women's talent.

Sexuality and Prejudice

Societal prejudice can also be a factor in terms of the sexual orientation of politicians. For instance, Wynne stated she felt a responsibility as the first lesbian premier (Brennan, 2015). She maintained that having a lesbian premier is a positive issue for social justice. Young women write to Wynne, declaring they are no longer afraid to come out, so different from her own upbringing in the 1950s. Indeed, in the last decade, there has been a mas-sive shift in Canadian public opinion in terms of prejudice against sexual minorities; most Canadians do not regard a person's sexuality as an impedi-ment to a political career (Everitt & Camp, 2014).

On the surface, there seems little prejudice against a gay woman or man being elected. Where sexuality is a problem is with political neophytes. Everitt and Camp (2014) argued that candidates who are open about being gay before their election are less likely to succeed. Their longitudinal study revealed that when a political incumbent talks about being gay, it is less like-ly to matter to their constituents. For most political hopefuls, however, stay-ing in the closet may be a better strategy. Wynne knows this prejudice well, for, in 1993, she failed to be elected to provincial office and was labeled as an "extremist lesbian" by political opponents. It appears that prejudice against LGBT individuals who run for office has not disappeared. Hence, it would be wrong to state that it is easy for homosexual candidates to be elected to public office. So, it would seem that prejudice may have lessened toward gays but it has not been eradicated. Thus, societal prejudice is a fac-tor in terms of the political success of politicians.

Sexuality is relevant to politics but in different ways depending upon the context. Bargel et al. (2013) examined sexuality within contemporary French politics. Until recently, the French media was respectful of politicians' privacy. Nonetheless, ignoring sexuality leads to "emotionless politics" (Bargel et al., 2013, p. 664). These scholars maintain that sexuality is significant because it affects who gets elected and their subsequent treatment by the media.

Recent legislative changes are encouraging greater gender parity in French politics (Bargel et al., 2013). Yet media accusations suggest some women politicians use their sexuality to prosper. Such rumors are more likely to damage a woman's political career than a man's, as we see from Bargel et al.'s study focusing on two women elected to municipal government. The first, Samira Foé, is a young African woman married to a popular footballer. The mayor of this unnamed French municipality made Foé his deputy, placing her in charge of an underprivileged area of the city. In a few years, she achieved a meteoric political rise, becoming a member of the National Socialist Committee. Yet, as her political career advanced, Foé's media coverage changed, as did the mayor's assessment of her. Where Foé was once described as refreshing, she later became depicted as aggressive and inconsiderate. Accusing her of incompetence, the mayor replaced Foé with Malika Sebti. A mother of three, Sebti was having an open affair with the mayor. Media and political rumors suggest this liaison led to her promotion. In an interview, Sebti explained that her affair with the mayor was politically expedient (Bargel et al., 2013). At fifty, when the next elections occur, some voters may consider her too old for politics. Thus, Sebti viewed her affair with the mayor as a strategy to help her win reelection.

This study raises two important issues relevant to our inquiry. First, the average age of French deputies is 58 (Bird, Saalfeld, & Wüst, 2011), yet Sebti declared people would view her as too old for politics, even though she would still be younger than most politicians. An intersectional analysis enables us to see the double standard at work; here it is age, coupled with gender prejudice that serves to devalue a woman's worth (Ross & Comrie, 2011).

Furthermore, sexuality is relevant to politics, because it affects political careers, but it does so in a gendered way. That is, reporters and politicians disparage these two women for using their sexual wiles to gain political power. Nevertheless, there is no discussion of how the mayor misuses his political office to gain sexual favors. He is not called to account for his unethical action, but the women are called immoral. This gender dissymmetry toward politicians' sexual conduct reflects the different moral standards for men and women.

Not only are women politicians held to higher moral account, but they also receive less media coverage than men (Bahadur, 2013), and the coverage they receive is often personality-based rather than issue-driven (Trimble et al., 2014). What is more, the media often judges women politicians through feminine values even when they are undertaking traditionally masculine roles. As such, media reporting reinforces "masculinised constructions of political leadership, governance, and citizenship"

(Adcock, 2010, p. 151). Women politicians would seem to do better when they downplay gender and highlight traits that are perceived as masculine, such as analytical skills, as in the case of Kathleen Wynne. However, not all women politicians want or are able to undo their femininity; some women appear more feminine than others. Must they be seen as lesser politicians as a result (Mavin et al., 2010)?

In order to improve gender equity in politics, we need to challenge how particular styles of being, or the lack thereof, influence success. One way might be to reconsider the dominant political discourse. Examining how certain forms of language, such as rhetoric, privilege some voices over others may afford insight. I do not suggest that all women and visible minorities are less able to do rhetoric. Nevertheless, I am suggesting that rhetorical discourse may hamper a desire for diverse political voices.

The Problem With Rhetoric

An Arendtian analysis offers a rich paradigm through which to understand political actions. I say *actions* deliberately, since we cannot know a politician's intentions (Arendt, 1961). We surmise their intentions from their actions. Thus, whether a politician is lying or telling the truth is not something that we can know with certainty. We watch the performances of politicians; we do not gain access to their interior monologues. This distinction is important to acknowledge, as Arendt (1961) shows in her essay, "Truth and Politics."

Arendt (1961) argued that lying dominates the political landscape. This situation is dangerous because without access to truth, we are unable to ascertain what matters to us as a community. She maintains there is a difference between truths we cannot change, such as the sun rising, and those determined by historical or social facts. Arendt offers the example of how Joseph Stalin sought to eradicate Leon Trotsky from the Soviet memory. Trotsky represented a challenge, a factual truth, distasteful to Stalin's dictatorship; not only was it necessary to kill Trotsky, all mention of his worldly presence had to be destroyed. Thus, Stalin's regime did its utmost to destroy all references to Trotsky. Nevertheless, evidence remains that Trotsky existed. What Arendt wants us to recognize through this example is that factual truths are vulnerable since those in power can change them (or at least, attempt to). Yet the problem with trying to destroy evidence is that facts are stubborn and have a habit of reappearing. Ultimately, Arendt argues, factual truth will outlast political lies and deception.

For Arendt (1961), truth-telling is anathema to politics. The reason for this state of affairs is that rhetoric, rather than dialogue, is the main form of political discourse. Political rhetoric is a problem, according to Arendt, because it is dependent upon opinion. As public opinion changes so, too, do the stated beliefs of the politician. The politician alters her opinions in keeping with what she perceives as popular sentiments. Arendt suggests it can be damaging to factual truth if politicians keep changing their minds out of expediency.

Moreover, a politician's eloquent rhetoric is a powerful device because it enables the politician to use her powers of persuasion to change others' minds. Thinking back to Olivia Chow's campaign, one problem, according to media reports, was that she was not a particularly gifted orator. Although her responses appeared heartfelt, in politics it is the sound bite that counts. Sound bites, rather than reasoned reflections, are easy to understand. Indeed, political sound bites are vital to a news industry that feeds upon simplistic messaging. One reason for the success of politicians such as Rob Ford is their manipulation of the media through the use of simple slogans. Chow did not manipulate the media in this manner. When under attack, she did not throw the verbal punches that seasoned politicians are renowned for throwing. Some reporters argued her discomfort with political debate was because English was her second language. Given that Chow has been a politician for close to 20 years, this suggestion seems unlikely, yet she did not do rhetoric well. But does this mean that she did not do politics well?

DISCUSSION AND CONCLUSION

The media, and many voters, tend to judge politicians on their rhetorical ability, or lack thereof. One might wonder why Chow's aides did not help her craft a message that would better resonate with the public. After all, it is what a person says, rather than what she believes, that is important in the political milieu. However, what if the reason for her failure was that she wanted to engage in genuine dialogue, rather than rhetorical posturing? Media reports note that Chow's inability to use rhetoric was a severe drawback to her campaign (Moore, 2014). In the game of politics, rhetoric privileges superficiality over depth and insincerity over truthfulness. Nonetheless, why must we deem it necessary for all politicians to be rhetoricians?

For Arendt (1958), the essence of the political is an agonistic space where people propose their views and listen to different opinions. Dialogue and debate are the crux of Arendtian politics, whereby each person is willing to propose and defend their opinion. This leads to a diversity of viewpoints and the potential for an inclusive politics. Yet a political realm where rhetoric dominates may attract a particular kind of individual. Rather than diverse viewpoints, representative of the populace at large, such a political space may encourage sameness. At times, then, rhetoric may be to the detriment of truth in politics, since it serves to privilege some voices over others. If we want broader political representation, perhaps we need to reassess our penchant for political rhetoric.

In recent times, the electorate has become jaded with the spin-doctoring and mastery of the media that are perceived critical skills for political success, but perhaps it is time to rethink the political in such a way that truth would have a place. This investigation into media prejudice has also been an examination into political prejudice. Thinking about prejudice does not begin and end with the Fourth Estate. Rather, we need to explore how political discourse—and here I am referring specifically to rhetoric—may serve to negate a diversity of viewpoints. This is why, alongside an intersectional analysis, we must pay attention to the language of politics.

The dual lenses of intersectionality and Arendtian phenomenology reveal how media prejudice affects political success. Some women politicians, as Kathleen Wynne demonstrates, use political rhetoric to their advantage. In being willing to take responsibility and to apologize for mistakes, she showed leadership. But Wynne showed, *contra* Arendt, that sometimes truth can find a place in politics, even though her truth may have been no more than political strategy. Others do not do rhetoric well. Political insiders say Chow is "a 'conversation communicator' instead of a 'combative one'" (Moore, 2014, para. 8). It may be that she is not a good rhetorician, but voices like hers may be good for politics.

Arendt may not have been surprised to learn that Chow trained as a philosopher. Philosophers, Arendt declared, often fail in politics, preferring the comfort of a life of the mind to the rough and tumble of the political realm. Yet maybe there is a problem with the dominant political discourse that may serve to constrain genuine dialogue. Chow's unsuccessful political campaign revealed media prejudice against those deemed different. It also illustrated the limitations of political posturing: Not resorting to rhetorical flourishes and sound bites might encourage different conversations to emerge. Finally, changing the political tone is not only an option for women; it is also an alternative that men could take.

If we want a political realm in which marginal voices are better represented, there is much work to do. The notion that equal numbers of men and women will change parliamentary discourses is insufficient (Phillips, 1995). Using intersectionality alongside Arendtian phenomenology illustrates how media prejudice reaffirms the political status quo. To mitigate the effect of prejudice, we need to ask different questions to encourage new avenues of inquiry. Questions for further reflection might include: In what ways can we alter our physical and virtual space to better enable other forms of speech? And how can we provide solutions to the problem of the public as passive consumers rather than participants in electoral processes? Ultimately, respect for different voices could result in a new style of politics, one that is more responsive to diverse ways of being-in-the-world.

REFERENCES

Adcock, C. (2010). The politician, the wife, the citizen and her newspaper: Rethinking women, democracy and media(ted) representation. *Feminist Media Studies, 10*(2), 135–160. doi:10.1177/1464884911433255

Adler, N. (1996). Global women political leaders: An invisible history, an increasingly important future. *Leadership Quarterly, 7*(1), 133–161.

Adler, N. (2015). Women leaders: Shaping history in the 21st century. In F. Wambura Ngunjiri & S. R. Madsen (Eds.), *Women as global leaders* (pp. 21–53). Charlotte, NC: Information Age.

Arendt, H. (1958). *The human condition.* Chicago, IL: Chicago University Press.

Arendt, H. (1961). Truth and politics. In H. Arendt & J. Kohn (Eds.), *Between past and future: Eight exercises in political thought* (pp. 227–265). London, UK: Penguin.

Bahadur, N. (2013, July 8). Women in politics: Coverage focuses more on personality traits, less on issues, study finds. *The Huffington Post.* Retrieved from http://www.huffingtonpost.com/2013/07/08/women-in-politics-mediacoverage_n_3561723.html

Bargel, L., Fassin, E., & Latté, S. (2013). Illegitimate affairs: The sex of politics and the politics of sex in French contemporary politics. *Current Sociology, 61*(5–6), 661–676. doi: 10.1177/0011392113486659

Benzie, R. (2013, June, 10). Wynne defends "professional" dress code in office. *Toronto Star.* Retrieved from http://www.thestar.com/news/canada/2013/06/09/wynne_defends_professional_dress_code_in_office.html

Bird, K., Saalfeld, T., & Wüst, A. M. (Eds.). (2011). *The political representation of immigrants and minorities: Voters, parties and parliaments in liberal democracies.* London, UK: Routledge.

Blanchford, C. (2014, January 17). Olivia Chow's "My Journey" an exhausting attempt at legacy building. *National Post.* Retrieved from http://news.nationalpost.com/full-comment/christie-blatchford-olivia-chows-my-journey-an-exhausting-attempt-at-legacy-building

Bligh, M. C., & Kohles, J. C. (2008). Negotiating rhetorical leadership and women in the U.S. Senate. *Leadership, 4*(4), 381–402. doi:10.1177/1742715008095187

Blizzard, C. (2013, June 22). Premier Kathleen Wynne's softer summer image. *Toronto Sun.* Retrieved from http://www.torontosun.com/2013/06/22/premier-kathleen-wynnes-softer-summer-image

Brennan, R. (2015, April 8). Kathleen Wynne feels "responsibility" as first lesbian premier. *Toronto Star.* Retrieved from http://www.thestar.com/news/queenspark/2015/04/08/kathleen-wynne-feels-responsibility-as-first-lesbian-premier.html

Chow, O. (2014). *My journey: A memoir.* Toronto, ON: Harper Collins Canada. Retrieved from http://oliviachow.ca/

Doolittle, R. (2014, March 15). Toronto mayoral election profile: Olivia Chow. *Toronto Star.* Retrieved from http://www.thestar.com/news/city_hall/toronto2014election/2014/03/15/toronto_mayoral_election_profile_olivia_chow.html

Dunaway, J., Lawrence, R. G., Rose M., & Weber, C. R. (2013). Traits versus issues: How female candidates shape coverage of senate and gubernatorial races. *Political Research Quarterly, 66*(3), 715–726. doi: 10.1177/1065912913491464

Eagly, A. (2005). Achieving relational authenticity in leadership: Does gender matter? *The Leadership Quarterly, 15*(3), 459–474. doi: 10.1016/j.leaqua.2005.03.007

Everitt, J., & M. Camp. (2014). In versus out: LGBT politicians in Canada. *Journal of Canadian Studies, 48*(1), 226-251. doi:10.1355/jcs.2014.0013

Gardiner, R. (2015). *Gender, authenticity and leadership: Thinking with Arendt.* London, UK: Palgrave MacMillan.

Genovese, M., & Steckenrider, J. S. (Eds.). (2013). *Women as political leaders: Studies in gender and governing.* London, UK: Routledge.

Honderich, J. (2014, October 30). *Where's the outrage over racist treatment of Olivia Chow? Toronto Star.* Retrieved from http://www.thestar.com/opinion/commentary/2014/10/30/wheres_the_outrage_over_racist_sexist_olivia_chow_cartoon_honderich.html

Jervis, B. (2014, October 14). Costume drama: Olivia Chow's many vote-courting fashion statements. *Toronto Life.* Retrieved from http://www.torontolife.com/informer/toronto-politics/2014/10/10/olivia-chow-costume-drama/

Jones, S. (2015). What kind of leader was Margaret Thatcher? In F. Wambura Ngunjiri & S. R. Madsen (Eds.), *Women as global leaders* (pp. 289–305). Charlotte, NC: Information Age.

Kulich, C., Ryan M. K., & Haslam, S. A. (2014). The political glass cliff: Understanding how seat selection contributes to the underperformance of ethnic minority candidates. *Political Research Quarterly, 67*(1), 84–95. doi:10.1177/1065912913495740

Mallick, H. (2014, October 31). Olivia Chow cartoon tests Canada. *Toronto Star.* Retrieved from http://www.thestar.com/news/gta/2014/10/31/racist_olivia_chow_cartoon_tests_canada_mallick.html

Mavin, S., Bryans, P., & Cunningham, R. (2010). Fed-up with Blair's babes, Gordon's gals, Cameron's cuties, Nick's nymphetes. Challenging gendered media representations of women politicians. *Gender in Management: An International Journal, 25*(7), 550–569. doi: 10.1108/17542411011081365

Moore, O. (2014, October). Olivia Chow's fall from grace. *The Globe and Mail.* Retrieved from http://www.theglobeandmail.com/news/toronto/olivia-chows-fall-from-grace-in-the-toronto-mayoral-race/article21341350/

Phillips, A. (1995). *The politics of presence.* Oxford, UK: Oxford University Press.

Preville, P. (2013). No. 3: Because Kathleen Wynne is one of us. *Toronto Life.* Retrived from http://torontolife.com/city/reasons-to-love-toronto-2013/4/

Ross, K., & M. Comrie. (2011). The rules of the (leadership) game: Gender, politics and news. *Journalism, 13*(8), 969–984.doi:10.1177/1464884911433255

Ryan, M. K., Haslam, S. A., & Postes, T. (2007). Reactions to the glass cliff. *Journal of Organizational Change Management, 20*(2), 182–197. doi: 10.1108/09534810710724748

Von Wahl, A. (2011). A "woman's revolution from above"? Female leadership, intersectionality, and public policy under the Merkel government. *German Politics, 20*(3), 392–409. doi: 10.1080/09644008.2011.606569

PART III

WOMEN IN FILM AND TELEVISION

CHAPTER 10

THE "GOGGLEBOX" AND GENDER

An Interdiscursive Analysis of Television Representations and Professional Femininities

Helen Rodgers, Liz Yeomans, and Sallyann Halliday
Leeds Beckett University

Professional career expectations (and trajectories) are constructed and ne-gotiated by decisions based upon individual experiences and interactions with the external social world (Bolton & Muzio, 2008; Elliott & Stead, 2008; Hirschorn, 1989). Numerous researchers have argued that the construction and perpetuation of gendered occupational stereotypes have an important influence on career choice by imparting powerful visual and textual imag-ery of what it is to be professional and what it is to be gendered in the work-place (Czarniawska, 2010; Gill, 2006; Mavin, 2009). Further, subtle social processes underlie the disparities and inadequacies in women's profession-al progress (Carli & Eagly, 2007; Critchett, 2010; Howells, 2014), with gen-dered media representations influencing constructs of gendered identities

Gender, Media, and Organization, pages 169–196
Copyright © 2016 by Information Age Publishing
All rights of reproduction in any form reserved.

and career choices over time (Gill, 2006; Kelan, 2012; Mavin, 2009; Rehn, 2008; van Zoonen, 1994).

This chapter explores the experiences of women in educational and work settings across three different professions, where gendered identities—and in particular femininities—have been represented in complex and controversial ways in the media: public relations (PR), criminology/police, and politics/government. In so doing, we respond, empirically, to the "calls for a research agenda which critically examines how women and femininity are now being included in the organisational sphere" (Billing, 2011 cited in Lewis, 2014, p. 1848).

Using the framework of the "circuit of culture" (du Gay, Hall, Janes, Madsen, Mackay, & Negus, 2013), we sought to explore the shaping of cultural meaning via television representations (the "gogglebox"[1]) of gender in relation to professional careers and gendered professional identities (Davis, 2015; Kelan, 2012; Yeomans, 2014).

THE PROFESSIONS AND POPULAR CULTURE

The media—and specifically television representations of gendered professional work—chronicles a flourishing set of discourses on sexism, ageism, racism, lookism, and so on, across time and across organizations. A brief examination of public relations (PR), the police, and political professions and their representations in popular culture provides the context for our study. While the study draws primarily upon research from professionals in the United Kingdom (UK), the television shows used as illustration are drawn from across Europe, Australia, and the United States of America (U.S.) and were viewed in the UK by research participants.

Public relations, as a relatively new profession, entered popular culture in the early 1990s. The excesses of consumerism, and PR's role within it, were parodied in the UK television sitcom *Absolutely Fabulous* (Spiers, Humphreys, French, Perkins, & Saunders, 1992–2012), which was first broadcast in 1992 (Rhodes & Westwood, 2008). *Absolutely Fabulous*, or "*Ab Fab*," depicts the often self-destructive exploits of two middle-aged women, PR agent Edina Monsoon and her best friend, the magazine editor Patsy Stone, and their pursuit of a hedonistic lifestyle. In parodying the world of PR and media, however, *Ab Fab* unwittingly created one of the most pervasive PR gender stereotypes: that of the "PR girl" and its image of fun, champagne, and launch parties where "very little 'real work' is actually done and zero contribution made to society" (Rhodes & Westwood, 2008, p. 115). Further, a feminist analysis of *Ab Fab* reveals its contradictions: While intended as a knowing critique of the narcissism arising from consumer culture, Rhodes and Westwood (2008) argued that its focus on image and fashion could be reproducing among some viewers the "very desires and longings it mocks and works against" (p. 115). If *Ab Fab* signaled the emergence of the PR girl during the 1990s, the highly popular romantic sitcom *Sex and the City* (Bushnell, King, Coulter, Engler, & Star, 1998–2004) could be said to embody the stereotype through its portrayal of the independent, glamorous, and sexually liberated character Samantha Jones, who runs her own PR business. For McRobbie (2008), *Sex and the City* exemplifies the post-feminist ideology of *girl power* but in doing so finds "embedded within these forms of feminine popular culture, a tidal wave of invidious insurgent patriarchalism which is hidden beneath the celebrations of female freedom" (p. 539). As forms of popular culture that are subject to contradictory feminist and post-feminist readings, both *Ab Fab* and *Sex and the City* are open to multiple interpretations (Krijnen & van Bauwel, 2015). The hidden aspects of patriarchy, as Elliott and Stead (2014) observed in their research into the pedagogical value of media representation, merely "reproduce gendered power relations and position women as outsiders" (p. 5).

PR men, by contrast, are stereotypically represented as political "spin doctors" in screen portrayals (Johnston, 2010). These include the popular British television satire *The Thick of It* (Ianucci et al., 2005–2012) and its abrasive, manipulative character of Malcolm Tucker, who is the Prime Minister's director of communications, and the less well-known *Absolute Power* (Morton, Shapeero, Tavener, & Lawson, 2003–2005), in which the amoral Charles Prentiss runs a government relations consultancy. While our focus is necessarily on challenging media mis(s)representations of women leaders and managers, it is important to be aware of male occupational stereotypes because they often function to represent masculine organizational power, thus shaping popular perceptions and expectations of the professional role in everyday life (Billing, 2011).

We now turn to a discussion of televised representations of women in the police. A career in the police, and the role of a police officer, is often presented as exciting and challenging within popular television series and other forms of popular culture. Some early portrayals of policewomen in television drama arguably helped to break down some of the barriers in terms of the perception held by the public about the capability of women police; examples of such portrayals are Angie Dickinson as Pepper Anderson in *Policewoman* (Collins, DeBlasio, Ganzer, Newland, & Shear, 1974–1978) and the cast of *Charlie's Angels* (Donnelley, Baron, Goff, & Roberts, 1976–1981, cited in Martin, 1996). However, gendered differences continue to be reflected in the portrayal of the power and competence of men and the assertive and ambitious nature of women. Modern crime dramas over the last 10 years portray main characters as people who "eat, sleep and drink their work" (Shepherdson, 2014, p. 4) their work and often putting their job first, sometimes at great cost to themselves (Heath & Gilbert,

1996; Shepherdson, 2014). For example, in television series such as *Forbrydelsen* [*The Killing*] (Sveistrup, Hoppe, Horsten, Nyholm, & Wullenweber, 2007–2012), *Engrenages* [*Spiral*] (Landois et al., 2005–2014), *Scott and Bailey* (Wainwright et al., 2011–2015), and *The Fall* (Cubitt & Verbruggen, 2013–2015), policewomen are portrayed as being single, separated, or divorced (Martin, 1996) and as existing on the boundaries of societal norms. Indeed, Helen Mirren's groundbreaking character Detective Chief Inspector (DCI) Jane Tennison in the 1990s UK TV crime drama *Prime Suspect* (LaPlante & Menual, 1991; LaPlante, Cubitt, & Strickland, 1992; LaPlante, & Drury, 1993), while considered one of the most realistic portrayals of a policewoman, depicted the success she had at work at the expense of her personal life. Men and women are more likely to be represented as equal in sitcoms like *The Thin Blue Line* (Elton & Birkin, 1995–1996), but in crime drama men are much more likely to play dominant roles (Martin, 1996).

For the last professional grouping, throughout the last three decades, careers in politics and government represented in television move through myriad representations of the satirical, chaotic, dysfunctional *Twenty Twelve* (Morton, 2011–2012); bucolic, comedic, and bumbling *Yes, Prime Minister* (Jay, Lynn, Lotterby, & Whitmore, 1986–1987); through to the serious, dramatic, and globally engaged. The serious genre of political television drama often portrays women and men as scheming, dark, and self-serving in nature; *House of Cards* (Willimon et al., 2013–2015) and *Scandal* (Rhimes, Bryne, Verica, Bokelburg, Zisk, & Liddi-Brown, 2012–2015) are both popular examples of this genre. In this arena, work may also be undertaken at a super-human pace and on heroic scale, as represented in the American fast-paced political thriller, *24* (Cochran, Surnow, Cassar, & Turner, 2001–2010) or the UK television spy series *Spooks* (Wolstencroft, Riley, & Nalluri, 2002–2011). In both of these series, women and men are shown to work equally in countering crime and terrorism. A popular role in the dramatization of political life in the world of counter terrorism is that of "M," portrayed in the James Bond series of films. The Bond franchise has navigated the decades of popular culture, from the early representations of Fleming's novels in 1965 through to the current portrayals of the archetypal, heroic fictional intelligence operator, James Bond. In the film *Casino Royale* and the three subsequent films (Wilson & Broccoli, 2006, 2008, 2012, 2015), Bond, played by the actor Daniel Craig, experiences life working for a female boss, "M," played by the actor Judi Dench. Of academic note within this series of Bond films is the representation of complex and strong female characterizations emerging in response to a modern form of Bond, who is still firmly situated in patriarchy, yet starting to experiment with moments of vulnerability and *femininity* (Funnell, 2011; Neuendorf, Gore, Dalessandro, Janstova & Snyder-Suby, 2010). Furthermore, Dench's character "M," in transgressing normative gender and age stereotypes, stands as a "cultural symbol of defiance, where her mere presence disrupts Bond's traditional notions of gender (and sexuality) and normative temporality" (Krainitski, 2014, p. 37). Thus, increasingly in film and television drama, women are portrayed at senior levels in political and government dramas as smart, self-disciplined, committed, determined, and courageous, yet in reality, the broader media scrutiny of women in "real" senior political positions is often impoverished, overlooked, scrutinized as negative and much maligned for emphasis on style and appearance over substance and policy (Ross, 2004; van Zoonen, 2006). Interestingly, women in senior positions in the UK's Foreign and Commonwealth Office (FCO) are rarely directly evaluated or represented in the mainstream media (Rahman, 2012).

The question remains: How is meaning actually shaped for those working in these professions and consuming television as a cultural commodity? Researchers in the field of social sciences and cultural studies (Acosta-Alzuru, 2003; Coleman, 2009; Gill, 2006; Gurevitch & Scannell, 2003; Hall, 1982; Johnson, 1986; McRobbie, 2008; Yeomans, 2014) remind us that the communication process is never neutral. Indeed, Acosta-Alzuru (2003) argued: "Writers, actors, media executives, texts and audiences are caught in a ritual process of establishing shared meanings, which is embedded in culture and power differentials" (p. 288). Television and other media representations of women in work play an important yet permeable role in the (re)construction and (re)negotiation of gendered professional identities.

A FRAMEWORK FOR THE STUDY: WHAT CAN WE LEARN FROM THE FIELD OF CULTURAL STUDIES?

The use of the circuit of culture framework (du Gay et al., 1997, 2013) comprising five aspects of a cultural artifact or *text* (regulation, representation, identity, production, and consumption) allows us to explore the interplay of media representation or (mis)representation on the (re)construction of professional identities through culturally situated and (always) gendered lenses (Figure 10.1). Initially developed to explore processes of modern cultural change and practice in a digitalized world for the Sony Walkman case study,[2] this relational model depicts the cultural process (of meaning making) as a complex and interdependent set of moments that are distinct, but not discrete, and accepts Johnson's (1986) proposition that the study of individual moments only gives us a partial view of how the meanings associated with a particular cultural product are produced, negotiated, and contested (du Gay et al., 1997, 2013).

For us, the interesting aspect of the circuit of culture is that these moments contribute to a shared cultural space in which meaning is created, shaped, modified, and recreated, mirroring organizational meaning

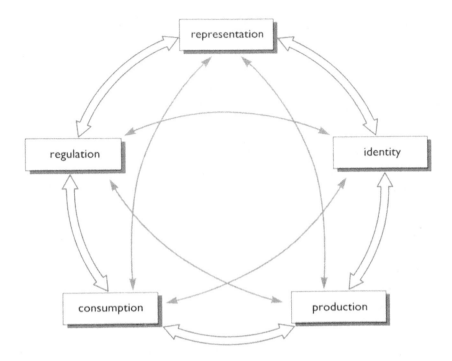

Figure 10.1 Du Gay et al.'s (1997, p. 3) Circuit of culture. *Doing cultural studies: The story of the Sony Walkman* by Du Gay, Paul et al., Reproduced with permission of Sage Publications, Incorporated in the format Book via Copyright Clearance Center.

making as "multi-directional, socially interacted" (Collinson, 2003, p. 142, cited in Elliott & Stead, 2008, p. 164).

"Regulation" comprises controls on cultural activity (e.g., legal, institutionalized systems, to the informal controls of cultural norms and expectations); it governs what is culturally acceptable and practicable. "Representation" is the form an object takes and the socially constructed meanings encoded in this. The moment of "identity" refers to the meanings that are created by communities/audiences within their own social networks and memberships. The "production" moment outlines the process by which creators of cultural products (e.g., writers, directors, actors, and television production teams) encode their own meanings. For the purposes of this research, we wanted to focus on the shaping of cultural meaning as relevant to women within these professions. However, we see the investigation of the production of cultural meaning as an important next stage in our research, in line with previous studies that have adopted the circuit of culture framework (Acosta-Alzuru, 2003; O'Reilly, 2005). The moment of "consumption" is where audiences decode messages (reinterpreted according to social and cultural contexts).

The circuit of culture emphasizes the relationship between culture and meaning, which is "constructed—given, produced—through cultural practices; it is not simply 'found' in things" (du Gay et al., 2013, p. 8). Within this perspective, television representations of women in work play a central and permanent role in the (re)construction and (re)negotiation of gendered professional identities and, there is a compelling need to examine the social engagement, associations, and gendered responses to such media representations (Mavin, 2009; Rehn, 2008).

RESEARCH DESIGN

Our research explored three different professions to see what phenomena arose in relation to the themes of gender, media, and professional identities. The research sample was drawn from three courses of academic study related to these professions (UCAS, 2014; Universities UK, 2012), at one university in the north of England, and from the study's three professions (public relations, psychology/criminology, and government/politics), with participants at four different stages of their professional careers—senior (females with fifteen or more years of professional experience, operating at senior level), middle level (females with between six to fourteen years of professional experience, operating at mid-level), beginners or early career (females with between one to five years of professional experience, operating at junior level), and student prospectors (university undergraduates, both male and female).

The professions that we chose to study had important distinctions in their gendered demography: One profession (PR) was predominantly female in its demographic (yet men occupied the majority of senior positions within the field); one profession was historically perceived as predominantly male (politics and government), with many recent lobbyists calling for greater and urgent gender rebalancing;[3] and one profession had been historically male dominated but was demonstrating a steady rise in numbers of female professionals moving into senior roles (criminology and the police).[4] By researching the three professions, we sought insights into the relationship between television representations and women's professional identity across career stages. Moreover, we wanted to test the robustness of the circuit of culture as a framework for examining the interplay between television representations and (re)constructions of professional gendered identities.

METHODOLOGY

We adopted a qualitative methodology with two phases to our investigation. Phase one involved three one-hour, face-to-face interviews with course leaders in PR, criminology/psychology, and government/politics to establish agreement for research and to gain an understanding of key parameters of interest for each course in relation to gender and media. Data from these initial interviews helped us to set a consistent research approach and interview design for the student focus groups and the practitioner interviews. Subsequently, we conducted three focus groups, each an hour in length, with undergraduate students enrolled in three courses: PR, criminology, and politics. The second phase involved face-to-face or telephone interviews with practitioners operating at senior, middle, and early career stages within the three professions (nine in total). In the case of politics and government, FCO government officials who were working overseas for the British government, rather than politicians, were interviewed. Each interview lasted 30 to 40 minutes. All participation was voluntary and compliant with the university's research protocols of informed consent, confidentiality, and anonymity.[5] Table 10.1 outlines the sampling frame and the pseudonyms assigned for each of the participants.

All participants were given the same set of questions in advance, examining general career influences and professional experiences initially and then narrowing into questions concerning the role of the media in general and television representations in particular. Data collected were rich in nature and highlighted participants' personal career motivations and experiences, with a specific focus on the role or influence of media representations in relation to the participants own professional identity.

We probed for ways in which media had an influence in terms of choices and decisions concerning careers, beliefs and values, and the emotions of individuals, and we explored barriers to working within the profession, including notions of prevailing stereotypes, unlikely jobs for a woman, reality versus representation, and senior role requirements. Prior to the focus groups and interviews, participants were asked to give some thought

TABLE 10.1 Research Participants				
Profession/ subject	Student Focus group Student prospectors	Early-career professional (1–5 years)	Mid-career professional (6–14 years)	Senior-career professional (15+ years)
Politics	Sarah, Ann, and Tom	Tom		
FCO			Penny	Isabella and Maddy
Criminology/ Police	Josh and Louisa	Amy	Lucy	Natasha
PR	Hannah, Emma, and James	Victoria	Rebecca	Tracey

to image(s) that represented a form of influence on their own choice of career/profession. Thus, we were careful to encourage the participants to relate their own associations to popular television representations in order to examine their personal identification with these representations, rather than use prompts of any kind. Cultural references were therefore offered by the participants from their own cultural standpoints. Only later in the research interviews and focus groups did we offer specific images of television portrayals, and (if recognized by the participant) these examples were used to probe for further response in relation to the circuit of culture. Although small in scale, our study was focused, inductive, and exploratory, providing participants with the opportunity to reflect on the complex interplay between representation, consumption, identity regulation, and, to a lesser extent, production offered by the circuit of culture in relation to television portrayals, thus adding flesh to our research interests and questions about the role of media in (re)constructing gendered professional identities.

CRITICAL DISCOURSE ANALYSIS

In analyzing our data, we adopted approaches from critical discourse analysis (CDA) defined as "emancipatory" and "politically committed to social change" (Jorgensen & Phillips, 2002, p. 64). If discourse is understood to be social action through text and talk, then the concepts relevant to our analysis are "interdiscursivity" and "intertextuality" (Fairclough, 1992, p. 117). Interdiscursivity might occur when, for example, the policy discourse of gender mainstreaming is reaffirmed, contradicted, or mixed in with other discourses surrounding gender and work, found in cultural texts (i.e., TV shows), and participants' talk, which is, in turn, mediated by discourses in policy and media.

Intertextuality is a type of interdiscursivity, in which the emphasis is "the influence of history on a text and to a text's influence on history" (Jorgensen & Phillips, 2002, p. 74), referring to what has been said before using manifest words and phrases. Fairclough (2010) observed that discourse is related to ideology and hegemony, such that some discourses will be privileged over others at a given point in time, and these can be signs of social stability or social change/resistance to dominant discourses. CDA enabled us to identify dominant ideologies (e.g., feminism and post-feminism) evident in our participants' talk about media representations and discourses, including support, resistance, or ambivalence towards these discourses. Analyzing the interdiscursive and intertextual features of our data enables the interplay of the five moments in the circuit of culture to be articulated.[6]

KEY FINDINGS AND DISCUSSION
FROM THE EMPIRICAL RESEARCH

The primary research uncovered a wide range of experiences and expectations within the different career and professional contexts. We continue with an exploration of themes as they emerged from the primary data. Issues concerning regulation; professional identity; early career influences; the influence of media; and the response to requirements on appearance, looks, and media scrutiny were evident in the focus group and individual interviews. In addition, some of the professional practitioners noted emerging career stage barriers and variable responses to the circuit of culture framework. The richness and subtleties of the data are presented and discussed using the nodes from the circuit of culture as a reference point.

REGULATION

Aspects of regulation in social structures that have facilitated women's progression into senior positions in two of the professions studied are well documented. Initiatives within the police profession have sought to address gender balance and to understand barriers to female career progression at managerial and leadership positions.[7] In the UK, the Gender Agenda was launched in 2001 and sought to "start a dialogue and increase understanding of the reality of being a woman officer in today's police service" ("Gender Agenda," n.d., para. 1). The Gender Agenda was followed by an updated, second version in 2006 ("Gender Agenda 2".[8] The aim throughout Gender Agendas 1 and 2 was to develop a common understanding of the issues affecting women, and the ability to achieve the potential within the Service. Gender Agenda 3 was launched in October 2014 ("Gender Agenda 3," 2014) and is seeking to build on the work that has already been undertaken through the implementation of Gender Agendas 1 and 2.

The hard work involved in this structural, long-term change was acknowledged by Lucy, working in the police profession, as well as Isabella and Maddy, working in the FCO. As Lucy commented:[9]

> There are those sort of stereotypes and unfortunately a lot of the stories that go in the media don't really help. Obviously we as a force, as other forces do, have roles that for whatever reason don't tend to attract women and we have to work really hard to understand why that is and break down some of the barriers.

Within government, women in senior, decision-making posts have been encouraged by the concept of gender mainstreaming (Booth & Bennett, 2002; Rawlings, 2013). Researched and developed into policy in the late

1990s, all UN member states are required "to ensure increased representation of women at all decision-making levels in national, regional and international institutions" as legitimated in 2000 by the UN Security Council Resolution, 1325 (UN S/Res/1325, 2000, p. 2, note 1).[10]

Although criticisms of old boys' networks in senior levels of the FCO still existed, exclusionary practices were seen to be changing, with signs of a significant shift that focused on a more open and diverse culture in which formal and collaborative mentoring and shadowing schemes helped early and mid-career female professionals to develop and grow toward senior appointments. One of the participants, Isabella, explained: "Things are changing slowly, we've been promoted, there are more female directors and we have a female high commissioner coming in now. It is opening up, but there are still a lot of Oxford/Cambridge types too."

Regulation was less pronounced in the PR profession, but in 2015, the UK's Chartered Institute of Public Relations (2016) launched a manifesto to help narrow the 20% gender pay gap. This included steps to support organizations and individual members and to lobby government on flexible working initiatives.[11]

IDENTITY

Issues relating to both gender and professional identity were apparent, with differing foci and concerns, across all three professions. There also seemed to be awareness of the effect of polarized stereotypes (Carli & Eagly, 2007; Czarniawska, 2010; Mavin, 2009) and the need to negotiate through different gendered and sociocultural contexts (Elliot & Stead, 2008; Kelan, 2012).

PR, as a relatively new profession, was observed to be attempting to establish an identity in the business world, leaving an abundance of space for gendered media portrayals and popular perceptions of PR to flourish. One of the participants, Victoria, summarized the female stereotype: "If you say you are a PR girl, I think that people automatically think you're a party girl; that you're up for a good time, that you're not particularly intelligent, maybe." Rebecca concurred with this view: "In a comms role, everyone around you brings their own perceptions and they want to you to fulfill a role that they want comms to be." Finally, Tracey linked a lack of confidence within the industry to a lack of *voice*, or agency, among young female practitioners, commenting: "We don't know what we stand for. We're not confident as an industry about what we're offering. If we haven't got that voice as an industry, then as a young woman how *do* you find a voice?"

Within the data related to the police profession, there were issues relating to the traditionally gendered notions and professional requirements for the job. Natasha commented on the way in which women police professionals may find themselves having to adopt perceived male traits within their roles or to progress through the ranks:

> Sometimes women feel that in particular roles or to achieve promotion or get on, they almost kind of have to take on male traits, and I don't think everybody can do that and [that] everybody is comfortable doing that. If they have children, they are generally the primary carer, and some of these environments require you to be on call and have quite complex shift patterns, and if you don't have a partner or family who are able to provide that care, it's very difficult. Because where do you get childcare at 3 a.m. when you're on call? So I think there are some barriers certainly that are more challenging [for women].

Clearly, Natasha perceived conflicting demands of work and home roles for women police professionals. By contrast, professional representation for Penny at the FCO was seen as out of the view of the general public, as she reflected on the low public profile of the role: "I don't think I've seen much, by way of the media, about being in public policy. It's almost silent on that as a career option, and many others." Later in the interview, Penny acknowledged the professional requirements for a low profile and the subsequent impact that this had on media perceptions: "That's how they [the media] see us, as faceless bureaucrats. Bureaucrats try to stay out of the media a lot, they're not in the media a lot."

Sensitivities about the links to political life, public service, and the negative public connotations associated with politicians were also apparent; as a result, professional identity performed through femininity was managed differently in different contexts, splintered, culturally situated, and multilayered (Genz, 2009; Lewis, 2014). Penny explained her lived experience of this:

> So part of it is, I've splintered it a bit, so I can say, I can present myself in different ways to people. I can say, look (umm) I'm a civil servant, which they assume bureaucratic, blah blah blah, or I can say I work on climate change issues and then that definitely gets a reaction as well (umm). So I will and do talk about the things I'm doing rather than my job description for instance, as a different way of connecting to people.

Establishing and maintaining identity, particularly gendered professional identity, while associated with elements of media production, representation, and consumption presented deep personal connections to lived experience and cultural histories. As Maddy voiced: "Why do they assume that I am going to make the tea? Because I'm not, I'm chairing the meeting!" Within this, women professionals worked through the complexities and challenges presented in their social world (Elliott & Stead, 2008; Genz, 2009), within a popular culture that seemed to perpetuate stereotypes (Mavin, 2009) of women's roles within the workplace.

MEDIA CONSUMPTION

Regarding professional career choice, the role of early life influences and personal conviction was very strong for the majority of participants: parents, family dynamics, teachers, and lecturers were seen to play a key role in influencing career expectations and choices. Maddy reflected, "I always wanted to be a fighter pilot, dad was in the Royal Air Force, and the fact that I can't see (laughter) was bit of a drawback. I thought, Foreign Office, next best thing. What's not to love?" The analysis of the data made clear that media consumption was an addition to, or embedded within, these key influences (Elliot & Stead, 2008). Across all three professions, career choices were closely linked to perceptions of skills matched to personal interests (e.g., big-picture thinking skills, negotiating, and advocacy skills for the government and FCO; creative and writing skills for PR; and social, critical, and organizational skills for police). In comparing "creative" PR work with the "aggressive" image of marketing, Rebecca appeared to express a more explicitly gendered career choice: "Public relations offered something creative, involving writing. A better fit than marketing, which was a more aggressive thing; PR seemed to capture that creativity." By contrast, the potential to make a difference in the world infused Penny's narrative: "What drew me to climate change was the commitment to doing something about a very big global problem. I've always cared about environmental issues, even at school."

As the interviews progressed, the relation between media and career expectations became clearer. Police work, as represented through popular crime dramas and programs, was described as adding meaning and generating interest in a career in the police, particularly for young females; however, the choice of role within the service was often gendered and the challenge to (re)construct this was acknowledged. As Amy described:

> Things are portrayed and you perceive them as, "yeah, that's a male, that's a female job," and when you do come to make a choice for work, you do choose you might think to yourself as well, "I'm not like that, I couldn't be hard like that." So that imagery that was portrayed to me at the time, maybe by the media stopped me from making that career choice.

The media role in portraying occupational stereotyping was also recognized by Natasha:

> I still think in the media they don't portray women as equal to men in most stories that you read. There'll be that slant that if it involves a man it'll be a big piece, if it's about a woman it'll be a smaller piece. There are still clues that you'll see all of the time. I'm still not convinced that society sees it as equal either in terms of the role.

One of the politics undergraduates, Ann, noted that for her the media stereotypes had a counterinfluence, encouraging female students to opt for a traditionally male subject area: "It [the media] definitely influences how we feel about the course that we're doing, due to the fact that it's [politics], it's seen as a male dominated subject." While professional identity and career interest among FCO professionals was closely connected with passion, an interest in big picture issues and the need to make a difference, with a very limited association to popular television portrayals of their occupation, even though a specific political sitcom, *Yes, Minister* (Jay, Lynn, Lotterby, Whitmore & Allen, 1980–1984), was mentioned by Penny, who observed:

> I don't think many people choose this career option, based on because they've watched *Yes Minister* or anything (laughs). So unlike, say, medicine, or law or something that is on television, or is in the news media much more. I think this kind of profession attracts people for different reasons than the media.

Interaction with differing forms of media varied between groups; of particular note among our findings was the marked difference in the discourses of media use or consumption between the undergraduate participants and the more senior practitioners across all three professions. Undergraduates talked animatedly of being heavily involved in social media and thus being more likely to interact with, produce, represent, consume, and identify through newer forms of media (Twitter, Buzz-feed, Instagram, Netflix, etc.) than all other participants. This finding was very pronounced in the politics and PR students; for example, Sarah, from the politics course, recounted: "So, for instance, on Twitter, I've had responses to my tweets saying that they are going to fuck the feminist out of me; it's horrific, it's disgusting." While social media enabled younger women to contribute to powerful online discussions, negative feedback had the propensity to harm emotionally, even from a distance.

Conversely, an indication that television consumption had a positive influence on professional career choice and gendered identities was also notable and apparent in PR practitioner responses. Victoria offered an example of this kind of influence:

> Two of my favorite shows are *Absolutely Fabulous*: I *love* that show. And Patsy in there, she runs a magazine and Edina has her own PR agency. And in *Sex and the City*, you've got Samantha and she doesn't need a man. Whereas, the other two, they are desperate. But what they have in common is that they are very strong, opinionated women. I think I may have subliminally chosen a career path off the back of [these shows], while identifying with characters like that. Yes, I watched both of them as I was growing up.

Television consumption, then, was individual, distinct, and differently contextualized for the different research participants, where situated realities and traditional norms were consumed, contested, and interpreted in myriad forms. Undoubtedly, the role of early life and other external influences figured largely, creating powerful cultural associations, yet media representations also had the power to entice, inspire, and sometimes horrify.

Associations with new forms of media, among them Twitter and Buzzfeed, presented innovative opportunities in the shaping of cultural meaning. The opportunity to both produce and consume, or "prosume"[12] (Krijnen, T., & van Bauwel, 2015), placed within the hands of all, meant a potential to construct more meaningful cultural realities with the power to emancipate and to challenge existing hegemonies.

REPRESENTATION

Television representations of the respective professions drew some of the strongest reactions from the focus groups and interviews. Some of the PR practitioners and students expressed resentment at the disconnect between the representations produced by certain forms of media and their own realities. Rebecca summarized this frustration: "I've always resented the media portrayal because it looked like a lot more fun and a lot less hard work." Similarly, Tracey attributed popular perceptions of PR work as well as exploitative work practices to media stereotypes, commenting: "A lot of women coming through still think PR is fluffy and consumer driven and that's why a lot of cosmetic agencies and fashion agencies get away with things such as unpaid internships."

Yet complex cultural contexts were differently consumed and negotiated, as demonstrated by Emma in her narrative about the character of Samantha Jones in *Sex and the City*:

> I don't think she is [a PR bunny]; I think she's quite authoritative. I think she's quite a strong woman but because of the niche of the show, it doesn't really focus on what she does specifically. I think if they did a show on her being in control of the business, it would be a very different TV show. But whenever everyone talks about *Sex and City* and Samantha Jones, they do go for the PR bunny, going out for cocktails, et cetera. I think that can be quite frustrating being in PR yourself to kind of see those and that's what people think you do, which is far from the truth.

Although the gendered media stereotypes of the "PR girl" and male political "spin doctor" (represented by the character of Malcolm Tucker in the UK television satire, *The Thick of It*) were interpreted and consumed differently (Kelan, 2012), this was largely situated within a dominant discourse of traditional authority and power (P. Lewis, 2014; Simpson & Lewis, 2005). Television representations were not only widely acknowledged to influence popular perceptions of the PR role, but Victoria who worked in consumer PR, felt compelled to actively play up to the PR girl stereotype as represented by Samantha in *Sex and the City*:

> You know when we talk to our friends, you say "what have you been up to?" You never talk about the day [job] doing coverage reports, or doing content calendars or any of this kind of stuff. Or writing press releases. You talk about the amazing campaign you are about to launch; the event I went to last month.

By contrast, Rebecca, working in local government, found herself unfavorably compared to the well-known political spin doctor Alastair Campbell, who worked as communications director to UK Prime Minister Tony Blair during the 1990s. Rebecca explained that she was expected to both meet and be constrained by the demands of the masculine stereotype of the political spin doctor:

> People would use the language they had seen on the television. They would use things like, "I'm going to take this line." I used to find a lot of Alastair Campbell-isms played back at me. I definitely felt I wasn't living up to that and because of that they didn't get where I was coming from. You sometimes felt you had failed expectations if you hadn't successfully managed to demonstrate media manipulation.

The interplays of representation, consumption, and associative identity between professional work and media television representation displayed in dynamic and fluid forms confirms the subtle processes at play in the creation of cultural meaning, viewed through the circuit of culture. It supports the view of the power of television in "representing and shaping the actual behaviour of people" (Mavin, Bryans, & Cunningham, 2010, p. 556). Moreover, we found in these "representations a likeness of organizations suffused with a creative rendition of their location in culture;...much of this culture is focused on satirising or condemning the office, the boss, the factory and so on" (Rhodes & Parker, 2008, p. 632).

Media focus on dress, femininity, and appearance and looking the part played to and against women's career expectations in two of the professions researched (politics and government; PR). For example, Sarah was fully aware of the cultural contradictions evoked by women female leaders in the public eye (Mavin et al., 2010; van Zoonen, 2006), commenting with disdain: "I'm so sick of Theresa May's shoes being discussed rather than her actual policies and what she does in Parliament. If you go to the *Daily Mail*, there's pages and pages on her different outfits." Further concerns were expressed by Sarah over media critiques:

Hillary Clinton was referred to so much as a bitch during her [2008] campaign...when all she was doing was asserting herself. If you're a man and you're asserting yourself you're confident, you're charismatic, and you've got style, whereas if you're a woman doing it [asserting yourself] you're a bitch, you're manipulative.

These concerns over media scrutiny of women in public roles were echoed by Penny at the FCO, with somewhat negative implications for those with political aspirations:

And I think it's pretty clear, in Australia anyway, if you're a female politician, you're going to have to deal with a whole set of issues about appearance and very, quite frankly, sexist things that a male politician just won't have to deal with.

Paradoxically, in PR, Tracey expressed disaffection with younger women's unawareness of the competitive nature of the profession and the hard work required to progress. Her perception that younger practitioners reinforced sexualized stereotypes through their dress and behavior, while lacking in confidence and agency, or "voice," could be attributed to societal pressures to look feminine: "The young women need to dress and act for the part. Some of them look like Miss Whiplash.... There's an issue of young women having a voice full stop. I think that it maybe feels unfeminine to be more business-orientated."

However, research participants were keen to identify with positive images of women professionals, where a closer and perhaps more "real" association between production, representation and professional identity was evident, as Natasha explained:

TV images of women in crime programs have a positive effect. A lot of them portray women in a very positive light. The women in a lot of the police crime dramas are senior women.... What it does do is generates people's interest and makes people believe that you can actually join as a woman and achieve a certain rank or grade.... So I think those seem to be a lot more positive for women the ones that have currently been out there.

Recent UK television portrayals were perceived to show more solid and realistic possibilities for professional women in complex roles across the professions. For example, Rebecca observed: "I was really pleased to see *Babylon* (Boyle, El Hosaini, Baird, Bain, Armstrong, & Brown, 2014) because it showed a [PR] woman operating in a complex series of relationships that had to be managed, as well as the work itself. She's glamorous; she's self-contained." Similar was Sarah's description of Gillian Anderson's portrayal of Stella in *The Fall* (Cubitt & Verbruggen, 2013–2015): "She's amazing, she's strong, she's powerful, she's confident, she's sexually active, . . . and she's leading the investigation."

Representations of and associations with glamor, sexual liberation, and über femininity—for example Gillian Anderson's portrayal of Stella in *The Fall*, and Kim Cattrall's portrayal of Samantha Jones in *Sex and the City*—appear to offer emotive, compelling constructions of professional femininities for professionals and for female student prospectors—a space where overly "feminine femininities" are valued by some consumers of television and bestowed with an emancipatory form of power.

Affirmative discourses, arising from study participants in different disciplines and age groups, emerged not only because these female television characters are depicted as highly professionally competent; they also retain glamour and overt sexuality, seemingly prerequisites for contemporary popular culture in its appropriation and successful commercialization of feminist discourse (McRobbie, 2008). Within this discourse, the "hierarchical relationship existing between the different modes femininity" (Lewis, 2014, p. 1859) is demonstrable, with some representations aligned with a new form of feminized power like Stella, in *The Fall*, while others still search for a powerful or convincing voice in connection with Samantha, in *Sex and the City*.

In producing representations that appeared to be closely matched to lived experience. In the example of *Happy Valley* (Lewis, Lyn, Wainwright & Fywell, 2014), the leading actor spoke to local police offers close to the set, and the television representation was deemed to be "much more real," as Natasha described:

> I think they've got better at it . . . as a force . . . one of the ones that was filmed in our Force area was the *Happy Valley* series with Sarah Lancashire. . . . Sarah actually came and spent a significant amount of time with officers on patrol so that the role that she portrayed was much more real, and I think that's the key—she spoke to people doing that job and spent time with people and saw firsthand what it really is like rather than trying to portray a role that in her own mind should look like.

This connection to emotive realism to what Coleman (2013) refers to as interactive mirrors has the ability to "move us, make us feel moved" (Featherstone, 2010, p. 195), and this resounds back into the professions. Here, there are attractive possibilities for the future. Media representations are perceived as plausible and able to reach and touch the aspirations of professional women; as such, the possibility exists for emancipatory change (Jorgensen & Phillips, 2002). In the professional world, Penny expressed optimism about future professional opportunities:

> There's been a real focus on diversity and hearing different voices, so I get the sense that maybe once the organization was very monocultural, which is sort

of straight White men...old...[laughter], and they had all the leadership positions and did all the talking, but it's quite clearly, everyone's decided that that can't happen in this world anymore.

CONCLUSION

In this chapter we have explored how television representations of gendered identities are negotiated by undergraduates and professionals in the three areas: criminology/police, politics/government, and public relations (PR). The framework of "the circuit of culture" (du Gay et al., 2013) enabled us to analyze how predominantly post-feminist discourses in television representations of gendered identities were affirmed or contested by our participants in relation to their lived experiences. Our findings reflected that while key influences for women's careers are fostered at an early stage via family, at school, or at university (Elliott & Stead, 2008), media representations can and do help to affirm or contest traditional stereotypes for women in the professions. Moreover, these representations are an important influence in (re)constructing cultural meaning and norms in an emancipatory way. Importantly, however, media influence is complex, and our study documented that media representations may be differentially consumed and negotiated in relation to ideas of gendered professional identity (Kelan, 2012), notions of seniority and leadership (Elliott & Stead, 2008), and notions of femininity (Lewis, 2014; McRobbie, 2008).

We also noted an unfolding or broadening of professional identities within the cultural sphere of professional life, in the "location between liberal feminism and femininity" (Lewis, 2014, p. 1857). Television representations, in nurturing the ambitions of women leaders and professionals, cannot be overlooked. The attraction of a career in the PR industry, while parodied by two very different television representations, was a key career influence and continues to inform some associations of identity development within the profession.

In support of Lewis's (2014) research, we find that these discourses contribute to a "resignification of femininity, making available to organizational actors a range of emerging femininities" (Lewis, 2014, p. 1848). Our research with these professions both builds and challenges the emerging post-feminist discourse by offering empirical insight into the emerging multiplicity of femininities (Lewis, 2014) lived out in reality, within an apparently broadening, more inclusive and open cultural space. Moreover, the transformational possibility of what one of the research participants, Penny, referred to as "splintered identities" presents a powerful way of (re)constructing professional meaning that has the propensity to reach out and connect with a wider and often skeptical set of stakeholders.

There is still a long way to go, but the opening up of cultural space in which gendered, professional identities, and in particular femininities, may be enacted and developed makes us optimistic for the future. Within this, the television representations examined appear to offer positive influences when identifiable associations are consumed, or indeed "prosumed." This emancipatory potential for cultural change is strong when there is a realistic prospect of attainability of identity for the women consuming these television representations.

Moreover, while these women demonstrated most of the features associated with a post-feminist regime, in which feminism and femininity co-exist (Baumgardner & Richards, 2004; Hinds & Stacey, 2001 in Lewis, 2014, p. 1851), they are not "retreating to home as a matter of choice" (Lewis, 2014, p. 1851); rather, they remain solidly and proudly within the public sphere.

The research study considered three very different professions; two of these established professions (police and politics and government) had benefitted from a progressive, transformational regulatory environment, mirrored to some extent in recent television portrayals. The other profession, PR, in its infancy, was still struggling with identity and voice in terms of gender equality. Across all three professions, tensions between gendered ideologies and lived realities are played out within the multilayered responses of participants navigating through complex and often clashing cultural constructs. Within this, for those researching gender, media, and the professions—and, indeed, those researching gendered representation and the digital world (Coleman, 2009)—it is clear that there is pressing need for further research, across professional and educational contexts. Indeed, we need to acknowledge the limits of our own study as relatively small and focused in nature, overly reliant on the UK context, and weak in exploring cultural production. Further, we have not reflexively examined the cultural artifacts—the TV shows—in terms of our own relationship to them as viewers, as advocated by Rhodes and Westwood (2008). We accept our findings and limitations as the starting point for further research and discussions.

What of the circuit of culture? The merits of the circuit of culture as a framework for exploring the nature of cultural meaning, of television representations, and gendered professional identities, lie in its multidirectional, socially interactive, emancipatory potential. Certainly, it helps an understanding of how professional identities may be reconstructed, co-constructed, shaped or reshaped over time, and across social and organizational contexts. The framework is complemented by an interdiscursive analysis, allowing for myriad discourses through which a multiplicity of femininities may be considered and debated openly and at length as "articulation[s]" (Rhodes & Westwood, 2008, p. 50) of popular culture. It is also clear that the power of emotive and associative media representations is critical in shaping and mediating discourse, for many in the professional world (Coleman, 2009; Featherstone, 2010). This critical aspect of the role of emotion and emotive association within culture formation is perhaps less theorized within the circuit of culture. Indeed, where there appears to be congruent, deep emotional and associative engagement between regulation, representation, identity, production, and consumption of professional identity, there is a powerful stimulus for enabling myriad women's professional identities to flourish in senior public life: a stimulus that is being seized from within the professions and from a few enlightened producers and regulators of popular culture.

NOTES

1. Gogglebox is a UK colloquial term for the television set.
2. In the UK in the 1990s, du Gay et al. (1997) used the Sony Walkman as a material cultural artifact to develop a case study text for pedagogic use in an Open University course, Culture, Media and Identities. The course was tasked with operationalizing the logic behind an emerging set of theories and methods in the social and human sciences, known collectively as the "cultural turn." The "circuit of culture," a framework, or framing device, to explore complex cultural formations was born out of this, and despite criticism it continues to be useful as a pedagogic device for exploring the making of cultural meaning.
3. For example, the change.org-led 50:50 campaign in the UK calling for 50:50 gender balanced representation in Parliament prior to the May 2015 General Election.
4. More females have reached senior ranks and grades across the UK police force, with women more represented in all specialist areas of the service (British Association for Women in Policing, n.d.).
5. Participants retained the right to withdraw from the research at all stages of the research and writing-up phases of the project up to final draft submission
6. Articulation refers to the linkages between the five nodes or "moments" of the circuit of culture that explain how a cultural artifact is constructed. In our study, the cultural artifact is a TV show of any genre that represents women in a profession. Importantly, an articulation, or linkage, is at a given point in time; therefore, our study must be seen as a mere snapshot of how the cultural artifacts are understood rather than "absolute or essential for all time" (du Gay et al., 2013, p. xxx).
7. In terms of statistical progress, in March 2014, women made up 27.9% of police officer strength (35,653 full-time employed staff), an increase of 0.6% from 2013. 60.45% of staff and 30.8% of specials were women. There are currently eight women chief constables, two women assistant commissioners, and overall, 39 Association of Chief Police Officers are women.
8. Based on research led by Manchester Metropolitan University designed to assess how far the service has progressed since 2006.

9. In 2014, 38% of all UK senior civil servants were women, and the gender breakdown across the Civil Service was becoming increasingly balanced across all grades: 58% of administrative officers and assistants were women, 46% of senior and higher executive officers were women, and 43% of Grade 6 and 7 posts were held by women ("Civil service employment," date). Other statistics on women in Whitehall show further breakdowns of senior posts (Cabinet Office, 2014). Across the numerous departments in 2013, 39% of deputy director posts were held by women, a 9% increase since 2005; 33% of director posts, a 7% increase since 2005; and 28% of director general posts, a 10% increase since 2005. Longitudinal data demonstrate a consistent upwards trend. Currently, the UK FCO employs about 14,000 people globally, of which 11,000 are locally engaged staff and 3,000 are UK-based staff (Diplomatic Corps based both in the UK and overseas). In 2013, the FCO board had about 40% female representation, 45% of the Fast Stream intake for 2012 were women, and there were 39 female heads of post across a global network.

10. Today, gender mainstreaming concepts are tied very closely to human rights initiatives advocated by the UN through international laws such as the Convention on the Elimination of Discrimination against Women (CEDAW) and Security Council Resolution 1325 (SCR 1325). Historically, the passing of SCR 1325 in October 2000 became the first celebrated resolution that acknowledges the political contribution of women in the context of peace and security. By placing gender concerns within the UN's official mandate, SCR 1325, complemented by resolutions 1820, 1888, and 1889, provides legitimate state duties in ensuring that women have equal access and full participation to power infrastructures.

11. Today's UK public relations industry, comprising PR consulting firms as well as in-house corporate communication departments, is now estimated to employ 61,600 practitioners (Gorkana Group, 2011). While public relations is predominantly female (64%), women's positions are not evenly distributed: men in PR are more likely to hold an owner or director-level position (52%); women are more likely to hold middle (70%) and junior level positions (72%)—an arrangement perpetuated in screen parodies such as *Absolute Power* and *In the Loop, UK* (Chartered Institute of Public Relations [CIPR], 2015; Johnston, 2010; Tandy, Loader, & Iannucci, 2009). Further, "gender has the third largest overall impact on salary, after level of seniority and years in industry" (CIPR 2015, p. 21).

12. The notion of the "prosumer" is said to challenge traditional relations between media industries and their audiences. The term, first coined by Alvin Toffler (1980), signifies a combination of producer and consumer. Nowadays, social media presents a blurring of the means of production and the act of consumption across digital networks potentially acting as an emancipatory force from traditional industry structures and norms.

REFERENCES

Acosta-Alzuru, C. (2003). "I'm not a feminist...I only defend women as human beings": The production, representation, and consumption of feminism in a *telenovela*. *Critical Studies in Media Communication, 20*(3), 269–294. doi: 10.1080/0739318032000112127

Baumgardner, J., & Richards, A. (2004). Feminism and femininity: Or how we learned to stop worrying and love the thong. In A. Harris (Ed.), *All about the girl: Culture, power and identity* (pp. 59–68). New York, NY: Routledge.

Billing, Y. D. (2011). Are women in management victims of the phantom of the male norm? *Gender, Work and Organization, 18*(3), 298–317. doi: 10.1111/j.1468-0432.2010.00546.x

Bolton, S., & Muzio, M. (2008). The paradoxical processes of feminization in the professions: The case of established, aspiring and semi professions. *Work, Employment and Society, 22*(2), 281–299. http://dx.doi.org/10.1177/0950017008089105

Booth, C., & Bennett, C. (2002). Gender mainstreaming in the European Union towards a new conception and practice of opportunities? *European Journal of Women's Studies, 9*(4), 430–446. doi:10.1177/135050680200940401

Boyle, D., El Hosaini, S., Baird, J. S., Bain, S., Armstrong, J., & Brown, J. (2014). *Babylon.* [Television series]. London, UK: Nightjack Productions.

British Association for Women in Policing. (n.d.). *The gender agenda: Women officers clearing hurdles together.* London, UK: BAWP. Retrieved from http://www.bawp.org/Resources/Documents/Gender%20Agenda%201.pdf

Bushnell, C., King, M. P., Coulter, A., Engler, M., & Star, D. (1998–2004). *Sex and the City.* [Television series]. U.S.A.: Darren Star Productions.

Cabinet Office. (2014). *Women in Whitehall, culture, leadership, talent.* Retrieved from https://www.gov.uk/government/publications/women-in-whitehall-culture-leadership-talent

Carli, A. H., & Eagly, L. L. (2007). *Through the labyrinth. The truth about how women become leaders.* Boston, MA: Harvard Business School.

Chartered Institute of Public Relations. (2015). *The state of the profession survey.* London, UK:

Chartered Institute of Public Relations. (2016).*Gender pay.* London, UK: CIPR. Retrieved from http://www.cipr.co.uk/content/policy-resources/policy/gender-pay

CIPR. Retrieved from http://www.cipr.co.uk/sites/default/files/SOPR15_Research Report_FINAL_UPDATE.pdf

"Civil service employment in the United Kingdom (UK) on March 31, 2015, by responsibility level and gender." (date) Statista: The Statistics Portal. Retrieved from http://www.statista.com/statistics/285092/uk-civil-service-employment-by-responsibility-level-and-gender/

Cochran, R., Surnow, J., Cassar, J., & Turner, B. (2001–2010). *24.* [Television series]. U.S.A.: 20th Century Fox., Imagine Entertainment., Realtime Productions., & Teakwood Lane Productions.

Coleman, R. (2009). *The becoming of bodies: Girls, images, experience.* Manchester, UK: Manchester University Press.

Coleman, R. (2013) Sociology and the virtual: Interactive mirrors, representational thinking and intensive power. *Sociological Review, 61*(1), 1–20. doi/10.1111/1467-954X.12002

Collins, R. L., DeBlasio, E., Ganzer, A., Newland, J., & Shear, B. (1974–1978). *Angie Dickinson: Police Woman.* [Television series] U.S.A.: Colombia Pictures Television, & David Gerber Productions.

Collinson, D. L. (2003). Identities and insecurities: selves at work. *Organization, 10*(3), 527–547. doi: 10.1177/13505084030103010

Critchett, K. (2010). *Comparative study into the under-representation of women in the police.* Fulbright Commission. Report completed for 2010–11 Fulbright Police Research Fellowship awarded by the U.S. –UK Fulbright Commission.

Cubitt, A., & Verbruggen, J. (2013–2015). *The Fall* [Television series]. Northern Ireland, UK: BBC Northern Ireland., & Artists Studio.

Czarniawska, B. (2010). The construction of business women in the media. Between evil and frailty. In L. Chouliaraki & M. Morsing (Eds.), *Media, organizations and identity* (pp. 185–208). London, UK: Palgrave.

Davis, G. (2015). Addressing unconscious bias. Does lopsided male representation in media skew our perceptions? *McKinsey Quarterly.* Retrieved from http://www.mckinsey.com/insights/organization/addressing_unconscious_bias

Donnelley, D., Baron, A., Goff, I., & Roberts, B. (1976–1981). *Charlie's Angels.* [Television series]. U.S.A.: Spelling-Goldberg Productions.

du Gay, P., Hall, S., Janes, L., Madsen, A. K., Mackay, H., & Negus, K. (1997). *Doing cultural studies: The story of the Sony Walkman.* Culture, media and identities series. London, UK: Sage.

du Gay, P., Hall, S., Janes, L., Madsen, A. K., Mackay, H., & Negus, K. (2013). *Doing cultural studies: The story of the Sony Walkman* (2nd ed.). Culture, media and identities series. London, UK: Sage.

Elliott, C., & Stead, V. (2008). Learning from leading women's experience: Towards a sociological understanding. *Leadership, 4*(2), 159–180. doi: 10.1177/1742715008089636

Elliott, C., & Stead, V. (2014, June). *Pedagogies of power: Women leaders' media representations and their pedagogical value.* Refereed paper presented at the 15th Universities Forum for Human Resource Development, Cork, Ireland.

Elton, B., & Birkin, J. (1995–1996). *The Thin Blue Line.* [Television series]. London, UK: BBC., & Tiger Aspect Productions.

Fairclough, N. (1992). *Discourse and social change.* Cambridge, UK: Polity Press.

Fairclough, N. (2010). *Critical discourse analysis: The critical study of language* (2nd ed.). Abingdon, UK: Taylor & Francis.

Featherstone, M. (2010). Body, image and affect in consumer culture. *Body Society, 16*(1), 193–221. doi: 10.1177/1357034X09354357

Funnell, L. (2011). I know where you keep your gun. Daniel Craig as the Bond–Bond Girl hybrid in Casino Royale. *Journal of Popular Culture, 44*(3), 455–472. doi: 10.1111/j.1540-5931.2011.00843.x

"Gender agenda." (n.d.). British Association for Women in Policing. Retrieved from http://www.bawp.org/GA

"Gender agenda 2: Women making their full contribution to policing." (n.d.). British Association for Women in Policing. Retrieved from http://www.bawp. org/Resources/Documents/GA2%20Mark2.pdf

"Gender agenda 3." (2014). British Association for Women in Policing. Retrieved from http://www.bawp.org/Resources/Documents/BAWP%20Gender%20 Agenda%203%20final%20%2016-oct-2014.pdf

Genz, S. (2009). *Postfemininities in popular culture.* Basingstoke, UK: Palgrave Macmillan.

Gill, R. (2006). *Gender and the media.* Cambridge, UK: Polity Press.

Gorkana Group. (2011). 2011 *PR census.* London, UK: PR Week/PRCA.

Gurevitch, M., & Scannell, P. (2003). Canonisation achieved? Stuart Hall's encoding/decoding model. In E. Katz, M. Gurenich, & J. D. Peters (Eds.), *Canonic texts in media research* (pp. 231–247). Cambridge, UK: Polity Press.

Hall, S. (2006). The rediscovery of 'ideology': Return of the repressed in media studies. In J. Storey (Ed.), *Culture theory and popular culture. A reader* (3rd ed.). Essex, UK: Pearson, Prentice Hall.

Heath, L., & Gilbert, K. (1996). Mass media and fear of crime. *American Behavioral Scientist, 39*(4), 379–386. doi: 10.1177/0002764296039004003

Hinds, H., & Stacey, J. (2001). Imagining feminism, imagining femininity: The bra burner, Diana and the woman who kills. *Feminist Media Studies, 1*(2), 153–177. doi: 10.1080/14680770120062114

Hirschhorn, L. (1989). Professionals, authority and group life: A case study of a law firm. *Human Resource Management, 28*(2), 235–252. doi: 10.1002/ hrm.3930280209

Howells, L. (2014). *"Why do we need the expert women" campaign and what impact has it had? The power of gendered media representations.* Paper presented at the Challenging Mis(S)Representations of Women Leaders and Managers seminar series. Durham University Business School, UK.

Ianucci, A., Martin, I., Armstrong, J., Blackwell, S., Gray, S., Roche, T., & Smith, W. (2005–2012). *The Thick of It.* [Television series]. London, UK: BBC.

Jay, A., Lynn, J., Lotterby, S., & Whitmore, P. (1986–1987). *Yes, Prime Minister.* [Television Series]. London, UK: BBC.

Johnson, R. (1986). The story so far: and for the transformations. In Punter, D. (Ed.), *Introduction to Contemporary Cultural Studies* (pp. 277–313). London, UK: Longman.

Johnston, J. (2010). Girls on screen: How film and television depict women in public relations. *Prism, 7*(4), 1–16. Retrieved from http://www.prismjournal.org/ fileadmin/Praxis/Files/Gender/Johnston.pdf

Jorgensen, M., & Phillips, L. J. (2002). *Discourse analysis as theory and method.* London, UK: Sage.

Kelan, E. K. (2012). The becoming of business bodies: Gender, appearance and leadership development. *Management Learning, 44*(1), 45–61. doi. 10.1177/135050761269009

Krainitski, E. (2014). Judi Dench's age-inappropriateness and the role of M: Challenging normative temporality. *Journal of Ageing Studies, 29,* 32–40. doi: 10.1016/j.jaging.2014.01.001

Krijnen, T. & van Bauwel, S. (2015). *Gender and media: Representing, producing, consuming.* Abingdon, UK: Routledge.

Landois, A., Clert, A., Sainderichin, G. P., Depambour, T., de Barahir, E., Brac, V., (Writers) Brondolo, J. M., Boursinhac, M., Triboit, P., & Jardin, F. (Directors). (2005–2014). *Engrenages [Spiral].* [Television series]. France: Canal + & Son et Lumiere.

LaPlante, L., & Menual, C. (1991). *Prime suspect.* [Television mini-series]. Manchester, UK: Granada Television.

LaPlante, L., & Cubitt, A., & Strickland, J. (1992). *Prime Suspect 2.* [Television mini-series]. Manchester, UK: Granada Television.

LaPlante, L., & Drury, D. (1993). *Prime Suspect 3.* [Television mini-series]. Manchester, UK: Granada Television.

Lewis, P. (2014). Postfeminism, feminities and organisation studies: Exploring a new agenda. *Organization Studies, 35*(12), 1845–1866. doi: 10.1177/0170840614539315

Lewis, K. (Producer), & Lyn, E., Wainwright, S., & Fywell, T. (Directors). (2014). *Happy valley.* [Television series]. UK: Red Production Company.

Martin, L. (1996, July). *Women police in the media: Fiction versus reality.* Paper presented at the Australian Institute of Criminology Conference, First Australasian Women Police Conference, Sydney, AU.

Mavin, S. (2009, June). Gender stereotypes and assumptions: Popular culture constructions of women leaders. *Gendered Issues in HRD.* Full refereed paper presented at the 10th International Conference HRD Development Research and Practice Across Europe, HRD: Complexity and Imperfection in Practice. Newcastle Business School, Northumbria University, UK.

Mavin, S., Bryans, P., & Cunningham, S. (2010). Fed-up with Blair's babes, Gordon's gals, Cameron's cuties, Nick's nymphets: Challenging gendered media representations of women political leaders. *Gender in Management: An International Journal, 25*(7), 550–569. http://dx.doi.org/10.1108/17542411011081365

McRobbie, A. (2008). Young women and consumer culture. *Cultural Studies, 22*(5), 531–550. doi: 10.1080/09502380802245803

Morton, J. (2011–2012). *Twenty twelve* [Television series]. London, UK: BBC.

Morton, J., Shapeero, T., Tavener, M., & Lawson, M. (2003–2005). *Absolute power.* [Television series]. London, UK: BBC.

Neuendorf, K. A., Gore, T. D., Dalessandro, A., Janstova, P., & Snyder-Suby, S. (2010). Shaken and stirred: A content analysis of women's portrayals in James Bond films. *Sex Roles, 62*(11), 747–761. doi: 10.1007/s11199-009-9644-2

O'Reilly, D. (2005). Cultural brands/branding cultures. *Journal of Marketing Management, 21*(5–6), 573–588.

Rahman, T. (2012). *Women in diplomacy. An assessment of British female ambassadors in overcoming gender hierarchy, 1990–2010.* Chapel Hill NC: American Diplomacy Publishers. Retrieved from_http://www.unc.edu/depts/diplomat/item/2011/0104/comm/rahman_women.html#note26

Rawlings, M. (2013, June 13). Foreign office broadens its appeal to women, *The Guardian.* Retrieved from http://www.theguardian.com/women-in-leadership/2013/jun/13/foreign-office-encourages-women-to-join

Rehn, A. (2008). Pop (culture) goes the organization: On highbrow, lowbrow and hybrids in studying popular culture within organization studies. *Organization, 15*(5), 765–783. http://dx.doi.org/10.1177/1350508408093652

Rhimes, S., Bryne, M., Verica, T., Bokelburg, O., Zisk, R., & Liddi-Brown, A. (2012–2015). *Scandal.* [Television series]. USA: ShondaLand & ABC Studios.

Rhodes, C., & Parker, M. (2008). Images of organizing in popular culture. *Organization, 19*(5), 627–637. doi: 10.1177/1350508408093645

Rhodes, C., & Westwood, R. (2008). *Critical representations of work and organization in popular culture.* Routledge advances in management and business series. Oxford, UK: Routledge.

Ross, K. (2004). *Women framed.* Oxford, UK: Blackwell.

Shepherdson, D. (2014). "Policing in Great Britain has always been as much a matter of image as much as of substance": The changing nature of media representations of the police and the effect on public perceptions: From mass media to social media. *Internet Journal of Criminology, 2*(22), 1–22. Retrieved from http://www.internetjournalofcriminology.com/Shepherdson_The_Changing_Nature_of_Media_Representations_of_the_Police%20_IJC_Jan_2014.pdf

Simpson, R., & Lewis, P. (2005). An investigation of silence and a scrutiny of transparency: Re-examining gender in organization literature through the concepts of voice and visibility. *Human Relations, 58*(10), 1253–1275. doi: 10.1177/0018726705058940

Spiers, B., & Humphreys, D. (Directors), & French., D., Perkins, S., & Saunders, J. (Writers) (1992–2012). *Absolutely fabulous.* [Television series]. London, UK: French & Saunders Productions., & BBC.

Sveistrup, S., Hoppe, T., Horsten, M.W., Nyholm, K., & Wullenweber, F. (2007–2012). *Forbrydelsen, trans. The Killing* [Television series]. Denmark: Danmarksradio., Norsk Rikskringkasting., Sveriges Television., ZDF Enterprises., Nordvision., & Nordisk Film.

Tandy, A. & Loader, K. (Producers), & Iannucci, A. (Director). (2009). *In the Loop* [Motion picture]. UK: BBC Films.

Toffler, A. (1980). *Future shock: The third wave.* New York, NY: Bantam.

UCAS. (2014). *U.K. application rates by country, region, sex, age and background* (2014 cycle, January deadline), UCAS Analysis and Research, 31 January 2014. Retrieved from https://www.ucas.com/sites/default/files/jan-14-application-rates.pdf

United Nations. (2000). Resolution 1325 Adopted by the Security Council on 31st October 2000. Retrieved from http://www.securitycouncilreport.org/atf/cf/%7B65BFC9B-6D27-4E9C-8CD3-CF6E4FF96FF9%7D/WPS%20SRES1325%20.pdf

United Nations. (2004). *Report on Women, Peace and Security.* Office of the Special Advisor on Gender Issues and Advancement of Women, OSAGI. Retrieved from http://www.un.org.osagi

Universities U.K. (2012). *Patterns and trends in U.K. higher education: Higher education: Analysing a decade of change.* London, UK: Universities UK. Retrieved from http://www.universitiesuk.ac.uk/highereducation/Documents/2012/PatternsAndTrendsinUKHigherEducation2012.pdf

van Zoonen, L. (1994). *Feminist media studies.* Thousand Oaks, CA: Sage.

van Zoonen, L. (2006). The personal, the political and the popular. A woman's guide to celebrity politics. *European Journal of Cultural Studies, 9*(3), 287–301. doi: 10.1177/1367549406066074

Wainwright, S., Taylor, D., Jones, S., Lindsay, S., & S. Bullmore, A. (Writers), & Fullerton, M., Moo-Young, C., Walker, P., May, J., & Delaney, S. (Directors). (2011–2015). *Scott and Bailey.* [Television series]. Manchester, UK: Red Production Company, Ingenious Broadcasting, Veredus Productions, & Ipomen Productions.

Willimon, B., Wright, R., Coles, J. D., & Franklin, C., (Directors), & Davies, A., Dobbs, M., Eason, L., Barnow, K., & Forman, S. (Writers). (2013–2015). *House of cards.* [Television series]. U.S.A.: Media Rights Capital., Panic Pictures., & Trigger Street Productions.

Wilson, M. G., & Broccoli, B. (Producers), & Campbell, M. (Director). (2006). *Casino Royale* [Motion picture]. UK: Eon Productions.

Wilson, M. G. & Broccoli, B. (Producers), & Forster, M. (Director). (2008). *Quantum of Solace.* [Motion picture]. UK: Eon Productions.

Wilson, M. G. & Broccoli, B. (Producers), & Mendes S. (Director). (2012). *Skyfall.* [Motion picture]. UK: Eon Productions.

Wilson, M. G. & Broccoli, B. (Producers), & Mendes, S. (Director). (2015). *Spectre* [Motion picture]. UK: Eon Productions.

Wolstencroft, D., Riley, A., & Nalluri, B. (2002–2011). *Spooks.* [Television series]. London, UK: Kudos Film and Television & BBC.

Yeomans, L. (2014). Gendered performance and identity work in PR consulting relationships: a UK perspective. In C. Daymon & K. Demetrious (Eds.), *Gender and public relations: critical perspectives on voice, image and identity* (pp. 87–107). London, UK: Routledge.

CHAPTER 11

MEDIATING THE FUTURE

Women Political Leaders
in Science Fiction Television

Kimberly Yost
Lourdes University

Science fiction narratives have long been considered the domain of boys and men. From the earliest days of science fiction television in the United States, with *Captain Video*, *Tom Corbett—Space Cadet*, and *Space Patrol*, the protagonists were heroic White males. Leading or recurring female characters seemed nonexistent or relegated to the Amazonian set-dressing of nonhuman women, as seen in *Flash Gordon*, or the ubiquitous damsels in distress saved by the hero: too bland and passive to be remembered as individuals. Accordingly, our collective knowledge of women in science fiction narratives suffers from our consideration of science fiction as a predominantly male genre. Yet, as Melzer (2006) points out, science fiction is a space where "we seem to reimagine gender relations most radically" (p. 1).

In our thinking about images of women in science fiction television, we might equally consider the competent professionalism of Lieutenant Nyota Uhura of *Star Trek*, Commander Susan Ivanova of *Babylon 5*, or Captain

Gender, Media, and Organization, pages 197–208
Copyright © 2016 by Information Age Publishing

Katherine Janeway of *Star Trek: Voyager.* From the 1960s to the 1990s, female characters in science fiction television were no longer absent or relegated to passive supporting roles but moved to positions of military command, a historically male function. Within our own century, the advance continues as female characters inhabit the highest positions of political leadership, such as Colonial President Laura Roslin of *Battlestar Galactica* and American President Allison Taylor of *24*. Thus, the evolution of the formal organizational positions of female characters and the implication of their portrayals in a science fictional context is an area deserving of study to help us make sense of the role of women in organizations and society.

Although there have been dozens of female heads of government across the world—ranging from Sirimavo Bandaranaike of Ceylon, elected in 1960; to the iconic Margaret Thatcher of the United Kingdom elected in 1979; to Saara Kuugongelwa of Namibia, elected in March 2015—some people in the United States consider the election of a woman president to be a novel concept, if not an outright impossibility or potential mistake in judgment by the electorate. Zaslow and Schoenberg (2012) noted that attitudes toward women and the presidency are slowly changing, but feelings about women being capable leaders remain less than fully positive. Science fiction television narratives offer a means by which we can contemplate the representations of female political leaders in a way that is not readily found in reality or nonfiction contexts and can be regarded, along with other popular culture texts, as "critical records and shapers of meaning about American understandings of the U.S. presidency" (Parry-Giles, 2014, p. 207).

We contextualize narratives historically and determine whether they are similar to or divergent from the dominant culture (Furia & Bielby, 2009). For science fiction, this includes characters or relationships different from the time/environment of the author and reader (Suvin, 2010). Thus, the depiction of a female president in American popular culture is always placed in a future context, the milieu of science fiction. While some television narratives with female American presidents may not seem to abide by conventional science fiction clichés, such as the inclusion of aliens or spaceships, the presentation of a future world is sufficiently accomplished through the embodiment of the presidency as female.

This understanding of the portrayal of legitimate political authority in science fiction narratives allows us to observe and contemplate the gendered expectations of political leaders. This occurs in what Suvin (2010) characterized as a "feedback oscillation," where the imagined world of the author allows the audience to reflect upon their own reality and then meet the narrative again to see it with a fresh perspective. It is within this process that we are able to contemplate contemporary social issues and challenge our understandings. As with all modes of storytelling, science fiction stories "are crucial tools for shaping cultural identities," and their "'realness'…enable individuals (and groups) to relate to and recognize the debates as relevant to their own lives" (Melzer, 2006, p. 4). Moreover, science fiction serves a particular social function to examine the dichotomy of our rational/technoscientific and spiritual/transcendent natures by mediating the tensions of our desires and fears concerning the future (Roberts, 2007). Indeed, Curtis (2010) identified our time as one in which "thinking about the end has fully suffused the popular culture" (p. 3) and the resultant "postapocalyptic fiction speaks both to our deepest fears and to our desire to start over again" (p. 5).

Importantly, science fiction narratives often present situations of cataclysmic change. Bad things happen in science fiction narratives—from the nuclear destruction of planetary systems to hostile alien invasions to pandemics that decimate the global population by 90%. In these situations, not only is leadership required for immediate sense making, the restoration of order, and a vision for the future, but the situation also needs those who can lead during an unimaginable crisis where the physical and social infrastructure is destroyed and the survival of the human species is at stake. Leading during a crisis requires basic competencies and is often discussed in terms of personal qualities such as integrity, confidence, and transparency, which are modeled behaviors and interactions with others when there is no preplanned strategy; however, they can often be abandoned during the overwhelming stress of a crisis and result in controlling, if not tyrannical, behaviors (Yost, 2013). Wheatley (2007) suggests that leaders, during turbulent times, are trapped in a dictatorial scenario by their strong desire to serve and the pressures from their followers to relieve uncertainty at nearly any cost. Of particular note in science fiction narratives is this sense of mortality salience among followers, which causes them to confer leadership authority to a divinely inspired charismatic leader (Yost, 2013) and often results in the depiction of the dark-side of leadership and leaders locked into an identity script, as described by Sinclair (2007), which proves ineffective.

General wisdom suggests that people want a strong leader during times of crisis, and the concept is usually expressed in a male body. The traits strong leaders possess can be coded masculine, such as individualism, need for control, assertiveness, and the skills of advocacy and domination (Fletcher, 2004). Leadership traits, in contrast to these, can be coded feminine and require an emotional skill-set based on relational abilities and qualities, such as self-awareness, empathy, vulnerability, and an openness to learn from others (Fletcher, 2004). While leadership studies may inhabit this postheroic paradigm, the general sociocultural landscape has not quite embraced this concept when judging leadership qualities in general, nor during a crisis. Herein lies the conundrum when examining women leaders in science fiction narratives: the prevalence of bias against women who demonstrate assertive or dominant qualities stereotypically attributed to men.

Stereotyped social roles based on gender continue to inform our understanding of leaders. Role congruity theory explains that women who behave in agentic ways that fulfill the expectations of leaders are viewed less positively than their male counterparts (Eagly & Karau, 2002). Moreover, Bongiorno, Bain, and David (2014) suggested, as agentic behavior on the part of women gains greater social acceptance, a new, and subtler, form of prejudice and disapproval has emerged for women who fail to exhibit masculine coded leadership behaviors. Both theoretical predictions could influence the ways in which we perceive women political leaders portrayed in science fiction television and those perceptions could manifest in our decision making and attitudes about potential female presidents in our real world.

Numerous female leaders exist in science fiction narratives, and often the narrative dispenses with discussions or dialogue on the question of gender. There appears to be little novelty of a female political leader in the future, which suggests a projection of a positive future on this account. Nevertheless, while there may be silence from the narratives on open discussions of gender, the qualities and behaviors of female political leaders still reverberate for our own reality and may have an impact on viewer perceptions, if not their own agentic behaviors per Bandura's (2001) social cognitive theory. In addition, as Collins (2011) suggested, we should not expect that seeing more women represented will "produce 'better,' 'fair,' or realistic portrayals" (p. 295).

For the purposes of this discussion, I have limited my examination to portrayals of female politicians in science fiction television series who are human and function within a democratic system of governance—that is, they were raised to their position of authority and held accountable by an electorate or followers. In addition, these characters operate within a crisis leadership mode in which the challenges are significant and the consequences for failure are more severe. The choice to examine the long-form narratives of television series provides us with the opportunity to gauge leadership qualities and effectiveness over time. A single crisis that is solved within the timeframe of a theatrical film can be constricted in its portrayal of leadership. In contrast, episodic television allows for nuance and growth—or at least change—in a leader and, especially in post-apocalyptic television series, the constant barrage of crises offers more than one observable situation in which the leader is tested.

To begin, I explore female political leaders who demonstrate the masculine-coded leadership qualities of individualism, assertiveness, advocacy, and domination through Colonial President Laura Roslin of *Battlestar Galactica* (Eick & Moore, 2003) and Prime Minister Harriet Jones of *Doctor Who.*

In the reimagined *Battlestar Galactica*, Secretary of Education Laura Roslin is sworn in as President of the Colonies after a surprise nuclear attack by enemy Cylons destroys the 12 colonial planets and their billions of inhabitants. The only survivors, approximately 50,000 people, are those who were traveling in space at the time of the attack. As the direness of the situation becomes clear, she begins to organize the passengers of the ship on which she is traveling to prepare for a lengthy stay onboard. She assigns people to assess the food and medical supplies, prepares the hold for sleeping quarters, and tries to calm everyone's anxieties. Roslin's authority is almost immediately challenged by a passenger, Doral, but she calmly and bluntly explains that because she is the highest-ranking government official aboard a government ship, she gets to be in charge. That does not quite pacify Doral, who later speaks to Captain Lee Adama, a fighter pilot assigned to escort the ship and complains about who is in charge of the ship. When Lee accompanies Doral to evaluate what is happening, Roslin is continuing to put people to work and assess the situation. She is calmly authoritative and demonstrates a realistic understanding of the seriousness of their situation even though there is a substantial amount of ambiguity. Lee simply tells Doral, "The lady's in charge" (Miniseries, 2003).

While Lee Adama is satisfied with the leadership capabilities and legitimate authority of Roslin, his father, Commander William Adama of the Galactica, is not. When Adama orders his son to return to the Galactica to help in the fight against the Cylons, Lee refuses and explains he is involved in rescue operations with the president. Adama is incredulous, commenting: "We're at war and you're taking orders from a schoolteacher?" (Miniseries, 2003).

In this first episode of *Battlestar Galactica*, there is a very subtle subtext of Roslin being unfit to lead due to her gender. From Doral's confrontation and attempt to remove her from giving orders to Adama's perception of her as a schoolteacher, which can be coded as an inconsequential female occupation, and initial rejection of her authority, the narrative provides a portrayal of a president who must not only take command during a crisis, but also overcome objections to her authority. Yet the text stays close to the idea of her questionable authority stemming from being 34th in line to the presidency prior to the destruction of the 12 colonies rather than the idea that as a woman she is unsuitable to lead.

As a crisis leader, Roslin's doubts and fears are private. While she seeks advice from others, she finds it difficult to develop deep interpersonal relationships. She appears to walk a path where she is determined to make tough decisions, all in service to the survival of the human species. A reading of Roslin suggests that her method of crisis leadership is to compromise her integrity and morality, although they are considered effective leadership qualities. As a consequence of solidifying her political power, she is able to make decisions that are ethically questionable but rationalized through her concentration on human safety and survival as a means of upholding human values and communality. These decisions include promising a Cylon his life will be spared if he gives up information and then ordering him tossed out of an airlock when he complies; kidnapping the human/Cylon child and concealing her actions by telling the parents the child died; ordering Commander Adama to assassinate Admiral Cain, whom she views as a threat to the safety of civilians and military, not to mention her own political efficacy; being complicit in the pharmaceutical torture of scientist Gaius Baltar for information on his collaboration with the Cylons; and authorizing the use of a biological weapon against the Cylons that would result in genocide. All of these actions point to an assertive leadership but oppose the sense of rightness and the virtuous qualities we desire in our leaders.

Concern for ethical action is also depicted in the long-running television series *Doctor Who* (Davies, 2005–2008) through Harriet Jones, a recurring character introduced as a rather endearingly annoying member of parliament (MP) from a small constituency who helps The Doctor defeat an alien invasion of the government and eventually rises to prime minister (PM). From these experiences, she is constantly vigilant to protect the British people against extraterrestrials. In the imagined world of *Doctor Who*, threats of alien attacks are near constant, so her vigilance cannot properly be described as paranoiac. The threats are very real and the consequences are considerable. Jones first becomes acquainted with The Doctor when a race known as the Slitheens kill and take over the bodies of the PM and several other political and government officials and she inadvertently discovers the conspiracy. Jones is elected PM, primarily on the strength of her handling of this crisis (Davies & Boak, "Aliens of London," 2005; Davies & Boak, "World War Three," 2005). Later, in "The Christmas Invasion" (Davies & Hawes, 2005), The Doctor negotiates through single combat with another group of aliens, the Sycorax, to leave Earth in peace. The Doctor is victorious and the alien ship leaves Earth but cannot escape before PM Jones orders the ship destroyed. The Doctor is furious and determines to end her political career through a whisper campaign about her health. While a female British prime minister is not a novelty—and the tenure of Margaret Thatcher in the 1980s demonstrated that women political leaders could be dominant and assertive while serving their constituents—this episode of *Doctor Who* questions the ethical actions of Jones's decision to destroy an enemy as they willingly retreat.

Jones does step down as PM, but she does not stop her vigilance toward protecting the planet. In "The Stolen Earth/Journey's End" (Davies, Nation, & Harper, 2008), she appears again and gathers the companions who have traveled with The Doctor in the past in an effort to find him and return Earth to its proper place in the universe after the evil Daleks whisk it away. Everyone is in despair over the hopelessness of the situation and the inevitability of their deaths at the hands of the Daleks, but Jones will have none of that and barks orders to motivate them to action. Even though she does not enjoy legitimate political or military authority, she behaves as if she does and is given this authority by the former companions. When questioned why Jones wants to find The Doctor after he deposed her, Jones admits she wondered whether her decision to destroy the Sycorax ship was wrong. Yet she stands by her actions because she knew one day Earth would be in danger and The Doctor would not be there. Jones then describes her plan for combining forces to become The Doctor's secret army. They decide to boost the telephone signal to call The Doctor. Jones says the signal will be discovered and traced back to her by the Daleks, but if it means Earth will be saved, she considers it a worthwhile risk. Once the Daleks trace the call to Jones, they descend upon her home. She defiantly rises to meet them and is resigned to her death, which is ultimately an act of redemption to protect the people of Earth until The Doctor can arrive.

While Roslin and Jones portray female heads of government as strong, assertive, dominant political leaders comfortable in their position and decision making, other science fiction television series depict female political leaders as more tentative in their approach, with the expectation of these portrayals as manifesting the subtle form of prejudice and disapproval described by Bongiorno et al. (2014). This understanding is evident in the character roles of President Allison Taylor of *24* and Samantha Willis of *Survivors*.

The television series *24* (Cochran & Surnow, 2001–2010) is set in a contemporary America and is, perhaps, more accurately described as an action-thriller series rather than a science fiction series. However, the events of the series, such as nuclear detonations in the southwest and a female president, inform the story in a way that clearly takes place in the future—even if that future is only moments away. Jack Bauer is the protagonist of the series as an agent of the Counter Terrorism Unit and each season (or day) is dedicated to Jack saving the country from terrorist attacks. Presidents play an important role in the narratives and allow us a mediated depiction of the American presidency.

In *24* Seasons 7 and 8, President Allison Taylor must contend with terrorist attacks, being held hostage in the White House, imprisoning her daughter for treasonous offenses, and her determination to leave a legacy of bringing about peace in the Middle East. Taylor's presidency follows the depictions of two male presidents, David Palmer (Seasons 2 and 3) and Charles Logan (Seasons 4 and 5), who exist on opposite ends of the virtue spectrum. Palmer is seen as competent and courageous; he is eulogized as one of the greatest American presidents. In contrast, Logan is unprincipled and complicit in the terrorist attacks that occur during his presidency. Parry-Giles (2014) characterizes Taylor's presidency as one of uncertainty and ambivalence. Taylor begins her presidency by seeking the virtuous path modeled by Palmer but eventually makes a deal with the disgraced Logan to obtain help in securing the peace treaty and her legacy. In effect, Taylor is admitting she does not have the power or is not willing to wield the unsavory power necessary to meet her goal, which lies in contrast to Jones of *Doctor Who*. Eventually, her tentativeness increases, her mistakes grow, her credibility is diminished, and she resigns from office. As Parry-Giles (2014) remarks, "Her uncertainty and mistakes undermine the presidentialist messages usually found in *24* and other popular culture texts… [and] invites viewer deliberation about the connections of that presidentialism with the prevailing sense of America's 'national manhood'" (p. 220). In essence, Taylor's presidency does not fit with the collective understanding of what a president should be, including the sense of the position being a male prerogative.

Similarly disapproving in its representation of female political leaders, the British television series *Survivors* (Hodges, 2008–2010) portrays a woman government official, Samantha Willis, who is a survivor of a pandemic and attempts to restore order and rebuild society. Her prepandemic position was as a government spokesperson, but now she is one of the sole remaining government officials, much like Roslin in *Battlestar Galactica*. As the population is decimated, government and military control is nonexistent, infrastructure is no longer operational, and her own immediate family is lost to the disease, we discover that Willis has made her way to a scientific ecosphere that was experimenting with self-sufficient living. This small group of survivors has power, food, water, medicine, defense systems and weapons, and even some hot water for bathing. In comparison to the rest of the landscape, they have an almost idyllic life. Willis intends to act communally and gather other survivors to develop a provisional government.

However, her followers are hostile and anxious about a gang that has repeatedly tried to steal their goods, even though Willis intends that supplies should be shared. When two of the gang members are caught stealing, Willis determines to uphold the democratic principles and conduct a trial. However, she is feeling pressured by those who disagree with her vision of rebuilding community, and her hold on power is tenuous. At the trial, the two are found guilty by the members of the community. Willis intends justice to be swift and, with a shaking hand, unexpectedly shoots one of the thieves, to the horror of those watching. Because the other thief tried to give back the goods when caught, she commutes his sentence, stating that the law is just and merciful; yet she stumbles away, demonstrating the emotional toll of her actions. Nevertheless, by carrying out the execution, she reasserts her leadership authority and demonstrates an ability to be ruthless, even if it is clear this is not her preferred style (Gunn & Chiappe, Episode 3, 2008). Similar to Taylor in *24*, Willis is perceived to be uncertain by apparently regretting her decisions, thus seeming less of a leader for displaying non-agentic behaviors.

Beyond the clear indication that Willis is in a crisis leadership situation beyond her abilities, the depiction of Willis as a tentative and emotionally vulnerable leader is in stark contrast to Abby Grant, a nonpolitician, who survives and gathers other survivors to reestablish a post-apocalyptic community.

Grant's followers confer leadership to her because of her ideological perspective of collaboration and her insistence that people are essentially good, worthy of help, and desire a sense of belonging to a community. In essence, Grant is a mother figure for the group, even to the point that she insists on hugs and birthday parties, but she disapproves of violent acts and holds her power confidently through personal integrity and moral authority. Grant is unmistakably coded with feminine leadership qualities, but this does not make her ineffective. It is Willis who is seen as ineffective and corrupt as she attempts to lead through domination, violence, and political machinations.

When contemplating the images of women political leaders in fictional narratives, we must acknowledge the implications of science fiction's post-apocalyptic scenarios. In a post-apocalypse, institutions are destroyed, and the system of checks and balances afforded by American-style democratic governance is absent. Therefore, the role of the head of government is by necessity increased, and followers have a greater identification of authority residing in the body of a single person. Followers' desire for someone to make sense from unimaginable catastrophe, provide them with basic physiological needs, and give them a sense of belonging and direction can be overwhelming for someone who takes up the role of leader, which can lead to dictatorial practices. Kellerman (2005) explains that people follow "bad leaders" because of their greater need for stability and self-interest. As seen in the narratives discussed, the choices made by leaders are often unilateral and predicated on the need to protect followers at any cost, but when a leader's political power is threatened, these same justifications become self-serving.

Interestingly, when science fiction narratives present a female political leader, the question of her gender is not a consideration for exploration, but her public actions and behaviors are assertive, dominant, and she feels she knows the best solution to challenges and the vision for the future. These are specifically agentic behaviors. These leaders can also be seen as engaging in unethical, if not illegal, activities. These women pay for their ethical lapses by losing their position of authority through impeachment, imprisonment, or the abandonment of their followers. However, female political leaders, such as Willis and Taylor, who display non-agentic behaviors, similarly engage in disreputable behaviors to maintain their power and, ultimately, become characters whom the audience can disapprove. Kellerman (2005) has suggested that we can learn from examples of bad leadership, both as leaders and followers, and avoid becoming or enabling one. However, within a fictional depiction, our power to rationally understand what we are viewing and apply broad understandings can be derailed by the emotional impact of the story in front of us and our immediate reactions.

This is the challenge in assessing mediated depictions of female political leaders in science fiction television. Do agentic behaviors in women coincide with being unscrupulous? Do non-agentic behaviors in women leaders simply reinforce the social construct of women as unsuitable for political office? In private moments of the narratives, we witness the doubts and fears the agentic characters possess. Perhaps these moments make agentic women leaders seem more authentic, but this could simply be a pretense for making them seem more feminine and not as outside the acceptable social norm. Each of the leaders discussed here is ultimately involved in the feminine coded quality of being communal in her objectives and justifications of her actions and decisions. Nevertheless, the depictions provide a nuanced display of the emotional and physical cost that could arguably undermine the understanding of their agency and further the biased construct of female authority and leadership.

Beyond the potential for audiences to view women political leaders with a prejudicial bias, either against their assertive leadership or their tentative and weak leadership, we must also reflect on the ways in which these narratives are no longer strictly bound to a specific sociohistoric context. With the proliferation of on-demand streaming video, DVDs, and other entertainment delivery systems, we can no longer consider the portrayals of women in television or film as eking out a linear progression toward positive changes in the depiction of their political or social positional power. Viewers can access narratives from any decade and may not be aware of the textual uniqueness of a certain depiction or how that depiction moved the boundaries of socially acceptable gender roles. Mediated depictions of women can be jumbled together within a person's viewing habits and the messaging, understanding, and attitudes of viewers toward the characters—and thus what is projected back to the real world—can stall, at best, and at worst, retreat. When juxtaposed against viewing other visual texts of heroic male leaders from various periods of cultural production, the complexity of contextualizing leadership progression within a gendered framework becomes increasingly problematic.

The challenge is to understand how we engage with visual texts differently than in previous generations. Our expectations of leadership behavior and the ways in which women have the capacity to lead are complicated by potentially concurrent viewings of agentic and non-agentic women. Concurrent viewings may obscure the ways in which cultural identity is formed and understood, as well as how we are able to perceive the relevance of the texts to our lives. While scholars may be fluent in theoretical paradigms and research on women's leadership, the literature itself rarely reaches those in society who ultimately provide the impetus for social change on micro or macro levels. Science fiction and other popular culture texts do, and we, as scholars, must remain cognizant of this as we move forward. Nevertheless, post-apocalyptic science fiction television offers a mediated depiction of the future with women at the forefront of crisis leadership, continuing to speak to our desires for a future founded in community, which can continue to be leveraged in the enduring dialogues on imagining gender and leadership.

REFERENCES

Bandura, A. (2001). Social cognitive theory: An agentic perspective. *Annual Review of Psychology, 52*, 1–26. doi: 10.1146/annurev.psych.52.1.1

Bongiorno, R., Bain, P. G., & David, B. (2014). If you're going to be a leader, at least act like it! Prejudice towards women who are tentative in leader roles. *British Journal of Social Psychology, 53*(2), 217–234. doi: 10.1111/bjso.12032

Cochran, R., & Surnow, J. (Producers). (2001–2010). *24* [Television series]. USA: Fox.

Collins, R. L. (2011). Content analysis of gender roles in media: Where are we now and where should we go? *Sex Roles, 63*, 290–298. doi: 10.1007/s11199-010-9929-5

Curtis, C. P. (2010). *Postapocalyptic fiction and the social contract: We'll not go home again.* Lanham, MD: Rowman & Littlefield.

Davies, R. T. (Producer). (2005–2008). *Doctor Who* [Television series]. Cardiff, Wales: BBC.

Davies, R. T. (Writer), & Hawes, J. (Director). (2005). The Christmas invasion [Television series episode]. In R. T. Davies (Producer), *Doctor Who.* Cardiff, Wales: BBC.

Davies, R. T., Nation, T. (Writers), & Harper, G. (Director). (2008). The stolen Earth/Journey's end. [Television series episode]. In R. T. Davies (Producer), *Doctor Who.* Cardiff, Wales: BBC.

Eagly, A. H., & Karau, S. J. (2002). Role congruity theory of prejudice toward female leaders. *Psychological Review, 109*(3), 573–598. doi: 10.1037//0033-295X.109.3.573

Eick, D., & Moore, R. D. (Producers). (2003–2009). *Battlestar Galactica* [Television series]. USA: David Eick Productions.

Fletcher, J. K. (2004). The paradox of postheroic leadership: an essay on gender, power, and transformational change. *Leadership Quarterly, 15*(3), 647–661. doi: 10.1177/1742715009354235

Furia, S. R., & Bielby, D. D. (2009). Bombshells on film: Women, military films, and hegemonic gender ideologies. *Popular Communication, 7*(4), 208–244. doi: 10.1080/15405700903046369

Hodges, A. (Producer). (2008–2010). *Survivors* [Television series]. London, UK: BBC.

Kellerman, B. (2005, Winter). How bad leadership happens. *Leader to Leader, 35*, 41–46. doi: 10.1002/ltl.113

Melzer, P. (2006). *Alien constructions: Science fiction and feminist thought.* Austin, TX: University of Texas Press.

Parry-Giles, T. (2014). Presidentialism, political fiction, and the complex presidencies of Fox's *24. Presidential Studies Quarterly, 44*(2), 204–223. doi: 10.1111/psq.12110

Roberts, A. (2007). *The history of science fiction.* New York, NY: Palgrave Macmillan.

Sinclair, A. (2007). *Leadership for the disillusioned: Moving beyond myths and heroes to leadership that liberates.* Crows Nest, NSW: Allen & Unwin.

Suvin, D. (2010). *Defined by a hollow: Essays on utopia, science fiction and political epistemology.* Bern, Switzerland: Peter Lang. (Original work published in 1977)

Wheatley, M. (2007). *Finding our way: Leadership for an uncertain time.* San Francisco, CA: Berrett-Koehler.

Yost, K. (2013). *From starship captains to galactic rebels: Leaders in science fiction television.* Lanham, MD: Rowman & Littlefield.

Zaslow, E., & Schoenberg, J. (2012). Stumping to girls through popular culture: Feminist interventions to shape future political leaders. *Women and Language, 35*(1), 97–116.

CHAPTER 12

THE RUNWAY-READY RINGLEADER AND OTHER MEDIA MYTHS

An Analysis of Common Television and Film Stereotypes of Women Leaders

Shana Matamala and Stephanie Abrahim
University of La Verne

Decades before I became Dr. Shana Matamala, professor and director, I was a girl growing up in a small town in the 1970s—a time before Netflix and other on-demand programming sites. Watching television back then, viewers were lucky if they had six choices. The women leaders I saw portrayed included Carol Brady from *The Brady Bunch* (Schwartz, 1969), Daisy Duke from *The Dukes of Hazard* (Picard, 1979), and Marion Cunningham from *Happy Days* (Marshall, 1974). Did these images exert a force on my internal belief system of how I perceived myself and other women? I would say they did, but I also had the voices of my family, where I grew up, and my educational experiences to influence these perceptions. My question is: What if

Gender, Media, and Organization, pages 209–224
Copyright © 2016 by Information Age Publishing
All rights of reproduction in any form reserved.

other girls do not have strong counter voices? What if the myths they see permeating the media remain the strongest voices? What kinds of stories do we want our girls seeing and believing about themselves?

Myths are nothing new, with Gilgamesh dating back to 2100 BC and the Greek myths in c. 700 BC, but the medium through which they travel changed dramatically with the development of film and television. The stories we repeat about ourselves and each other give meaning to how we feel about and categorize people, places, and events (Campbell, 1988; Merskin, 2010). Societal myths often become taken for granted and operate like a pair of glasses through which we view the world from our own distorted lenses (Bennett, 1980). Stereotypes stem from myths as an oversimplification and typecast a person by getting hold of a few "widely recognized characteristics about a person, reduce everything about the person to those traits, exaggerate and simplify them, and fix them without change or development" (Hall, 1997, p. 248).

Gender stereotypes pertain to both men and women and ascribe particular characteristics of how they should operate. Both descriptive and prescriptive in nature, they not only describe gender-specific traits, but also prescribe how men and women should act; men should be assertive and women should be submissive (Burgess & Borgida, 1999; Glick & Fiske, 1999). Individual men and women do not exemplify masculinity and femininity; rather, they become defined through thousands of years of socially expected behaviors and ideas (Merskin, 2010). Today men are often stereotyped as being competitive, resolute, autonomous, and analytical, while women are characterized as approachable, nurturing, motherly, and caring (Heilman, 2001). Often stereotypes do not come from first-hand knowledge, but from stories told by others or the media (Seiter, 1986).

This chapter delves into common media stereotypes of women leaders and how this influences the self-concepts of women, along with pervasive biases and prejudices. These negative views perpetuated by media include the perception of women leaders being less valued and not as effective as their male counterparts (Heilman, 2001; Phelan & Rudman, 2010; Ridgeway, 2001; Schein 2001). While many factors may contribute to a woman's difficulty in attaining and working in leadership positions, media stereotypes stand out as ubiquitous influencers. In a study by Simon and Hoyt, the research found that "women exposed to images depicting counterstereotypical roles subsequently reported stronger nontraditional gender role beliefs than women exposed to images depicting stereotypical roles" (2012, p. 232).

METHOD

In looking at media myths of women leaders, a thematic analysis approach was used in identifying and reporting stereotypes (Braun & Clarke, 2006:

Guest, MacQueen, & Namey, 2012). While women in the media permeate radio, magazines, television, movies, and news broadcasts, this chapter narrows the focus by centering on American film and television from the 1950s to the present. Thematic analysis serves as a qualitative method for finding and analyzing themes in a data set, in this case film and television. This method goes beyond looking for precise words and phrases and delves into implicit and explicit patterns and ideas (Guest et al., 2012). Specifically, theoretical thematic analysis was used in this study to code the data driven by the research question, which led to identifying themes.

We began with the initial research question of how women leaders are portrayed in film and television from the 1950s to the present. In generating initial codes, we found three main categories of the motherly leader, the woman with stereotypical male leadership qualities, and the woman who could do it all and look beautiful. Identifying these codes took place by separately looking for relevant data points on women leaders and then looking for similarities and differences. Within our three main themes, we also identified pronounced ethnic stereotypes in women. These ethnic stereotypes overrepresented one racial group within the three main categories. For instance, we found Latina women leaders overwhelmingly portrayed as the sassy and hot Latina. Lastly, we found a fifth category of positive portrayals of women leaders, which will be discussed towards the end of the chapter.

At this stage, the three themes were defined and named. The motherly leader became the *communal caretaker* theme as a way to emphasize women in follower roles focused on caretaking within their community. The coding of woman with stereotypical male leadership qualities became the *devil woman* theme in order to embody the women leaders portrayed with traditionally male characteristics of assertiveness, competitiveness, and independence. Lastly, the woman who could do it all and look beautiful was named the *runway-ready ringleader* as a picture of the women leader who was dressed like and looked so much like a model that she could walk the runway one minute, but she could also successfully lead a Central Intelligence Agency (CIA) team the next minute. The following provides exemplars of film and television programs from each of the identified themes that paint a picture of the current landscape of the portrayal of woman leaders.

ANALYSIS OF COMMON MEDIA STEREOTYPES

The communal caretaker stereotype centers on the continuing portrayal of women in follower roles, which stems from the bias that women take care and men take charge (Hoyt & Chemers, 2008). Television moms in the 1950s, like Jane Wyatt from *Father Knows Best* (Rodney, 1954), epitomized the caretaker myth as they kept a spotless house, made sure dinner was on the table when their husband came home, and solved family quarrels, all while keeping every hair in place. While sitcoms now include more women in empowered positions than in the 1950s, many shows like *Desperate Housewives* (Cherry, 2004), *The Bachelor* (Fleiss & Levenson, 2002), and countless commercials continue to depict women in follower roles. Soap operas stand out as a medium for the communal caretaker myth. Women viewers of soap operas empathize with characters who rarely live a life outside stereotypically imposed boundaries based on gender roles. Female soap opera characters often avoid or run away from their problems instead of confronting them directly (Byerly & Ross, 2008).

The media consistently depict men and women in traditional gender stereotypes with the man as the breadwinner and the woman as the caregiver (Coltrane & Adams, 1997; Ganahl, Prinsen, & Netzley, 2003; Goffman, 1977; Reichert, 2008; Reichert & Carpenter, 2004; Rounder, Slater, & Domenech-Rodríguez, 2003). Bias toward female leaders stems from a misconstrued lack of fit between traditional masculine views of leaders and the communal caretaker stereotype of women portrayed in the media (Simon & Hoyt, 2012). In the documentary *Miss Representation* (Siebel-Newsom & Costanzo, 2011), an aspiring actress, Jennifer Siebel-Newsom, shares the pressure she felt to mold herself into the myth of the communal caretaker stereotype. While she graduated from Stanford University with an MBA, she was pushed to remove this degree from her resume for fear of appearing too threatening to prospective directors and filmmakers. In addition, she found minimal, multidimensional roles as options; the female characters often lacked the depth and complexity exhibited in male protagonists of films.

Some movies, like *Three Men and a Baby* (Field, Cort, & Nimoy, 1987) and *Kindergarten Cop* (Reitman, Grazer, & Reitman, 1990), portray men in the archetypal woman's role of the caretaker. At first glance, this may seem like a step toward gender equality, but upon further examination the viewer sees the communal caretaker myth being retold through the misfit of a man unsuccessfully trying to fill a traditional female role. This bumbling father role remains a common staple in sitcoms, such as Bob Duncan from *Good Luck Charlie* (Baker & Vaupen, 2010) and Hal from *Malcom in the Middle* (Boomer, 2000). Men in these shows are depicted as lacking in basic skills and amusing when they stumble through and make myriad mistakes. A woman depicted as stumbling through mothering or caretaking would never be viewed as humorous (Macdonald, 2009).

An ethnic subcategory within the communal caretaker myth focuses on the Black woman character as helper to the White main character. This helper storyline gets retold both as the best friend role and as the magical sage. The magical sage, referenced in African American criticism as the "Magical Negro," can be seen in characters like Oda Mae Brown played by Whoopi Goldberg in *Ghost* (Weinstein & Zucker, 1990) and the Oracle played by Gloria Foster in *The Matrix* (Silver, Wachowski, & Wachowski, 1999). These characters do exhibit amazing leadership in their wisdom and advice to the main characters, but upon closer examination we see they hold no personal goals or motivation besides guiding the main character. Their seemingly magical powers focus on assisting the protagonist out of predicaments (Glenn & Cunningham, 2009). The best friend storyline continues this theme of nurturing the main character without consideration for their own interests or ambitions. Exemplars of this myth include Delia played by Viola Davis as best friend and advice expert to Julia Robert's character in *Eat Pray Love* (Kleiner, Pitt, Wlodkowski, & Murphy, 2010) and Tracie Thomas as Anne Hathaway's sidekick in *The Devil Wears Prada* (Finerman & Frankel, 2006). Television executive Rose Catherine Pinkney asserts that "historically, people of color have had to play nurturing, rational caretakers of the white lead characters" (Braxton, 2007, para. 9).

One of the courses I, Shana, teach on a regular basis is a master's level class for teachers called "Leadership, Worldviews and Contemporary Issues in Education." A significant portion of students in this course tell me or write in their papers that they do not consider themselves leaders. All the students who shared this have been female, while not a single male has said it. When I push for why, most of them share their stereotypical image of a leader being the charismatic, male speaker inciting a group to action. I found this surprising for college-educated women, and it made me wonder how many more women without the experience of higher education have internalized the communal caretaker stereotype.

The runway-ready ringleader myth portrays women with model-like beauty, but also the physically aggressive leadership of a male hero character like the fictional character of James Bond. This stereotypical masculine aggressiveness and stereotypical view of female attractiveness gives us mixed messages about female leadership (Taylor & Setters, 2011). Some researchers have termed these attractive protagonists as counterstereotypical; however, "in light of the importance of physical appearance for such figures, it may be more accurate to characterize them as both challenging and reinforcing gender stereotypes" (Taylor & Setters, 2011, p. 35). Television shows produced in the 1970s, which include *Charlie's Angels* (Spelling & Goldberg, 1976), *Policewoman* (Gerber, 1974), and *Wonder Woman* (Baumes & Cramer, 1975) did "showcase women in lead roles, although the women actors still conformed in very obvious ways to the stereotypes of normative femininity, being beautiful, slender, and white" (Byerly & Ross, 2008, p. 25). Women in these shows embraced strong leadership roles, but the actresses' physical appearance still appealed to the male fantasy. The runway-ready ringleader myth is retold in current roles like Jane Smith in *Mr. and Mrs. Smith* (Goldsman, Milchan, Foster, & Liman, 2005), Nikita in *Nikita* (Silverstein, 2010), and Kate Becket of *Castle* (Bernstein & Bowman,

2009). Siebel-Newsom (2011) stresses that "even though women are placed in action roles and doing things supposedly on her own terms, she very much is objectified and exists for the male viewer" (29:20).

In analyzing the runway-ready ringleader category, we found that if a Latina character was present in a film or television show, she overwhelmingly fit into the runway-ready ringleader category. This is seen in the characters played by Eva Longoria in *Desperate Housewives* (Cherry, 2004), Sophia Vergara in *Modern Family*, (Levitan, 2009) and Eva Mendes in *The Women* (English, Jagger, Johnson, Pearman, & English, 2008). In a study of the hot Latina stereotype, Merskin (2010) found that Eva Longoria's "prime time pinup status and promotional positioning in magazines reinforce the already prominent, oversexed, under-dressed decisive and divisive character she embodies on *DH*" (p. 157). In other words, Eva's role as the sassy Latina did not stop with her character, Gabrielle Solis, but continued into Eva's real-world persona with strategic marketing and promotional appearances. Additionally, the media often stereotypes Latina characters into one pan-Latino identity, instead of recognizing the unique experiences of Central, Caribbean, and South American Latinas (Davila, 2001; Guzman & Valdivia, 2004). Merskin (2010) claimed that if "Anglos, by the way of media-supplied information, come not to expect much of Latinas and, because of the function of internalized oppression, Latinas do not expect much for themselves, the cycle of oppression continues uninterrupted" (pp. 172–173).

For all ethnicities, this hypersexualizing of women in the runway-ready ringleader myth affects young girls' perception of achieving positions of leadership. Young women often begin believing their physical appearance, which consists of physical attractiveness along with masculine aggressiveness, is their only path to power, leadership, or success (Siebel-Newsom & Costanzo, 2011). Taylor and Setters (2011) found, in their study, that women viewers held higher expectations for the runway-ready ringleader than their male counterparts. After viewing media with stereotypical masculine leadership roles along with stereotypical feminine beauty, women viewers maintained heightened superwomen or "ideal women" biases—the belief that women need to be able to do it all and look like a model in the process.

The devil woman stereotype has been made prominent in movies such as *The Devil Wears Prada*: "Okay, she's tough, but if Miranda were a man, . . . no one would notice anything about her, except how great she is at her job" (Finerman & Frankel, 2006, 1:26:21). This quote by Anne Hathaway's character in the movie, Andrea Sachs, captures the complexity of women in high power positions. If Miranda were a man, would she be characterized as a devil or as an assertive and effective leader? Traditionally, the underlying belief persists that female leaders must take on masculine leadership qualities that include being analytical, competitive, hierarchical, rational, unemotional, strategic, and assertive. Fitting into this mythical model, women need to both look like and act like a man (Court, 2005; Kruse & Prettyman, 2008).

This stereotype is often reinforced in the media with woman-to-woman conflict: the myth of only one devil woman running the show. If two women work in the same position and achieve an equally noticeable amount of success, they automatically become classified as enemies. For example, American journalists Katie Couric and Diane Sawyer were often discussed in the media emphasizing the "feud" between the two women (Siebel-Newsom & Costanzo, 2011). Shows like *Ally McBeal* (D'Elia, & Kelley, 1997) used this woman conflict theme as a recurring story line. Two arguing male characters are likely characterized as debating, in contrast to female characters being labeled as having a catfight.

Within this myth of the devil woman, we found the *dragon lady* stereotype of Asian Americans to be pronounced. This myth portrays Asian woman leaders as domineering, ruthless, and underhanded. While our study did not focus on 1920s film, we found it interesting that actress Anna May Wong played numerous dragon lady roles during this era. She moved to Europe for a time as an escape from this type cast. In a 1933 magazine interview, she explained her move: "I was so tired of the parts I had to play. Why is it that the screen Chinese is nearly always the villain of the piece, and so cruel a villain—murderous, treacherous, a snake in the grass? We are not like that" (Sakamoto, 1987, para. 10). More recent characterizations of this myth include Kimmy-Jin in *Pitch Perfect* (Brooks, Handelman, Banks, & Moore, 2012) and Sun from *Lost* (Abrams, 2004). Madame Gao from *Daredevil* (Goddard, 2015) takes the myth to the extreme as a shrewd crime boss that employs blind Chinese workers to process her heroin and even sends them to kill her enemies as suicide bombers.

THE IMPACT OF MEDIA MYTHS

While the masculine stereotype of leadership has lessened in recent years, it continues to permeate both the media and our internal belief systems (Koenig, Eagly, Mitchell, & Ristikari, 2011). The United States reality show, *The Apprentice* (Burnett, Trump, & Bienstock, 2004), looks at leadership from a competitive vantage point with male and female leaders vying for the top spot. Sung (2011) conducted a study of viewers of this show and found that women who embraced both masculine and feminine qualities in their leadership styles were viewed more negatively than their male counterparts. Sung (2011) explored the various characteristics associated with "masculine speech styles" and "feminine speech styles" (p. 90). In the observation and analysis of both male and female managers' leadership approaches, Sung found a mixing of masculine and feminine styles. Although both genders engaged in this *mixing* of discourse, the female and male managers were viewed differently by the viewers. The female manager was characterized as "overly aggressive," ultimately illustrating that "women in general may be under more constraints in enacting leadership than men when they transgress stereotypical gendered expectations for their speech patterns" (Sung, 2011, p. 101). As leaders, women are often confronted with the paradox that they should be masculine but not lose their femininity (Hoyt, 2013).

For many of us, the ability to analyze the underlying myths of women and leadership in the media remains inhibited by the idea that it is *just entertainment*. While entertaining, these media portrayals can additionally be used as powerful vehicles for either reinforcing traditional roles and values, or challenging them (Kruse & Prettyman, 2008). With the average American watching 34 hours of television per week, this media exerts itself as a powerful force in contemporary myth telling (Hinckley, 2012). In two studies by Simon and Hoyt (2012) they found that "female participants who viewed images of women in counterstereotypical roles as a part of an ostensibly separate study then reported lower negative self-perceptions and greater leadership aspirations after performing a leadership task than participants who viewed images of women in stereotypical roles" (p. 241).

Hoyt (2005) stressed that for women to respond against stereotypes or engage "in behaviors or thoughts counter to those prescribed by the stereotype, is likely only to be a response of those who have high, as opposed to low, leadership efficacy" (p. 3). Self-efficacy describes a person's self-concept of their own ability to effectively lead. Numerous studies have highlighted leadership self-efficacy as a key indicator of individual, group, and organizational successes (Chemers, Watson, & May, 2000; Hoyt, Murphy, Halverson, & Watson, 2003; Murphy, 2001). Strong self-efficacy can be worn down if myths become the dominant soundtrack in the back of our minds.

While becoming Dr. Matamala impacted my life dramatically, becoming a mother brought the importance of media images home. My son taught me one of my most dynamic lessons in the power of the media myth and self-efficacy. When he was around the age of three, I took him to a new park in the area. He ran to the park from the car, excited about the new play equipment. He stopped short and stared at the large sign at the entrance, and, running back, he grabbed my hand to show me the sign. "Look, Mom, it's me!" he yelled, touching the sign. The sign portrayed drawings of a young boy with black hair and a brown complexion demonstrating the play equipment. Gripped by the sign, he spent a good five minutes, an eternity for a three-year-old at a park, looking at and talking about it. As I shared in his excitement, I also felt sadness. From my own dominant culture lens, I thought we had done a good job of exposing our adopted Guatemalan son to his culture in a positive way. My husband is Hispanic, so my son has a father who looks like him along with his grandparents and extended family. I read him books about adoption from a variety of countries. What I had not stopped to consider was the consistent media images and myths he saw told over and over again. I now wore a new pair of lenses in viewing the world. We went to an outdoor mall later that week, and I saw that every mural decorating the buildings was of 1950s' White families. The characters in children's shows and commercials he saw were also predominately White. If they did show a Hispanic character, he or she held a secondary role. As a parent, I need to counter the media myths my son and my daughter hear and see because I do not want these to be the stories they believe concerning themselves.

CHANGING MEDIA PERCEPTIONS

Some current television shows and movies are attempting to portray positive roles of females in leadership positions. One example is Leslie Knope from *Parks and Recreation* (Daniels, Klein, & Schur, 2009). Leslie depicts various leadership qualities, including ambition, genuinely caring about her work and her employees, authenticity, and optimism. She portrays openness about her areas of needed growth, which include perfectionism and trouble delegating (Hamsmith, 2014). The television show *Commander in Chief* (Botchco, 2005), depicted a female political figure who played the role of a wife, mother, and leader of the free world. While the show was cancelled after one season, a survey distributed after the release of the show showed 68% of viewers were more likely to accept a female president (Siebel-Newsom & Costanzo, 2011).

The lead actress on *Commander in Chief* (Botchco, 2005), Geena Davis, launched a think tank a few years ago after seeing a lack of strong female characters on shows she watched with her daughter. The Geena Davis Institute partnered with professors from the University of Southern California in conducting a study on media gender roles. The study looked at more than 11,000 characters and showed that 44.3% of female characters in primetime television are employed, which closely mirrors the real world figure of 46.7%. This is a step in the right direction, but, in sharp contrast, the study showed that 81% of jobs are held by men in shows that are geared toward children. Another interesting discovery showed that almost none of the female leads were also mothers while, in reality, 60% of working women are mothers. Additionally, the study looked at the antiheroes like the characters in *The Shield* (Ryan, 2002), *Breaking Bad* (Gilligan, 2008), and *Nip/Tuck* (Murphy & Robin, 2003) and found that women were not embraced as an antihero in the same way as a male character. Concerning leadership, the study found primetime shows depicting women company heads only 14% of the time, with the real-world statistics at 25% (Ulaby, 2013).

While not a focus of this study, it is interesting to note that some commercials are leading the way in changing media perceptions. The Proctor and Gamble feminine products brand Always™ began a campaign named #LikeAGirl to combat a survey which found 72% of girls do feel society restricts them. In this commercial, young girls discuss their beliefs about how their culture views girls. One girl mentions that girls are always being rescued; they are never the ones to rescue. After the girls express their personal feelings, they write a stereotype on a plain white box. The white boxes begin to accumulate with stereotypical phrases about girls written on them. The young girls are then asked to push away or knock down the boxes as a symbolic action of empowering them to defy the stereotypes.

DISCUSSION

Evidence points to the discordant views of leadership and female gender stereotypes (Eagly & Karua, 2002). The aim of this study focused on contributing to the field of women and leadership by highlighting pervasive themes of incongruence of women leaders in film and television. One of the most interesting discoveries from this study was the repackaging of the communal caretaker stereotype. The 1950s saw this housewife stereotype blatantly retold in television shows like *Father Knows Best* (Rodney, 1954) and *Leave It to Beaver* (Connelly & Mosher, 1957). Currently, primetime television shows approximately 44% percent of female characters as employed, which does show a shift from the 1950s' stereotype. Today the communal caretaker myth is told more often through the bumbling father. Homer from *The Simpsons* (Groening & Brooks, 1989). epitomizes the man making mistake after mistake when he tries to fulfill traditional female roles. This not only perpetuates the communal caretaker role for women, but it also reinforces the stereotype that men cannot venture out of their own stereotypical roles.

The study also found the runway-ready ringleader myth gaining popularity in the 1970s and continuing strong today. We feel this myth might be one of the most damaging for young women because it does highlight women in strong leadership roles, but with unrealistic model-like beauty. Young women are told the story of the need to have traditionally male leadership qualities, but keep their femininity by looking and dressing for the runway. Lead female characters in shows like *Nikita* (Silverstein, 2010) are often depicted running in high heels through action scenes as intense as those in *Mission Impossible* (Cruise, Wagner, & De Palma, 1996).

Additionally, the study found a large subcategory of films and television shows highlighting woman-to-woman conflict within the theme of the devil women. In these portrayals, not only is the woman leader portrayed as a devil, but she also cannot collaborate with other women. *Ally McBeal*

(D'Elia & Kelley, 1997), *Desperate Housewives* (Cherry, 2004), and *Melrose Place* (Spelling, 1992) use this theme as a recurring storyline. We often hear women say they would much rather work for a male leader than a female, and this myth continues to retell the story that high-power women cannot get along with other high-power women.

While ethnic stereotypes were not the central focus of this study, we felt the need to include these myths. With media myths of women leaders permeating film and television, myths based on ethnicity further categorize otherness. Rocchio (2000) states, "The contemporary status of race in mainstream American culture is intimately bound to the process of representations within and through the mass media" (p. 4). We were particularly struck by the magical sage myth, as the Black character's sole purpose is to assist the main White character.

Research on women in leadership found common characteristic threads of collaboration, reflection, problem-solving, relational, and personal high expectations (Brunner, 1999; Grogan, 1999; Sherman, 2005; Tallerico, 2000). A study by Eagly, Johannesen-Schmidt, and van Egen (2003) found women strong in transformational leadership. This kind of female leader displays a sharp contrast to the media myths of the communal caretaker, the runway-ready ring leader, and the devil woman. What would it look like to see more of these types of women leaders depicted in the media? Creating media images "that challenge these assumptions and present alternative models might allow for the public and particularly young women, to consider different paths to and for leadership, different ways to use and dislodge power, and different ways of being in the world" (Kruse & Prettyman, 2008, p. 462).

According to Sharma (2012), "Most women, especially in developing countries, are not able to access effectively the expanding electronic information highways and therefore cannot establish networks that will provide them with alternative sources of information" (p. 3). Even in the Matamala house as I write this chapter, my son is watching the bumbling father on *Good Luck Charlie* (Baker & Vaupen, 2010) as my 14-year-old daughter flips through her Instagram, where I see pages of young women posting model-like selfies. My children come from a home where both my husband and I hold doctorates and leadership positions, but countering these waves of media images can be daunting and exhausting. What child wants a discussion on gender myths with their mom after watching their favorite family sitcom? Changing the dominant media myths themselves will shift the stories we believe about ourselves.

REFERENCES

Abrams, J. J. (Producer). (2004). *Lost* [Television series]. New York, NY: American Broadcasting Company.

Baker, P., & Vaupen, D. (Producers). (2010). *Good luck Charlie* [Television series]. Burbank, CA: Disney Channel.

Baumes, W. L., & Cramer, D. S. (Producers). (1975). *Wonder woman* [Television series]. New York, NY: American Broadcasting Company.

Bennett, L. W. (1980). Myth, ritual, and political control. *Journal of Communication, 30*(4), 166–179. doi: 10.1111/j.1460-2466.1980.tb02028.x

Bernstein, A., & Bowman, R. (Producers). (2009). *Castle* [Television series]. New York, NY: American Broadcasting Company.

Boomer, L. (Producer). (2000). *Malcolm in the middle* [Television series]. Los Angeles, CA: Fox Broadcasting Company.

Botchco, S. (Producer). (2005). *Commander in chief* [Television series]. New York, NY: American Broadcasting Company.

Braun, V., & Clarke, V. (2006). Using thematic analysis in psychology. *Qualitative Research in Psychology, 3*(2), 77–101. doi: 10.1191/1478088706qp063oa

Braxton, G. (2007, August 29). Buddy system. *Los Angeles Times*. Retrieved from http://articles.latimes.com/2007/aug/29/entertainment/et-bff29

Brooks, P., Handelman, M., & Banks, E. (Producers), & Moore, J. (Director). (2012). *Pitch perfect* [Motion picture]. USA: Universal Pictures.

Brunner, C. (1999). *Sacred dreams: Women and the superintendency*. New York, NY: Albany State University of New York Press.

Burgess, D., & Borgida, E. (1999). Who women are, who women should be: Descriptive and prescriptive gender stereotyping in sex discrimination. *Psychology, Public Policy, & Law, 5*(3), 665–692. doi: 10.1037/1076-8971.5.3.665

Burnett, M., Trump, D. J., & Bienstock, J. (Producers). (2004). *The apprentice* [Television series]. New York, NY: American Broadcasting Company.

Byerly, C. M., & Ross, K. (2008). *Women and media: A critical introduction*. Oxford, UK: Blackwell.

Campbell, J. (1988). *The power of myth*. New York, NY: Anchor.

Chemers, M. M., Watson, C. B., & May, S. (2000). Dispositional affect and leadership effectiveness: A comparison of self-esteem, optimism and efficacy. *Personality and Social Psychology Bulletin, 26*(3), 267–277. doi: 10.1177/0146167200265001

Cherry, M. (Producer). (2004). *Desperate housewives* [Television series]. New York, NY: American Broadcasting Company.

Coltrane, S., & Adams, M. (1997). Work–family imagery and gender stereotypes: Television and the reproduction of difference. *Journal of Vocational Behavior, 50*(2), 323–347. doi: 10.1006/jvbe.1996.1575

Connelly, J., & Mosher, B. (Producers). (1957). *Leave it to beaver* [Television series]. New York, NY: American Broadcasting Company.

Court, M. (2005). Negotiating and reconstructing gendered leadership discourses. In J. Collard & C. Reynolds (Eds.), *Leadership, gender and culture in education: Male and female perspectives* (pp. 1–21). New York, NY: Open University Press.

Cruise, T., & Wagner, P. (Producers), & De Palma, B. (Director). (1996). *Mission: Impossible* [Motion picture]. USA: Paramount Pictures.

Daniels, G., Klein, H., & Schur, M. (Producers). (2009). *Parks and recreation* [Television series]. New York, NY: National Broadcasting Company.

Davila, A. (2001). *Latinos Inc. The marketing and making of people*. Berkeley, CA: University of California Press.

D'Elia, B., & Kelley, D. E. (Producers). (1997). *Ally McBeal* [Television series]. Los Angeles, CA: Fox Broadcasting Company.

Eagly, A. H., Johannesen-Schmidt, M. C., & van Engen, M. (2003). Transformational, transactional, and laissez-faire leadership styles. A meta-analysis comparing women and men. *Psychological Bulletin, 129*(4), 569–591. doi: 10.1037/0033-2909.129.4.569

Eagly, A. H., & Karau, S. J. (2002). Role congruity theory of prejudice toward female leaders. *Psychological Review, 109*(3), 573–598. doi: 10.1037/0033-295X.109.3.573

English, D., Jagger, M., Johnson, B., & Pearman, V. (Producers), & English, D. (Director). (2008). *The women* [Motion picture]. USA: Picturehouse.

Field, T., & Cort, R. W. (Producers), & Nimoy, L. (Director). (1987). *Three men and a baby* [Motion picture]. USA: Buena Vista Pictures.

Finerman, W. (Producer), & Frankel, D. (Director). (2006). *The devil wears Prada* [Motion picture]. USA: 20th Century Fox.

Fleiss, M., & Levenson, L. (Producers). (2002). *The bachelor* [Television series]. New York, NY: American Broadcasting Company.

Ganahl, D. J., Prinsen, T. J., & Netzley, S. B. (2003). A content analysis of prime time commercials: A contextual framework of gender representation. *Sex Roles, 49*(9/10), 545–551. doi: 10.1023/A:1025893025658

Gerber, D. (Producer). (1974). *Police woman* [Television series]. New York, NY: National Broadcasting Company.

Gilligan, V. (Producer). (2008). *Breaking bad* [Television series]. New York, NY: AMC.

Glenn, C. L., & Cunningham, L. J. (2009). The power of black magic: The magical Negro and White salvation in film. *Journal of Black Studies, 40*(2), 135. doi: 10.1177/0021934707307831

Glick, P., & Fiske, S. T. (1999). Sexism and other "isms": Independence, status, and the ambivalent content of stereotypes. In W. B. Swann, Jr., & J. H. Langlois (Eds.), *Sexism and stereotypes in modern society: The gender science of Janet Taylor Spence* (pp. 193–221). Washington, DC: American Psychological Association.

Goddard, D. (Producer). (2015). *Daredevil* [Television series]. Los Gatos, CA: Netflix.

Goffman, E. (1977). The arrangement between the sexes. *Theory & Society, 4*(3), 301–331.

Goldsman, A., Milchan, A., & Foster, L. (Producers), & Liman, D. (Director). (2005). *Mr. & Mrs. Smith* [Motion picture]. USA: 20th Century Fox.

Groening, M., & Brooks, J. L. (Producers). (1989). *The Simpsons* [Television series]. Los Angeles, CA: Fox Broadcasting Company.

Grogan, M. (1999). Equity/equality issues of gender, race and class. *Educational Administration Quarterly, 35*(4), 518–536. doi: 10.1177/00131619921968743

Guest, G., MacQueen, K. M., & Namey, E. E. (2012). *Applied thematic analysis.* Thousand Oaks, CA: Sage.

Guzman, I. M., & Valdivia, A. N. (2004). Brain, brow, and booty: Latina iconicity in U.S. popular culture. *The Communication Review, 7*(2), 205–221. doi: 10.1080/10714420490448723

Hall, S. (1997). *Representation: Cultural representations and signifying practices. Culture, media and identities.* London, UK: Sage.

Hamsmith, R. (2014). Leadership lessons from Leslie Knope of "Parks and Recreation." *Employee and Workplace, Entrepreneur Resources, Informational, Personal Branding.* Retrieved from https://www.qualitylogoproducts.com/blog/leadership-lessons-leslie-knope-parks-and-recreation/

Heilman, M. E. (2001). Description and prescription: How gender stereotypes prevent women's ascent up the organizational ladder. *Journal of Social Issues, 57*(4), 657–674. doi: 10.1111/0022-4537.00234

Hinckley, D. (2012). Americans spend 34 hours a week watching TV, according to Nielsen numbers. *NY Daily News.* Retrieved from http://www.nydailynews.com/entertainment/tv-movies/americans-spend-34-hours-week-watching-tv-nielsen-numbers-article-1.1162285

Hoyt, C. L. (2005). The role of leadership efficacy and stereotype activation in women's identification with leadership. *Journal of Leadership and Organizational Studies, 11*(4), 1–14. doi: 10.1177/107179190501100401

Hoyt, C. L. (2013). Women and leadership. In P. G. Northouse (Ed.), *Leadership: Theory and practice* (pp. 349–382). Thousand Oaks, CA: Sage.

Hoyt, C. L., & Chemers, M. M. (2008). Social stigma and leadership: A long climb up a slippery ladder. In C. L. Hoyt, G. R. Goethals, & D. R. Forsyth (Eds.), *Leadership at the crossroads: Leadership and psychology* (Vol. 1, pp. 165–180). Westport, CT: Praeger.

Hoyt, C., Murphy, S., Halverson, S., & Watson C. (2003). Group leadership: Efficacy and effectiveness. *Group dynamics: Theory, Research, and Practice, 7*(4), 259–274. doi: 10.1037/1089-2699.7.4.259

Kleiner, J., Pitt, B., & Wlodkowski, S. (Producers), & Murphy, R. (Director). (2010). *Eat pray love* [Motion picture]. USA: Columbia Pictures.

Koenig, A. M., Eagly, A. H., Mitchell, A. A., & Ristikari, T. (2011). Are leader stereotypes masculine? A meta-analysis of three research paradigms. *Psychological Bulletin, 137*(4), 616–642. doi: 0.1037/a0023557

Kruse, S. D., & Prettyman, S. S. (2008). Women, leadership, and power revisiting the wicked witch of the west. *Gender and Education, 20*(5), 451–464. doi: 10.1080/09540250701805797

Levitan, S. (Producer). (2009). *Modern family* [Television series]. New York, NY: American Broadcasting Company.

Macdonald, M. (2009). *Representing women: Myths of femininity in the popular media.* London, UK: Bloomsbury Academic.

Marshall, G. (Producer). (1974). *Happy days* [Television series]. New York, NY: American Broadcasting Company.

Merskin, D. (2010). *Media, minorities, and meaning: A critical introduction.* New York, NY: Peter Lang.

Murphy, R., & Robin, M. M. (Producers). (2003). *Nip/tuck* [Television series]. Los Angeles, CA: FX.

Murphy, S. E. (2001). Leader self-regulation: The role of self-efficacy and multiple intelligences. In R .E. Riggio & S. E. Murphy (Eds.), *Multiple intelligences and leadership* (pp. 163–186). Mahwah, NJ: Lawrence Erlbaum Associates.

Newsom, J. S., & Costanzo, J. (Producers), & Newsom, J. S. (Director). (2011). *Miss representation* [Motion picture]. United States: Girls' Club Entertainment.

Phelan, J. E., & Rudman, L. A. (2010). Prejudice toward female leaders: Backlash effects and women's impression management dilemma. *Social and Personality Psychology Compass, 4*(10), 807–820. doi: 10.1111/j.1751-9004.2010.00306.x

Picard, P. R. (Producer). (1979). *The dukes of hazard* [Television series]. New York, NY: Columbia Broadcasting System.

Reichert, T. (2008). *Investigating the use of sex in media promotion and advertising.* New York, NY: Routledge.

Reichert, T., & Carpenter, C. (2004). An update on sex in magazine advertising: 1983 to 2003. *Journalism & Mass Communication Quarterly, 81*(4), 823–837. doi: 10.1177/107769900408100407

Reitman, I., & Grazer, B. (Producers), & Reitman, I. (Director). (1990). *Kindergarten cop* [Motion picture]. USA: Universal Pictures.

Ridgeway, C. L. (2001). Gender, status, and leadership. *Journal of Social Issues, 57*(4), 637–655.

Rocchio, V. F. (2000). *Reel racism: Confronting Hollywood's Construction of Afro-American Culture. Thinking through cinema.*. Boulder, CO: Westview.

Rodney, E. B. (Producer). (1954). *Father knows best* [Television series]. New York, NY: Columbia Broadcasting System.

Rounder, D., Slater, M. D., & Domenech-Rodríguez, M. (2003). Adolescent evaluation of gender role and sexual imagery in television advertisements. *Journal of Broadcasting & Electronic Media, 47*(3), 435–454. doi: 10.1207/s15506878jobem4703_7

Ryan, S. (Producer). (2002). *The shield* [Television series]. Los Angeles, CA: FX.

Sakamoto, E. (1987, July 12). Anna May Wong and the dragon-lady syndrome. *Los Angeles Times.* Retrieved from http://articles.latimes.com/1987-07-12/entertainment/ca-3279_1_dragon-lady

Schein, V. E. (2001). A global look at psychological barriers to women's progress in management. *Journal of Social Issues, 57*(4), 675–688. doi: 10.1111/0022-4537.00235

Schwartz, S (Producer). (1969). *The brady bunch* [Television series]. New York, NY: American Broadcasting Company.

Seiter, E. (1986). Stereotypes and the media: A re-evaluation. *Journal of Communication, 36*(2), 14–26. doi: 10.1111/j.1460-2466.1986.tb01420.x

Sharma, A. (2012). Portrayal of women in mass media. *Media Watch: An International Journal in Media and Communication.* Retrieved from http://www.mediawatch global.com/wp-content/uploads/2012/04/Portrayal-of-Women-in-Mass-Media .pdf

Sherman, W. H. (2005). Preserving the status quo or renegotiating leadership: Women's experiences with a district-based aspiring leaders program. *Educational Administration Quarterly 41*(5), 707–740. doi: 10.1177/0013161X05279548

Siebel-Newsom, J., & Costanzo, J. (Producers), & Siebel-Newsom, J. (Director). (2011). *Miss Representation* [Motion picture]. USA: Girls' Club Entertainment.

Silver, J. (Producer), & Wachowski, L., & Wachowski, L. (Directors). (1999). *The matrix* [Motion picture]. USA: Warner Bros.

Silverstein, C. (Producer). (2010). *Nikita* [Television series]. Burbank, CA: The CW Television Network.

Simon, S., & Hoyt, C. L. (2012). Exploring the effect of media images on women's leadership self-perceptions and aspirations. *Group Processes & Intergroup Relations, 16*(2), 232–245. doi: 10.1177/1368430212451176

Spelling, A. (Producer). (1992). *Melrose place* [Television series]. Los Angeles, CA: Fox Broadcasting Company.

Spelling, A., & Goldberg, L. (Producers). (1976). *Charlie's angels* [Television series]. New York, NY: American Broadcasting Company.

Sung, C. C. M. (2011). Doing gender and leadership: A discursive analysis of media representations in a reality TV show. *English Text Construction, 4*(1), 85–111. Doi: 10.1075/etc.4.1.05sun

Tallerico, M. (2000). Gaining access to the superintendency: Headhunting, gender and color. *Educational Administration Quarterly, 36*(1), 18–43. doi: 10.1177/00131610021968886

Taylor L. D., & Setters, T. (2011, July). Watching aggressive, attractive, female protagonists shapes gender roles for women among male and female undergraduate viewers. *Sex Roles* [serial online]. *65,* 35–46. doi: 10.1007/s11199-011-9960-1

Ulaby, N. (2013, May 18). *Working women on television: A mixed bag at best. NPR.* Retrieved from http://www.npr.org/blogs/monkeysee/2013/05/18/184832930/working-women-on-television-a-mixed-bag-at-best

Weinstein, L. (Producer), & Zucker, J. (Director). (1990). *Ghost* [Motion picture]. USA: Paramount Pictures.

CHAPTER 13

WORKING IN SHONDALAND

Representations of African American Women in Leadership

Carrie Wilson-Brown and Samantha Szczur
Eastern Illinois University

Thursday evening programming holds a special significance in American television. Networks command high prices for advertising slots on Thursday nights as companies make one last marketing attempt before the weekend. Currently, ABC's Thursday night programming consists entirely of dramas produced by ShondaLand, the production company of Shonda Rhimes. The lineup of *Grey's Anatomy*, *Scandal*, and *How to Get Away with Murder* draws millions of viewers each week. A striking theme among these shows is the inclusion of strong female roles portraying women who are successful in their respective professional arenas. Further, many of Rhimes's key characters are African American women.

In the chapter that follows, we perform an analysis of representations of African American women in leadership positions on two interrelated levels. First, we examine the phenomenon of Shonda Rhimes as auteur and successful African American businesswoman. We consider her own creative

Gender, Media, and Organization, pages 225–242

vision and self-representations and also how she is represented in various media venues. Second, focusing on *Grey's Anatomy, Scandal,* and *How to Get Away with Murder* (HTGAWM), we suggest that despite Rhimes's downplaying of race and sex, pivotal (female African American) characters in each show both portray and face significant challenges related to race and gender. Specifically, we consider Dr. Miranda Bailey (an attending physician on *Grey's Anatomy*), Olivia Pope (a political image consultant on *Scandal*), and Annalise Keating (a criminal law professor on *How to Get Away with Murder*). Despite rhetoric that Rhimes's shows (and our society at large) are postfeminist and postrace, the texts can be read in a way that demonstrates the very real and significant challenges that African American women in leadership positions face. Thus, representations of Bailey, Pope, and Keating evidence the reality that expectations related to race and gender greatly influence and shape the work and lives of African American women. Further, we attend to the flows of political economy as they relate to who and what can or cannot attain success in the televisual entertainment industry. We argue that though the representations of Rhimes's and ShondaLand's African American female leads be what they may, the discourse surrounding the shows must attempt to sell a benign (lack of) racial politics. We employ literatures from media studies and critical organizational communication to theoretically ground and perform our analysis.

RACE, REPRESENTATION, AND TELEVISION

Television has a storied history of aligning products, consumption, and national programming. Over the decades, successful television series were those that appealed to broader cultural sentiments, largely reinscribing dominant ideologies and stereotypes. For example, television's role in constructing a postwar, 1950s national identity was dependent on reaffirming sameness by omitting difference, and reaffirming gender, familial, and sexual roles in the growing White suburban middle class. Spigel's (1992) cultural history of television argues that TV physically and ideologically constructed domestic space and what happened, in thought and practice, in that space. Thus, as the ideal consumer emerged, early 1950s programming relied on reformist fantasies of mammies and servants. Shows like *Beulah*, a comedy about a maid for a White family who is commonly referred to as the *queen of the kitchen*, were crucial in constructing representations of African Americans in the mass media. Gray (1995) stated: "It [1950s television] remains the moment against which all other television representations of blackness have reacted. And it is the defining moment with which subsequent representations...remain in dialogue" (p. 74). Televisually in the 1950s, Blackness was the distinct other and labored for White domestic happiness.

The civil rights movement and the Black power movement seemed to challenge the national identity constructed in the 1950s. Television had to accommodate a growing resistance to racial and political segregation, and socially, minorities began to explore racial identity. With this shift in national consciousness, African American representations on TV became less stereotypical and more benign. Since the 1960s, the industry has strived to create an economic and representational structure aligned with what Gray (2005) characterized as the "logic of assimilation...codified into a social project of color blindness, a legal project of equal opportunity, and a moral project of individualism and self-responsibility" (p. 101). Shows such as *Julia* and *I Spy* placed their Black leads in all-White worlds of work, community, and home, rendering all cultural referent points that do not read as "White" invisible.

As Hunt (2005) observed in his survey of representational politics and market practices, by the 1970s and 1980s African American activist groups and community leaders demanded that TV produce representations of people of color that were relevant to their community. The success of activists in arguing that African American audiences are political consumers of TV drew a response from creators and programmers to provide authentic and realistic representations of African Americans. During the 1970s largely White male producers, such as Norman Lear, moved African Americans representationally out of the suburbs and into an authentic urban experience. Television shows such as *Good Times* and *What's Happening* satisfied the political forces calling for authentic representations and the market forces by not alienating Whites. This management of containment, which offers a separate but equal space where Black lives parallel Whites, maintains the fiction of the ideal White audience/consumer-populated mediated culture (Gray, 1995, 2005). Within this urban landscape, Black men are buffoons, single Black mothers replace Black fathers, and the sassy Black woman makes her ideological home. Additionally, to offset representations of urban poverty, shows like *Gimme a Break* and *The Jeffersons* tellingly reinforce the importance of ascending to the middle class.

Gray (1995) contended that, as in the 1970s, television shows in the 1980s mediated between the site of the Black home and the realism of urban spaces. The TV industry was legislatively left vulnerable by the Federal Communications Committee (FCC), which sought to break the power base of the top three networks by limiting hours that networks could produce programming. In this environment, independent producers such as Carsey-Werner (*Cosby, Different World*) and Stephen Bochco (*Hill Street Blues, LA Law*) representationally corrected stereotypical depictions of the Black family and African American demonstrations of work and authority. Springer (2007) identified the *Cosby Show* as an important site of middle-class respectability for the Black middle class and noted that Claire Huxtable in particular is the consummate

"Black lady," the modern mammy who is appropriately subordinate to White male authority yet maintains a level of ambition and the aggressiveness needed to ascend into the middle class. *Hill Street Blues* began a trend that continued into the 1990s and 2000s of multicultural casts in the insular world of work where discussions of race are diffused by representational equity (Harris, 2006). These multicultural procedural ensemble dramas continued with *LA Law* and *St. Elsewhere* in the 1980s and *ER* and *Chicago Hope* in the 1990s.

By the 1990s, with increased consolidation of the media industry and despite the entrance of a fourth network, Fox, there was a significant decrease in African American-centered shows. Historically, the industry's response to legislative and economic threats by civil rights and media activist organizations questioning the exclusion of minority representation at all levels of the media industry has largely been met with public relations solutions. Exemplified by the signing of 1999 Network Diversity Agreement by all four networks, temporary scholarships, grants, internships, and training programs, designed to grow the ranks of minority creative professionals in the industry, have been largely unsuccessful and unsustainable. Few African American executive heads and producers emerged during the early 2000s. Though *The Wire* received accolades as one of the most complex shows in its exploration of race and diverse casting, most network shows remained committed to half-hour situation comedies such as the CW's *Girlfriends* and *The Game,* or police procedurals such as the *Law and Order* franchise.

The television landscape rewards transmedia storytelling and audience participation in a global marketplace. Like the cinema, which is under increasing pressure to produce films that are profitable overseas, television producers in the U.S. must create a commodity that can sell domestically and to overseas cable and satellite providers. Havens (2013) identified *Grey's Anatomy* as successful in overseas markets for its adherence to middle-class professional values that appeal to viewers in the European marketplace. Diverse workplace environments are also appealing to middle-class and upper-middle-class minority audiences in smaller markets such as Brazil and South Africa. According to Barraclough (2014), *Grey's Anatomy* was airing in 238 international markets and *Scandal* was airing in 227. *HTGAWM* was recently sold to 158 territories including most of Europe, Vietnam, South Africa, China, all of Africa, and Israel. Warner (2014) argued that Rhimes's practice of blind-casting—when race is not written into the script—is a disavowal of racially specific politics and, conversely, her cast of characters practices a similar strategy that results in limited racial identification.

AFRICAN AMERICAN WOMEN AND LEADERSHIP

As an intellectual project, critical theory complicates social and cultural flows of power. Growing out of the critical tradition, feminist organizational analyses examine networks of power, sex, gender, and organizational materiality and discourse. Much of early feminist organizational research focused on professional women and their lived experiences in organizational settings. In other words, this research sought to articulate what it was like for women at work. For example, in her classic work *Men and Women of the Corporation*, Kanter (1977) outlined four archetypal stereotypes of women in workplaces. The "pet" is seen as a novelty. The "sex object" is present for viewing and physical pleasure. The "mother" nurtures in feminized ways, while the "iron maiden" is tough and enacts masculine characteristics.

Subsequent work in critical organizational communication studies has elaborated upon the challenges faced by working women. Much has been written about the seemingly insurmountable glass ceiling, difficulties managing work and home life, and the informal ways in which women are excluded in organizational settings (Medved & Kirby, 2005; Tracy & Rivera, 2009). Further, in light of postmodern and poststructural turns, contemporary critical organizational research focuses on the social construction and fluidity of sex and gender (Bordo, 1993; Butler, 2006). In this vein, the body is considered a key site where mechanisms of power play out. Nadesan and Trethewey (2000) offered one such analysis in their examination of popular success literature targeted toward women. Ultimately, they unpacked the gendered performances of professional women in relation to the success literature in which "discourses of enterprise and therapy intersect to discipline women's bodies and selves" (p. 224). Similarly, Trethewey (1999), using a feminist Foucauldian approach, suggested that discourses of "professionalism" come to bear on women's bodies by positioning the professional body as a text to be read that is fit and sexualized. Further, Buzzanell and Liu (2005) performed a poststructuralist feminist analysis of women negotiating maternity leave policies, complicating the implications of the pregnant body in professional settings where masculine corporate discourses were privileged over caring and nurturance.

In terms of the leadership literature, a similar trend emerges. When researchers turned their attention to sex and gender in relation to leadership, studies often sought to distinguish discursive strategies and psychological differences between men and women. Turner and Henzl (1987) evidenced this approach in their study of the intersections among sex, gender, power position, and message construction. Similarly, Hirokawa, Kodama, and Harper (1990) examined the persuasive strategies of male and female managers in varying degrees of authority. Subsequent research underscores the social construction of both leaders and leadership. Fairhurst and Grant (2010) highlighted the fluid, social, and communicative features of leadership by suggesting that "leadership is co-constructed, a product of sociohistorical and collective meaning making, and negotiated on an ongoing basis through a complex interplay among leadership actors, be they designated or emergent leaders, managers, and/or followers" (p. 172). Carroll and Levy (2010), recognizing the social fabrication of leadership, linked the co-constitutive process of leadership development to identity. They ultimately suggested that discourses of leadership not only regulate identity, but they also construct identity.

In recent decades, building on feminist and critical organizational literature, academic work has addressed intersectionality—the ways in which multiple facets of identity come to bear upon individuals. Much of this research emerges from feminist standpoint perspectives that also foreground race. This work draws from Collins' (2000) notion of the "outsider within," suggesting that members of nondominant groups cultivate sophisticated understandings of social structures since they are at once included and excluded among them. For example, Allen (1998) recounted her experience as the sole female and person of color in an academic department. She discussed her discomfort in meetings, feeling unable to voice concerns for fear of being too assertive—hence, a "bitch" on one hand or viewed as the stereotypical "loud Black woman" on the other. Allen (2000) provided another standpoint analysis in her treatment of organizational socialization processes, examining the raced and gendered implications of how African American women learn to be full members of an organization. She argued that the literature on organizational socialization assumes the default "White male" positionality and unpacks the ways in which African American women's socialization experiences are shaped by identities of sex and race. Further, Gates (2003) offered a standpoint account in her analysis of the experiences of African American women and men negotiating organizational roles. Her co-researchers (interview participants) reported general feelings of tension and hostility in their working environments growing from differences in race, class, and gender. Yet another example is Forbes's (2009) examination of the persistent sexualization faced by nine Black women in organizational settings. She drew on the broad framework of Black feminist theorizing to address the commodification and sexualization of African American women. Stemming from the racist colonial history in the U.S., African American women have been positioned as the sexual playthings of (White) men (Forbes, 2009). Thus, Forbes described the paradox experienced by her nine participants of being simultaneously hypervisible (sexually available) yet invisible (lacking voice and intellect).

Critical organizational communication theorists have specifically addressed leadership challenges faced by African American women. Parker (2001, 2002) performed several analyses of African American women who are senior executives in their respective organizations. Parker's (2002) study examined the perceived challenges executive African American women face when dealing with White male colleagues and other African Americans. In regard to White male colleagues, participants identified the primary challenges as interpersonal conflict, ignored or co-opted ideas, and exclusion from networks. However, related to their positions of leadership, they also faced challenges from other African Americans, including perceptions of unmet expectations and attacks on character. In a similar study, Parker (2001) examined the reconceptualization of control as a strategy employed by executive African American women to manage their positions of leadership within dominant-culture organizations. Subsequent work, such as Ospina and Su's (2009) article on leadership in social change organizations, continued to interrogate the myriad ways race intersects and influences leadership processes.

To summarize, critical organizational communication scholarship attends to experiences of organizational life in relation to various identity positions. Our analysis builds upon the aforementioned theory as we examine the simultaneity of race and sex in the media representations of Miranda Bailey, Olivia Pope, and Annalise Keating in relation—and sometimes contrast—to Shonda Rhimes's purported strategies of colorblind casting. We stand at the intersection of critical media and organizational communication scholarship to examine and problematize these representations while linking them to larger social and cultural sentiments.

ANALYSIS—SHONDA, SHONDALAND, AND THANK GOD IT'S THURSDAY

ABC's Thursday night programming, dubbed Thank God It's Thursday (TGIT), features three of ShondaLand's wildly successful series. Back to back, *Grey's Anatomy, Scandal,* and *HTGAWM* provide three hours of televised entertainment spliced with heavy-handed advertisements to prep viewers/consumers for the upcoming weekend.

Grey's Anatomy is a medical drama that follows the lives and careers of surgical interns and doctors at Seattle Grace Hospital. The series began in 2005 concluded its 11th season in 2015. The show's protagonist is Meredith Grey, who enters the residency program with a cohort of other residents who quickly become her friends and support structure. Meredith and her cohort are assigned to work under the tutelage of Dr. Miranda Bailey, a general surgery resident. Dr. Bailey, the character upon which we focus, has the notorious reputation of being hard on her interns, prompting the nickname "the Nazi" for her curt and assertive demeanor. Throughout the series, the character evolves in her work and life. Professionally, Dr. Bailey worked in both general surgery and pediatrics, launched a free clinic and a genome mapping project, and eventually filled the role of attending physician. Personally, her first marriage ended shortly after the birth of her son, largely due to her commitment to her job. She eventually remarries another doctor with whom she worked but faces struggles with that marriage as well.

Scandal, premiering in 2012, is a political thriller focusing on Olivia Pope, a former White House communications director who founded her own political crisis management firm. Olivia is known as DC's best "fixer," a whiz at problem solving and image management. She is surrounded by a team of fiercely loyal employees, each of whom Olivia has helped in the past. Olivia is direct, authoritative, and confident. Her professional successes are apparent throughout the series. In addition, her character enters into multiple romantic relationships with high-powered men, the most notable being Olivia's relationship with Fitzgerald "Fitz" Grant, the president of the United States, whom Pope helped to win office. Her character is based upon Judy Smith, the press secretary for George H. W. Bush. Upon her departure from the White House, Smith founded her crisis management organization, Smith and Company. Smith currently co-produces and advises for the series.

How to Get Away with Murder is a legal thriller following Annalise Keating, a criminal law professor at a prestigious Philadelphia university. The show concluded its first season in February 2015. Keating manages her own firm and recruits talented students to work in her practice. Keating's law practice is located on the first floor of the house she shares with her husband, Sam. Keating's professional and personal lives begin as intertwined and become stronger throughout the season. Sam, a Caucasian man, is involved in an extramarital affair with one of his young, White students. This relationship serves as the starting point for a series of murders that are related in convoluted ways. Annalise is known for her unshakable demeanor, shrewd legal prowess, and calculated decision making.

While each of ShondaLand's series includes racially and sexually diverse casts, Rhimes has always maintained that both casting and writing are colorblind processes. Despite such claims, much has been written in the popular press about ShondaLand's assumed emphasis on casting and representing minority populations. For example, speaking to such sentiment, a recent *Deadline Hollywood* article, "Pilots 2015: The Year of Ethnic Castings" details how "the pendulum might have swung a bit too far" (Andreeva, 2015, para. 13) in minority casting for the fall 2015 television season. The *Deadline* piece chastises networks for socially engineering "ethnic casting" (para. 19) by employing an aggressive affirmative action-like a quota system instead of championing a colorblind meritocracy. Unlike the film industry, which has been criticized for a lack of gender and racial diversity among Academy Award nominees, three networks—NBC, ABC, and Fox—currently have a higher percentage of African Americans in primetime than are in the general population (Bauder, Elber, & Moore, 2015). Yet, as television shows with diverse casts have increased, the University of California–Los Angeles'

(UCLA) Hollywood Diversity Report highlights diversity concerns at the executive level (Hunt, Ramon, & Price, 2014). During the 2010–2011 season, only 4% of broadcast comedies and dramas were credited to minority producers. The report specified that a large percentage of this programming is credited to Shonda Rhimes and ShondaLand Productions.

Rhimes's public profile as a producer, writer, and production head semantically, symbolically, and biographically collide with the three Black female characters most closely associated with her production company: Dr. Miranda Bailey, Olivia Pope, and Annalise Keating. The comparison between Rhimes and the character Annalise Keating is highlighted in the racially tinged profile of Rhimes by Alessandra Stanley in the *New York Times*, which opens, "When Shonda Rhimes writes her autobiography, it should be called 'How to Get Away with Being an Angry Black Woman'" (Stanley, 2014, para. 1). The comparison of Rhimes and Annalise Keating in similar stereotypical brush strokes is made despite the fact that a White man is the show's creator and executive producer.

Rhimes's status as super-producer stems from her entrance into a select group of showrunners who are closely identified discursively with the shows they produce. These TV auteurs, like their counterparts in film, are critically lauded for their unique approach to storytelling, aesthetic vision, autobiographical leanings, and differentiated product. A showrunner is typically the series creator who has varying roles—producer, writer, and financial advocate—throughout the run of the series. The modern showrunner is viewed as the public conscience of the show, a conduit for the creative and financial alike. Similar to the emergence of the filmic author, the modern showrunner is a product of institutional, creative, and technological changes in the television industry since the 1970s. Also, like the auteurs identified by Andre Bazin and his protégés in Cuhiers du Cinema in the 1950s, and theorized in the U.S. by Andrew Sarris in 1962, showrunners remain primarily White and male (Rosenberg, 2015; Warner, 2015).

The FCC's passage of the Financial Interest Syndication (fin-syn) Rule in 1970, which barred networks from owning primetime programming, led to the rise of independent producers in the 1980s and 1990s such as Stephen Bochco (*Hill Street Blues, LA Law, NYPD Blue*) and Chris Carter (*The X Files*). Two factors by the 1990s—the repeal of fin-syn and Hollywood's grab for the American teenager—left cable networks and premium cable channels like HBO ready to court the White middle class. These institutional shifts brought creative changes and modified audience tastes that favored serialized novelization, cinematic scope, thematic consistency, and strong narrative throughlines that span the entire series. David Chase (*The Sopranos*) is the prototype for more contemporary showrunners on cable, such as Mathew Weiner (*Mad Men*) and Vince Gilligan (*Breaking Bad*), and Joss Whedon (*Buffy the Vampire*

Slayer, Agents of S.H.I.E.L.D.) is the forerunner to network television showrunners like J. J. Abrams (*Lost, Fringe*) and Shonda Rhimes.

Despite or because of this new media landscape that demands textual flexibility, strong fan-based social media collaboration, and global reach, these shows are discursively produced, promoted, and received as author-identified branded quality entertainment. This contradiction or collision of two fictions—a fiction of autonomous creation with the fiction of an increasingly democratized media—is the environment in which Rhimes thrives. For instance, since the first season of *Scandal*, Rhimes has crafted a social media strategy that has consistently made the series a mainstay in the top 10 watched shows of the week. Moreover, as diverse journalistic outlets like *Salon, The Washington Post, The Atlantic,* and academic researchers have begun to write about the cultural and political might of Black Twitter, Rhimes has harnessed this network since 2013 to make *Scandal* the highest-rated scripted drama among African Americans by live tweeting with the *Scandal* cast during each episode. According to Rhimes, she hosted these live parties to ensure that the cast and fans can "watch together" (Vega, 2013, para. 15).

Rhetorically, Rhimes's aligns her authorial voice with fan feedback via social networks. When Rhimes was asked about her television industry mentors at the Deutsche Bank's Women on Wall Street Conference, she replied that she didn't have any television mentors and credited her fans as mentors: "I learned what works by listening to the audience" (Kohli, 2014, para. 4). This informality and lack of pretension is a reflection of her television origins story. Rhimes, since her early press tours promoting *Grey's Anatomy*, recounts that she learned how to write for television while watching television when she was at home caring for her then two-year-old daughter. Again, this story gets recycled in the press for *HTGAWM* in outlets like National Public Radio (NPR). These two ideological strands, can-do individualism and a postracial universalism, also discussed earlier in the chapter, are discursively redirected through Bailey, Pope, and Keating. Specifically, Pope and Keating share no particular political or ideological allegiances. Olivia Pope works for both Republicans and Democrats, and Annalise Keating will represent the rich or poor, corrupt or clean, White or Black. They simply work within the immediacy of the now and function ahistorically in worlds where diversity gives way to banal multiculturalism.

In terms of general representations, the gendered expectations for each character reflect the arguments presented in feminist organizational communication literature. Bailey, Pope, and Keating each enact a predictable masculinity in professional settings. They are bold, assertive, aggressive, and unapologetically committed to their careers. Just as Nadesan and Trethewey (2000) suggested, professional settings discursively privilege masculinity, and women are often positioned so they must enact masculine behaviors in order to succeed in professional realms. This is especially true for women in positions of leadership who may encounter great difficulties being taken seriously. Dr. Miranda Bailey provides a telling example of the (un)acceptability of pronounced femininity. We are occasionally offered glimpses of Miranda early on in her residency. Contrary to The Nazi she becomes, Miranda arrived at Seattle Grace (the only female in her cohort) as wide-eyed, bubbly, eager, and hesitant to step on toes. However, she was quickly advised to speak up and become more aggressive. She morphs into a hardened professional and, despite the fact that all of Seattle Grace's doctors are direct and curt, it is only Bailey who is colloquially referred to as The Nazi. Similarly, in the first episode of *HTGAW*, a student of Keating referred to her as a "ball buster" (Nowalk, 2014, 3:03), and her own husband asked a student if Annalise had "gone full terrorist" yet (Nowalk, 2014, 26:35). Clearly, Bailey and Keating are conceptualized as "bitchy Black women," a persistent stereotype faced by many African American women in positions of leadership (Allen, 1998), despite commentary about a supposed postrace society.

In recent decades, the image of the superwoman has pervaded popular imagination, prompting the idea that women can, should, and should want to "have it all." For example, Sheryl Sandberg's best-seller *Lean In* (2013), depicted an idealized image of working women with children and a loving partner. In Rhimes's shows, Bailey, Pope, and Keating demonstrate counternarratives to this superwoman discourse, contrarily suggesting the impossibility of such an existence. In her respective way, each character effectively fails at having it all. Bailey, while professionally successful, sees the end of her marriage to Tucker after his repeated assertions that Bailey prioritized work over her family. Olivia Pope is without children and her primary relationship with Fitz is secretive, covert, and tenuous. Annalise Keating, also without children, has an unfaithful husband whom she literally loses when he is killed by her students. Each instance connotes that professional success is only possible with the absence or sacrifice of close familial relationships. Thus, the personal is portrayed as a barrier to a high-powered career.

While the sexed challenges are apparent for Bailey, Pope, and Keating, the racial intersections are largely underscored in *Grey's Anatomy* and *Scandal*. It is not until *How to Get Away with Murder* that themes of race become more overt, prodding the speculation that it is only at the present that large-scale audiences can metabolize more direct conversations about racial inequities. In one of the most powerful scenes in *HTGAWM*, we see Annalise Keating, sitting in front of her bedroom mirror, presumably performing her presleep ritual. In this scene, she transitions from her professional self to her private self. Keating is visibly distraught. In contrast to her unbreakable professional persona, Annalise is crying and is literally taking off her professional identity. However, this disrobing is far more nuanced than a simple clothing change from business suit to pajamas. Keating begins by removing her false eyelashes and her straight-haired bobbed wig. She proceeds by wiping all traces of make-up from her face. In an instant, Keating moves from the epitome of (White) masculine professionalism, to a private self that is broken, emotional, and transgressing all norms of the professional body. In other words, the scene demonstrates that professional women of color must not only project masculine gendered performances in order to obtain success, but are additionally subject to White norms of feminine beauty (Forbes, 2009). She is stripped of her power, leadership, and success as she sheds her professionalism, masculinity, and White beauty.

Racial and gender archetypes from the antebellum and reformation periods (mammy, jezebel, sapphire, and matriarch) and more recent entries to the lexicon of racism (welfare queen, crack mother, loud, and angry Black woman) continue to populate the cultural landscape (Springer, 2007). The strength and attraction of these stereotypes is, first, their historic depth and breadth, which makes them easy to use as a shorthand in storytelling and, secondly, their utter malleability. Scholars and critics continue to identify these archetypes in the media and cultural landscape in general, and the shows Rhimes produces specifically. First, all three characters are a form of Black matriarchy in that they are strong women who play both mother and father. Further, they are surrogate mothers to damaged strivers who gain trust through manipulation, fear, and power. Dr. Miranda Bailey is read concurrently as both a mammy and the sassy Black woman. Bailey is in service only to her White medical charges and exists in a fantasy life without code switching. As Wanzo (2013) observed about Bailey, she is allowed to publicly call out the errors and failings of her superiors to the benefit of the White medical students and doctors without any fear of retribution.

At times, Rhimes herself has interwoven the criticisms of her characters as 21st-century archetypes into her scripts. For instance, critics have noted that Olivia Pope can be read as a well-dressed, well-educated version of the "house slave." Kerry Washington's character, Olivia Pope, compares her relationship with Fitz to Thomas Jefferson and Sally Hemings's relationship—one of master and slave. Another example is the scene of Khandi Alexander (playing Maya Pope, Olivia Pope's mother), when confronted as a terrorist and a traitor to her country, counters, "Maybe. But I'd rather be a traitor than what you are, Livie. Cleaning up those people's messes, fixing up their lives. You think you're family, but you're nothing but the help" (McGhee, 2014, 21:23). Though press and critics sometimes read Annalise Keating as a sophisticated form of the angry Black woman most commonly associated with reality television contestants such as Omarosa Manigault-Stallworth from the first season of *The Apprentice* and the cast of *Bad Girls Club*, the collision and circulation of various archetypes can be present simultaneously. This is best illustrated with the controversial live tweet posted by *People*

Magazine (Rose, 2014) during the first episode of *HTGAWM*: "Waiting for Viola to break into 'You is Kind. You is Smart. You is Important'" quoting Viola Davis's character, a maid in the 1960s, from the film *The Help* (Columbus & Taylor, 2011). Though Davis's character in *HTGAWM* is a prominent lawyer, Davis's role as a maid in *The Help* and seemingly the archetype of the maid in general remains a dominant identifying marker of African American women televisually.

In essence, we can gather that in order for Rhimes's shows to be viable successes, they must be palatable in terms of their "raced and sexed" political statements. In the context of the United States in regard specifically to race, we can examine the contemporary movement of Black Lives Matter. Over the past few years, there have been several high-profile instances where African Americans have been murdered, often at the hands of the police. In response to the Trayvon Martin case, in which an unarmed African American boy was killed by a neighborhood watch patrolman, Black Lives Matter was established to draw attention to and ideally overcome the disproportion of violence and poverty among Black populations. Black Lives Matter is a self-described movement that attempts to reignite the Black liberation movement.

For some, Black Lives Matter provides a platform to bring to light systemic and institutionalized racism. However, there are those who resist foregrounding the racial nuances of violence and poverty, countering instead that "all lives matter." This is evidenced, for example, in the Twittersphere where the call #blacklivesmatter is countered by #alllivesmatter. Similarly, Black Lives Matter signs and banners are routinely altered to blank out or cut out entirely the word "Black"—leaving only "Lives Matter." Numerous public figures have also uttered the phrase "all lives matter," including Hillary Clinton, a divisive figure in American politics, when speaking to a historically Black church in Missouri. Toney Armstrong, the Memphis Police Chief, also utilized that terminology during his eulogy of murdered police officer Sean Bolton.

The backlash against Black Lives Matter, evidenced in the emergence and prevalence of the "all lives matter" counter, demonstrates a popular desire to lowlight or outright erase issues of race. In an American context, even when an outcry for justice highlights race, it must be reigned in and appropriated to continually render African Americans invisible. Ostensibly, the American political and cultural landscape craves a colorblindness that, in itself, is markedly raced and racist. As Dvorak (2015) succinctly states:

> "All Lives Matter" or "Lives Matter" is the opposite of colorblind. It is not about racial harmony. It is not a clever call-out on reverse discrimination. It is not a way to give other groups equal importance. It tried to erase one of this country's most pernicious and persistent shortcomings: its ugly racism. (paras. 5, 6)

Ugly as it is, this is the landscape Rhimes and ShondaLand must navigate in order to attain commercial success. However, Rhimes's programs and others featuring African American leads are, indeed, successful. Crediting the continued and growing success of Rhimes's production company and the ratings success of African American-led shows such as Fox's *Empire* and ABC's *Black-ish*, *Indiwire* announced in March 2015 that there are 73 pilots/series with African American actors in lead or supporting roles for the 2015–2016 television season across broadcast and cable networks (Obenson, 2015). This growth in African American casting, and by extension textual representations, is connected to a shifting range of politically nuanced business practices.

In this vein, our chapter concurrently analyzes Rhimes's characters as both "speaking in" and "speaking to" a tradition of African American female representation and Rhimes herself as working "inside" and "outside" a set of media business practices. We argue that Rhimes's construction of Black female leadership is at once read contextually within a history of African American textual representation in both racial and postracial contexts and paratextually through press reports and industry profiles of Rhimes as producer, auteur, and showrunner. This reading of Rhimes's shows through the raced and sexed body of Rhimes herself can both help White and Black audiences read her shows as authentic, but they also may fall into a form of reductionism that both recreates archetypes or, more problematically for television executives greenlighting programming in a competitive and global environment, labels her as an African American producer of African American shows. We argue that these two strands are defused by strategic production practices such as multicultural casting and colorblind casting. As Warner (2015) noted, representation is not solely what reaches the television screen but is a byproduct of decision-making practices during production. We extend this logic beyond production and also interrogate Rhimes's audience-based reception strategies that include second-screen viewing and social media campaigns.

With the rise of video streaming services and cross-platform production practices, the landscape of African American media professionals and talent has numerically and creatively shifted. As a *New York Times* (Wortham, 2015) profile of Issa Rae, the star, writer, and director of the YouTube series *The Misadventures of Awkward Black Girl*, observed, networks are no longer the primary creators, distributors, and producers of content for the small screen: television, computers, tablets, and phones. This leads to two distinct shifts in the future analysis of televisual representation of women and people of color. First, speaking to both quantitative and qualitative analysis, short-form and long-form programming from media and technology firms such as Vimeo, Snapchat, Vine, Yahoo, and Amazon may cater to niche, age-specific audiences and provide a platform for innovative, bold programming. Secondly, a shift in programming alters forms of creation *and* reception. As film scholars contend with the erosion between film and television, television studies continue to wrestle with what constitutes tele-visual programming and practices. This is evident in the *People Magazine* live-tweet example mentioned earlier in our analysis, which concurrently referenced Davis's filmic work alongside her television work. This intertex-tual reading also extends to viewing practices and reception. Once again, using this example, audiences access *The Help* and *HTGAWM* on a variety of on-demand streaming platforms and video-sharing sites in their home, which challenges traditional viewing and production practices.

CONCLUSION

In this chapter we have examined representations of African American women in positions of leadership in both fictional and actual realms. As an African American woman of immense success, wealth, and cultural capital, Shonda Rhimes has carefully navigated an industry that rests upon innocu-ous diversity. Her claims to colorblind casting, whether truthful or not, do not obscure how the content and characters in ShondaLand's Thursday night programming demonstrate sexed and raced stereotypes and struggles that Black women face. As such, reading the representations of Bailey, Pope, and Keating alongside industry, cultural, and social trends offers significant insight into the contemporary moment—and this moment is certainly nei-ther postfeminist nor postrace, not even on Thursday nights.

REFERENCES

Allen, B. J. (1998). Black womanhood and feminist standpoints. *Management Com-munication Quarterly, 11*(4), 575–586. doi: 10.1177/0893318998114004

Allen, B. J. (2000). "Learning the ropes": A black feminist standpoint analysis. In P. M.Buzzanell (Ed.), *Rethinking organizational and managerial communication from feminist perspectives* (pp.177–208). London, UK: Sage.

Andreeva, N. (2015, March 24). Pilots: 2015. The year of ethnic castings. *Deadline Hollywood.* Retrieved from http://deadline.com/2015/03/tv-pilots-ethnic-casting-trend-backlash-1201386511/ed

Barraclough, L. (2014, October 12). Mipcom: Disney sells "How to get away with murder" to 158 territories. *Variety.* Retrieved from http://variety.com/2014/tv/global/mipcom-disney-sells-how-to-get-away-with-murder-to-158-territories-1201328329/

Bauder, D., Elber, L., & Moore, F. (2015, January 20). How TV networks made un-equal progress toward on-screen diversity. *Huffington Post.* Retrieved from http://www.huffingtonpost.com/2015/01/20/tv-networks-unequal-progress-on-screen-diversity_n_6509818.html

Bordo, S. (1993). *Unbearable weight: Feminism, western culture, and the body.* Berkeley, CA: University of California Press.

Butler, J. (2006). *Gender trouble: Feminism and the subversion of identity.* New York, NY: Routledge.

Buzzanell, P. M., & Liu, M. (2005). Struggling with maternity leave policies and practices: A poststructuralist feminist analysis of gendered organizing. *Journal of Applied Communication Research, 33*(1), 1–25. doi: 10.1080/00909880042000318495

Carroll, B., & Levy, L. (2010). Leadership development as identity construction. *Management Communication Quarterly, 24*(2), 211–231. doi: 10.1177/0893318909358725

Collins, P. H. (2000). *Black feminist thought: Knowledge, consciousness, and the politics of empowerment.* New York, NY: Routledge.

Columbus, C. (Producer), & Taylor, T. (Director). (2011). *The help* [Motion picture]. USA: Touchstone Pictures.

Dvorak, P. (2015, August 6). The ugly message behind erasing "Black" from "Black Lives Matter" signs. Retrieved from http://www.washingtonpost.com/local/the-ugly-message-behind-erasing-black-from-black-lives-matter-signs/2015/08/06/1d87a892-3c57-11e5-9c2d-ed991d848c48_story.html

Fairhurst, G. T., & Grant, D. (2010). The social construction of leadership: A sailing guide. *Management Communication Quarterly, 24*(2), 171–210. doi: 10.1177/0893318909359697

Forbes, D. A. (2009). Commodification and co-modification: Explicating black female sexuality in organizations. *Management Communication Quarterly, 22*(4), 577–613. doi: 10.1177/0893318908331322

Gates, D. (2003). Learning to play the game: An exploratory study of how African American women and men interact with others in organizations. *Electronic Journal of Communication, 13*(2/3). Retrieved from http://www.cios.org/

Gray, H. (1995). *Watching race: Television and the struggles for "Blackness."* Minneapolis: University of Minnesota.

Gray, H. S. (2005). *Cultural moves: African Americans and the politics of representation.* Berkeley, CA: University of California Press.

Harris, G. (2006). *Beyond representation: Television drama and the politics and aesthetics of identity.* Manchester, UK: Manchester University Press.

Havens, T. (2013). *Black television travels: African American media around the globe.* New York, NY: New York University Press.

Hirokawa, R. Y., Kodama, R. A., & Harper, N. L. (1990). Impact of managerial power on persuasive strategy selection by female and male managers. *Management Communication Quarterly, 4*(1), 30–50. doi: 10.1177/0893318990004001003

Hunt, D. M. (2005). Making sense of Blackness on television. In D. M. Hunt (Ed.), *Channeling Blackness. Studies on television and race in America* (pp. 1–24). New York, NY: Oxford University Press.

Hunt, D., Ramon, A.-C., & Price, Z. (2014). 2014 Hollywood diversity report: Making sense of the disconnect. Retrieved from http://www.bunchecenter.ucla.edu/wp-content/uploads/2014/02/2014-Hollywood-Diversity-Report-2-12-14.pdf

Kanter, R. M. (1977). *Men and women of the corporation.* New York, NY: Basic Books.

Kohli, S. (2014, October 8). Shonda Rhimes never had a mentor—she had her fans and Twitter instead. *Quartz.* Retrieved from http://qz.com/278491/shonda-rhimes-never-had-a-mentor-she-had-her-fans-and-twitter-instead/

McGhee, Z. (Writer), Goldwyn, T. (Director), & Rhimes, S. (Producer). (2014). *Scandal.* USA: ABC Studios.

Medved, C. E., & Kirby, E. L. (2005). Family CEOs: A feminist analysis of corporate mothering discourses. *Management Communication Quarterly, 18*(4), 435–478. doi: 10.1177/0893318904273690

Nadesan, M. H., & Trethewey, A. (2000). Performing the enterprising subject: Gendered strategies for success (?). *Text and Performance Quarterly, 20*(3), 223–250. doi: 10.1080/10462930009366299

Nowalk, P. (Writer), Offer, M. (Director), & Rhimes, S. (Producer). (2014). *How to get away with murder.* U.S.A.: ABC Studios.

Obenson, T. A. (2015). 73 new TV pilots & series with Black actors in starring and/or supporting roles ordered for next season. The full list. *Indiwire.* Retrieved from http://blogs.indiewire.com/shadowandact/71-new-tv-pilots-series-with-black-actors-in-starring-and-or-supporting-roles-ordered-for-next-season-heres-the-full-list-20150310

Ospina, S., & Su, C. (2009). Weaving color lines: Race, ethnicity, and the work of leadership in social change organizations. *Leadership, 5*(2), 131–170. doi: 10.1177/1742715009102927

Parker, P. S. (2001). African American women executives' leadership communication within dominant-culture organizations: (Re)conceptualizing notions of collaboration and instrumentality. *Management Communication Quarterly, 15*(1), 42–82. doi: 10.1177/0893318901151002

Parker, P. S. (2002). Negotiating identity in raced and gendered workplace interactions: The use of strategic communication by African American senior executives within dominant culture organizations. *Communication Quarterly, 50*(3–4), 251–268. doi: 10.1080/01463370209385663

Rose, R. (2014, September 25). *People* magazine deletes offensive tweets about Viola Davis and *Scandal. Jezebel.* Retrieved from http://jezebel.com/people-magazine-deletes-offensive-tweets-about-viola-da-1639390681

Rosenberg, A. (2015, May 14). How Hollywood stays white and male. *The Washington Post.* Retrieved from https://www.washingtonpost.com/news/act-four/wp/2015/05/14/how-hollywood-stays-white-and-male/

Sandberg, S. (2013). *Lean in: Women, work, and the will to lead.* New York, NY: Knopf.

Spigel, L. (1992). *Make room for TV: Television and the family ideal in postwar America.* Chicago, IL: University of Chicago.

Springer, K. (2007). Divas, evil Black bitches, and bitter Black women: African American women in postfeminist and post-civil rights popular culture. In C. Brundson & L. Spigel (Eds.), *Feminist television criticism: A reader* (pp. 249–276). New York, NY: Oxford University Press.

Stanley, A. (2014, September 18). Wrought in Rhimes' image. Viola Davis plays Shonda Rhimes' latest heroine. *The New York Times.* Retrieved from http://www.nytimes.com/2014/09/21/arts/television/viola-davis-plays-shonda-rhimess-latest-tough-heroine.html

Tracy, S. J., & Rivera, K. D. (2009). Endorsing equity and applauding stay-at-home moms: How male voices on work–life reveal aversive sexism and flickers of transformation. *Management Communication Quarterly, 24*(1), 3–43. doi: 10.1177/0893318909352248

Trethewey, A. (1999). Disciplined bodies: Women's embodied identities at work. *Organization Studies, 20*(3), 423–450. doi: 10.1177/0170840699203003

Turner, L. H., & Henzl, S. A. (1987). Influence attempts in organizational conflict. *Management Communication Quarterly, 1*(1), 32–58. doi: 10.1177/0893318987001001003

Vega, T. (2013, January 16). A show makes friends and history. "Scandal" on ABC is breaking barriers. *The New York Times*. Retrieved from http://www.nytimes.com/2013/01/17/arts/television/scandal-on-abc-is-breaking-barriers.html

Wanzo, R. (2013). Can the black woman shout? A meditation on "real" and utopian depictions of African American women on scripted. In D. L. Leonard & L. A. Guerro (Eds.), *African Americans on television: Race-ing for ratings* (pp. 373–389). Santa Barbara, CA: Praeger.

Warner, K. J. (2014). The racial logic of *Grey's Anatomy*: Shonda Rhimes and her "post-civil rights, post-feminist" series. *Television & New Media*, 1–17. doi: 10.1177/1527476414550529

Warner, K. J. (2015). *The cultural politics of colorblind TV casting*. New York, NY: Routledge.

Wortham, J. (2015, August, 4). The misadventures of Issa Rae. *The New York Times Magazine*. Retrieved from http://www.nytimes.com/2015/08/09/magazine/the-misadventures-of-issa-rae.html?_r=3&referrer=

CHAPTER 14

THE MARGIN AS A SPACE OF RESISTANCE

Transforming Gendered Leadership Through Popular Film

Alexia Panayiotou
University of Cyprus

This chapter uses popular films from the last 30 years to explore how executive women—outliers in the organizational hierarchy—are portrayed in organizational spaces. Starting from the premise that popular culture is a powerful tool for management and leadership learning, the chapter explores protagonists' spatial practices as these are used to subvert, intentionally or unintentionally, patriarchal structures. Findings show that, although on the surface organizational spaces marginalize women, certain practices can hybridize the workspace and transform the margin into a *space of radical openness*, thus offering new potential for how leadership is practiced by women in organizations. In this sense, popular film itself can also serve as a site for resistance and subversion.

Gender, Media, and Organization, pages 243–258
Copyright © 2016 by Information Age Publishing
All rights of reproduction in any form reserved.

GENDER, SPACE, AND LEADERSHIP

The idea that space tells a story of power in organizations is perhaps not new in management research (Berg & Kreiner, 1990; Dale & Burrell, 2008; Kornberger & Clegg, 2004); that this power has gender(ed) dimensions has also been somewhat addressed by the literature (Panayiotou & Kafiris, 2010; Tyler & Cohen, 2010). We know that space is not gender neutral; on the contrary, it can be said that *all* spaces are gendered spaces. But what happens when *marginal actors* such as female executives challenge the symbolic spatial order through their otherness? This is the guiding question of the current chapter.

To explore this question, I rely on Butler's (2000) concept of "gender performativity" to highlight that gender is not something we *are* but something we *do*. I employ a performative lens to the study of both gender and space to stress that subjects continually *perform* identities (of gender and sexuality) as these may be prescribed by hegemonic discourses, including a dominant spatial discourse (see also Panayiotou, 2014; Tyler & Cohen, 2010). It is in this context, then, that I use the verbs *gendering* and *spacing* (Beyes & Steyaert, 2011) to denote the performative processes through which both are enacted; in other words, I am less interested in space and gender as products and more interested in the material and social processes that produce them. Working within this performative processual approach, I explore how the very processes of othering executive women in the workplace can also be used as a form of resistance to gendered spaces. Can the gendering or, more explicitly, the feminizing of space enable women's resistance rather than restrict it? And, ultimately, what do these processes tell us about women and organizational leadership?

Gendering as a social and spatial process is not only something that happens to women, of course, so my focus on female executives should not be misconstrued as essentializing. My choice lies on two premises—bodies matter and female bodies matter even more. In other words, not only is the physical body often curiously absent from organizational theory and should be addressed, but the female body, which has been regarded as *at odds* with the modern workplace (McDowell & Court, 1994) and leadership in particular (Kenny & Bell, 2011), deserves a research focus. As Sinclair (2011) notes, "[B]odies and physical performances often play central roles in establishing power and credentials for leadership.... [B]odies activate unconscious processes...that reinforce or undermine authority, power and socially constructed credibility" (p. 118). The body seems to be missing from leadership studies, potentially because leaders are assumed to be male, and male bodies have been made invisible for "particular ideological purposes" (Sinclair, 2011, p. 120). As several researchers have noted, managers are actually *man*-agers (Collinson & Hearn, 1996; Panayiotou, 2010) and the "managerial body" is often assumed to conform to the "masculine bodily norm" (Kenny & Bell, 2011, p. 163). Therefore, the question of how female executives embody organizational spaces, as well as how these spaces are altered due to the presence of female executives, has rich epistemological potential.

In addition, female executives are marginal actors not only because statistically they are by far a minority ("Women in the workplace," 2013), but also because their very presence in the organizational hierarchy is seen as an anomaly and a challenge to the dominant patriarchal ethos (Martin, 1996). This is not to say that I regard executive women—or even women— as a category with fixed features, nor do I see them as the only marginal actors within organizations. I do think, however, that much can be learned from analyzing the representations of these executives in film and the processes of gendering, spacing, and leading, as these unfold in the featured storyline (see also Panayiotou, 2014). As I argue below, media representations are both assumed to be "normal" and act as "normalizing" in daily life; as such, they offer a fruitful ground through which to study leadership and organizations.

METHODOLOGICAL APPROACH

To explore the questions raised, I use Hollywood films in the tradition of many organizational researchers. As Denzin (1995) wrote, contemporary society seems to be undergoing a process of "cinematization," in which we come to "know ourselves, collectively and individually, through the images and stories Hollywood produces" (p. 24). In fact, film can be seen as "a persuasive cultural artifact" (Brewis, 1998, p. 86), greatly influential in constructing perceptions, attitudes, and even behaviors. In addition, as a "cultural text," film offers "politically mobilizing representations of leadership to audiences" and provides spectators with "role models of embodied organizational behavior which they may choose to emulate" (Bell & Sinclair, in press, p. 2). This is particularly useful in understanding gendered power relations in organizations because of the difficulty of using conventional research methods for studying inequality (Czarniawska, 2011). As Bell and Sinclair (in press, p. 2) stressed, film allows audiences to "literally and metaphorically 'freeze-frame' vivid moments, giving space and opportunity to explore their meaning and impact." This not only enables the questioning of gender norms, it also potentially offers a means of doing leadership differently. In this sense, film teaches practices (reported or invented) by offering interpretive templates or *strong plots* that may be more influential for the actual practice of leadership than what happens in classrooms or boardrooms (Czarniawska & Rhodes, 2006).

Czarniawska and Rhodes (2006, p. 198) describe strong plots as "folk tales" acting as "interpretive templates" through which we make sense of the world. Strong plots are, in essence, a culturally derived meaning-making device which provides possible blueprints for the management of meaning in organizations: "abstract models do not teach you what to say or how to act during your first management meeting, a movie might" (Czarniawska & Rhodes, 2006, p. 199). Strong plots can be subverted, of course, and popular films seem to offer a fruitful ground through which this can happen.

Specifically, then, to track films with a female in an organizational leadership role, I followed previous work in the field (Panayiotou, 2010, 2014; Panayiotou & Kafiris, 2011) and conducted an extensive keyword search on IMDb, the largest and most comprehensive movie industry database, visited by over 60 million users per month and the recipient of several user awards. My search was conducted using IMDbPro (a specialized member service of the database) and focused on full-length English-language films produced for the big screen in the last 30 years (1985–2014) that scored at least 6/10 in IMDb's popularity measure (a proxy definition for "popular") and included any combination of keywords in their plot summary from the following two lists: firm, company, corporation, corporate, business, office, work *and* female protagonist, businesswoman, female executive, female business executive, and female leader (based on the keywords available on IMDb). The search yielded 13 films that were screened in terms of suitability. Films that did not provide enough material for analysis, had different institutional contexts (e.g., political office or the army), or were mistakenly chosen through the keyword search were dismissed. The final list included five films: *Baby Boom* (Myers, Block, & Shyer, 1987), *Working Girl* (Wick & Nichols, 1988), *Disclosure* (Crichton & Levinson, 1994), *What Women Want* (Cartsonis et al., 2000), and *The Devil Wears Prada* (Finerman & Frankel, 2006). It is clear that despite the lengthy time period chosen, films with women in a central executive role, with the storyline materializing in a corporate work space are very limited. Of course, this may be a reflection of organizational reality: in 2014, for example, women represented a mere 13% of on-screen leaders when looking at the top 100 gross-producing films of that year, 30% of all speaking characters, 29% of major characters, and only 12% of protagonists (Silverstein, 2014). Nonetheless, if such portrayals are few and far between, it becomes even more important to study the implicit messages they convey. Cinematographic details of the films chosen are found in Table 14.1. Plot summaries can be found on IMDb.

To analyze the films, I worked within a variation of Rose's (2001) methodology that sees film as "visual narrative." Specifically:

1. I watched the films several times and made notes of key points, with an initial focus on the overall *narrative structure.*

TABLE 14.1   Films Chosen

Film	Year	Genre (Imdb)	Director	Production Company	Main Cast	Popularity Index (Aug. 2015)
Baby Boom	1987	Comedy	Charles Shyer	United Artists	Diane Keaton, Sam Shepard	6.1
Working Girl	1988	Comedy	Mike Nichols	Twentieth Century-Fox	Melanie Griffith, Sigourney Weaver, Harrison Ford	6.7
Disclosure	1994	Drama	Barry Levinson	Warner Bros	Demi Moore, Michael Douglas	6.0
What Women Want	2000	Comedy	Nancy Meyers	Paramount	Helen Hunt, Mel Gibson	6.4
The Devil Wears Prada	2006	Comedy	David Frankel	Twentieth Century-Fox	Meryl Streep, Anne Hathaway	6.8

2. I watched the films, pausing in instances where organizational spaces were featured, and used the still frame to transcribe all details. I also paused in instances in which the executives' homes were featured, to detect whether these were simply an extension of their workspace.
3. I recorded information on how the characters interacted with the built environment.
4. I used open coding to find common themes and patterns in what I had noted in (2) and (3) above.
5. I constructed a cross-case analysis chart based on the common themes found both in regard to how space was presented but also in regard to the spatial practices of the protagonists. From this chart I also constructed the strong plots (a lengthier discussion of the methodology can be found in Panayiotou, 2014).

FEMINIZING ORGANIZATIONAL SPACES: AN ACT OF RESISTANCE?

The findings are twofold. First, I describe the female protagonists' offices, then the protagonists' spatial practices. In the subsequent section, I analyze the implications of these findings for organizational leadership.

The Feminine Office

Women's offices are atypical in regard to the rest of the company, even when they hold executive power. As different as the films may be in regard to time periods, as different as the industries may be in which the organizations are found (from high tech, to investment, to the creative industries of advertising and fashion), and as different as the characters may be, the space executive women inhabit is almost ubiquitously the same. Taking Yanow's (1995) analytical dimensions as a guide for exploring physical space, I focused on the office layout; décor, including furniture and lighting; and doors and windows.

Firstly, one notices that all offices are laid out in a similar manner, with large windows, light-colored carpets or colorful rugs, soft furniture and lighting, and ostensibly placed flowers and other decorative objects. Unlike other areas of the organizations, which tend to be heavy, unadorned (or adorned with awards, prizes, expensive artwork), and dark both in regard to light and the color of furniture, carpets, and drapes, women's offices are colorful, decorated and, by corporate standards, *homey*. Katharine's (Sigourney Weaver) office in *Working Girl* features a large window facing towards the Hudson River, light peach-colored walls, translucent curtains, and a large, dominant, rosewood desk. Soft leather chairs and a large brown sofa are found alongside exercise equipment, blurring the distinction between company/office space and personal/home space. Bowls and other ceramic household objects adorn the shelves beside personal photographs, statues, and flower pots. This scenery is repeated in all the films, adjusting for the time period and the industry. Darcy's (Helen Hunt) office in *What Women Want* is distinctly different both from Nick's (Mel Gibson, playing the high-level executive seen as her rival) and the company CEO, as well as from other organizational spaces such as the board room; her office is brighter, ornate, colorful, and filled with flowers and personal objects such as candles, photographs, even a fruit bowl. Interestingly, this space is not quite fitting for Darcy's corporate image as "man eater" or "bitch on wheels," in the same way that Miranda Priestley's (Meryl Streep) office in *The Devil Wears Prada* is not what one would expect from the "Snow Queen" or even from J.C. Wyatt (Diane Keaton), the "Tiger Lady" of *Baby Boom*. Miranda's office may be orderly, minimalist, and largely white, but it is, again, decorated with soft, rounded furniture, including a comfortable red chair, a silver hexagonal mirror, an old bureau with photographs and flowers, and colorful books by the window. It is also interesting to note that photographs of her husband and children are prominent on her desk. Less homey and bright is Meredith Johnson's (Demi Moore) office in *Disclosure*, the tale of sexual harassment by a female boss towards a male subordinate, but the darker image of this office is potentially concomitant to Meredith's shady character. Despite this, and like most of the other offices, Meredith has a comfortable leather sofa, cluttered corners, flowers and vases on her shelves, and a rustic colorful rug, reminiscent more of a home than an office.

It is clear from these shots that, regardless of what the rest of the corporation looks like, a woman's office looks a particular way: adorned, comfortable, and homey.

Leaky Boundaries

Moving on to spatial practices, it is interesting to note that organizational boundaries are both kept and negotiated by the women in the films. Firstly, although executive women are found behind closed doors, most women in the organization are found in open-floor arrangements, behind cubicles or lined-up desks. The boundary separating those with power from those without is marked and visible, and boundary-keeping processes are evident in many situations. Managers buzz their assistants in, assistants knock on the door before entering, and perhaps no image is more telling of boundary-keeping than Miranda Priestly throwing her bag and coat to her assistant who must then place them in their proper place.

Yet the fact that boundaries are maintained through everyday habitu-
al practices by both managers and assistants is somewhat less interesting
than the acts of crossing these boundaries, creating what can be seen as
"leaky boundaries" (Panayiotou, 2014, p. 433). Through mostly deliberate
actions, female protagonists transgress the norms of masculine space, blurring not only the boundaries of public and private, but also allowing the
feminine spaces described above to "leak" into the rest of the organization.
So, although the visible spatial boundary between female manager–female
assistant is maintained, another boundary, that of the public–private, is not.
For one, the very fact that traditional office spaces look less like offices
and more like living rooms could be seen as an act of resisting traditional
norms and distinctions. When Meredith lies on the couch, heels off, shirt
untucked, scotch in her hand, she is making a statement not only about
the office being *her* space but also about the boundary between office and
home being less distinguishable. Katharine's exercising in her office is unexpected. However, perhaps the most obvious indication of blurring private and public space is J.C.'s act of bringing her child to work. The scene
in which she is interviewed for a partner position, child attached to her
side, fussing with her hair and creating multiple disturbances is, at the same
time, a question about her belonging in this space (can women really be
executives?) as it is a form of resistance to the home–work dichotomy.

In the films we also see that not only is the office–home boundary blurred,
so too is that of home–office. In other words, just as the home is brought into
the office, the office is brought into the home. Home life and work life are
not separate at all: Miranda's assistant is asked to deliver the proofs of *Runway*
to her home for approval; Katharine's assistant is asked to bring her medica-
tion when she breaks her leg. In these instances, those with power are found
by their subordinates in compromised positions, be it in sweatpants (Darcy), a
negligee (Katharine), or a nightgown (Miranda). It is in these instances, however, that yet another boundary is crossed: The visible boundary of the office
that keeps assistants outside of the boss' closed door is negated in the home,
signifying, perhaps, a crossing of the invisible boundary of power as well. It
is not that power is transferred or questioned but that boundaries in these
female relationships are fluid, leaky. Moreover, while it may be the case that
who allows whom in what space is always indicative of power structures, we see
that these structures are not rigid, allowing the possibility for transformation.

The Gendered Body as a Disruption in Space

Women in the films seem to uniformly conform to the traditional sex stereotype, as this is applied to their bodies, clothes, demeanor, and sexuality.
They carry themselves in expected ways, leaving no doubt that their body

is a gendered, sexualized, female body—which, as Sinclair (2013) notes, is also antithetical to leadership. We take cues about the executives' feminine status from J.C.'s fuzzy sweaters and pink scarves, Katharine's lingerie, Meredith's short suits and stiletto heels, Darcy's form-fitting dresses—even Miranda's pencil skirts, tight belts and lavish jewelry. All protagonists wear high heels, often red, never sensible, always glamorous. Bare legs are shown. Hair is tended to. Nails are always manicured. Makeup is a must, and, even when subtle, lipstick is obvious. Through clothes, jewelry, accessories, and shoes, the adorned body is distinctly *marked* as female.

At the same time, movement in and through space is also gendered—even sexualized at times. Every time Meredith Johnson sits down, we have a view of her bare, suggestively-crossed legs, her high-heeled shoe dangling as she playfully moves her ankle. Darcy leans over the conference room table while giving a presentation, and her button-down shirt gives a glimpse of her cleavage. And Miranda, legs always crossed, softly touches her lips when she is concentrating, waving her hands in graceful, ballerina-like movements, even while dismissing a subordinate.

Of course, it can be argued that what we, the viewers, receive is simply the voyeuristic gaze (Mulvey, 1975) of the filmmakers since all films, except *What Women Want*, were directed by men (see Table 14.1). While this is an interesting discussion, in this study I want to analyze further the *representations* to which we are exposed. I argue that female protagonists act in expectedly gendered ways in order to "resolve the doubts of external actors as to their presence in the company" (Bruni, Gherardi, & Poggio, 2004, p. 424). It is perhaps only through gender-appropriate practices where women executives can become accepted.

Nevertheless, there is also something else worth exploring here: Women's spatial practices may be expectedly gendered, but they are also simultaneously and unexpectedly disruptive, changing not just the way that things are normally done but also how leadership is done, as I explain later. In *What Women Want*, for example, our first glance of Darcy is given through a camera focusing first on her slim legs then working its way up to her face—perhaps signaling her other-ness in the space and framing her as a gendered subject. The next few shots, however, center around Darcy's marketing-savvy actions to bring (her) feminine world to the decision-making table: She hands all her new colleagues a pink box with products "familiar to the women in the room, but for the men let's briefly run through them" (Cartsonis et al., 2000, 18:06), such as anti-wrinkle cream, an at-home waxing kit, a light blue wonder bra, pore cleansing strips, and control-top pantyhose. Darcy has at once created an acceptable frame of reference for herself because of the way she looks, maybe even because of what she is talking about (women's products for which, as a woman, she may be authorized to talk about)—so she is not defying social expectations of her gendered self—but at the same time she seems to disrupt these references by laying out a bra and pantyhose on the boardroom table.

This disruption is also evident in *Disclosure,* even if the film has been criticized for its misogynistic slant (Brewis, 1998; Denzin, 1995). Leaving this debate aside, however, it can be argued that Meredith's outward sexuality at the office is at once fitting with social stereotypes of women in top positions—undeserving, conniving, ruthless, exploitative of her femininity—*and* subversive to the organizational order. In the scene where she forces herself upon Sanders, at once claiming her office space but also resisting corporate power, she is both working within stereotypical views of powerful women (a temptress) but also changing them (sex forced by women on men in an office setting). Again, I am not examining here the dynamics portrayed in the film, or Meredith's positioning as sexual object or subject; I am merely suggesting we go beyond the interpretive frame given to explore whether women's organizational otherness is what transforms corporate spaces and our notions of leadership.

In *Baby Boom,* J.C. quits her job, moves to a 62-acre country estate in Vermont, and starts her own business of gourmet baby food. Here, J.C. does not make as much a statement of rejecting the corporation or even the corporate world, as she does of rejecting its office space and the life that this space entails. As she poignantly states, "I have a crib in my office and there's a mobile over my desk and I really like that" (Meyers & Block, 1987, 102.04), referring to her new home office hybrid space. Even though she admits she is no longer the "tiger lady," she seems to have negated her boss' comment, "You just can't have it all" (Meyers & Block, 1987, 98.07), and in fact tells him so. And perhaps no scene is more powerful regarding female executives transforming corporate space as the scene in which J.C.'s former boss, holding a teddy bear, waits for J.C. to arrive with her baby to the negotiation meeting about buying out her new food company: an older man in a dark, pinstriped suit holding a baby toy.

THE MARGIN AS A SPACE OF RESISTANCE

In the aforementioned examples, women seem to blur if not transgress physical and metaphorical boundaries. With their presence and acts—from spilling baby formula on a company partner (*Baby Boom*) to laying out pantyhose on a conference room table (*What Women Want*)—women subversively spill their femininity into an otherwise masculinist corporate space, to borrow a term from Tyler and Cohen (2010, p. 187). Thus, although the women seem to act initially in what these authors call "a selective, bounded way" (Tyler & Cohen, 2010, p. 188) by playing up their femininity, even "mak[ing] explicit connections between gender performativity and the presentation of office space" (p. 190), later on they use these expectations to disrupt business as usual. In the process of this disruption, intentionally or unintentionally, they transform not only the office–home/public–private boundary, but also flip otherness on its head. In other words, by existing on the *hyphen* (of office–home), women's initial otherness brings them a sense of belonging in the organizational space not just physically but symbolically as well.

The hyphen is, of course, a tough place to be. And, to survive here, women seem to resort to gender switching (Butler, 2000): by acting both within a socially ascribed image (feminizing space through their practices) but also outside of it (through exerting power and control) they simultaneously upheld and challenged the "workplace performance that constructs them as honorary men" (McDowell & Court, 1994, p. 745). And this is exactly where resistance to the masculinist organization is enabled. By dressing as women but acting as managers, displaying flowers and personal photographs on their desks but frightening those around them, wearing high heels but climbing the ladder of success, these women question both the performance of femininity that they outwardly display *and* the traditional masculinist notion of leadership. Their at-once abidance to their ascribed gender and their questioning of it by going outside of their acceptable, bounded spatiality, creates a new kind of "organizational creature" (Brewis, Hampton, & Linstead, 1997, p. 1296), which also disturbs the idea of one-gender leadership, as I discuss below.

Subverting Space, Transforming Leadership

To return to my question of marginal actors challenging the symbolic spatial order, it seems that films show precisely the process through which this change occurs. The margin (both symbolic and material) through which women lead becomes what bell hooks (1989, p. 203) calls "a space of radical openness" in which all transformation is possible. Women in power, an organizational anomaly as statistics show, may tell a story of otherness. But through this story, women resist not only the symbolic gender order of the corporate world but also *reconstruct* the story that space tells.

Is it possible, then, that this *space of radical openness* can subvert the traditional *strong plot* of the career woman—the Snow Queen, the Tiger Lady, the Man Eater—who is nothing more than a demonic seductress or a boss from hell, thus transforming both *what* we know and *how* we know in organizations (Swan, Stead, & Elliott, 2009)? I argue that what we see in the films is the introduction of a new strong plot, a new interpretive template that flips old stereotypes on their head, and that this is exactly where the subversive—and educational—power of popular films lies.

But first, what is the superficial story told by the films? On the surface, the films analyzed could be seen as propagating the myth of the career woman who cannot have it all. The prototype given is one where a strong-willed, highly educated, powerful woman must choose between work and family. If she chooses her leadership role she should be aware of the consequences: unfulfilled, perhaps frigid, less than a woman, an imposter in organizations, maybe even in life. The female executive is as unnatural as her ambition and it is only when she makes the "right" decision to drop out of the organizational world, or at least out of the organizational hierarchy, that she can find happiness. But is it really so?

On the one hand, it can be argued that the *cost* of power is obvious and quite high for women; after all, four of the five protagonists are fired or lose their jobs, and Miranda only saves hers through questionable maneuvers. Relationships are an issue for all, with references to a biological clock and to the need/duty to procreate for all the childless women (Miranda has twins but two failed marriages). The choice between a partner and work is again obvious in all films, as is the need for a partner—with implications that when it comes down to it, women should choose the husband.

It is here, however, that the twist in the plot reveals the subversive potential of popular films. Even though J.C. loses her job, for example, she redefines organizational reality by negating binaries: she *can* have it all in the end by changing the rules of the game to suit her. She is happy with her adopted child and new partner, at the same time that she is the owner of a multimillion-dollar entrepreneurial business (which, as a side note, is also beneficial to society). In *Working Girl*, Katharine may be fired but she is replaced by another woman, Tess. Even in *Disclosure*, it is a woman who takes over Meredith's position, not Tom Sanders. Perhaps the last lines in *What Women Want* are the most telling about the reversal of the strong plot. Although Darcy is fired, she is rehired when the truth is revealed about Nick Marshall stealing her ideas. Nick is then fired, but Darcy will not allow that: "What kind of knight in shining armor would I be if I let the man I love walk out that door?" To which Nick replies, "My hero" (Cartsonis et al., 2000, 1:56:50).

So it seems that a new kind of heroine or leader is developed in these films. If we assume that otherness is not embodied by specific individuals in organizations, but rather see it as broadly materialized through gender, what we discover through the films is that gendered practices need not be oppressive and that the symbolic gender order can indeed be resisted, even transformed—not in spite of gender but *because* of gender and, in this case, gendered spatial practices. The margin is no longer a site of deprivation but a space of resistance and ultimately power. It is not "a marginality one wishes to lose—to give up or surrender as part of moving into the center—but rather of a site one stays in, clings to even, because it nourishes one's capacity to resist" (hooks, 1989, p. 207). The margin enables us to imagine alternatives and new worlds. And it is here, perhaps, that the foundations for a new organizational strong plot are laid.

In this new strong plot, executive women are no longer outsiders to organizational spaces, not because they become insiders but because they manage to transform space itself. They are empowered, not through a direct attack on patriarchal and organizational norms, but by calling into question these norms. Through their gendered spatial practices, women manage to change both the spaces they inhabit and the way others experience these spaces as well. And at the same time that they transform space, they also transform gender identity and gendered leadership. While they are acting acceptably feminine, through their various spatial practices they are able to simultaneously step out of fixed gender boundaries and, in the process, destabilize both the category of woman and the category of leader as one-dimensional and antithetical.

As such, the new kind of organizational creature created calls into question the multiple either–or dualisms that we often hold as obvious in the Western world—man–woman, work–life, home–office, body–space, insider–outsider—including woman–leader. The double bind that women leaders often face (Ely, Ibarra, & Kolb, 2011; Hall & Donaghue, 2013) is, after all, an outcome of these socially constructed tensions. Yet, when the hyphen is reimagined as a (physical and metaphorical) space of resistance that allows us to explore identities more fully, we move beyond the gendered minefield (Kenny & Bell, 2011) towards a new imaginary of leadership, not as an *either–or* construct but as an integrative, synthetic, flexible, dynamic, *both–and* type of organizational practice. And leaders are no longer disembodied, homeless creatures abiding to strict norms of clothes, demeanor, discipline, and sexuality (Sinclair, 2013) but real, multifaceted human beings with needs, conflicts, and desires.

This is perhaps the greatest contribution of the new strong plot: The executive women in the films have shown us, the audience, an alternative, potentially subversive conception of leadership. Interestingly, this conception may be just what is needed in today's complex organizational world. As Putnam (2015) says, despite our clinginess to an outdated version of leadership-as-control, leaders today need to manage the constant interplay between order and disorder, to hold opposites together, and to utilize the energy generated from naturally occurring tensions as a way to transform, not to hinder, organizational development. In fact, this paradoxical notion of leadership may be the only way forward, she says. This view of leadership is exactly the story told—and embodied— by the female protagonists in the films analyzed.

We have, then, an unexpected twist in the plot: Whereas traditional notions of leadership would have us believe women's identities, gender, and bodies are antithetical to leadership (Sinclair, 2013), it may actually be the case that executive women—existing on the hyphen—are in the best possible position to enact the type of leadership that is necessary today. Leadership exists, after all, outside established boundaries or, at the very least, *on* the boundary of what is acceptable/established and what is not. So, it seems that leadership, too, is found *on a hyphen.*

It may be that the hyphen I describe resembles what Janssens and Steyaert (1999) have previously called a "third space": a liminal space of disruption and invention that engages contradictions and allows people to develop dialogic relationships that enable them to live with paradoxes. Interestingly, and as a final twist in the story of this chapter, popular films may be the most fitting methodology for studying this hyphen/space—as a kind of third space in and of themselves, they provide a way through which we can work through widely held social contradictions. It seems that as an accessible, even if untapped source of leadership wisdom (Clemens & Wolff, 1999), films provide the critical testing ground through which we can explore and reimagine the way we perform both gender and leadership.

REFERENCES

Bell, E., & Sinclair, A. (in press). Re-envisaging leadership through the feminine imaginary in film and television. In T. Beyes, M. Parker, & C. Steyaert (Eds.), *Routledge companion to reinventing management education.* London, UK: Routledge.

Berg, P. O., & Kreiner, K. (1990). Corporate architecture: Turning physical settings into symbolic resources. In P. Gagliardi (Ed.), *Symbols and artifacts: Views of the corporate landscape* (pp. 41–67). New York, NY: Aldine de Gruyter.

Beyes, T., & Steyaert, C. (2011). Spacing organization: Non-representational theory and performing organizational space. *Organization, 19*(1), 45–61. doi: 10.1177/1350508411401946

Brewis, J. (1998). What is wrong with this picture? Sex and gender relations in *Disclosure.* In J. Hassard & R. Holliday (Eds.), *Organization-representation: Work and organization in popular culture* (pp. 83–100). London, UK: Sage.

Brewis, J., Hampton, M. P., & Linstead, S. (1997). Unpacking Priscilla: Subjectivity and identity in organization of gendered appearance. *Human Relations, 50*(10), 1275–1304. doi: 10.1177/001872679705001005

Bruni, A., Gherardi, S., & Poggio, B (2004). Doing gender, doing entrepreneurship: An ethnographic account of intertwined practices. *Gender, Work and Organization, 11*(4), 406–429. doi: 10.1111/j.1468-0432.2004.00240.x

Butler, J. (2000). *Gender trouble: Feminism and the subversion of identity.* New York, NY: Routledge.

Cartsonis, S., Davey, B., Matthews, G., Meyers, N., Williams, M. (Producers), & Meyers, N. (Director). (2000). *What women want* [Motion picture]. U.S.A.: Paramount Pictures.

Clemens, J., & Wolff, M. (1999). *Movies to manage by: Lessons in leadership from great films.* Chicago, IL: Contemporary Books.

Collinson, D. L., & Hearn, J. (1996). Breaking the silence: On men, masculinities and managements. In D. L. Collinson & J. Hearn (Eds.), *Men as managers, managers as men: Critical perspectives on men, masculinities and managements* (pp. 1–24). London, UK: Sage.

Crichton, M., Levinson, B. (Producers), & Levinson, B. (Director). (1994). *Disclosure* [Motion picture]. USA: Warner Bros.

Czarniawska, B. (2011). How to study gender inequality in organizations? In E. L. Jeanes, D. Knights, & P. Y. Martin (Ed.), *Handbook of gender, work and organization* (pp. 81–108). Chichester, UK: Wiley.

Czarniawska, B., & Rhodes, C. (2006). Strong plots: Popular culture in management practice and theory. In P. Gagliardi & B. Czarniawska (Eds.), *Management education and humanities* (pp. 195–218). Cheltenham, UK: Edward Elgar.

Dale, K., & Burrell, G. (2008). *The spaces of organization and the organization of space: Power, identity and materiality at work.* Basingstoke. UK: Palgrave.

Denzin, N. (1995). *The cinematic society: The voyeur's gaze.* London, UK: Sage.

Ely, R., Ibarra, H., & Kolb, D. (2011). Taking gender into account: Theory and design for women's leadership development programs. *Academy of Management Learning and Education, 10*(3), 474–493. doi: 10.5465/amle.2010.0046

Finerman, W. (Producer), & Frankel, D. (Director). (2006). *The devil wears Prada* [Motion picture]. USA: 20th Century Fox.

Hall, L., & Donaghue, N. (2013). Nice girls don't carry knives: Constructions of ambition in media coverage of Australia's first female prime minister. *British Journal of Social Psychology, 52*(4), 631–647. doi: 10.1111/j.2044-8309.2012.02114.x

hooks, b. (1989). Choosing the margin as a space of radical openness (from Yearnings: Race, gender and cultural politics, 1989). In J. Rendell, B. Penner & I. Borden (Eds.), *Gender space architecture: An interdisciplinary introduction* (pp. 203–209). London, UK: Routledge.

Janssens, M., & Steyaert, C. (1999). The world in two and a third way out? The concept of duality in organization theory and practice. *Scandinavian Journal of Management, 15*(2), 121–139. doi: 10.1016/S0956-5221(98)00010-4

Kenny, K., & Bell, E. (2011). Representing the successful managerial body. In E. L. Jeanes, D. Knights, & P. Y. Martin (Eds.), *Handbook of gender, work and organization* (pp. 163–176). Chichester, UK: Wiley.

Kornberger, M., & Clegg, S. R. (2004). Bringing space back in: Organizing the generative building. *Organization Studies, 25*(7), 1095–1114. doi: 10.1177/0170840604046312

Martin, P. Y. (1996). Gendering and evaluating dynamics: Men, masculinities and managements. In D. L. Collinson & J. Hearn (Eds.), *Men as managers, managers as men: Critical perspectives on men, masculinities and managements* (pp. 186–209). London, UK: Sage.

McDowell, L., & Court, G. (1994). Performing work: Bodily representation in merchant banks. *Environment and Planning D: Society and Space, 12*(6), 727–750. doi: 10.1068/d120727

Meyers, N., & Block, B. A. (Producers), & Shyer, C. (Director). (1987). *Baby boom* [Motion picture]. USA: United Artists.

Mulvey, L. (1975). Visual pleasure and narrative cinema. *Screen, 16*(3), 6–18. doi: *10.1093/screen/16.3.6*

Panayiotou, A. (2010). 'Macho' managers and organizational heroes: Competing masculinities in popular films. *Organization, 17*(6), 659–683. doi: 10.1177/1350508410366275

Panayiotou, A. (2014). Spacing gender, gendering space: A radical "strong plot" in film. *Management Learning, 46*(4), 427–443. doi: 10.1177/1350507614541200

Panayiotou, A., & Kafiris, K. (2010). Firms in film: Representations of organizational space, gender and power. In A. van Marrewijk & D. Yanow (Eds.), *Organizational spaces: Rematerializing the workaday world* (pp. 174–199). Cheltenham. UK: Edward Elgar.

Panayiotou, A., & Kafiris, K. (2011). Viewing the language of space: Organizational spaces, power and resistance in popular films. *Journal of Management Inquiry, 20*(3), 264–284. doi: 10.1177/1056492610389816

Putnam, L. (2015, July). *Moving beyond "both-and" approaches: Alternative strategies for managing paradoxical tensions.* Paper presented at the European Group for Organizational Studies Colloquium, Athens, Greece.

Rose, G. (2001). *Visual methodologies: An introduction to the interpretation of visual materials.* London, UK: Sage.

Silverstein, M. (2014). *Statistics on the state of women and Hollywood* [web log]. Retrieved from http://blogs.indiewire.com/womenandhollywood/statistics

Sinclair, A. (2011). Leading with body. In E. L. Jeanes, D. Knights, & P. Y. Martin (Eds.), *Handbook of gender, work and organization* (pp. 117–130). Chichester, UK: Wiley.

Sinclair, A. (2013). Can I really be me? The challenges of women leaders constructing authenticity. In D. Ladkin & C. Spiller (Eds.), *Authentic leadership: Clashes, coonvergences and coalescences* (pp. 239–251). New horizons in leadership studies. Cheltenham, UK: Edward Elgar.

Swan, E., Stead, V., & Elliott, C. (2009). Feminist challenges and futures: Women, diversity and management learning. *Management Learning, 40*(4), 431–437. doi: 10.1177/1350507609336709

Tyler, M., & Cohen, L. (2010). Spaces that matter: Gender performativity and organizational space. *Organization Studies, 31*(2), 175–198. doi: 10.1177/0170840609357381

Wick, D. (Producer), & Nichols, M. (Director). (1988). *Working girl* [Motion picture]. USA: 20th Century Fox.

Women in the workplace: A research roundup. (2013, September). *Harvard Business Review.* Retrieved from https://hbr.org/2013/09/women-in-the-workplace-a-research-roundup

Yanow, D. (1995). Built space as story: The policy stories that buildings tell. *Policy Studies Journal, 23*(3), 407–422. doi: 10.1111/j.1541-0072.1995.tb00520.x

ABOUT THE EDITORS

Carole Elliott is professor of human resource development at the University of Roehampton Business School in London, UK, and visiting fellow at George Washington University, Washington, DC. She is editor-in-chief of the Taylor and Francis journal *Human Resource Development International* and principal investigator for the Economic and Social Science Research Council (ESRC) seminar series, "Challenging Gendered Media (Mis)representations of Women Professionals and Leaders."

Carole's principal research interests are in management and leadership learning, with a primary focus on the critical examination of women's leadership and women's leadership learning. Recent collaborations with Valerie Stead have involved conducting qualitative research and narrative interviews with women leaders, resulting in scholarly articles in journals such as *Management Learning* and *Leadership*, including the research monograph *Women's Leadership* (2009). With Gareth Edwards, Marian Iszatt-White, and Doris Schedlitzki, she recently co-edited a special issue of *Management Learning*, "Critical and Alternative Approaches to Leadership Learning and Development" (2013), and an issue of *Advances in Developing Human Resources* titled "Using Creative Techniques in Leadership Learning and Development" (2015). Current research projects with Valerie Stead include an examination of the mobilization of textual and visual representations of women's leadership in the media. Other projects include collaborations with Sarah Robinson and Ron Kerr focused on the development of critical hermeneutic and visual methods, leading to papers published in *Management Learning* and book chapters published in *The Routledge Companion to*

Gender, Media, and Organization, pages 259–261
Copyright © 2016 by Information Age Publishing
259

Visual Organization. This work is now extending to examinations of the role of websites in creating revisionist histories of organizations.

Carole regularly presents her research at national and international conferences, is a member of the *ILA, European Group for Organizational Studies,* the *British Academy of Management,* and is an academic member of the *Chartered Institute of Personnel and Development* as well as a fellow of the Leadership Trust Foundation in the UK.

Valerie Stead is senior lecturer in management learning and leadership at Lancaster University Management School, Lancaster, UK and visiting fellow at George Washington University, Washington, DC. She is associate editor for the *International Journal of Management Reviews* and co-investigator for the ESRC seminar series "Challenging Gendered Media (Mis)srepresentations of Women Professionals and Leaders."

Valerie's research interests are in leadership, learning, and critical approaches to research, with a primary focus on the critical examination of women's leadership and women's leadership learning. Recent research projects, including collaborations with Carole Elliott, have involved conducting qualitative research and narrative interviews with women leaders leading to scholarly articles in the journals *Management Learning* and *Leadership* and the research monograph *Women's Leadership* (2009). Valerie has also published on women's leadership and learning in the entrepreneurial context, in journals *Human Resource Development International* and *International Small Business Journal,* and with Ellie Hamilton in the *Research Handbook on Entrepreneurship and Leadership.* Current research projects include working with Carole Elliott to examine the mobilization of textual and visual representations of women's leadership in the media, and with Claire Leitch, Carole Howorth, and Caroline Parkinson to examine gender, power, and leadership in family business. Related to her research interests, Valerie has established and coordinates the Lancaster University Management School Academy for Women, Diversity, and Leadership, the first research forum of its kind in the UK.

Valerie regularly presents her research at national and international conferences and is a member of the British Academy of Management and the Academy of Management. She is also a Fellow of the Chartered Institute of Personnel and Development and a Fellow of the Leadership Trust Foundation in the UK.

Sharon Mavin is professor of organization and human resource management and director of the Roehampton Business School, London, UK. Sharon was previously associate dean and dean of Newcastle Business School (2003–2013), where she made a significant contribution to the school's successful accreditation to the Association to Advance Collegiate Schools of Business (AACSB) for business and management as well as accounting.

Sharon is chair of the University Forum for Human Resource Development and has been awarded fellow of the British Academy of Management for outstanding contributions to the academy. She is co-editor of *Gender in Management: An International Journal* and an associate editor of the *International Journal of Management Reviews*.

Her research has contributed toward advances in understanding women's experiences of organizations, management, and leadership and the changes necessary to advance gender equality in the UK. Sharon is leading a qualitative research project involving over 80 women elite leaders from UK organizations. She is also an ambassador for the Board Apprentice Scheme and apprentice to an investment trust public limited company for the Board Apprentice Scheme, which aims to increase diversity on corporate boards. Her research has been published in the *British Journal of Management* with Gina Grandy and Jannine Williams and in *Human Relations* with Gina Grandy. Sharon was awarded the Alan Moon University Forum for Human Resource Development best conference paper for "Woman as Project" with Jannine Williams, Nicola Patterson, and Trish Bryans. Research into female misogyny won Best Paper in the Gender in Management Track at the British Academy of Management Conference 2015 with Gina Grandy and Jannine Williams. Sharon leads the Association of Business Schools Diversity Impact Group and is a visiting professor at the International Centre for Women's Leadership at Cranfield University, and York St. John University.

Jannine Williams is a lecturer in human resource management and organizational behavior at University of Bradford School of Management, Bradford, UK. After completing her PhD on disabled academics' career experiences at Newcastle Business School, Jannine worked there as lecturer and senior lecturer in organizational behavior. Jannine coordinated two research projects while serving as a lecturer: a Senior Women at Work project that explored senior women's working relationships with other women, and a Gender, Media, and Leadership project that investigated women's perspectives on media representations of women and leadership in a UK region. From her background in working with disabled people, combined with her PhD on disabled academics' career experiences and gender projects, Jannine has developed research interests that are broadly underpinned by critical management studies using qualitative research methods including: categories of social relations—constructions of disability as negated difference, ableism and impairment effects, and gender; career studies with a focus on career boundaries; and women's intragender relations, friendship at work, and media representations of women and leadership.

ABOUT THE CONTRIBUTORS

Stephanie Abrahim received her bachelor's in psychology and social behavior from the University of California–Irvine. She is currently a graduate student at California Baptist University pursuing her master's in education and multiple-subject teaching credential.

Pasi Ahonen is a lecturer in management at Essex Business School, University of Essex, UK. Pasi's research interests include diversity and difference in organizations; temporality, history, and memory in organizational settings; and organizations in the media and media organizations. His work has been published in management and organization journals, including *Human Relations* and *Organization,* as well as edited collections.

Lisa Baker-Webster is an associate professor in the School of Communication at Radford University. Her research interests include communication pedagogy, women's studies, Appalachian studies, and media and culture. Lisa holds undergraduate and graduate degrees from the University of Virginia at Wise, the University of Alabama, and Bowling Green State University.

Scarlett Brown is a PhD student in the department of management at King's College London, UK, where she is undertaking an Economic and Social Sciences Research Council-funded CASE studentship, with King's College London and Sapphire Partners. Her research reveals gender bias in how nonexecutive directors are appointed to corporate boards of directors in the UK. The research is longitudinal and based on repeat interviews with men and women seeking board roles. This show how their accounts of what

Gender, Media, and Organization, pages 263–269
Copyright © 2016 by Information Age Publishing
All rights of reproduction in any form reserved.

makes an "ideal" board member are gendered; how candidates' relationships with others facilitate their appointment, and how their networking practices are gendered; and how they make sense of success and failure.

Judith Clair is an associate professor at Boston College in the department of management and organization, located in the Carroll School of Management. Judith writes on gender and diversity, identity, and the professions; working women's transition into motherhood; stigma management in the workplace; and women and leadership. Her publications have appeared in journals such as *Academy of Management Journal, Academy of Management Review, Human Relations, Academy of Management Executive,* and *Academy of Management Learning and Education.*

Sandra L. French is an associate professor in the School of Communication at Radford University. She earned her B.S. at Radford University, M.A. at Wake Forest University, and PhD at Pennsylvania State University. Sandy teaches leadership courses for the State Department's Middle Eastern Program Initiative and serves as an associate editor of the *International Journal of Business Communication.* Her research has been published in the *Journal of Applied Communication,* the *Southern Communication Journal,* the *Journal of Business Communication,* and *Business Communication Quarterly.*

Maria E. Gallego-Pace is a doctoral candidate in applied organizational psychology at Hofstra University and an industrial and organizational psychology business consultant at BeamPines, Inc. She earned her M.A. in general psychology from New York University, completing her thesis on gender roles in the workplace. Her research interests include work–family issues, employee attitudes, motivation, and engagement.

Rita A. Gardiner teaches women's studies and leadership at the University of Western Ontario and King's University College, London, Ontario. Her research examines the intersection among gender, authenticity, and leadership. In addition to publications on gender and leadership, Rita has published several articles on Hannah Arendt and Simone de Beauvoir. Her book is entitled *Gender, Authenticity and Leadership.*

Sallyann Halliday is a research fellow at the Policy Research Institute and co-module leader of the Postgraduate Dissertation Scheme in the Faculty of Business and Law at Leeds Beckett University, Leeds, UK. Sallyann has 14 years of experience in academic and applied social policy research and consultancy. She has extensive experience of undertaking research exploring changes in behavior and attitudes, particularly in relation to work/employment and skills. She has conducted extensive research involving professionals working in a wide range of organizational contexts. Sallyann has a particular interest in organizational behavior and culture, leadership, and management.

Elisabeth Kelan is professor of leadership at Cranfield School of Management, Bedford, UK. During the 2014–2015 academic year, she was a British Academy Mid-Career Fellow, exploring how middle managers can drive gender change in organizations. Her research focuses on women and leadership, generations in organizations, leadership and diversity, and inclusion. She has published two books: *Rising Stars—Developing Millennial Women as Leaders* and *Performing Gender*, both with Palgrave and numerous peer-reviewed articles in academic journals. She is an associate editor of the journal *Gender, Work and Organization* and is on the editorial board of the *British Journal of Management*. Her research has been recognized through various academic and practitioner awards. She is also regularly providing thought-leadership to businesses and international organizations. She sits on the advisory boards of the Women's Empowerment Principles, a partnership initiative of UN Women and the UN Global Compact, as well as the National Society of High School Scholars Foundation.

Helena Liu is a lecturer in organization studies at Swinburne Business School, Victoria, Australia. She holds a PhD from the University of Sydney Business School. Her research focuses on the discursive construction of leadership. This approach has led her to examine how leaders account for failure and the social construction of authenticity amongst banking CEOs during the global financial crisis. Central to her work is a critical disposition towards the gendered, racialized, and classed nature of how we have come to understand "leadership." Helena's work has been published in *Gender, Work, and Organization; Journal of Business Ethics;* and *Management Communication Quarterly.*

Shana Matamala is Director of Teaching Fieldwork Experiences and assistant professor at the University of La Verne. She spent 11 years teaching in K–12 private, public, and charter school settings before moving to the university level in 2007. After receiving her master's in education from Azusa Pacific University, she earned her doctorate in organizational leadership from the University of La Verne in 2013.

Maura J. Mills is an assistant professor and director of internships for industrial/organizational psychology at Hofstra University, Hempstead, as well as an adjunct assistant professor at the Frank G. Zarb School of Business at Hofstra University. Her research interests include the work–family/work–life interface, gender in the workplace, and positive organizational behavior. In addition to her forthcoming edited book, *Gender and the Work–Family Interface: An Intersection of Two Domains*, Dr. Mills has worked in organizational consulting and has published in a variety of notable outlets including *Gender in Management: An International Journal, Human Relations, Journal of Occupational Health Psychology,* and *Diversity Executive,* among others.

Caela McCann is an undergraduate research fellow in the Carroll School of Management at Boston College. Her current research focuses on discourses about "having it all" in a time of debate regarding women, work, and the "will to lead." Her research examines the development of a genre and area of literature, media, and public dialogue referred to as "pop" women's leadership literature.

Alexia Panayiotou is assistant professor in the department of business and public administration at the University of Cyprus. She completed undergraduate and graduate studies at Stanford University and has a doctorate in human development and psychology from Harvard University. Her current research interests include the role of paradox in (organizational) life, the role of discourse in shaping "reality," the power of the visual, management and popular culture, gender and work, and organizational space and symbolism. Her work has appeared in journals such as *Organization, Management Learning, Journal of Management Inquiry* and the *Journal of Corporate Citizenship,* as well as in several edited volumes.

Alison Pullen is professor of management and organization studies at Macquarie University, Sydney, Australia. An internationally renowned scholar, Alison focuses her research on the intersections between gender, identity, corporeality, and ethics as they relate to work organizations. In pursuing her research, Alison works with feminist philosophy as a means to engage in an ethical politics that challenges marginalization and oppression in the workplace. Alison has published six books and many articles in leading journals; she serves on the editorial boards of many journals including *Organization Studies, Organization, Gender, Work and Organization,* and *Management Communication Quarterly.* She regularly contributes to leading edited collections, reference works, and encyclopedias. Alison's recent work on leadership critiques the inherent stereotypes found with gendered leadership, especially as it relates to female masculinity, and ethics, embodiment, and leadership.

Ann Rippin is a reader in management in the department of management at the University of Bristol, Bristol, UK. Her research interests are in gender in organizations, particularly women's relationships with particular brands and the way that textiles have helped them to shape and maintain their identities. She is also interested in textile art as a research method and often uses textiles as her primary method of inquiry. She is also interested in the patchwork and quilting industry and in women's identity formation through the pursuit of their serious leisure activities. Her blog can be found at www.annjrippin.wordpress.com.

Helen Rodgers is a senior lecturer and course leader for the MSc Leadership and Change, Leeds Beckett University, Leeds, UK. Helen has 20 years of experience teaching and researching in the areas of organizational behavior, gender and diversity, leadership and change, and governance, focusing on how these areas are translated into organizational contexts. Previous research studies have focused on gender and post bureaucracy; leading comparator contexts in health, education and local government; the Future of the Professions—Council for Excellence in Management and Leadership; and Women into Work Sector Pathways Initiative. Helen has a PhD in gender and organizational transformation from the University of Kent. Prior to working in higher education, Helen was a marketing manager in the telecommunications industry.

Harriet Shortt is senior lecturer in organization studies at Bristol Business School, University of the West of England, Bristol, UK. She researches organizational space, aesthetics, and identity and has expertise in ethnography and participant-led photography. Harriet has conducted research projects in public and private sector organizations, examining spatial change and the impact of work space on employees' well-being. Her research has been published in journals including *Human Relations, Management Learning, Visual Studies*, and the *International Journal of Work, Organisation and Emotion*. She is a member of inVisio (the International Network for Visual Studies in Organization).

Samantha Szczur is an assistant professor in the communication studies department at Eastern Illinois University. She received her PhD in communication studies from the University of North Carolina at Chapel Hill. Her research focuses on the cultural politics of work and takes a critical approach to organizational life, analyzing mechanisms of power, control, and resistance. Her research is heavily influenced by critical theory and cultural studies. Current research projects include an analysis of corporate campuses using Foucault's framework of governmentality, a critique of strict bureaucratic forms and their potential undermining of diversity goals, and an examination of the intentional blurring of work/life on behalf of organizations that further inserts employees into capitalist production.

Lucy Taksa is professor of management and head of the department of marketing and management at Macquarie University in Sydney, Australia. She is internationally recognized for her work on management history; gendered workplace cultures in transport and finance; nicknaming, embodiment, emotions, and misbehavior; and migrant employees, multiculturalism, identity, and diversity management. Current projects include the Australian Research Council-funded "Affinities in Multicultural Australia" and the industry-funded "Exploring the Socioeconomic Impact of Living with Lymphoedema." She is on the Australian Research Council College of Experts, serves as an associate editor for the *European Management Review*, and she is area editor for gender on the *Economic and Labour Relations Review*. Lucy's work on masculine work cultures and on identity negotiations and representations has focused on how naming and representation sustains processes of inclusion and exclusion of the other.

Janne Tienari is professor of organization and management at Aalto University, School of Business, Helsinki, Finland. Janne's research and teaching interests include gender studies, media, managing multinational corporations, mergers and acquisitions, strategy work, and cross-cultural management. His latest passion is to understand management, new generations, and the future. His work has been published in leading organization and management studies journals.

Leanne M. Tortez is a doctoral candidate in applied organizational psychology at Hofstra University, Hempstead. She earned her M.S. in industrial/organizational psychology from California State University, San Bernardino, focusing her thesis on leadership and organizational culture. Her research interests include the work and family interface, leadership, and employee attitudes.

Samantha Warren is a professor at Cardiff Business School, Wales, UK, where she is currently researching creative economy as it plays out in the lives and work of underground techno disc jockeys. She writes predominantly on visual methodologies and the aesthetic dimensions of organizational life. Her work spans a broad range of marginalized organizational topics, including smell in the workplace, drug-testing at work, flashmobs, and workplace fun. She is a founder member of the International Network for Visual Studies in Organizations (www.in-visio.org) and is a co-editor of the *Routledge Companion to Visual Organization* (2014).

Carrie A. Wilson-Brown is an instructor in the communication studies department of Eastern Illinois University. Her teaching is influenced by her interdisciplinary background in film and media theory, visual communication and video production, cultural studies, gender studies, and Latino/a studies. Her interests include the study of youth media, subcultures, and consumptive practices. She is a member of the Eastern Illinois University Film Studies Advisory Board and the coordinator of the department's student multimedia contest.

Liz Yeomans is principal lecturer at Leeds Beckett University, Leeds, UK. Liz has taught and researched in public relations and communication for over 20 years. Her doctoral work developed perspectives in public relations, drawing on gender and emotional labor theories within the sociology of work. Liz's diverse interests include emotion and empathy in promotional culture, gendered identities in public relations, student internships, blogger relationships, and critical-interpretive research methods. Liz is the co-editor of the popular international student textbook, *Exploring Public Relations*, which is now in its third edition.

Kimberly Yost is currently visiting professor in the College of Business and Leadership at Lourdes University in Ohio. She has explored depictions of leaders in science fiction narratives to discover the ways in which these images influence our thinking about crisis leadership and the ethical leadership principles of love, forgiveness, redemption, and inclusion. She is the author of *From Starship Captains to Galactic Rebels: Leaders in Science Fiction Television* (Rowman & Littlefield, 2013). Kimberly received her PhD in leadership and change from Antioch University.

Made in the USA
Middletown, DE
31 October 2020

23107363R00157